AF856128

INTERNATIONAL PATENT-LEGISLATION AND DEVELOPING COUNTRIES

INTERNATIONAL PATENT-LEGISLATION AND DEVELOPING COUNTRIES

by

ULF ANDERFELT

MARTINUS NIJHOFF / THE HAGUE / 1971

© 1971 by Martinus Nijhoff, The Hague, Netherlands
All rights reserved, including the right to translate or to reproduce this book or parts thereof in any form

ISBN 978-94-011-8492-2 ISBN 978-94-011-9218-7 (eBook)

DOI 10.1007/978-94-011-9218-7

"To Hilda and to my parents"

TABLE OF CONTENTS

THE INTERNATIONAL PATENT-LEGISLATION AND DEVELOPING COUNTRIES

A major concern today in many fields of international cooperation is the development of the nonindustrialized part of the world. This was not always so. Until fairly recently contacts among States were basically limited to diplomatic intercourse. The concept of State sovereignty naturally led to the application of the principle of legal reciprocity between States. In the few areas outside diplomatic relations where international cooperation developed during the last century the same principle of legal reciprocity was applied. The cooperation that did take place was mostly among a limited number of Western States. In case countries outside this group wished to participate they were free to do so on accepting the traditional standards for such cooperation. Though a few countries, which today would have been or are known as developing countries, did join in various schemes of international cooperation, the majority of them remained outside. Moreover, a large number of States, which today are known as developing, did not exist as sovereign States at the time.

One of the areas in which a system of international cooperation was set up in the latter part of the nineteenth century was that of patent protection. The major objectives of this study are (1) to examine the extent to which certain existing rules of international patent protection can usefully serve the industrialization of developing countries, (2) to identify the principal obstacles against desirable changes, and (3) to suggest some modifications of existing rules which may favorably influence the industrialization of developing countries.

The Problem.

The one facet of the development process, which today receives the most attention, is the industrialization of less developed countries. A major requirement in this respect is the supply of technological knowledge. It is often held that one advantage of countries developing later than others is their possibility to draw on the accumulated experience and knowledge of already developed countries. If this wealth of knowledge, technical and other, is to be put to efficient use, appropriate channels have to be furnished for its flow. A large part of technological knowledge is free in the sense that its transfer is "merely" a problem of documentation and adaptation. This is usually so for the technological knowledge required for very simple industrial activities and for branches of industry based on a more or less static type of technology. It is with the so-called growth industries, relying on a continuously evolving dynamic type of technology for their efficient operation, that special problems related to patent protection may arise.

The principles, upon which present international patent cooperation is based, are those originally established in the latter part of the nineteenth century. Can these principles be advantageously applied today to the relations between industrialized countries and those that are not, either because the same considerations for participation in international patent cooperation apply to all countries, or because specific considerations of developing countries still favor the application of the established rules? Or do the special conditions and requirements of developing countries suggest modifications of the present system? These are some of the questions to which answers will be sought.

Organization of Study

The study is divided into two parts. Its first part, *The Evolution of Patent Legislation and Practices under Patent Rights, Nationally and Internationally*, will examine three aspects of the patent institution, the understanding of which are essential in dealing with the problems facing developing countries in the field of international patent protection today.

Chapter I, *Society and the Inventor*, will contain a brief review of the origins and the evolution of the patent institution. Its objective is to clarify the rationale of patent protection, as seen through the different theories on patent rights, which are connected with their appearance in different countries and at different times. The two main theories – the one that holds that patent protection is extended in the interest of society, and the other that holds that such protection is mainly granted by society in recognition of a pre-existing "natural right" of the inventor – are often contradictory. The knowledge of the origin of patent protection and its evolution will make it possible to evaluate certain recurring propositions concerning the historical role of the patent institution and its relevance today for developing countries.

Chapter II, *The Role of Patents Today,* will contain an analysis of some aspects of the working of the patent institution today. Do contemporary conditions of inventive activity invalidate the original reasons given for the granting of patent rights? Have modern conditions surrounding the process of invention and innovation given rise to new motivations for granting such rights? The answers to these questions, together with an examination of some principal criticism of the patent institution, will show that the patent system today is functioning in a way, which is often far removed from the idealistic terms in which it is sometimes described. This finding will make it easier for an objective study of the requirements of developing countries, without the burden of a preconceived idea, that the patent system in general is ideally suited for its contemporary setting.

Chapter III, *The Development of an International Patent Legislation,* will serve as an introduction to the present international patent system as it operates within the Paris Union for the International Protection of Industrial Property. Attention will focus on the various conferences for the revision of the original convention, and in particular on instances where disagreements among countries have appeared as a consequence of their different stages of economic and industrial development. Other international agreements concerning patent cooperation will be mentioned.

The second part of the study, *Effects of the International Patent Legislation on Developing Countries and Possible Remedies to Disadvantages due to Their Underdevelopment,* will analyse certain aspects of the influence of the international patent system on the transfer of technology to developing countries and suggest some measures, that would increase the net benefits to these countries from the operation of that system.

Chapter I, *The Status of Developing Countries in Patent Matters,* will show the position of developing countries with regard to both national and international patent legislation. For the latter case, the emphasis will be on the States that are members of the Paris Union and the extent to which non-members apply similar rules to those prescribed by the Convention.

Chapter II, *Direct Effects of the International Patent System,* will examine the effects that derive from obligations stipulated by the Convention. The relevance of arguments advanced concerning the benefits of joining the international system, with emphasis on the arguments that are specifically directed at developing countries, will be analyzed in the light of certain disadvantages suffered by these countries.

Chapter III, *Indirect Effects of the International Patent System*, will call attention to the effects of certain practices, which, while not directly the results of obligations imposed by the international patent system, often rely on the existence of that system for their exercise. In this case there is, for all practical purposes, little difference between members and non-members of the Paris Union.

Chapter IV, *The Activities of Various International Organizations*, will examine the positions taken by and within some international organizations on the question of developing countries and international patent protection. Besides the activities of various United Nations organs and those of the Secretariat of the Paris Union, the positions and opinions of two non-governmental organizations will be treated.

Chapter V, *Possible Remedies within the Existing System*, will examine the extent to which certain disadvantageous effects may be remedied under the present substantive rules of the Convention, and the extent to which developing countries, in practice, could hope to obtain more favorable rules.

Chapter VI, *Remedies outside the Existing System*, finally, will suggest the justification for changes, favorable to developing countries, in derogation to the basic principles of the present international patent system. Special emphasis will be put on the fact that developing countries today have been given a special status within certain areas of international cooperation. The evolution in the field of international copyright protection will be shown as constituting a possible precedent. It will also be observed that a change in patent legislation alone will not be sufficient to remove the gap separating industrialized and developing countries in the field of industrial technology.

Definitions and Limitations

Developing countries. Since the present study is concerned with the principles of the effects of the international patent legislation, rather than with a quantitative measurement of such effects, it has been found convenient to use the classification of developing countries adopted by the United Nations Statistical Office, i.e., all Sovereign States of Economic Class II.

International Patent legislation. When not otherwise specified, this expression refers to the rules of the Paris Convention subscribed to by the Member States of the Paris Union. This expression is used interchangeably with the *International Patent System.*

Working or Exploitation of Patented Inventions. The Paris Convention and often other international agreements on industrial property rights regulate a wide range of aspects on patent rights and other industrial property rights. The present study will deal exclusively with problems concerning the working or exploitation requirements of patented inventions.

Previous Studies.

There exists a vast literature on the subjects of national and international patent legislation. With few exceptions, the authors have been lawyers treating the subjects almost exclusively from a legal point of view. The following studies analyzing the economics of patent protection in general represent some notable exceptions: A. Plant, *The Economic Theory Concerning Patents for Inventions;* L. LeGrand, *Etude économique de la propriété industrielle, fondement et fonction de cette "propriété";* M. Börlin, *Die volkswirtschaftliche Problematik der Patentgesetzgebung unter besonderer Berücksichtigung der Schweizerischen Verhältnisse;* Institut de Science Economique Appliquée (I.S.E.A.) *Les brevets d'invention dans l'économie: Caractères institutionelles et problématique économique.*

As far as the international patent system is concerned, only one treatise on the economics of international patent protection has appeared: E. T. Penrose, *The Economics of the International Patent System.*

The existing literature is even smaller on the particular problems encountered by developing countries in connection with patent protection. Though a number of articles on industrial property and developing countries have appeared during the last decade, with few exceptions they can hardly be considered adequate for the present purpose, since they rarely even question the adequacy of the existing system for the particular needs and requirements of developing countries. A notable exception is S. Pretnar, *The International Protection of Industrial Property and the Different Stages of Economic Development of the States.* The only substantial treatment of the subject from the point of view of a developing country appears to be a report prepared for the Indian Government by R. Ayyangar, *Report on the Revision of the Patents Law.**

* The material underlying this work has been updated to include developments up to January 1st, 1969.

PART I

THE EVOLUTION OF PATENT LEGISLATION AND PRACTICES UNDER PATENT RIGHTS, NATIONALLY AND INTERNATIONALLY

CHAPTER I

SOCIETY AND THE INVENTOR

The early history of the patent institution shows that, while most of the motives underlying contemporary patent legislation were already then considered, the relative weights given these respective motives differed considerably from those during the system's later evolution. The fact, nevertheless, that most motives behind contemporary patent legislation existed already several centuries ago, may indicate that the developments of the late eighteenth century, with their heavy emphasis on the "natural rights" of inventors, were a passing thing rather than the birth of the patent institution. It is of particular interest to the contemporary problems concerning the acquisition of foreign technology by the developing countries to see how some of the now industrialized countries themselves secured foreign technology during their own period of economic development.

A. EARLY ORIGINS OF PATENTS FOR INVENTIONS

Until fairly recently it was generally believed that patents for inventions originated in England in the late sixteenth century and were later introduced in other countries as a mere imitation of an English institution.[1] It has been established, however, that the English patent system had antecedents in several countries of continental Europe. In particular, a Venetian law preceded the English Statute of Monopolies, the first statutory regulation of patents in England, by one hundred and fifty years.

The belief that patents originated in England can be explained at least partly by the fact that patent granting has always been linked to

[1] Cf. M. Frumkin, *The Early History of Patents for Invention, Paper presented at a joint meeting of the Chartered Institute of Patent Agents and the Newcomen Society* (London, 1947) p. 1.

the idea of industrial progress, which was generally non-existent during the period prior to the sixteenth century. One outstanding exception to this state of affairs was the situation of the Italian city-states of Florence and Venice.[2] The former is generally credited with issuing the first patent for an invention in 1421. It was, according to Frumkin, "a real invention patent, as good in subject matter as any of those dealt with in 1947 by the [British] Patent Office."[3] In Venice, the first patent grant, showing all the features of a modern patent for invention, was given in 1443.[4] From that date on, an increasing number of patent grants were recorded. The crowning event of this evolution was the promulgation of the Venetian Patent Act of 1474. Its preamble reads in part:

> And if it were provided that others may not make nor take unto themselves, to increase their own honor, the works and artifices they may have seen so discovered ... such men would use their minds, and would discover and make things, which would be of no little utility to our State.[5]

and the law states that:

> It is enacted by the authority of the present Council that whoever will make in this city any new and ingenuous artifice, not made previously in our State, will be obliged to registrer it at the Office of our prov-editors of the Commune ... It shall be forbidden to anyone else in any our land and place to make any other artifice to the image and similarity of that one without consent and license of the author during the term of ten years ....[6]

The texts quoted above show that the Venetian patent law contained the essential elements of any contemporary patent law. Of the four motivations usually said to underlie the patent institution, i.e., utility to society, encouragement of inventive activity, refund of costs incurred by the inventor, and the inventor's right to the fruit of his mind, all are already present in this old Venetian Act.[7]

The heavy emphasis on the promotion of a social interest as the ratio-

[2] *Ibid.*, pp. 6–7.

[3] *Ibid.*

[4] *Ibid.*, p. 8.; G. Mandich, "Venetian Patents (1450–1550)," *J.P.O.S.*, 30 : 172, March, 1948.

[5] Quoted by Frumkin, *op. cit.*, p. 8.

[6] *Ibid.*, p. 9.

[7] Mandich, *op. cit.*, pp. 177, 184, while recognizing that the Venetian Act begins by declaring patents a means to a social end, points out that it also takes cognizance of an "honor" to safeguard. After examining individual patent applications the author concludes that "apparently at least a vague feeling is involved that the supplicant has the right to the products of his mind". see also F. D. Prager, "A History of Intellectual Property from 1545 to 1787," *J.P.O.S.*, 26 : 733, November, 1944. M. Silberstein, *Erfindungsschutz und merkantilistische Gewerbsprivilegien*, (Zürich: Polygraphischer Verlag, 1961) pp. 23–24, states that the protection of the inventor's rights was the major objective of the law.

nale of the patent grant is particularly significant. The first sentence of the law-text quoted above makes it the inventor's duty to register his invention with the authorities.[8] Another indication of the social interest involved is the concept of novelty referred to in the law, the significance of which Mandich stresses when he says, in part:

> Novelty has been conceived in the sense of what is new for Venice. We now understand the full significance of this concept; it has to do with the utilization and public use of the invention. The right to a patent belongs to the person who is the first, in the territory of Venice, to actively exploit some "ingenuous device"; it is the compensation for the advantages derived by the Commonwealth from such exploitation.[9]

Two further reasons to believe that the social interest was the major rationale behind the Venetian patent law merit our attention in considering present-day problems concerning the exploitation of patented inventions. One is given in the last paragraph of the law providing that it shall be within the power and discretion of the government to use any patented invention on the condition, however, that only the inventor should be allowed to operate it.[10] The other is the fact that, according to F. Machlup, there existed an obligation to exploit the patent. The author points out that, besides the existence of this implicit rule in the law, the Venetian Senate recalled patent grants in those cases in which the inventions were not exploited.[11]

The fact that the patent grant often also meant an authorization to activity in a particular field, in the face of existing guild-privileges, seems to emphasize the dominant interest of the State in the expected benefits from the patent system. It is this preponderant economic interest of society, together with the absence of any specific reference to an unqualified right of the inventor to protection, that makes the Venetian Patent Act such an interesting precedent of modern patent law. In the contemporary debate on the patent institution one frequently raised problem is that of reconciling the often conflicting interests of society and those of the inventor. It is then often held that an essential feature of the patent institution is the right, sometimes referred to as the "inherent right," of the inventor in his invention. This

[8] Though the same text as quoted by Mandich, *op. cit.*, pp. 177–78, reads "shall give notice" instead of "will be obliged to register," the author interprets the wording in the imperative sense.

[9] *Ibid.*, p. 195.

[10] Cf. Frumkin, *op. cit.*, p. 9; Mandich, *loc. cit.*

[11] F. Machlup, "Patentwesen – I. Geschichtliche Uberblick [und] II. Wirtschaftsteoretische Betrachtung," *Handwörterbuch des Sozialwissenschaften, Vol. XLII.* (Göttingen: G G. Fischer, J. C. B. Mohr, 1962), p. 233.

philosophy has created the term "immaterial property rights" to express man's right to the creations of his mind, including inventions. Against the background of the Venetian law, the development of the idea of "immaterial," or, as they are also called "intellectual," property rights, is clearly seen as a later occurrence.

The existence of the Venetian Patent Act, and of early patent systems in some other continental countries, is interesting from another point of view. The idea, so cherished by the patent advocates, that there exists a more or less organic relationship between the existence of a patent law and the economic and industrial performance of a country, cannot be supported at all by this early experience. In Venice the patent system was introduced when that State was already at the height of its development.

That the Venetian patent system a century later slowly fell into disuse was certainly an effect of rather than a contributory cause to the economic decline of the City State. The same development appeared in the early German experience with the patent system.[12]

The patent institution spread from Italy to the countries of Western Europe. The clear influence of the Italian patent system can be seen in the fact that invariably, in all countries which adopted some sort of patent system during the fifteenth and sixteenth centuries, the first few patentees were Italians. Furthermore, the time limit as first introduced was generally the Venetian ten-year term.

The patent institution first spread to Germany, in the Empire as well as in the particular States, from the Italian city-states.[13] It later made its way to Holland, Belgium, France and England in that order. The German experience seems to be the only one in which an established system grew up before the English Statute of Monopolies was enacted in 1624. H. Pohlmann, in his thorough study, "The Inventor's Right in Early German Law," describes not only the existence of patent grants in the fifteenth and sixteenth centuries, but also analyzes the legal foundation of the German patent institution.[14] The author shows convincingly that, contrary to early beliefs, the patent

[12] M. Frumkin, "Les anciens brevets d'invention: les pays du continent européen au XVIIIe siècle," *Bijblad bij De Industriële Eigendom*, 23 : 46–49, April, 1955. In a study of the birth and decline of early patent systems in some continental countries, the author compares their evolution with the emergence and decline of particular countries as centers of culture and economic activity. The author's conclusion appears to be that the patent institution followed (rather than preceded) the economic and cultural development and later lost its importance when these activities became less intensive.

[13] *Ibid.*, p. 46.

[14] H. Pohlmann, "The Inventor's Right in Early German Law," *J.P.O.S.*, 43 : 121–35, February, 1961.

system as applied both in the Empire and in some of the particular States, was not just a system of privileges and royal favors but was indeed based on established customary law.

B. THE STATUTE OF MONOPOLIES OF 1623

The custom of granting privileges to inventors became known in England around the middle of the sixteenth century, although a few cases of such grants have been recorded even before that date. As had been the case in Venice, as well as on the continent, monopoly privileges were granted by the Crown for various reasons. Popular reaction to this use of the royal prerogative, often motivated by pure favoritism, was translated into a parliamentary measure, the promulgation of the Statute of Monopolies of 1623. It was not a patent law in the sense that it did not represent a new regulatory system. It did, however, abolish the royal prerogative to grant monopoly privileges, excepting only the privileges granted for a term of fourteen years for "the sole working or making of any manner of new manufacture."[15] From the quoted text, the social interest that is to be served by the patent system is obvious. E. W. Hulme, the pioneer of research on the origins of the patent institution in England, stated that "the undertaking to work the grant constituted the essential consideration in the early monopoly system."[16] E. Blum, after examining the motives underlying the Venetian law, says on the Statute of Monopolies:

> The later English forerunners of the patent law too, at the beginning of the seventeenth century, are all based on the thought that those should be granted a monopoly who introduce new industries and thus acquire merits with the industry and the entire community.

This author concludes his historical survey of the patent institution, up to and including the English Statute of Monopolies, saying that "this historical survey makes it clear where the real source of patent law lies and why it considers in the first instance not the inventor but the invention."[17]

There are principally two explanations why numerous authors have held that the origin of the patent institution is the English Statute of

[15] From Section VI of the statute quoted by W. Jarratt, "The English Patent System," *J.P.O.S.*, 26 : 761–68, November, 1944 , p. 761.

[16] E. W. Hulme, "On the Consideration of the Patent Grant, Past and Present," *Law Quarterly Review*, 13: 314, 1897, quoted by E. T. Penrose, *Economics of the International Patent System* (Baltimore: Johns Hopkins, 1951), p. 138.

[17] E. Blum, "Abuse of Monopolies and its Prevention," *Souvenir – Indian Patents Centenary 1856–1956* (Calcutta: Patent Office, 1956), p. 55.

Monopolies of 1623. The first is that the findings of Frumkin and Mandich have become known only recently. Prager has pointed out, however, that much earlier observations have been made, when he states that "the patent laws of France along with those of England and the United States, are branches of a single system of jurisprudence, and that they all go back to a system of privileges, developed in Venice."[18]

The other explanation is based on the opinion that, although the English Statute did not inaugurate the practice of granting monopoly privileges to inventors, qualitatively it was so different from earlier practices that it constituted an original system.

Many authors have pointed out wrongly, as will be shown below, that the Statute was the first law to lay down the principle that only "the first and true inventor" was to be granted a monopoly privilege and have designated the Statute of Monopolies the "Magna Carta" of inventors.[19] That this was not correct becomes clear when a comparison is made of the texts of the Venetian Act and the English Statute. To judge from a textual comparison, the Venetian law concerns itself only with the protection of inventions made in the State of Venice,[20] and includes a qualification that only "the first and true inventor" is eligible for a patent grant, whereas the English law also permits patent grants to those who introduce foreign inventions.[21]

The claim that the concept of the "first and true inventor" was a novelty, when it appeared in the Statute and, correctly interpreted, meant that only an inventor (and not someone who introduced a foreign-made invention) was to be granted patent protection, has also influenced the belief that the modern patent institution originated in seventeenth century England. Though all authors agree that technically the patent grant remained a privilege bestowed upon the inventor by royal prerogative, several writers have concluded that, in fact, the law implied a recognition of the inventor's right to claim protection.[22] The only support for this contention seems to be the fact that,

[18] Prager, *op. cit.*, p. 711, referring to J. Kohler, *Lehrbuch des Patentsrechts* (Leipzig: J. Bensheimer, 1908).

[19] Penrose, *op. cit.*, p. 7.; J. Vojáček, *A Survey of the Principal National Patent Systems* (New York: Prentice Hall, 1936; addenda: 1951, 1956) pp. 97–98.

[20] Machlup, "Patentwesen ...", p. 234, expresses this opinion saying that the concept of "true and first inventor" was used in the Venetian Act in the purer form of "geistigen Urheber."

[21] Cf. Penrose, *op. cit.*, p. 7.; Silberstein, *op. cit.*, pp. 99–100.

[22] In this sense, see Vojáček, *op. cit.*, p. 6.

in practice, all requests for patent protection were granted.[23] If by "the right of the inventor" it is merely meant that he was given legal protection after fulfilling the requirements of the law, no objections can be raised to the use of that term.[24] But if it is used to imply that the mere fact of intellectual creation entitled the inventor to protection by the State, it can only be the result of a backward projection of the evolution in the late eighteenth and early nineteenth centuries on the English practice in the seventeenth century. The development of the theory of "inherent rights" of the inventor was definitely a later occurrence.[25]

Thus it can be concluded, that the Statute of Monopolies had, to at least the same degree as the Venetian law, the economic interest of the State as its rationale, and that the right of the inventor was merely the result of the patent protection that was granted in the interest of society. Just as the Venetian authorities required that the patented inventions be worked, so was it obligatory in England that the invention be exploited.[26] One more indication is provided by the text of section VI of the Statute which contains, in its final paragraph, the observation that patent grants should be used in such manner as not to be "mischievous to the State by raising prices of commodities at home or hurt of trade."[27]

The long-standing belief that the Statute of Monopolies was the first legal enactment in the history of the patent institution, and that the English practice in patent matters constituted an original development, has certainly influenced the patent doctrine. For one thing, was not the readiness with which the theory of the inventor's "inherent" rights was later accepted, partly at least based on that belief? The enactment of the Statute of Monopolies was viewed as a reaction against the privilege system, and the exception of patent grants from the general prohibition to accord privileges, may have been seen as a recognition of the inventor's right to claim protection.

[23] A. Troller, Immaterial-güterrecht (2 vols., Basel: Helbing und Lichtenhahn 1959–62), vol. 1, p. 21.

[24] In that case there is no difference between the English and Venetian systems. See F. Neumeyer, *Patent: reflexioner kring ,patent-institutionens uppkomst, utveckling och ställning i vår tid* (Studier och Debatt No. IV 1958; Stockholm: SNS, 1958) p. 7.

[25] Cf. P. Roubier, *Le droit de la propriété industrielle,* (Paris: Sirey, 2 vols, 1952, 1954), Vol. I., pp. 20, 63–64, and "Droits intellectuels ou droit du clientèle," *Revue Trimestrielle du Droit Civil,* 34: 255, No. 2, 1935; Prager, *op. cit.*, pp. 719–20, though he contends that an "embryonic" recognition of intellectual property first appeared in a French Copyright Statute of 1545, makes no mention of the existence of such a concept in England at the time of the Statute.

[26] Penrose, *op. cit.*, p. 138.

[27] *Supra*, n. 15.

The assumption that the patent system was born in the country where the industrial revolution was soon to start, and at a moment when the economy had been liberalized through the general abolition of the privilege system, easily led to the conviction that the patent institution was not only consistent with a liberal economy, but also that, in fact, it had been a vital, if not indispensable, means of stimulating the process of industrialization.[28] Today this argument has often been used to convince the developing countries of the "historical necessity" of adopting a patent system in order to achieve economic and industrial development. When developing countries, who are not members of the international patent system, are urged to join the Paris Union on the assumption that they will benefit from extending patent protection to foreigners, such an assumption cannot be based on this early historical experience. One of the purposes of the English Statute was to encourage its citizens to bring in foreign technology for the benefit of the national economy. This same consideration was also to play an important role in the American and French patent systems, which were introduced in the last decade of the following century.

C. THE PATENT DOCTRINE AT THE END OF THE EIGHTEENTH CENTURY: THE PATENT LAWS OF THE UNITED STATES AND FRANCE

The principal reason why many authors have not recognized, and why some still do not recognize, the early patent systems (sometimes including the Statute of Monopolies), as true patent systems comparable to those of today, is that the patentee did not have an "inherent" right to protection. It is generally supposed that this concept was introduced in the eighteenth century. Though the theory of the inventor's inherent right to protection retained its prominent position only until the middle of the nineteenth century, its influence can be observed far beyond that date. In fact, it would seem that this theory, though its theoretical foundations have been rejected, still plays a role in contemporary thinking on the patent institution. Therefore, it is important not only to briefly report the birth of this theory, but also to analyze its foundations. Did the reason for the existence of a patent institution change from a means of promoting the welfare of society – with any benefit gained by the inventor being only an accessory – to a protection due

[28] An illustrative example of this type of derivation is provided by H. Isay, *Die Funktion der Patente im Wirtschaftskampf* (Berlin: Franz Vahlen, 1927), pp. 6–10.

to the inventor in virtue of an "inherent right"? To what extent was the theory applied consistently? If an affirmative answer can be given to the first question, and if it can be supported by consistency in its practical application, then there exists a clear case for maintaining that developments in the eighteenth century and onwards marked a new departure in the field of patent protection. If, on the other hand, the answer is negative, there is no reason why the patent systems of the three preceding centuries ought not to be regarded as precedents to the contemporary patent institution.

The evolution of the theory that an inventor had an "inherent" and pre-existing right to the protection of his invention, construed as a property right, which was to reach its culmination in the French Patent Law of 1791, went through two stages. The first was the appearance of the concept of "intellectual property rights" which according to Prager were already taking shape in "embryonic" form in sixteenth-century France.[29] The theory of "intellectual property rights" was in the beginning an effort to strengthen the position of authors against their publishers. At the time, copyrights were given to the publishers with the result that the authors were totally dependent upon them. When a kind of property right of the writer to his product was recognized, the copyright was effectively transferred to him. The intellectual property theory was not limited to authors and copyrights but slowly came to envelop all products of intellectual activity, usually referred to as "creations of the mind." During the eighteenth century this theory of "industrial property rights," as it was later called, gradually came to determine the inventor's position. The developments in the United States and France during this same period present the best illustrations of the evolution of the patent doctrine of the time.

In the United States the patent institution first appeared in statute form in Massachusetts (1641) and Connecticut (1672). Both took their inspiration from the English Statute of Monopolies, emphasizing society's interest in such protection.[30] This changed, according to Neumeyer, after the Revolution when several states introduced patent systems recognizing the right of inventors to get protection.[31] By 1780 ten of the thirteen states had adopted copyright laws which provided that authors were to be granted protection in virtue of a natural right. Since copyright and patent protection provisions were frequently in-

[29] *Supra*, n. 25.

[30] F. Neumeyer, "Die historischen Grundlagen der ersten modernen Patentgesetze in den U.S.A. und in Frankreich," *G.R.U.R.*: *Ausl.*, 58: 242, June, 1956.

[31] *Ibid.*

cluded in the same law, and since often no distinction was made between the two concepts, Neumeyer seems to arrive at the conclusion that the inventor's right was recognized as a natural right.[32]

Paragraph eight of article one of the American Constitution empowers Congress to grant monopoly rights in order to "promote the progress of science and the useful arts." Although this provision, upon which the United States patent law (1790) is based, makes no reference to any "inherent" or natural right of the inventor, it has sometimes been interpreted as a recognition of such a right. Madison, one of the authors of this patent law, and whose commentary on the underlying constitutional provisions is the only contemporary analysis that exists, has expressed himself in this sense, while emphasizing at the same time the interest of society in promoting science. On the natural right of the inventor Madison said that the author's copyright was solemnly recognized as a part of the Common Law in Great Britain, and that the right to useful inventions seems with equal justice to belong to the inventor.[33] The problem of reconciling the interests of the individual and society does not exist for Madison, who merely asserts that the usefulness to society coincides in both cases, i.e. copyrights and patents, completely with the claim of the individuals.[34, 35] Prager says that "it is a well supportable theory that modern common law vests the inventor with property in his invention in the same manner that it vests the author with property in his book", though he points out that such a theory was rejected by the authors of the Patent Act of 1793. "According to this Act," says Prager, "the applicant for a patent had to signify, in his petition, a 'desire of *obtaining* an exclusive property' in his invention, not a claim to have an existing property *secured* to himself."[36] Shortly before the passing of the Patent Act of 1790, President

[32] *Ibid.*

[33] Commentary on Article I, par. 8 of the U.S. Constitution by Madison (1888) quoted by Neumeyer, "Die historischen Grundlagen ...," p. 244.

[34] *Ibid.* Other authors, including some contemporary ones, have no reservations at all to the recognition of "inherent" rights of inventors. One author quotes Daniel Webster [citation probably from the Great India Rubber Suit Case (in 1852) in which Webster successfully defended some Goodyear patents] to make his point: "The Constitution does not attempt to *give* an inventor a right to his invention ... No such thing. But the Constitution *recognizes* an original, pre-existing, inherent right of property in the invention, and authorizes Congress to secure to inventors the enjoyment of that right." H. G. Fox, *Monopolies and Patents: A Study of the History and Future of the Patent Monopoly* (Toronto: University of Toronto Studies, Legal Series, Extra Vol., 1947) pp. 200–01.

[35] One feature of the American patent law, which was introduced in 1793 and remained in force until 1836, which might have been taken to support the theory of "inherent" or "pre-existing" rights, was the absence of any provision requiring examination of the merits of patent applications.

[36] Prager, *op. cit.*, pp. 742–43.

Washington, in a speech to Congress, concerning the Patent Act, said in part:

The advancement of Agriculture, Commerce and Manufactures by all proper means will not, I trust, need recommendation, but I cannot forbear intimating to you the expediency of giving effectual encouragement as well to the introduction of new and useful inventions from abroad as to the exertions of skill and genious in producing them at home. [37]

A better illustration could not be found of the true rationale of the American Patent Act. The importance put on facilitating the importation of foreign inventions is particularly significant. The United States was at that time as little industrialized as are most of the developing countries today. Though today the latter may have to give protection to foreign inventors, in order to obtain their participation in the local exploitation of their inventions, following the American example, the developing countries need not feel obliged to protect foreign inventors out of mere concern for the rights of the latter.[38] In his interpretation of the passage quoted above from Washington's speech, Neumeyer says that in view of the scientific and technological backwardness of the United States at that time, Washington was more or less forced to recommend all measures to secure the importation of the great technological developments from abroad.[39]

It is possible to affirm then that as far as the American Patent Act is concerned, there can be no doubt but that its primary *raison d'être* was to give an incentive for working new inventions locally; the rights of local inventors were only the corollary of the monopoly conditions deemed appropriate for such exploitation, while the rights of foreign inventors were completely disregarded.

In France isolated patent grants were known before they appeared in England. Though the first French patent law did not appear until after the Revolution, Prager suggests that France had a patent system at least as developed as that of England in the sixteenth and seventeenth centuries.[40] Analyzing patent proceedings from the latter part

[37] G. Washington, Inaugural Adress, quoted by H. A. J. Toulmin, *Invention and the Law* (New York: Prentice Hall, 1936), p. 11.

[38] When developing countries today are told of the necessity of having an "adequate" patent system ("adequate" meaning accepting at least the minimum requirements of the international patent system) and the "historical examples" of the now industrialized countries are referred to in support, the fact that several of the latter at certain periods used their patent systems chiefly as an incentive to "importers" of foreign-made inventions is understandably never mentioned.

[39] Neumeyer, "Die historischen Grundlagen...," p. 244.

[40] Prager, *op. cit.*, p. 711.

of the seventeenth century until almost the middle of the eighteenth, the same author says: "They reflect a patent system containing all basic elements of our present one ... omitting only one essential feature – the legal right of an inventor to claim for a patent."[41]

It has been considered that the first developments towards the recognition of a property right in inventions took place in the early part of the eighteenth century.[42] These developments, however, were not consistent and opinions opposed to the idea of industrial property rights were manifested on several occasions. An edict of 1762, for example, regulating privileges to inventors, gave the stimulus to inventive activity and the development of industry as the only motive for such privileges. Furthermore, such grants were subject to the condition that the invention be worked within one year; in the case of non-compliance, the privilege would be revoked.[43,44]

The first French patent act came into force in 1791. It was clearly inspired by the ideas emerging from the Revolution and the resulting Declaration of the Rights of Man. Property was now thought to be a prolongation of the personality of the owner. In the same direction of thought the new principle was established, that every invention is the inventor's personal property, and, that the law guarantees its complete and unlimited enjoyment by its owner.[45] If one should judge merely by the above-mentioned principle as it appears in the text of the law[46], and the theoretical support for the property theory[47], one would con-

[41] *Ibid.*, p. 727.

[42] *Ibid.*, pp. 730, 734; Neumeyer, "Die historischen Grundlagen...," p. 249.

[43] Roubier, *Le droit de la propriété intellectuelle.* Vol. I., p. 69.

[44] For the development in the particular field of design patents during the 18th century, see Prager, *op. cit.*, p. 731. After several laws had been passed successively, contradicting each other on the question of the existence of a legal right to claim protection, a law of 1787 became, according to Prager, the immediate forerunner of the general patent law of 1791, in this respect.

In discussions of "inventor's rights" it is often unclear whether the terminology refers to the right of a patentee in his patent or the right of an inventor in his invention. It does not seem consistent to maintain that a right in the latter sense existed before 1789, while recognizing that up to that date, patent grants were given as a royal privilege.

[45] Neumeyer, *Patent* ..., pp. 10–11.

[46] Roubier, analyzing the juridical configuration of the rights of the inventor as recognized by this law, stated that besides being rights to exclusive exploitation for a limited period, these rights did not constitute just a concession by the State; they were created as a direct result of the invention and the State could only act in a declaratory manner. Roubier, "Droits intellectuels ou droit de clientèle," *Revue Trimestrielle du Droit Civil*, 34: 250, No. 2, 1935.

[47] F. Machlup, E. T. Penrose, "The Patent Controversy in the Nineteenth Century," *Journal of Economic History*, 10:2, January 1950, p. 11., n. 35, give a typical example of such theoretical constructions by quoting the principal author of the Law, de Boufflers: "If there is for a man any genuine property it is thought ... and the tree which grows on a field does not so incontrovertibly belong to the owner of the field as the idea which springs from a man's

clude that the French patent act of 1791 in effect marked a new departure in the field of patent rights. A closer examination, however, of the various parts of the law as well as of the motives behind its introduction, reveals inconsistencies in some features of the law and contradictions to the property theory, and indicates that the underlying motives were far removed from the sole concern for the inventor. For one thing, the law required the patentee to exploit his invention.[48] Another feature of the law was that it included so-called importation patents, which meant that the "importer" of foreign inventions was granted a patent.[49] Thus instead of recognizing any property right of the inventor, the law permitted that the latter's invention be brought into France and provided that its importer be vested with the same right as an original inventor. This provision clearly reveals the dominant interest behind the law. Yet another provision, seemingly peculiar to France, accentuates the social interest behind the law. It states that an inventor having a French patent would loose it the moment he took out a foreign patent for the same invention.[50,51]

The author of the French patent law project was de Boufflers. Besides presenting his philosophical arguments in favor of the property theory, de Boufflers also advanced materially-oriented reasons, which have a striking resemblance with the motives underlying the American patent law, and, it is also supposed that de Boufflers was much influenced by the American example.[52] According to Neumeyer, de Boufflers emphasized three basic motives in a report supporting the patent bill: (1) the backwardness of the French industry; (2) the English penetration of the French economy; and (3) the desire to ameliorate the situation of the French industrial worker.[53] The same author explains the inclusion of patents for importation, saying that during the century of the great discoveries and against the background

mind belongs to its author. Invention, the source of the arts, is also the source of property: it is primary property while all other property is merely conventional."

48 Vojáček, *op. cit.*, p. 59.

49 Machlup, *op. cit.*, p. 235; Neumeyer, *Patent* ..., p. 11.

50 S. Pretnar, "The International Protection of Industrial Property and the Different Stages of Economic Development of the States," [translation supplied by BIRPI of "La protection internationale de la propriété industrielle et les différents stades de développement économique des Etats," *P.I.*, 69: 213–221, December, 1953] 10 pp. [BIRPI library] p. 2.

51 As in the case of the U.S. patent law (between 1793 and 1836) the French law did not require examination of patent applications as to their merits (novelty, inventiveness, etc.), a fact which may have given support to the idea of "inherent" or "pre-existing" rights. Unlike the case of the U.S., French patent law still maintains this feature.

52 Neumeyer, "Die historischen Grundlagen ...," p. 251.

53 *Ibid.*, p. 249.

of the more advanced development in England, this type of patent was for France absolutely essential.[54]

What are the three basic motives mentioned in de Boufflers' report as quoted above and the explanation by Neumeyer of the ground for the "importation-patent" but the objectives of, and reasons for, modern economic development policy? In the case of patents for importation the difference is that today they are only acceptable if given to the original inventor or his assignee.

Thus, the French patent law, as was the case with the American one, was based not on the promotion of the position of inventors *per se* but on the promotion of the economic and industrial performance of the State.

Most authors have not drawn so far-reaching conclusions. They have generally contented themselves with pointing out certain inconsistencies in the application of the theory of an "inherent" property right in inventions, while maintaining that the French law of 1791 and, in a lesser degree, that of the United States of 1790, have given a new quality to the patent institution.

A few writers, and significantly perhaps, mainly economists, have discounted the idea of a property right in inventions. These authors have questioned the sincerity of de Boufflers' natural property theory. Louis Le Grand maintains that the use of the word property was employed for the purpose of avoiding opposition to the patent bill.[55] Machlup is of the opinion that de Boufflers deliberately used the vocabulary containing "property" as a substitute for "privilege", and states that the latter in his report on the bill openly admitted that the property theory was basically employed for propaganda reasons.[56] For de Boufflers knew "that there was no hope of saving the institution of patent privileges except under an acceptable theory."[57]

Although the main rationale of both the American and French patent laws has thus been found to be the economic interest of the State, for which "all means available" were employed, and although the theory of an "inherent" right in inventions has been discredited, this

[54] *Ibid.*, p. 251.

[55] L. Le Grand, *Etude économique de la propriété industrielle; fondement et fonction économique de "cette propriété"* (Paris: Sirey, 1937), p. 52; for the same opinion, see M. Plaisant, *Traité de droit conventionnel international concernant la propriété industrielle* (Paris: Sirey, 1950), p. 6.

[56] Machlup, *op. cit.*, p. 242.

[57] Machlup, Penrose, *op. cit.*, p. 16.

latter theory has had a powerful influence on the further evolution of the patent doctrine.[58]

D. THE DIFFERENT THEORIES ON PATENT RIGHTS AND THE EVOLUTION OF THE PRIVATE PROPERTY DOCTRINE

This comparative analysis of various theories on patent rights and the evolution of the doctrine on private property starts with the ideas made popular through the American and French Revolutions and the resulting Constitutions. The different theories on patent rights, which have appeared since the end of the eighteenth century, cannot be dirctly derived from the evolution of the private property doctrine. In terms of general evolution, however, certain parallels exist. Such a comparative analysis is of interest for several reasons. The theories on the proprietary nature of patent rights have considerably influenced the patent doctrine; putting the emphasis on the powers conferred by property rights and not on the objects of such rights, similarities, as well as dissimilarities, between the two groups of rights become obvious; such similarities can be observed notably in contemporary compromises between private and social interests.

1. Natural law doctrine – inherent rights in inventions

Out of the American and French Revolutions was born the concept of certain inherent and inalienable rights of individuals; among them was the absolute and total control over private property. This concept of private property rights is sometimes referred to as the "individualist doctrine."[59] M. Waline distinguishes between two aspects of this doctrine: "individualisme juridique" and "individualisme politique." While the former expression refers to the notion that the individual was the end of all law, the latter indicates that the legislator sacrifices national or social interests in favor of the interests of individuals.[60] Allowing for a certain measure of generalization, it may be said that while reaction against the part of the individualist doctrine described

[58] Machlup, *loc. cit.* After pointing out de Boufflers' deliberate use of the "property theory", Machlup says that "this tactical device has lead to century-long debates on intellectual property." See further below, and n. 65.

[59] See for instance, M. Waline, *L'Individualisme et le Droit* (Paris: Editions Domat Montchrestien, 1945).

[60] *Ibid.*, pp. 376 ff.

as "legal individualism" appeared almost at once, i.e. from the beginning of the nineteenth century, reaction against "political individualism" came only during the latter part of the last century.

The first reaction against the more or less unrestrained liberty of the individual found expression in the French Civil Code of 1804. Since such restrictions as were introduced were made more for the benefit of other property owners than for society as a whole, they cannot be taken to indicate a basic change in favor of the interests of society.[61] It was only towards the middle of the 19th century that a reaction set in against the very far-reaching liberty of the individual. The nascent democratic ideas of that period, proclaiming the right to a certain liberty and freedom for all, were not compatible with total individual liberty. For, according to Waline, such total individual liberty tends to support an abuse of power by the stronger against the weaker.[62]

The first patent acts of both France and the United States came shortly after the promulgation of the French Civil Code and the American Constitution. As we have seen in the preceding section, the French patent act wholly adopted the natural law theory on private property to patents, proclaiming the inventor's "inherent" right to protection, while the American patent act, it has sometimes been stated, implicitly recognized such a theory. That the adoption of the theory of "inherent" and "inalienable" rights to private property did not automatically lead to a similar theory concerning patents is well illustrated by the actions of de Boufflers, when he sponsored the French patent bill. The important fact is nevertheless that the theory of "inherent" property rights in inventions was in fact supposed to derive from the general doctrine on private property.

The theory of "inherent" property rights in inventions introduced two new concepts: that a patent grant constituted private property; and that an inventor had an "inherent" right to claim patent protection. Based on a notion that "creations of the mind" were equal or even superior to conventional property, there emerged the theory that the rights of inventors were not created by positive law through the granting of patents but existed from the moment an invention was made, and that the only task of the authorities was to recognize such rights.

The most obvious inconsistency in the application of the natural law doctrine to the rights of inventors is the notion of "inherent" or pre-

[61] G. Ripert, *Les forces créatrices du droit* (Paris: Librairie Générale de Droit et de Jurisprudence, 1955), p. 196.

[62] Waline, *op. cit.*, pp. 394–95.

existing rights. Although the theory may seem to be applicable in a system in which the State, upon receiving an application for a patent grant, issues such a grant without examination, as the case was, and still is, in France, it would hardly be compatible in systems in which examination (as to novelty, inventiveness, etc.) precedes the patent grant. And even in the case of non-examination, i.e. in cases in which the intervention of the State is only of a declaratory nature, the theory does not hold for the case in which a second, independent inventor obtains a grant in the place of the first inventor.[63]

The "inherent" rights theory, appearing at the same time as the notion of "legal individualism," was not, as the latter, applied consistently even in the beginning. As we have seen, the original French patent law prescribed an obligation to work the patented invention. The French Constitution of 1795 provided furthermore that an inventor should *either* be given a compensation *or* an exclusive patent grant.

The idea that an inventor had a pre-existing right to his invention, and, to a lesser extent, the notion that such a right was of a proprietary nature, may stem from a confusion of the moral and pecuniary rights of an inventor. The rights of a patentee include the two groups of rights, but it is essential to distinguish between them. The pecuniary or patrimonial rights are derived from the monopolistic exploitation of an invention made possible by a patent grant. The moral right, on the other hand, does not depend on whether an invention is patented or not, though patent laws often contain certain provisions regarding this right. If it were not so, how could one distinguish between patentable and unpatentable inventions or between two or more inventors claiming protection for the same invention. When, towards the middle of the last century, private property began to lose its position as "absolute", more subtle and fruitful methods of analysis were applied to define the nature of property rights. The same was to be the case for the nature of patent rights.[64] The terminology "industrial property," in-

[63] Roubier, "Droits intellectuels ou droit de clientèle," pp. 278–79.

[64] The first country after France and the United States to introduce a patent law was Austria, in 1810. The Austrian law expressly declared that inventors had neither any property rights in their inventions nor any rights to patents. The law also affirmed that "the government reserved its prerogative to grant privileges to restrict what was called their subjects' 'natural rights' to imitate an inventor's idea." F. Machlup, "An Economic Review of the Patent System," *U.S. Senate, Committee on the Judiciary, Study No. 15 of the Subcommittee on Patents, Trademarks and Copyrights* (Washington: Government Printing Office, 1958), p. 3. Thus within the span of twenty years from the date which, in the opinion of many authors, constitutes a landmark in the evolution of the patent institution, or even its birthdate, one is back to the system of "privileges," which had been in practice for over three hundred years. Admittedly it was so far the position of only one country, but it indicated the future

troduced by the theorists of "inherent property rights" in inventions, is still used today. Its contemporary meaning, however, is merely to designate the rights conferred on the patentee by the patent grant, without prejudice to the nature of such rights. The impact of its original meaning on the later development of the patent doctrine was great.[65]

2. *The advent of the collectivist doctrine – the social utility of patents*

By the middle of the last century the whole individualist doctrine began to decline. In its place, and as a reaction to it, appeared what Waline calls the "anti-individualist" or the "collectivist" doctrine.[66] It became acknowledged that the principle of equal treatment before the law was insufficient or even obstructive to achieving a minimum of social justice. Towards the end of the nineteenth century the concept of social equality was substituted for that of legal equality.[67] This development was to have a strong influence on the patent doctrine, supporting the theory that the patent institution is primarily based on its expected utility to society. The practical result was that it put more obligations on patent holders.

The most far-reaching departure from the classical theory on private property rights is represented by the doctrine of teleological interpretation of legal acts. As a consequence of this doctrine, an act which itself lies within the power of an individual to perform, may still be sanctioned, if the motives behind it are contrary to the interests of society.[68]

Once it had been admitted that the "absolute" protection of private property was a concept of the past, it became easier to analyze the

evolution. In France, the stronghold of the theory of property rights in inventions, a patent law of 1844 omitted any reference to such rights. Roubier, *Le Droit de la propriété industrielle*, p. 69. According to Roubier, the motives of the law expressly stated that its authors wished to leave the metaphysical speculations in order to take account of facts and realities. Roubier, "Droits intellectuels ou droit de clientèle," p. 277.

[65] Machlup, Penrose, *op. cit.*, pp. 16–17, referring to the use de Boufflers made of the theory of "inherent" rights when introducing the patent bill, have said: "This appraisal of popular ways of thinking was certainly correct. For more than seventy years afterwards scholars seriously debated the notion of a property in ideas, a notion first proposed, to put it bluntly, as a political ruse."

[66] Waline, *op. cit.*, p. 346.

[67] Ripert, *op. cit.*, p. 90.

[68] "Il ne s'agit plus seulement de condamner celui qui mésuse de son droit en agissant mal; ce qu'on veut c'est empêcher l'exercise des droits individuels, même légitimes, lorsque cet exercice paraît contraire à l'intérêt général." G. Ripert, *Le régime démocratique et le droit civil moderne* (Paris: Librairie Générale de Droit et de Jurisprudence, 1936) p. 229; A similar definition is given by Waline, *op. cit.*, pp. 411–412.

contents of private property rights and compare their effects with the socially desired ends. Instead of using an all-comprehensive formula, they were separated into the three constituent parts of private property rights, which since Roman law have been accepted as the characteristics of private property: the exclusive rights to use, to derive an income from, and to dispose of, an object. In doing so, one avoids the mistake of confusing the content of the property right, i.e. the powers over an object by virtue of such a right, with the object itself.[69] It was now possible to admit that a restriction on, or even suppression of, one of these principal powers did not amount to an abrogation of the whole property right. Instead, it may be seen as an adjustment called for in the general interest, due to new circumstances.[70]

It is especially the power of exclusive utilization of the object which became the target for criticism and changes.[71] Certain categories of property owners have had their power to decide exclusively over the use of their property restricted by legislation. This is the case, for instance, where landlords are restrained from evicting tenants without proper cause. Other categories of property owners have been forced by changing circumstances to give up their exclusive right to use their property. This is the case of shareholders in modern, capitalist corporations, who, in practice, only retain the right of recieving remuneration from and disposing of, their property.[72] Indeed, some authors seem to discern such a trend applying to all productive property, i.e., property having an economic value to society apart from its value to its owner.[73,74]

[69] "... whilst the right of property is normally a *definite set of powers*, the underlying good ... may be of the most varied kind." Kruse, *op. cit.*, p. 107; in the same sense R. Savatier, *Les métamorphoses économiques et sociales du droit civil d'aujourd'hui* (Paris: Librairie Dalloz, 3 vols., 1948–59). Vol. III, pp. 107–08, 145.

[70] This has been admirably expressed by Ripert, *Les Forces Créatrices du Droit*, p. 28, when he says: "Quand on modifie la portée d'une règle juridique pour l'étendre ou la restreindre à raison des considérations nouvelles, c'est à fin de la conserver et non de la détruire. On pourrait même soutenir qu'on maintient ainsi son véritable sens. Ainsi le droit à la propriété individuelle n'est pas atteint ou compromis si le législateur impose des restrictions nouvelles à son exercice, soustrait certains bien à l'appropriation privée ... Le réglementer, le limiter par la loi, c'est reconnaître son existence et sa nécessité, le sauver peut-être en empêchant des abus."

[71] See Waline, *op. cit.*, p. 345.

[72] A. Berle, "Property, Production and Revolution," *Columbia Law Review*, 50: 9, January 1965.

[73] "La transition du droit privé peut être formulée: substitution à un régime de possession d'un régime de valeurs." E. Levy, *Les fondements du droit* (Paris: Librairie Felix Alcan, 1933), p. 87; in the same sense, G. Ripert, *Aspects juridiques du capitalisme moderne* (Paris: Libraire Générale de Droit de Jurisprudence, 1946), p. 129.

[74] Ripert, *Les forces créatrices du droit*, p. 211, discarding the theory of intellectual property and emphasizing that only the exploitation of an activity gives value to a monopoly grant,

With the advent of collectivism, which stresses the interests of society and the identification of property rights with a set of powers which could change according to circumstances, the old property concept of patent rights and the excessive if not exclusive emphasis on the interests of patentees were bound to change. The idea that a patent represents a piece of property in its conventional sense was held to be untenable. For while the patentee had both the power of deriving a remuneration from his patent and the power of disposing of it, by definition, he cannot retain the power of using it exclusively.[75]

However, a very special incident in the history of the patent institution probably retarded the evolution towards the acceptance of the patent institution as being essentially justified by its expected social utility. The incident referred to is a controversy between advocates and opponents of the patent institution as such. It started around 1850 and continued for almost a quarter of a century. Parallel to the emergence of the free-trade movement a strong opposition towards the patent institution arose, mostly among economists. The monopolies created by patent grants were held to be injurious to economic activity on the national level and, through its protectionist effects, obstacles to international trade.[76] This movement of opposition against patent grants rapidly gained strength in the 1850's, only to disappear two decades later. The sudden disappearance of the patent controversy after 1873 seems due to the simultaneous weakening of the free-trade movement and the severe depression starting in the early 1870's.[77]

The results of the strong opposition to patent grants during this period were several. Though one country abolished patent protection[78] and two other countries delayed the introduction of a national patent system,[79] the more important effects seem to have been in other directions. The long-term effect was a greater awareness of the need to prevent abuses of patent monopolies and of the inadequacy of having purely national patent systems in view of the expansion of in-

says that one is led to ask whether a like consideration of the notion of exploitation ought not to be of primary importance for material property as well.

75 Roubier, "Droits intellectuels ou droit de clientèle," pp. 280–81.

76 The fact that while all of Europe was involved in the controversy, it did not spread to the United States with its strong protectionist policies, appears significant. Silberstein, a contemporary advocate of inventor's "inherent" rights, however, explains the non-participation of the United States in the controversy by stating that the conviction of the necessity of protecting inventors was more securely implanted. Silberstein, *op. cit.*, p. 279, n. 110.

77 Machlup, Penrose, *op. cit.*, p. 6.

78 The Netherlands abolished their patent system in 1869. It was reintroduced in 1910.

79 Germany introduced its patent system in 1871 and Switzerland in 1887, in both cases after initially strong opposition.

ternational trade. One immediate effect of this controversy, however, was to reinforce the "property" theory. The patent advocates during this period, just as the French legislators at the time of the Revolution, faced the task of rebutting the charges of obstructive monopolies and privileges. To dissociate the patent institution from the monopoly issue and the free-trade issue, the device was once more used to promote the case of patent protection as one of "natural law and private property and of man's right to live by his work."[80] Alternatively with the "property" theory, the so-called contract theory was advocated. This latter theory, like the property theory, can be traced back to the French and American patent laws,[81] though it was to gain more prominence later. When the impossibility of applying the theoretical ideas of the "inherent" property rights concept was recognized, when new notions of the rights and obligations of the individual towards society became accepted, and a more scientific analysis of the economic impact of the patent institution was introduced, the contract theory gained much support. This theory was based on the contention that through the patent system the inventor was given an incentive to disclose what otherwise would have remained secret. However, several objections were raised. As most arguments serving to reject or defend the patent institution during that period have also been raised in the contemporary debate, they will be examined in the next chapter.

Even though the original property theory, which held that the patent were of a nature comparable to that of conventional property, was abandoned, attempts were made to explain the proprietary nature of patents by the creation of a third class of patrimonial rights. Patent rights, copyrights and certain other rights which do not fit into the two conventional groups of property rights, were supposed to form a new class of property *sui generis*. This new class of property rights was termed "intellectual property" by Edmund Picard (1874) and "immaterial property" by Josef Kohler (1875).[82]

The efforts of Picard, Kohler and others have been convincingly criticized by Le Grand and Roubier, among others. The former stresses the mistake of confusing moral and pecuniary rights and through an economic and legal analysis of the monopoly grant arrives at the con-

80 *Ibid.*, p. 9.

81 C. Ackerman, *L'Obligation d'exploiter et la licence obligatoire en matière de brevet d'invention* (Paris: Sirey, 1936), p. 329.

82 E. Picard, "Embryologie juridique" *Journal du droit international privé*, 10: 565–85, November–December, 1883; J. Kohler, *Handbuch des Deutschen Patentrechts* (Mannheim: J. Bensheimer, 1900).

clusion that "the law of industrial property is based upon the idea of an economic value of exchange, based on the utility and rarity of things"[83] Roubier points out that not only are there all sorts of immaterial things, which may be legally protected without including the right of exclusive exploitation – he criticized the fact that the definition of the "intellectual" or "immaterial" property rights was only a negative one, i.e., it was only said what these rights were not – but also the fact that the contents of a right are not necessarily changed if it is attached to an "immaterial" thing rather than to a material object.[84]

For all the persistent efforts made to link patent rights to the personality of the inventor, the evolution of practical considerations as to the justification of the patent institution has moved parallel to that of the private property doctrine. In private law the notion of private property rights being subjective rights or simple prerogatives has been replaced by the idea of private property rights as encompassing a complex of powers and obligations, tying the recognition of a right to the imposition of various obligations; the same is fundamentally true for industrial property rights. These rights ought not only to serve the interests of title holders but also those of the community, subject also to considerations of national and international economics.[85] Industrial property rights, formerly the exclusive concern of private law, are now regulated by various provisions of public law.

This is the consequence of substituting the regulations of legal relationships by the authorities for the complete contractual liberty, which, by resulting in unequal positions of the parties, had often led to distortions in competition.[86]

This apparently signifies a return towards the original considerations underlying the patent institution, i.e., those existing before the end of the eighteenth century, namely that the State granted patent privileges on the basis of their expected social usefulness.[87] If there are still some

[83] "*La législation de la* 'propriété industrielle' *repose sur la notion économique de valeur d'échange, établie sur l'utilité et la rareté des choses.*" Le Grand, *op. cit.*, p. 75.

[84] Roubier, "Droits intellectuels ou droit de clientèle," p. 290.

[85] C. Magnin, "Une mise au point des notions de base de la propriété industrielle," *P.I.*, 68: 144, October, 1952; in the same sense P. J. Pointet, "Du défaut d'exploitation des brevets d'invention," *Revue Suisse de la Propriété Industrielle et Droit d'Auteur*, May, 1952, p. 28, 39. See also J. B. Brown, "The Situation Confronting Our Patent System," *J.P.O.S.*, 21: 159–94, March, p. 161 ff.

[86] Magnin, *loc. cit.*

[87] In this sense A. Van Der Haeghen, "Partage des droits intellectuels en propriété industrielle et en droit d'auteur," *L'Ingénieur Conseil*, 44: 198, Novembre-Décembre, 1954, whose conclusion is that: "Le but économique des brevets se rapproche de celui des privilèges de l'ancien régime, en ce qu'il vise la création de richesses par la mise en exploitation de

authors who maintain that the patent institution is primarily a response to an inventor's claim for protection,[88] this would appear to result from the confusion between moral rights, which basically exist independently of any legal provisions, and pecuniary rights created under patent law. And even the pecuniary rights, represented by the monopoly grant, are not protected without exception. In cases in which a patentee does not satisfactorily exploit his invention, almost every national legislation has provisions for granting compulsory licenses or even revoking patent grants. Furthermore, though no country has yet introduced a general system of compulsory licenses, the encouragement to giving volontary licenses and the exclusion of certain fields of technology may indicate an evolution for the future toward a situation in which the inventor-patentee can claim remuneration for the exploitation of his invention but not the exclusive control over its utilization.[89,90]

quelque chose d'intéressant. A cet égard, la nouveauté de l'invention n'a qu'une importance secondaire."

Le but économique de la loi sur les brevets ... apparaît encore en ce que c'est ne pas à l'inventeur qu'est réservé l'exclusivité."

[88] Cf., for instance, M. Plaisant, "De la protection international de la propriété industrielle," *Académie de Droit International, Recueil des Cours*, 39(I): 361, 1932, and Toulmin, *op. cit.*, p. 89.

[89] J-M. Mousseron, *Le droit de breveté d'invention – contribution à une analyse objective*, (Paris: Librairie de droit et de jurisprudence, 1961), p. 251: "Le droit du breveté défini comme une 'propriété' en 1791, un 'droit exclusif d'exploiter' en 1844, se transformera peu à peu à un simple droit de créance."

[90] With the exception of Roubier, no attempts seem to have been made to define the contents of patent rights further than as being rights to exclusive exploitation. Roubier, after criticizing all property theories, finds that, as the patent grant confers the right of exclusive exploitation of an industrial activity, the aim is to vest the patentee with certain prerogatives vis-à-vis the public, the consumers. Though it might appear that those rights are established vis-à-vis the consumer, Roubier maintains that, for all practical purposes, the right to monopolistic exploitation is established against the patentee's competitors. As therefore the rights conferred by patent grants provide certain favorable positions in the competition for the consumer, Roubier has suggested to name these rights "droit de clientèle." Roubier, "Droits intellectuels ou droit de clientèle," p. 295.

CHAPTER II

THE ROLE OF PATENTS TODAY

The following chapter is devoted to some aspects of the patent institution today. After a review of some of the fundamental changes in the conditions surrounding inventive activity that have taken place since the beginning of the last century, the following points will be treated successively: the appropriateness of the original motivations for the patent institution in contemporary circumstances; the value or relevance of motivations developed later; some of the principal arguments against contemporary patent practices; and finally, some suggestions for more or less radical changes of the patent institution.

As an introductory note to the present chapter, it may be useful to examine briefly some of the contentions made to show or even "prove" the value of patents today. Although a few authors, having analyzed the patent institution with the most refined tools, have come to the conclusion that, at present, it is not possible to arrive at a definite judgment as to the net benefits of the patent system,[1] the majority of the writers on the subject are much less guarded in their opinions. It is generally admitted today that the patent institution has its principal, if not sole, justification in the economic interest of society. A number of authors emphatically refer to "economic experience" or "history" to justify the patent institution today.[2] Fox, in his often-quoted *Monopo-*

[1] See, for instance, F. Machlup, "An Economic Review of the Patent System," *U.S. Senate, Committee on the Judiciary, Study No. 15 of the Subcommittee on Patents, Trademarks and Copyrights* (Washington: Government Printing House, 1958); J. W. Markham "Inventive Activity: Government Controls and the Legal Environment," *National Bureau of Economic Research, Special Conference Series*, Vol. XIII (Princeton: Princeton University Press, 1962) pp. 587–608; S. Melman, "The Impact of the Patent System on Research," *U.S. Senate, Committee on the Judiciary, Study No. 11 of the Subcommittee on Patents, Trademarks and Copyrights* (Washington: Government Printing House, 1958).

[2] See, for instance, H. Randon de Sanso "The Effect of Patent Protection on the National Economy of a Developing Country," *I.P.*, 4: 114, May 1965, and H. A. J. Toulmin, *Invention and the Law* (New York: Prentice Hall, 1936) p. 22.

lies and Patents; A Study of the History and Future of the Patent Monopoly,[3] writes:

It is my feeling that the attacks on the present patent system ... are the product of ignorance and a failure to know the necessity upon which history demonstrates the patent system to be based, coupled with an inability to understand the significance of the historical factors.[4]

The author states notably that "the patent system today is not the result of inspired thinking but is a dictate of historical necessity."[4a] Without supplying any specific proof, Fox concludes his study thus:

"The economic history of any country will show conclusively that a strong and efficiently working patent system has been coincidental and coterminus with the relative progress and development of that country scientifically and industrially ..."[4b]. Often, when efforts are made to demonstrate the importance of patents to economic development, the concepts of patents and inventions are not kept clearly apart, which gives the impression that the latter have appeared only because of the existence of the former. Despite the general application of scientific and sceptical methods of interpreting the relevance of historical comparisons in social research, in the particular field of patented inventions, these dubious statements continue to be made without reservations.[5] References to "historical experience" almost invariably appear when arguments are put forward for developing countries to institute patent systems or to bring their systems in line with the requirements of international conventions. The following quotation may serve as an example:

[3] H. G. Fox, *Monopolies and Patents: A Study of the History and Future of the Patent Monopoly* (Toronto: University of Toronto Studies, Legal Series, Extra Vol., 1947).

[4] *Ibid.*, pp. 6–7.

[4a] *Ibid.*, p. 190

[4b] *Ibid.*, p. 208

[5] "For contemporary opinion it is likely to appear axiomatic that patent protection has been one of the principal prerequisites for the splendid industrial development that we can look back upon." [translated from Swedish] G. Eberstein, "Det industriella rättsskyddet – Några aktuella synpunkter," *N.I.R.*, 28: 74–79, No. 1, 1959., p. 74.; "Durch die hinzukommende geschichtliche Bewährung steigert sich die Berechtigung des Patentrechts gerade zu Selbstverständlichkeit." R. Blum, M. Pedrazzini, *Das Schweizerische Patentrecht* (Bern: Stämpfli, 3 vols., 1957–61) Vol. I., p. 67; "What else other than the Patent System and the resulting competitive free enterprise has enabled the free world to stay ahead of Russia in scientific technology." C. Barnes, "Patents from the Inventor's Viewpoint," *IDEA*, 4: 74–80, Conference No., 1960, p. 75.

The history of the industrial growth of Europe and the United States indicates that the protection of property rights in inventions is one of the essential preconditions of rapid and spontaneous industrialization.[6,7]

This type of argument based on "historical experience", purporting to show the role of patent protection, is questionable for several reasons. Firstly, there are no scientific tools by which a comparison could be made between what has happened and what would have happened under different circumstances.[8] Secondly, even if it were possible to measure the impact that patent protection has had during a certain period, there are no means by which to derive its present or future impact. Thirdly, the correlation between the industrial development of a country and the development of its patent system, which has been used by several authors to show the importance of the patent system to the industrial performance of a particular State, could just as conceivably be held to show an inverse dependence. When it is said that "China grants no patents to foreigners, which probably is a factor in that nation's limited industrial development" (said in 1943),[9] a statement to the effect that China's limited industrial development has not favored that country's participation in the international patent system, would seem equally plausible. Finally, when "historical experience" has been referred to for justification of the patent institution, the factor of cost to society of granting patents is generally absent,[10] or explicitly excluded;[11] and even if that cost could be calculated it would vary according to the country and the period of time.

[6] D. L. Ladd, "The Industrial Property Revolution in the Common Market and the United States," *I.P.*, 2: 124–27, April, 1963, p. 127; R. Brown, "Whither Goes the United States Patent System?," *IDEA*, 9: 251–71, No. 2, 1965, p. 255, writes: "It is a general fact that the living standards of a country and its economic status are generally proportional to the sophistication of its patent system," and again (p. 256) that "... the effectiveness of the United States patent system has been strongly evidenced by the place the United States holds in scientific and industrial progress"; Cf. also Rondon de Sanso, *op. cit.*, pp. 114–16.

[7] As to the use of terms such as "necessary" or "essential preconditions," A. Gerschenkron, *Economic Backwardness in Historical Perspective* (The Belknap Press of Harvard University Press: Cambridge, Mass., 1962) p. 357, says: "There should be a fine on the use of words such as 'necessary' or 'necessity' in historical writings. As one takes a closer look at the concept of necessity as it is appended to pre-requisites of industrial development, it becomes clear that, whenever the concept is not entirely destitute of meaning, it is likely to be purely definitional: industrialization is defined in terms of certain conditions which then, by an imperceptible turn of the writer's wrist, are metamorphosed into historical preconditions."

[8] Cf. Machlup, *op. cit.*, p. 79; E. T. Penrose, *The Economics of the International Patent System* (Baltimore: Johns Hopkins, 1951) pp. 38–39.

[9] W. B. Bennett, *The American Patent System, An Economic Interpretation* (Baton Rouge: Louisiana State University Press, 1943), p. 227.

[10] Penrose, *op. cit.*, p. 198.

[11] For the allegation that "patent protection costs nothing to the public" and related problems, see *infra*, p. 46.

Even if the alleged historical impact of patent protection could be substantiated, efforts trying to justify existing regulations of social life by it, the environment of which is continuously changing, would still be lacking in scientific exactness. Such an approach gives the impression that the long existence of a certain order helps to provide its own justification.[12]

A. SOCIETY AND THE INVENTOR TODAY

From the foregoing it is clear that in order to evaluate how appropriate the patent institution is today, the circumstances under which it is supposed to function must first of all be examined. Since it is designed to further inventive activity, the conditions under which such activity is carried out today must be known.

At the time when the American and French patent laws were introduced and during most of the last century, when national patent laws were passed in the Western world, the position of the inventor and the organization of inventive activity were clearly not what they are today. The rationale of the patent system at that time was twofold: induce those with inventive capacity to undertake such activities and to bring such men to disclose the secrets of their inventions. It was thought that without the pecuniary rewards of monopolistic exploitation the inventor would either not risk the expenses involved in research or without the guarantee of exclusive control over his invention, would work it in secret. In the latter case, the invention would be lost to society through the death of the inventor. The inventor at that time was an individual, self-taught, working on his own projects, generally financed by his own resources, and exploiting the results himself. Furthermore, the inventive process for any particular invention was thought of as so endowed with the unique qualities of its inventor, that but for his individual genius the invention would not be made. This idea of the invention as an individualized creation was supported by the seemingly fortuitous manner in which inventions were made.[13]

[12] See L. Le Grand, *Etude économique de la propriété industrielle; fondement et fonction de cette propriété* (Paris: Sirey, 1937), p. 67; on the general problem of searching for the motives of laws, G. Ripert, *Les forces créatrices du droit* (Paris: Librairie Générale de Droit et de Jurisprudence, 1955), p. 83, has said: "La difficulté de cette étude est qu'elle exige une impartialité du jugement dont nous ne sommes pas capables. La loi, quand elle est mise en vigueur va diriger l'économie et créer les moeurs. On a beau jeu, quand elle s'est appliquée, pour déclarer qu'elle était nécessaire à l'économie ou imposée par les moeurs. On juge alors ses causes d'après ses effets et on la justifie par son existence même."

[13] The present section only summarizes the conditions and premises on which the patent

In order to find out the extent to which circumstances surrounding inventive activity have changed, the following three questions might be asked: (1) who is doing research today; (2) who is supplying the financial means; and, (3) who is exploiting the results? Furthermore, it might be useful to inquire into (4) the characteristics of the inventive process and whether any relation exists between the number of patents and the amount of research; and finally (5) the relation that exists today between inventor and innovator.[14]

1. Who is doing the research?

It is obviously still the inventor. His individual position has, however, largely disappeared. First of all, inventive activity is increasingly being carried out by inventors employed by industry or, to a much smaller extent, by special research organizations.[15] These inventors do not live from the particular results of their inventive activities but from a regular income. Secondly, few inventions today can be exclusively attributed to the work of a single individual. Though the question as to the extent to which inventions today can be attributed to individual conceptions in their final shapes is disputed, nobody can deny that the organization of contemporary research is increasingly in the form of teamwork, and often scientists from different fields cooperate on a particular project.[16] Modern organization and research has rendered the idea of a clear division between pure and applied science questionable.[17] Such a separation has always been used to distinguish between what is patentable and what is not. It has been held that whereas ap-

institution was originally based and compares them with contemporary conditions surrounding inventive activity. The criticism that may be raised against the underlying premises will be analyzed in the following section.

[14] For a detailed description of changes in the social environment of science, cf. I. de Sola Pool, "The Social Environment for Sustained Technological Growth," *Patents and Progress, The Sources and Impact of Advancing Technology* [eds. W. Alderson, V. Terpstra, S. J. Shapiro] (Homewood, Ill.: Richard D. Irwin, 1965).

[15] For the fiscal year 1961–1962, the following partition of total research activities has been reported for the United States: industry – 74 per cent, government agencies – 14 per cent, universities – 9 per cent, and non-profit research organizations – 3 per cent. B. Daudé, "L'Importance actuelle de la recherche dans l'économie et les caractéristiques de l'industrie de la découverte," *La rentabilité de la recherche, Cahiers de l'Institut de Science Economique Appliquée, No. 148* (Paris: I.S.E.A., April, 1964, pp. 107–70), p. 127.

[16] "Modern scientific and engineering research is increasingly caracterized by the integrated application of the work of various specialists. The resulting condition of interdependence in inquiry renders the concept of inventor obsolete to a considerable extent." Melman, *op. cit.*, p. 18.

[17] See, for instance, F. Walleser, *Die Patentfähigkeit als rechtsteleologisches Problem* (Bern: Stämpfli, 1963) p. 19.

plied research is directed towards the solution of practical problems, which would be of direct economic benefit to society and thus worthy of a monopoly grant, pure science was merely an extension of our general knowledge. As the borderline between the two disciplines disappears, the exclusion of "pure "scientists from the reward system will have to be arbitrary.

2. *Who is supplying the financial means?*

It has been mentioned above that the formerly self-employed inventor has to a large extent become an employee of industry. If industry and private research organizations had simply taken over the financial role of the formerly self-supporting individual, it might have been said that the former had merely replaced the latter and that the assumptions underlying the patent institution had not really changed in this respect. However, this is not quite the case. The growth of government-sponsored research since the beginning of the last world war is striking, and even more so is the increase in total research expenditures during the same period. In the United States, in 1940, total research expenditure was some U.S. $ 120 million,[18] of which an estimated 25 percent was supplied by the government. Total research outlay in 1965 amounted to some twenty billion dollars of which two-thirds are estimated to have been supplied by the government.[19]

3. *Who is using the results?*

First of all, the individual, inventing and exploiting his invention by himself has largely been replaced in both capacities by corporations. Secondly, and even more important, is the concentration of research effort and, for all obvious reasons, exploitation of the results obtained. In addition to the large portion of patents obtained by big corporations[20] must be added the unknown, but probably considerable number of

[18] P. J. Pointet, "L'influence sur le développement économique d'une législation appropriée en matière de brevets et de marques," *R.I.P.I.A.*, 69: 148, October, 1961.
[19] P. J. Pointet, "The Role of Industrial Property in the Economic Development of States," *I.P.* 6: 64, March, 1967.
[20] According to J.-M. Mousseron, *Le droit de breveté d'invention – contribution à une analyse objective* (Paris: Librairie de Droit et de Jurisprudence, 1961), p. 30, an American study shows that 60 per cent of patents are granted to large corporations with teamwork research and 40 per cent are granted to smaller firms and individuals.

patents taken out by small companies and individuals and later bought by larger companies.[21]

So far, it is clear that the individual inventor has, to a considerable extent, become an employee and a member of a research team, that the self-supporting inventor has been replaced by the employee-inventor largely supported by government subsidies, and that the exploitation of inventions by large corporations, which by their size would be expected to dominate the smaller companies in the exploitation of new technology, is relatively greater than that of their smaller competitors due to the uneven distribution of government subsidies.[22] This last point should be kept in mind when the frequent argument that the patent system is of particular importance to small business is put forward.

4. Characteristics of inventive activity

From having been the field of action of self-employed, individual inventors, inventive activity today occupies a significant position in the total economic activity of any country. For industry, sustained research has become an indispensable means without which it cannot remain competitive and still less hope to increase its activities. Governments, for their part, are increasingly realizing that without substantial subsidies to support technological research, the welfare and progress of their countries will be impaired.

Whatever correlation there might once have been between a country's patent system, the number of patents taken out and the amount of research undertaken, little such correlation can be found today. "It is sufficient to look at American statistics; the increase in the number of patents applied for by Americans over the last twenty years is extremely small although everyone knows that the sums devoted to research ... have increased to extraordinary proportions."[23]

The ever-expanding basis upon which research, in both pure and

[21] Statistics showing the recipients of governmental research funds demonstrate the concentration of research both as between branches of industry and by single firms. For American figures, see Daudé, *op. cit.*, pp. 131–32.

[23] G. Finniss, "The Impact of Research Policy upon Economic Expansion and the Standard of Living," *I.P.*, 5: 89, April, 1966.

[22] "Exploitation" of inventions is taken to mean controlling the technology involved, because all patented inventions are not commercially exploited. Especially among big corporations the policy of taking out patents may often be based on the consideration of forestalling competitors from acquiring them. For certain practices like this, *infra*, pp. 53–54.

applied science, is carried out today tends to diminish the relative importance of any one invention.[24] One author, challenging the basic assumption behind the patent system that "single real inventions are distinguishable, patentable, [and] usable" has said:

> The interpretation of all social institutions as the end results of an impersonal evolutionary process marked by the gradual accretion and gradual change has become part of the common sense of modern social science....
>
> The transformation of technology and of economic society during the last century negates completely the patent law assumptions as to the nature of the inventive process.[25]

The fact that, with rare exceptions, any single patent is only a minute addition to the accumulated technological knowledge together with the increasing complexity of contemporary technology have lead to a situation in which a single invention rarely can be used in isolation. This in turn means that inventions generally constitute only one link in a complex technical product. The lesser the importance of a single invention in relation to the total technology required in any field, the further one is removed from the concept of the invention as an individial piece of new technology. To that extent also the single invention may become identified before it is made and active research will then merely concentrate to define the missing link. This latter circumstance has certainly helped to shape contemporary research policies within single firms.[26] The increasing complexity of industrial technology and the costs involved, in addition to the fact that inventions can rarely be used in isolation, have led to mergers of smaller industrial units into large integrated corporations or other forms of cooperation in the field of research, such as the creation of joint research facilities or agreements to share the research results among several separate corporations, so-called patent-pooling agreements. The contrast between contemporary arrangements for industrial research and the original

[24] C. Akermann, *L'Obligation d'exploiter et la licence obligatoire en matière de brevet d'invention*, (Paris: Sirey, 1936), p. 384: "Quelle que soit l'importance de l'invention, elle ne peut constituer, dans l'état actuel de technique qu'un apport minime par rapport au capital de connaissances constituant le patrimoine scientifique et technique de l'humanité et dans lequel l'inventeur a puisé et dont il s'est servi pour créer son oeuvre."

[25] A. E. Kahn, "Fundamental Deficiencies of the American Patent Law," *A.E.R.*, 30: 479–81, September, 1940.

[26] "An invention today is seldom a surprise. To a large extent we identify a purpose and then undertake an R and D program to find the means to achieve that purpose." de Sola Pool, *op. cit.*, p. 23; for a similar opinion, cf. Kahn, *op. cit.*, p. 479; an illustration of contemporary conditions of corporate research is given by Ch. R. Whittlesey, *National Interest and International Cartels* (New York: Macmillan, 1946) pp. 87–88 (quoting from Potts et al. v. Coe 140F. 2d, 474–477): "The Corporate research laboratory of today has given us the greatest invention of modern times, the knowledge of how to invent."

assumptions underlying the patent-grant has lead Penrose to conclude that:

> In creating the patent-pool, industry has recognized that the assumption behind the patent system does not fit the facts of modern technology; the idea of an individual inventor rewarded by a monopoly patent on "his" invention is an anachronism in modern cooperative research.[27]

Another result of the expanding wealth of technological knowledge, which has also contributed to the organization of sustained research today, is the shortening of the "life-length" of any individual invention.[28] This phenomenon is of course both a cause and an effect of modern organized research.

5. *The inventor and the innovator*

Whereas formerly the tasks of the inventor and the innovator were performed by the same person, this is no longer the case. The patent system, designed to support the inventor in both respects, now splits its functions to the extent that the inventor, whether an individual or an enterprise, does not also exploit the invention. This, however, may not in itself invalidate the assumption underlying the patent system, which is that only be giving the innovator a competitive edge over his rivals could he hope to recuperate the costs involved in the exploitation of the invention. Though the argument that the innovator would enjoy a sufficient competitive advantage by being first on the market with the new product was early raised against this, the counter-argument that profits would be wiped out too fast, may have seemed plausible at a time when competition was assumed to be almost perfect.[29] Today, however, the competitive market structure has largely been replaced by conditions known as imperfect or monopolistic competition, and to the sole competitive weapon of earlier days – price – have been added several new devices such as trademarks and advertising. The latter means of competition often overshadow that of pure price competition.

From the foregoing it can be seen that conditions surrounding research and the inventive process have greatly changed since the principles of the patent institution were laid down. This rather cursory examination of some aspects of these changes is intended to provide a general back-

[27] Penrose, *op. cit.*, p. 191.
[28] Walleser, *op. cit.*, p. 35.
[29] F. Machlup, E. T. Penrose, "The Patent Controversy in the Nineteenth Century," *Journal of Economic History*, 10: 18–19, January, 1950.

ground of reference for the remainder of the present chapter. Some of the aspects mentioned here will be developed more fully in the following sections.

Most authors readily recognize the fundamental changes in the conditions surrounding inventive activity, but their conclusions differ widely, as will be shown below. Some hold that because the patent system was designed for the individual inventor, the shift of location of inventive activity, the changes in the inventive process and in competitive conditions, may have rendered the traditional patent system obsolete.[30] Other authors consider that the system remains applicable although its rationale has changed.[31] Others again question the applicability of certain of the original rules.[32] One of the foremost German patent authrorities, H. Isay, writing in 1923, held that since the patent institution had been conceived and developed under early capitalism based on individual enterprise, these conditions had shaped its legal character from the beginning, and that the use of the patent instituion for any purposes of cooperative enterprise would run counter to its very essence.[33]

B. VALIDITY OF TRADITIONAL CONSIDERATIONS FOR PATENT GRANTS

Four separate considerations are generally mentioned as the original motives underlying the patent institution: (1) the utility of disclosure to society, (2) the incentive to inventive activity, (3) the just compensation to the inventor, and (4) the inventor's right to his creation. The evolution of the patent doctrine has brought many shifts of emphasis among them – especially between the first two which represent the interests of society and the last two which relate to the interests of the individual. A number of more recent justifications have been advanced (which will be dealt with in the following section) and adaptations of the original considerations have been made in an effort to reconcile the system with contemporary conditions. Frequently one finds references

[30] See for instance Markham, *op. cit.*, pp. 597–602; Whittlesey, *op. cit.*, p. 87.

[31] Mousseron, *op. cit.*, p. 26.

[32] See for instance F. Russo, "Introduction," *Les brevets d'invention dans l'économie. I. – Caractères institutionnels et problématiques économiques, Cahiers de l'Institut de Science Economique Appliquée, No. 116*, (Paris: I.S.E.A., August, 1961, pp. 3–5) p. 4; Kahn, *op. cit.*, p. 475 ff.; J. B. Brown, "The Situation Confronting Our Patent System," *J.P.O.S.*, 21: 159–94, March, 1939.

[33] H. Isay, *Die Patentgemeinschaft im Dienst des Kartellgedankens*, (Mannheim: J. Bensheimer, 1923) pp. 25–26.

to the motives underlying the patent institution without indication of the exact interpretation given to them. For this reason it is necessary to examine the motives, both in their original sense and their later interpretations.

1. *Utility of disclosure to society*

In exchange for the temporary monopoly rights granted to the patentee, he should disclose his secrets. In this way it could be made certain that inventions were not being worked in secret and subsequently lost by the death of the inventor. The idea was that after the expiration of the patent anybody should be able to use the invention. Two other considerations have been added to this original idea: that scientists would learn of the technological advance at the time of the patent grant, when the required description is published, instead of later, if ever, when the product based on the invention appeared; and secondly, that the collection of published patent applications would serve the scientific community as an up-to-date source on the advance of science.

The idea behind the original "utility-of-disclosure" theory has been challenged by several authors. They argue that save for exceptional circumstances, the inventor would only apply for a patent grant when he feared that he would not be able to keep his invention secret or ran the risk that his invention would be duplicated, independently, within the period corresponding to the duration of the patent grant. "It would follow," says Machlup, "that the patent system can elicit only those secrets which ... without a patent system would be dispersed even sooner."[34] This argument, presented already during the patent controversy of the last century, would seem to have acquired even more force today in view of contemporary organized research, where duplicate inventions are bound to become more and more numerous, and where, as a consequence, individual creativeness as the source of any particular invention is often replaced by an evolutionary chain of events conditioned by the "state of the arts."[35]

[34] Machlup, *op. cit.*, p. 76; G. E. Frost, "Patent Rights and the Stimulation of Technical Change," *Patents and Progress, The Sources and Impact of Advancing Technology* [eds. W. Alderson, V. Terpstra, S. J. Shapiro] (Homewood, Ill.: Richard D. Irwin, 1965,) p. 68, an ardent defender of the patent system, mentions that "there are many fields where trade secrets are now the practical substitute or alternative for patent protection. To the extent," says Frost, "secrets such as these are relied upon and maintained, the patent system has failed. " In so saying, he appears to implicitly recognize the validity of Machlup's thesis.

[35] "The duplicated inventing of identical ideas is the perfect and sufficient proof for the theory of the social origin of inventions ... The enormous frequency of duplicate inventing

Another fact of modern industrial research is that a large and growing part of technology is not subject to patents, thus quantitatively reducing the importance of the technology disclosed through published patent descriptions. A further fact that appears to diminish the importance of the "incentive-to-disclosure" thesis relates to the claim that it is assumed useful to society to be able to freely exploit the invention after the expiration of the patent protection. The idea that an invention about twenty years old today will continue to be valuable may often seem doubtful considering the present-day speed of technological evolution.[36]

That the published patent descriptions may serve as a documentation on the advances of science is a clear advantage, though its usefulness must diminish to the extent that the non-patented part of technology increases in relation to the patented. In any case, this is a mere by-product of the patent system. If the establishment of an information service were a major concern, certainly a more effective and less costly system could be found.

2. *Incentive to inventive activity*

While the four traditional considerations for patent grants are dealt with separately, they are not independent of one another. If one believes, for instance, in the argument that without a patent system, new inventions would be kept secret, one would undoubtedly agree with E. Blum that if inventions are kept secret, the industry loses the necessary stimulus for development and scientific research.[37] Others hold, however, that without a patent system, the same end-result, as the one

is best shown by the fact that discovery of anticipations is the usual reason why half of all the patent applications are never granted." S. C. Gilfillan "The Root of Patents or Squaring Patents by Their Roots," *J.P.O.S.*, 31: 620, August, 1949; for a similar opinion, see, E. Dame, *Die volkswirtschaftliche Bedeutung des Systems des Ausführungszwanges im Patentwesen* (Berlin: Verlag Chemie, 1929), p. 53; M. Börlin, *Die volkswirtschaftliche Problematik der Patentgesetzgebung unter besonderer Berücksichtigung der Schweizerischen Verhältnisse* (Zürich: Polygraphischer Verlag, 1954), pp. 17–18, though making a similar analysis and recognizing the logic of this conclusion, favors patent protection for its alleged benefits in leading to as quick a disclosure as possible.

[36] In this sense S. Pretnar "More on the Legal Protection of Industrial Property," *I.P.* 71: annex, January, 1955 [translation supplied by BIRPI of "Nochmals zur Frage des gewerblichen Rechtschutzes in der Struktur des heutigen Weltwirtschaft, BIRPI Library] p. 4.

[37] "Where would the world be today if it had to renounce to the enormous number of inventions made in the United States of America, in Great Britain or in Germany, that is to say, if inventors in those countries so rich in creative genius had not had the assurance to have their inventions properly protected and had for that reason kept them secret?" E. Blum, "Abuse of Monopolies and Its Prevention," *Souvenir – Indian Patents Centenary 1856–1956* (Calcutta: Patent Office, 1956), p. 55.

suggested by Blum, would come about, but for the opposite reason: if the results of all scientific work were to become free for everybody, it would not pay anyone to exploit them and thus the inventions made available would be lost to society.[38] The former opinion is not consistent with what was shown in the previous paragraph. The tenability of the latter opinion will depend on whether unpatented inventions are exploited and on the importance of other possible incentives to industrial research.

Without questioning the historical role of the patent system as an incentive to inventive activity – and, not at least, as an incentive to the importation of foreign inventions – its effective value as an incentive under contemporary conditions may appear doubtful. What once might have been an appropriate means, despite its costs, to encourage long-term technological growth still in its infancy, might well be less appropriate under present-day conditions. There are two questions to answer: does the patent system today offer an effective incentive to inventive activity, and if so, is such an incentive necessary or even beneficial to society? The latter question will, of course, be of interest only if the answer to the first is affirmative. – In any case, the latter question will be treated in a subsequent section as it is intrinsically related to the calculations of private and social costs and benefits, the only scientific approach in appraising the patent institution. – Whatever incentive potential patent protection may have had earlier in encouraging the inventive spirit of scientists, such a role of the patent system would seem of less consequence today considering that invention and continual innovation is a *sine qua non* condition for industrial and economic growth.[39] From a financial point of view, however, the

[38] See for instance J. L. Kahn, "Découverte scientifique et propriété industrielle," *Les brevets d'invention dans l'économie. I. – Caractères institutionnels et problématique économique, Cahiers de l'Institut de Science Economique Appliquée, No. 116.* (Paris: I.S.E.A., August, 1961) p. 70.

[39] Börlin, *op. cit.*, p. 41; Mousseron, *op. cit.*, p. 37, states however: "Le brevet représente un stimulant actif pour le chercheur. Ce l'était en 1791 et 1844; ce l'est plus encore de nos jours .... La loi est donc un facteur important dans l'intensification des recherches dans un pays. Il y a là un argument puissant en faveur du renforcement du droit de breveté"; A. Troller, "Intellectual Property and Justice," *I.P.*, 3: 122, April 1964, in a similar analysis says: "If the patent system were abolished, all incentive to intellectual effort by those to whom we owe the kind of technical progress, which can be directly converted into practice, would be removed. They would never use and develop their talents with the same enthusiasm." The author continues with the following peculiar argument: "That would be detrimental not only to science but also to themselves and those around them .... A lot could be said to this and to the value of the community of each person's intellectual development ....

In their attack on patent legislation, economists have not ventured into the field where purely economic reasoning so easily goes astray."

patent may still be a strong incentive. The value of the patent incentive in this respect can only be estimated when it is compared to other forces inducing industry to invent and innovate. Only by continuously undertaking research can an industry remain competitive. These considerations make the assumption that without patents there would be no sufficient incentive for such research to take place rather doubtful. It is generally recognized that the volume of industrial research is influenced by strategic, competitive considerations. In such cases calculations of immediate profitability are less important than long-term prospects for the future.[40] It has been admitted that the influence of the patent system on inventive activity and technological change does not lend itself to any reliable scientific examination.[41]

A general feature of national patent laws is the partial or total exclusion from patentability of certain products. The most common use of such exceptions is made in the case of pharmaceuticals and foodstuffs. Sometimes an exception refers to patents for either products or processes. The usual reason for these exceptions is that there is a particular public interest in not restraining the supply of products essential to the general welfare. At first sight, such a motivation might well seem acceptable. Typical is the following comment on such restrictions, made by Roubier, when he says that one easily understands the motives of the legislator in not creating monopolies on goods of essential importance to the life and health of the people.[42] On closer scrutiny, however, the following questions inevitably arise:

> If patents are regarded as a means of stimulating technological progress, and if progress in the food and drug industries is not less desired than in other industries, why should these exceptions be made? Is the answer that monopolies in food and in medicine are intolerable, consistent with belief in the theory of the acceleration of progress through patent monopolies? Does it not reflect some doubt in the theory?[43]

[40] In this sense Börlin, *op. cit.*, pp. 55–56.

[41] See, for instance, J. W. Markham, J. S. Worley, D. S. Brothers, "The Value of the American Patent System: An Inquiry into Possible Approaches to its Measurement," *Patent, Trademark and Copyright Journal of Research and Education*, 1: 22, No. 1, 1957; S. C. Gilfillan, "The Prediction of Technical Change," *Review of Economics and Statistics*, 20: 378, November, 1952; see also J. Rossman, *Industrial Creativity: The Psychology of the Inventor* (New York: University Books, third ed., 1964) pp. 151–59, for an interesting analysis of the motives of a large number of individual inventors, and the questionable interpretation of these findings by Bennett, *op. cit.*, pp. 30–31.

[42] "On comprend la pensée à laquelle obéissent ces législateurs, à savoir de ne pas créer de monopoles sur des objets trop précieux pour la vie et la santé des personnes." P. Roubier, *Le droit de la propriété industrielle* (Paris: Sirey, 2 vols. 1952, 1954), Vol. II, p. 34.

[43] Machlup, *op. cit.*, pp. 8–9.

One reaction may be to propose to also grant patents in those fields, but making compulsory licences immediately available. Such is the rule, for instance, in India. In the case of this country, it has been said that:

> In ordering a compulsory licence in such a case, the Controller is guided by one principle, which is that ... [such inventions] should be available to the public at the lowest price consistent with the patentees' deriving a reasonable advantage from their patents.[44]

The Brazilian delegation to the Lisbon Revision Conference of the Paris Union (1958), explaining that country's policy of not granting patents on chemicals, foodstuffs and drugs, said that in refusing to grant patents for chemical, pharmaceutical, and food-products, the legislator had wanted to avoid increasing the cost of living in the most important sectors: nutrition and health. In so doing the legislator was motivated by social considerations so strong as to take precedence over any particular private interest.

"However," continued the Brazilean delegation, "the legislator has not neglected measures providing for an equitable compensation for those who do research and work for improvements in the sectors of health, nutrition and chemical products."[45]

Is not the deriving of a "reasonable advantage from the patent" (the Indian case) and the granting of "an equitable compensation" (in the case of Brazil) the principle which is supposed to underlie the whole patent institution? If the standards quoted above should amount to a lower remuneration than that expected from an ordinary patent grant, then notwithstanding such standards of reward, progress in areas considered particularly vital to the welfare of a nation will be given less incentive. If, on the other hand, such standards are supposed to ensure adequate progress, why should they not be applied generally?[46] The chemical field represents a special area. Though it cannot be said to be endowed with a particular public interest relating to the

[44] A. Bose, "Compulsory Licencing of Patents," *Souvenir – Indian Patents Centenary 1856–1956* (Calcutta: Patent Office, 1956), p. 59.

[45] Actes de la Conférence de Lisbonne (1958), p. 918. [translated from French]

[46] Akerman, *op. cit.*, p. 384, suggests that the international patent convention should stipulate that certain categories of inventions should, when patented, be immediately opened to general licensing. Such a solution does not, however, answer the theoretical problem involved. – "Expedients such as licenses of right ... cannot repair the lack of theoretical principle behind the whole patent system. They can only serve to confine the evils of monopoly within the limits contemplated by the legislators; and ... the science of economics as it stands today furnishes no basis of justification for this enormous experiment in the encouragement of a particular activity by enabling monopolistic price control." A. Plant, "The Economic Theory Concerning Patents for Inventions," *Economica*, 1: 51, No. 1, 1934; for fuller treatment of this point, see Section D below.

general welfare, there is an opinion against granting patents for chemical products on the theory that such monopoly grants restrict competition too much, whereas process patents will only force competitors to invent another way of producing an existing product. In Germany this has been the case for a long time, which has lead Roubier to the following conclusion: "There can be no doubt but that the nonpatentbility of chemical products has assured a great development of the German chemical industry."[47] The same author also mentions that many people today question whether patentability in general should not be restricted to means and methods of production while excluding the products themselves.[48]

Whether patents play any significant role as incentives to inventive activity cannot be tested scientifically. That they do induce some inventors is very probable. The reason for doubting that the contemporary patent institution provides a major, and still more, a decisive incentive to research, however, do suggest that competitive forces within industries and public financial support provide more powerful research incentives.

3. *Just compensation to the inventor*

The two justifications for the patent institution examined above were based on the interest of society to encourage technological progress. The "just reward" argument as well as that of the inventor's right to his creation both relate to the interests of patentees. The "just reward" theory is based on three assumptions: (a) justice demands that the inventor be rewarded for his services, (b) that this reward should be commensurate to the services rendered, that is, proportional to the welfare generated, and (c) that the only method of objectively measuring the required reward is to grant temporary monopoly privileges.

(a) In order that an inventor be rewarded for his services, there must exist an individual inventor and his creation must be an identifiable

[47] [translated from French] Roubier, *op. cit.*, Vol. II, p. 34; Frost, *op. cit.*, p. 84, seems to ignore the German exception of patentability for chemical products, when he takes the achievements of the German chemical industry as an example of the effects of patent protection, saying: "It is exceedingly doubtful that this intense research and new product competition would continue in the absence of a patent system." – Whatever is the weight of the opinion of Roubier it should be realized that patentability of chemical products has not hindered the chemical industries in, for instance, Great Britain and the United States from acquiring their powerful positions in this field.

[48] Roubier, *Loc. cit.*

piece of technology. As was suggested above, whatever the position of the inventor was formerly, today he is increasingly becoming an employee inventor and is often just one member of a research team. Thus, according to many, the concept of an individual inventor is to a large extent inconsistent with the actual organization of research today. Another change in the position of the inventor from that assumed originally by the patent doctrine is that he is to a large extent no longer the exploiter of his invention. Thus the inventor, instead of receiving his "reward" from what the consumers were prepared to pay for his products, will now often depend upon his bargaining strength vis-à-vis the corporation buying his invention. The more concentrated research ventures become, and the more numerous the sponsored research grants are, the more insignificant will become the power of the inventor.[49] As has been observed in a previous paragraph, a large and growing part of technology today is not subject to patents. By the relative increase of this type of technology, a system rewarding some inventions, even though they may be identifiable and attributed to one individual, while not rewarding a large, or major, part of new technological creations, would seem more and more arbitrary.

(b) Although reasons for serious doubt have been shown in the preceding paragraph concerning the validity of the concepts underlying the "just reward" theory, i.e. those of the generally existing individualized inventors and identifiable inventions, they will be disregarded in the following analysis. The assumption will be made that there are grounds for granting a special reward to individual inventors – patentees. When examining the justifications for such a reward as the patent grant is assumed to convey, one has to distinguish between two approaches: one in which the monopoly grant is simply thought to be the most equitable remuneration to the inventor, and another, in which the idea seems to be that the inventor is entitled to some particular remuneration above what a pure payment for his services would amount to. This latter approach seems to rest on a belief that a mystical, higher quality is attached to certain manifestations of intellectual achievement in comparison to the rest of human activity. This may probably be explained by the whole atmosphere surrounding the subject of inventions. The thought of all the wonders that technology has brought for-

[49] "Another way of describing this situation is to say that the inventor today instead of working for a wide market of consumers is selling his services to a monophsony which administratively decides what it wants." De Sola Pool, *op. cit.*, p. 25.

ward coupled with uncertainty of future inventions and a suspicion that if all efforts to encourage their appearance are not employed, they will remain hidden. While understandable during the infancy of technological development, such fears are hardly consistent with contemporary scientific approaches to inventive activity. Rondon de Sanso, stating that there is a need to protect the inventor, says that, "the lowest expression of such protection is the granting of patents."[50] Even Le Grand, after having shown in his very factual study that the patent institution has its foundation in the consideration of utility that society attaches to inventions, subscribes to this idea, saying:

"Just imagine the enthusiasm of the inventor in case ... he found himself considered a mere producer of ideas who would not be entitled to more than a salary."[51]

Walleser also supports the idea that monopoly privileges constitute a "just reward" to the successful inventor by the following curious argument:

On finally considering those inventors whose creations only resulted in disappointments and losses, and the unsuccessfulness of the duplicate inventors to whom protection had to be denied, one is forced to admit that the compensation that consumers pay to inventors in total, is less than due."[52]

Thus this author, while recognizing the inequalities of the patent system when it comes to rewarding inventors, uses these very facts in support of the system!

The approach to the "just reward" theory recognizing the patent system as the most preferable means of rewarding inventors has been expressed in the following way:

An exclusive privilege of temporary duration is preferable; because it leaves nothing to anyone's discretion; because the reward conferred by it depends upon the invention's being found useful, and the greater the usefulness, the greater the reward; and because it is paid by the very persons to whom this service is rendered.[53]

"This," say Machlup and Penrose, "became the standard argument in the defense of the patent system during the patent controversy as the most adequate method of securing just rewards to inventors."[54]

[50] Rondon de Sanso, *op. cit.*, p. 115.
[51] [translated from French] Le Grand, *op. cit.*, p. 199.
[52] [translated from German] Walleser, *op. cit.*, p. 52.
[53] Machlup, Penrose, *op. cit.*, p. 20, quoting J. S. Mill, *Principles of Political Economy* (London, 1852) p. 932.
[54] *Ibid.*

Despite present-day more refined approaches to economic analysis the same argument or variations of it, are still put forward today.[55]

(c) The argument that the price paid for a patented product or a product produced by a patented process reflects its usefulness to society implies that "the maximum total revenue that can be obtained in the market by a monopolist is a correct measure of the usefulness to society of an invention," and that "the moral deserts of the inventor are in proportion to the usefulness of the invention as so measured."[56] The idea that the price of a product equates social usefulness can only come from a confusion between usefulness and economic value expressed as the price paid for a good. However, the higher the price the more restricted will be demand, and the lower the price the more widespread will be the use of any good. This restatement of the paradox of value must be particularly obvious in the case of patented inventions, for in this case their scarcity-value does not stem from their limited supply, but is the result of a deliberate restriction put on their use. Thus they acquire an economic value or price and at the same time, their total usefulness are restricted.

The assumption that the achievement of the inventor is equal to the monopoly price paid for his creation has no logical foundation. The cases in which fairly simple inventions have rendered their inventors rewards out of all proportion to their efforts are too well-known to require elaboration.[57] The weakness of this assumption becomes particularly obvious in the case of inventions "ahead of time." When the "just reward" theory is treated, it is usually said that only in the case of an invention "ahead of time" may the reward not correspond to the social usefulness because society is not yet prepared to fully exploit it. The conclusion would then seem to be that while the system remunerates inventions, which have been more or less expected from the point of view of existing technology, and which would thus seem to need less

[55] See, for instance, Walleser, *op. cit.*, pp. 54–55; and A. W. Deller, "Social and Economic Impact of Patents," *J.P.O.S.* 46: 449, June, 1964.

[56] Penrose, *op. cit.*, pp. 26–27; see also F. Machlup, "Patentwesen – I. Geschichtliche Überblick [und] II. Wirtschaftsteoretische Betrachtung," *Handwörterbuch der Sozialwissenschaften, Vol. VIII.* (Göttingen: G. Fischer, J. C. B. Mohr, 1962) p. 242.

[57] There may also be cases in which an invention, though in itself a complex piece of technology, would, according to the norms, render its inventor(s) disproportionate rewards. A particularly striking case is mentioned by F. Neumeyer, *Patent: reflexioner kring patentinstitutionens uppkomst, utveckling och ställning i vår tid* (Vol. IV of Studier och Debatt, Stockholm: SNS, 1958) p. 51. For general considerations on the need to change the standards of reward, see de Sola Pool, *op. cit.*, pp. 24–26.

of an artificial incentive to be brought out, in the case of inventions representing real breakthroughs, the system fails to grant "adequate" recompense.

4. The inventor's right to his creation

The original idea behind this justification for the patent institution was that, by natural law, the inventor had a property right in his mental creation, born at the moment the invention was conceived and only to be recognized and protected by the State. Two concepts which developed later must be distinguished from this idea: that the inventor has a property right in his patented invention and the concept according to which the inventor has a property right in his patent.

The thesis of inherent property rights was the outcome of the natural law philosophy of the late eighteenth century. Although the theory as applied to inventions showed serious inconsistencies from the beginning, and although the general theory of inherent rights in private property belongs to history, its application to inventions is still advocated by a few authors today.[58] The flaws in the logical application of the inherent rights thesis to inventions appeared from the beginning, when "patents of importation" were admitted as well as the use of revocation of patent grants. In addition, the exclusion of certain products from patentability is inconsistent with such a theory.

When it was recognized that, whatever justification there might be in protecting the inventor, there was also a social interest to be taken account of, it was said that not only "natural justice" but also "economic expediency" demanded the protection of the inventor.[59] In order to give the patentee as secure a position as possible, the concepts of "intellectual" or "immaterial" property rights were created giving the patentee a property right in his patented invention. The theoretical

[58] Probably the most eloquent but nevertheless dubious defense of this thesis has been presented by Plaisant: "La mission de l'Etat est de restituer les inventions dans leur intégrité et de rétablir les inventeurs dans leur eminente dignité. L'invention nous apparaît comme la manifestation d'un épanouissement suprême de la personne; elle s'élève au sublime par la génie de la conception. Cette exaltation doit être attisée et protégée comme un droit de l'homme dans son essence la plus précieuse: l'homme demeure la richesse inépuisable. La personnalité humaine et le flux qui en émane doivent être placés au dessus du réseau des intérêts communs." M. Plaisant, "Le rôle des inventions dans l'industrie et des inventeurs dans l'Etat," *Revue Politique et Parlementaire*, 267: 3–10, April–June, 1952, p. 10; *cf.* S. C. Gilfillan, *The Sociology of Inventions* (Chicago: Follett, 1935), p. 119: "The only inherent right of an inventor . . . is that it may be expedient – or it may not be – to pay him more or less well for inventing."

[59] Fox, *op. cit.*, p. 200.

basis on which this rested was the much-used argument illustrated by Fox:

The patentee receives nothing from the law which he did not have before. The only effect of the patent is to restrain others from encroaching upon the private property of the patentee – property which is his by the highest possible title of natural right.[60]

There are two obvious flaws in this reasoning. Even if an invention can be thought of as so advanced with reference to previous technology as to be a proper creation of the inventor, there is still, during the duration of the patent grant, a prohibition on the exploitation of duplicate inventions. Secondly, there is a confusion between the nature of material and immaterial goods.[61] "The right to exclude others from the use of particular material things is necessary for their efficient use ... The rights to exclude others from the use of an idea demands a justification on alltogether different grounds."[62]

Without any theoretical foundation, the idea has been put forward that a patentee has a property right in his patent. A patent grant gives its holder certain legal claims concerning the exploitation of the patented invention. But there is hardly any justification to talk about a property right in a set of legal claims.

C. LATER JUSTIFICATIONS FOR THE PATENT INSTITUTION

Besides the four justifications for the patent institution dealt with in the previous section a number of other considerations have been developed later. Some of them are supplementary to the traditional ones and others are substitutions for them. These new points have been introduced to take into account the changes that have occurred in the field of inventive activity and in its environment. Three of these more recent justifications for the patent system will be briefly examined below. Though they may be regarded as the most significant, there exist others, some of which will be mentioned in the subsequent section.

[60] *Ibid.*, p. 203.

[61] *Ibid.*, p. 204. Fox illustrates this confusion, when he holds that "once it is admitted that property – private property – is an acceptable and proper incident of law of human life, then the argument against monopolies fails. For every property constitutes a monopoly."

[62] F. Machlup, *The Political Economy of Monopoly: Business, Labor and Government Policies* (Baltimore: Johns Hopkins, 1952), p. 281.

1. *Invention and innovation*

Given the contemporary organization of research, it is evident that inventive activity, up to and including the stage at which inventions are patented, today has both new incentives and sources of support, which are independent of the patent system. As a consequence, the emphasis today is often laid less on the support of inventive activity than on the encouragement of innovation. Originally, an invention to be patentable had to be developed to the state at which it could be practically exploited. Though such cases may still exist, in practice, patented inventions are often far from the commercial stage, and additional time and finances are needed to complete and launch the product on the market.[63] This may be explained both by efforts to seek protection as early as possible and so reduce the risk of independent "duplicate" inventions and by the immensely more complicated technology of today. Thus many authors recognize that the major part of the support provided by the patent system has shifted from the inventor to the invention, and that its incentive is more important for the innovative than for the inventive phase.[64] The majority of authors, after having established these changes, merely accept the new situation and see it as an indication that the patent institution has been able to adapt itself to new circumstances. This new situation, however, presents aspects of the appropriateness and usefulness of the patent institution which cannot be supported by the same arguments used for the creation of special incentives for inventive activity. The basic difference is that while inventive activity must precede the patent, innovating activity follows it. Whatever justifications there may be for subsidizing inventive activity – to the detriment of other activities – they cannot be valid without further qualification for financing the exploitation of patented inventions. Arguments in favor of such support will have to show that innovations based on patented inventions are socially more desirable than other innovating activity, whether in technology or any other field. When the uncertainty of what may or may not be invented under various incentive schemes is replaced by a situation in which some inventions might not be exploited without special support, then, if their exploitation is still desirable, would not a particular aid for such cases be more appropriate, i.e., less costly?

[63] A usual estimate today of total costs for inventing and marketing new products will allow for ninety percent for the latter stage.

[64] See, for instance, Bennett, *op. cit.*, p. 46; Machlup, "Patentwesen," p. 245.

2. *Means to support costly research*

The fact that a large and growing part of inventive activity is today carried out by corporate and other laboratories on a sustained and continuous basis has changed the original idea, that a patent grant would enable the inventor to recuperate his expenses for any particular invention. In the modern version of the cost-covering role of patent monopolies, the profits generated by successful inventions are also supposed to pay for less successful projects. Mousseron, considering the modern conditions of inventive activity, says that the firm which invests, multiplies its laboratories, recruits tens and hundreds of scientists, feels that it has a right to the invention and sees in its protection something due to the company.[65] Markham, on the other hand, considering the same situation, observes that while corporate enterprise has obviously not eliminated the risks of uncertainty, the large corporate laboratory can, on the insurance principle, reduce it.[66] It is sufficient to look at the proportions of successful and unsuccessful inventions to strongly doubt that it is at all possible for a firm to recover its research expenses in the way described above, or at least that it is a rational use of the patent system. Mousseron refers to a set of statistics which is often quoted, with minor variations: according to these figures, only one percent of patented inventions generates an income well above costs, nine percent give moderate returns, twenty percent merely cover expenses, while seventy percent of all patented inventions give rise to losses.[67] To the extent that firms do try to cover their research expenses by the profits from the relatively small number of successful patents, there can be no justification for using the patent system for such a purpose without, at least, redefining its role.

3. *Means to support individuals and small enterprise*

Of all justifications for patent grants introduced lately, the most frequently mentioned holds that although some large companies could continue their activities in the absence of a patent system, it would seriously affect the existence of individuals and small or new compa-

[65] Mousseron, *op. cit.*, p. 29.
[66] Markham, *op. cit.*, p. 600.
[67] Mousseron, *op. cit.*, p. 25. See however J. Schmookler, ***Invention And Economic Growth*** (Cambridge, Mass.: Harvard University Press, 1966) pp. 47–55, who, on the evidence of certain studies, claims a much higher proportion of economical and profitable inventions.

nies.[68] The general idea behind this argument is that financially weak patentees receive a strong competitive weapon through the patent grant with which they can fight the overwhelming financial and technological power of large corporations. Most advocates of this theory do not go further than this in their analysis. Börlin, however, has made a detailed examination of the factors involved in order to find out whether, in the end, the individuals and small firms are relatively better off with or without the patent system.[69] Comparing finally the sets of advantages and disadvantages found for weak and powerful patentees respectively, Börlin asks whether patent-induced growth of power is greater for the one or the other category of patentees and finally draws the conclusion, that the patent law has changed the unequal situation between weak and powerful competitors in favor of the former.[70] The author, however, arrives at this conclusion only by affirming that some of the abuses, which are a result of the patent system, would occur also if it were non-existant. The powerful corporations would have other means to subdue their weaker competitors. But the degree to which this power is increased by the patent system is not great enough to cancel out the benefits derived from it by the less powerful patentees.[71] Nevertheless, Börlin also concludes that the concentration-promoting effects of the patent system, only partially balanced by the protection of smaller companies, negates the guiding motive of the lawmaker that the monopolistic effect of the patent law should limit itself to exclusive privileges of exploitation.[72,73]

While leaving the technical questions of abuse of the patent monopoly for the next section, a more fundamental question is raised by the present justification for the patent institution. Even if individual inventors and small enterprises are supposed to be relatively more im-

[68] "Some of the larger industries could probably continue in much the same way as they operate today even if the patent system were done away with ... but such a change would seriously hamper the development of new industries." Opinions expressed by the presidents of the General Electric and the Owens Illinois Glass companies at hearings in the Temporary National Economic Committee, quoted by Bennett, *op. cit.*, p. 59; the same opinion is expressed by S. P. Ladas, *Propiedad Industrial y Desarrollo Económico* (Bogotá: Brigard y Hurrutia, 1963), p. 7.

[69] For the detailed analysis, see Börlin, *op. cit.*, pp. 145–50.

[70] *Ibid.*, p. 150.

[71] *Ibid.*; Another author making the same type of analysis, draws the opposite conclusion. Cf. G. Gather, "Reform der Patentgesetzgebung," *Jahrbuch für die Ordnung von Wirtschaft und Gesellschaft, Vol. II.*, [ORDO] (Godesberg: Helmut Küpper, 1949) pp. 294–303.

[72] Börlin *op. cit.*, p. 151.

[73] Mousseron, *op. cit.*, pp. 38–39, though recognizing the possible negative influences on the economy of patent-induced concentrations, uses such effects and an alleged insufficiency of industrial concentration, to justify a strengthening of the patentee's position!

portant for technological progress – a proposition often made though impossible to substantiate and perhaps contrary to reasonable expectations – is it the role of a system designed to promote technological progress in general to specifically support a quantitatively minor part of those who work towards this progress? The real reason – if indeed it represents more than a convenient argument[74] – for emphasizing the support of individuals and small businesses is probably the idea of safeguarding competition. But in view of the fact that such patentees only make a minor contribution to the total technological activity and that the larger corporations are also able to operate without the system, it can hardly be the role of a system once introduced to spur general technological advance, to steer economic activity along certain socially desirable lines. Instead, what seems to be called for is a system specifically geared to support weaker participants in the technological field without giving undue additional power to already strong competitors.[75]

D. CRITICISM OF THE PATENT INSTITUTION

Since the end of the patent controversy in the 1870's,[76] no similar movement against the patent system has appeared. Many of the objections then raised still continue to appear, often reinforced by the changes that have taken place in the conditions in which inventive activity is undertaken since the end of the last century. The patent controversy did not end because the theoretical arguments against it were convincingly refuted, but because the political debate, influenced by the protectionist feelings growing out of the severe depression of the early 1870's, ended with a victory for the patent advocates.[77] Never-

[74] "Those who defend in the name of the poor inventor, the abuses of the prevailing system had better devote their enthusiasm to increasing his bargaining power." W. H. Hamilton, "Patents and Free Enterprise," *Temporary National Economic Committee, Monograph No. 31* (Washington: Government Printing Office, 1941), p. 154.

[75] For to say that large patentees are more or less independent of the support of the patent system is not the same as saying that they do not profit by it. "Though the patent system today still serves this basic purpose [of stimulating individual inventiveness] it tends to funnel the major benefits of the monopolistic privileges it creates into the hands of large corporations which find these grants useful as an adjunct and aid in restraining competition." G. W. Stocking, M. W. Watkins, *Monopoly and Free Enterprise* (New York: Twentieth Century Fund, 1951), p. 450.

[76] *Supra*, p. 22.

[77] Machlup and Penrose, *op. cit.*, pp. 28–29; Rondon de Sanso, *op. cit.*, p. 114, is of the opposite opinion, stating that the question whether the patent system is beneficial or not to the economy of any country "is extremely simple, since the theory opposed to the granting of inventors' patents has died a natural death for want of any sufficiently enduring quality."

theless, as a reaction to the protectionist policies of the 1930's, when governments, if not actively encouraged restrictive business practices, at least condoned in many of them, criticism of the patent system mounted, especially of its use by large industrial corporations to stifle competition. This was notably the case in the United States. Though reactions against such practices arose during the war they have remained prominent since then[78].

This section proposes to examine briefly some aspects usually emphasized when the patent institution is criticized today. Although the legal and economic characteristics of the patent system are not really separable, the points mentioned below have been grouped according to whether the dominant feature concerns the legal or economic nature of the system.

1. *The legal foundations*

The appropriateness of investing the patentee with the exclusive rights that the patent grant gives rise to has been criticized principally from two points of view. Their common denominator is that the patent invests its holder with an unjustifiably strong position at the expense of his competitors: (a) a patent grant not only hinders later inventors with the same idea from enjoying the patent privilege but also prevents them from using their independently created inventions; and (b) the powers derived from the patent grant are often used to further objectives never intended by the lawmaker.

a. *Restraints inherent to the patent monopoly*

It has always been recognized that granting exclusive rights for the exploitation of a certain invention will have restrictive effects. The

78 The article "Champion of Competition," *The Economist*, July 16, 1966, p. 257, referring to some of the activities of the Anti-trust Division of the American Justice Department, mentions as one of its preoccupations "the question of monopolies built up through allegedly illegal uses of patents." Citing one big case in which the charge was the use of illegal tactics including threats to bring unjustified suits claiming infringement of patents, the article says that "a study of such [predatory patent] practices in a dozen major industries, something never undertaken before ... has just been ordered." As far as Europe is concerned, the opposition to patent abuses seems less strong. Nonetheless, at least within the Common Market, there appears to be a growing awareness of the possible detrimental consequences of certain restrictive agreements, often tied to the exchange of patent rights, for the inter-market competition. See C. Neme, "Pénétration de produits sous marque ou licence et unification des marchés dans la C.E.E.," *La propriété industrielle et le Marché Commun, Aspects économiques, Colloque Université – Industrie, 19–20 novembre 1965, Lyon* (Paris: Dunod, 1966), pp. 133–38.

argument, that a patent monopoly, as opposed to other monopolies, does not deprive the public of anything it previously could enjoy and thus is not harmful, has been convincingly criticized.[79] It was still admitted, however, that the probability of duplicate inventions was a price that had to be paid. With the evolution of research activity the price of denying independent inventors the use of their inventions has evidently increased. The "all-or-nothing" proposition inherent to the patent system of giving exclusive rights to the first inventor is sometimes claimed to be not only a necessary cost of the system, but also to actually constitute one of its advantages in that it creates competition among inventors.[80] The wastefulness implied by this approach has, however, been recognized by industry and devices have been found to avoid its costs, as will be shown below.

b. Abuse of the patent monopoly

The point developed above concerns the objective application of the patent system to contemporary conditions. The present paragraph concerns the subjective use to which the patent monopoly has been put, to further purposes never intended originally. Though all such practices are usually referred to as "abuse of the patent monopoly," the term "abuse" must be understood in a wide sense. It covers not only practices that are contrary to the law but also those that conflict with the basic intentions of the lawmakers. When dealing with abuses it should be recognized that some contemporary practices in patent matters are merely the results of more or less unavoidable adjustments of patent usage to fit modern conditions.

A patent-holder may extend the time limit of his monopoly power in several ways. Besides relying upon trademarks and goodwill, he can use particular patent devices to increase the duration and impact of his monopoly. Through successive patenting of improvements he can make the original, unimproved invention commercially unusuable after the expiration of its patent.

A device, designed to extend the functional limits of the patent monopoly, which is a clear violation of the patent grant, is the use of "tie-in clauses." By means of such provisions, a licensor may compel

[79] *Supra.* p. 46.

[80] Cf., for instance, S. P. Ladas, "The Fundamental Bases of the International Protection of Industrial Property," *P.I.*, 70: annex, April, 1954 [original text of "Les bases fondamentales de la protection internationale de la propriété industrielle," *P.I.*, 70: 93–97, April, 1954] p. 3.

the licensee to exclusively use certain unpatented materials in connection with the exploitation of the invention.

Bigness itself is the cause of the most evident anomaly in the operation of the patent system today. The organization of industrial society has given rise to a few very big corporate entities, which by the sheer size of their operations have tended to amass large numbers of patents. These companies have realized the fact that the power derived from a number of patents is greater than the sum of the powers conferred by each individual patent. This power has been extensively used for strategic reasons to enhance their position and to control markets.[81] Although these effects of large patent-holdings are generally recognized, some authors maintain that it is really not the patent institution that is at fault.[82] Though anti-trust legislation may be applicable when there is no direct violation of patent law, if one can find that even in such cases the same law, which was passed with the purpose of creating limited rights of exclusive exploitation of inventions, is also used to extend and perpetuate them, then this patent law is clearly responsible.

It has become the conscious policy of big corporations to collect large numbers of patents. This, of course, is partly a result of their inventive activities and of buying up patents from outside sources, with the intention of exploiting them later. Even though all patented inventions may not be commercially successful, the policy of amassing the greatest number possible of patents is actively pursued to stop others from using them. One such practice is known as "fencing-in." Besides patenting a product or process that will be exploited, the company also tries to patent as many alternative methods as possible of achieving the same result, in order to block competitors from "inventing around." The sheer size and extension of the patent holdings

[81] "A dichotomy which represents no one's conscious intent makes the nature of the patent. At law ... it is a letter which certifies invention and rewards the inventor. In fact ... it has become an asset to business, a fence about the corporate estate, a weapon of competitive strategy for private industrial government." Hamilton, *op. cit.*, p. 123.

[82] It is either said that abuses that may follow from the accumulation of patents do not concern patent law but rather antitrust law, or that the power that patentees hold does not derive from patents but from their economic strength and that patents are not a cause but an effect of such economic power. For support of the first opinion, see for example Walleser, *op. cit.*, p. 47. In any case, says this author, patent abuses are suprisingly rare, though no facts are provided in support of such a statement. In the opinion of Walleser, therefore, only a complete misunderstanding of the interrelationship between patents and competition can explain "why over-zealous economists," uncritically condemning every monopoly, would like to weaken or abolish the patent system. – For the second point of view, see for instance Blum, *op. cit.*, p. 56.

of large firms will often deter smaller firms from attempting aggressive competitive policies.

A second and similar device is known as "fencing off." This is a case in which a resourceful corporation tries to limit the usefulness of an invention made by an independent inventor by securing patents on every possible combination of elements surrounding it.

The most versatile instrument when it comes to intimidating competitors is the infringement suit. It can be used not only for legal action, but also as a method of control with a wide range of possibilities. A competing product or process is challenged without a clear basis for charges of infringement. If the two companies and their respective patents seem of equal weight, the result is likely to be a settlement out of court with a mutual agreement for the licensing of each other's patents. If, however, the challenged company is fairly small, and though its patent may be perfectly sound, it may be in no position to undertake a costly lawsuit. Instead the outcome is likely to be that it accepts a license under the challenger's patent, which sets rigid price and production limits.[83]

The most obvious manifestation of the insufficiency of the original concepts underlying the patent institution is the appearance of patent-pooling agreements. The parties to such agreements pool their patents by extending licenses to other members. So far this is merely a recognition that cooperation between inventors/patentees pays better than competition, which the patent system is supposed to stimulate.[84] However, the advantages of using these technical agreements as foundations for cartels are obvious. This device has been used on both the national and international levels. Whereas in most cases ordinary cartel agreements may be difficult to enforce, those that rely upon patent rights are normally more easily carried out. Besides the effect of keeping outsiders from sharing in the pool's inventions, a policy which tends even more than that of a single large company to extend the monopoly power over whole branches of industry, the patent cartel can restrict its members in several ways. Some of the ingredients of ordinary cartel agreements may be included such as market-sharing, price controls, controls on output, etc. Other parts of such agreements

[83] "A big corporation working from a base containing as many as 10,000 patents can usually, if it wishes, find a basis upon which to pursue almost any competitor." "War and Peace and the Patent System," *Fortune*, 51: 132, August, 1942. This article provides a rich illustration of various patent abuses. See also, Hamilton, *op. cit.*, pp. 46–48; Bennett, *op. cit.*, p. 189.

[84] *Cf. supra*, p. 34, for quotation from Penrose.

concern specifically the use of inventions and are of greater importance from the point of view of technological progress. One frequent clause concerns the limitation on the use of patents held by outsiders. The object of such a clause would be to hinder outsiders from increasing their bargaining power vis-à-vis the cartel members by making them dependent on patents of third parties. Another clause may provide that cartel members undertake not to challenge the validity of each other's patents. Yet another serious limitation is often present, in that cartel members agree (or are obliged) to include all their future inventions in the exclusive cross-licensing within the group.

All contemporary developments confirm the assumption that the principal impact of the patent system is no longer on the inventor but on the innovator. Even without a patent system today, it would only be natural to find that the bargaining position of the inventor would have weakened in favor of the innovator, considering the means required for effective exploitation of most inventions. But by using the patent-pool as a shield, larger companies may manage to restrict the inventor's choice even further by offering him only one buyer for his invention. The same fate may be reserved for less powerful firms, which find that the only possibility for their continued development is to come to terms with one or a few dominant corporations. These developments are hardly consistent with the thesis that the patent system is justified by its support for individuals and small firms. In addition, restrictive pooling agreements raise serious questions as to what degree they actually retard technological development by limiting the flow and utilization of inventions.[85]

2. *The economic foundations*

It must be clear from the foregoing sections of this chapter, that the cost to society of the patent system, when at all taken into account, has not been defined very precisely. The following brief examination of criticism raised against the economic premises of the patent system will study the costs involved from three different angles: (a) the patent system is supposed to induce inventions/innovations by covering the discrepancy between private and social net benefits; (b) monopoly conditions tend to divert resources from other employment; and (c) the patent monopoly restricts trade.

[85] See *infra*, Part II, Chapter III, "Indirect Effects of the International Patent System."

a. Private and social net benefits

The justification of the patent institution, in economic terms, is based on two assumptions: (i) by holding out the prospect of monopoly profits, inventors will be induced to produce and disclose inventions which otherwise would not have been made. As a result of subsidies for inventive activity, an additional number of inventions will become profitable to their producers, through the positive influence these subsidies will have on their cost/benefit calculations. (ii) The second assumption is that without such additional number of inventions, there will not be sufficient technological progress.

(i) Studying the probable effects of the patent system on inventive activity, one may divide inventions appearing under the patent system into three categories: (a) inventions which would have appeared even without the patent system; (b) inventions which, without the patent incentive, would have appeared later; and finally, (c) inventions that would not have appeared at all save for a special incentive.[86] It is, of course, not possible to measure either quantitatively or qualitatively any of these groups of inventions. In the opinion of many authors the patent system is largely a prop to individuals and small enterprises, whild larger corporations have other resources and incentives making them less dependant – if not independant – of the patent system.[87] Taking this into consideration, and further the fact that a majority of patents are taken out by large firms, it seems reasonable to assume that a large part of all patented inventions belong to group (a) above. One immediate disadvantage of a general patent system must follow from this consideration. In order to support groups two and three, the cost of which constitutes the minimum society would have to pay to obtain the inventions due to the patent system, one unnecessarily increases this cost by also supporting the first category mentioned above.

(ii) The second assumption referred to above is a simple hypothesis for which there exists no recognized proof despite the efforts to provide it by means of historical comparisons. The only reflection it may lead to is that, whatever its support might have been in the infancy of modern technological evolution, it seems far less convincing today.

b. Diversion of scarce resources

So far the gross advantages, which the patent system is supposed to procure, have been examined. To arrive at a meaningful judgment, it is

[86] Machlup, "Patentwesen ..." pp. 247–48;
[87] *Cf. supra*, pp. 49–50.

necessary to consider the social costs of the system. Among the variety of these costs, the one of greatest principal interest becomes discernable when the consequences of the patent institution are studied in the light of an alternative-cost analysis. Nobody would deny the truth of the general statement that monopoly conditions tend to promote the diversion of the scarce resources of production from a more to a less preferred utilization. Leaving aside the inventive activity that goes on independently of the patent system, it is obvious that resources for patent-induced activity will be withdrawn from somewhere. The diversion may be from other productive pursuits to "inventing" or from innovation or research activities in one field to the same kind of activities in another field in which the results receive patent protection. The crucial question then is the following: can the results of patent-induced activities be expected to be endowed with a higher social usefulness than other, foregone production? Plant, treating this question, has said:

> The only conceivable line for such an argument to take would seem to be that *ultimately* the inventions of a patentable type which will be made in response to the grant of a temporary monopoly will possess of sufficiently greater general usefulness than would result from the other inventions or other output immediately foregone, to outweigh the immediate loss. There surely exists no scientific reason for making any such claim for *patentable* inventions in general, as compared with alternative output.[88]

The patent system was introduced to spur competition between inventors. One item of "waste," that it has always given rise to, is the need for "inventing around" an already patent protected invention. The waste lies in the fact that one is forced to employ scarce resources in order to find other solutions to problems, which have already been solved.[89] Although this practice has been most often merely defended as unavoidable under the patent system, it is sometimes described as

[88] Plant, *op. cit.*, pp. 42–43. The author says elsewhere, "I suggest that such a conclusion runs counter to all general presumptions concerning the disposition of scarce productive resources in a regime of monopolistic control as contrasted with open competition." See also, Machlup, "An Economic Review ...," pp. 48–49; it is important to stress the fact that the redeployment of resources is not merely from "other activities" into "inventing" but also from one technological field to another; for a case may be made for special incentives for technological research assuming that such activities will generally have a higher usefulness. See C. F. Carter, "Economic Incentives for and Consequences of Technical Invention," *Scientific Change, Symposium on the History of Science, Oxford, 1961* (London: Heinemann, 1963, pp. 678–90), pp. 679.

[89] Frost, *op. cit.*, p. 81, minimizes this cost. "Usually the significance of even a very important patent – no matter how jealously enforced – is a modest cost of 'designing around' the patented subject matter." If this is so, one is inevitably led to ask what happened to the role of the patent rewarding its holder commensurably with the importance of the invention.

one of the principal advantages of the institution.[90] The cost of "inventing around" is further increased by the defensive and offensive tactics known as "fencing-in" and "fencing off."

d. Restrictions on trade

It has always been accepted that the principal cost of the patent system would be the restraint on trade caused by monopoly grants, although opinions have varied as to its importance. The evolution of industrial inventive activity, that has given rise to the various patent practices described above, has vastly increased such restraints. Many individual firms have grown so large and their patent-holdings so extensive, that the importance of any one patent may often be negligible, but the mass of patents taken together makes an effective weapon and creates conditions for the monopolistic control of markets. In many areas today only large-scale operations are profitable and in most fields not even big individual corporations find it profitable to operate on their own research alone, wasting their efforts on "competitive" research. Instead they have entered into patent-pooling agreements. Although the sharing of research among companies is an obvious rationalization of resources, when this is done by means of restricted patent-pools with all the secondary restrictions usually found in such agreements, the social value to society is considerably reduced.

E. ALTERNATIVES TO THE PRESENT PATENT SYSTEM

Whenever the principles of the patent institution have been criticized, more or less radical changes have been suggested. Though most of the criticism levelled against the patent system, and most of the remedies suggested for its alleged deficiencies, first appeared more than a century ago, no major changes have been implemented anywhere.[91] While it has been suggested that the patent doctrine was influenced by the

[90] See, for instance, Walleser, *op. cit.*, pp. 44–45; Akerman, *op. cit.*, pp. 376–77; Machlup, "An Economic Review . . .," p. 51, makes the following comment on this argument: "What may appear absurd to a disinterested observer, or unjust or unfair to one who lost the right to use the fruit of his own labor and investment, must to an economist appear as sheer economic waste."

[91] An exception is the system of "certificates of authorship" which exist in the Soviet Union and some other socialist countries. According to this system, the inventor, upon submitting his invention to the State, receives a monetary reward calculated upon the economic value of the invention from its exploitation. Though these countries offer inventors the choice between applying for a "certificate of authorship" and a patent, it would appear obvious that the present economic order in these countries is incompatible with the power of the patentee to exploit his patent.

evolution of the private property right concept, this has so far had little impact on patent legislation. Though it is true that the weight of emphasis on the various considerations underlying the patent system has shifted from the interests of individuals to those of society in theoretical discussions, it might even be maintained that the position of the patentee has become relatively stronger, at least to judge from the development of the international patent system.

When discussing various remedial steps to counter the alleged deficiencies of the patent system, ranging from merely attenuating the monopoly power of the patentee to the complete abolition of the system, one must be aware of two different points of departure. One may either limit the inquiry to whether or not the patent system today fulfills its original purpose, or whether, disregarding this, it plays a useful role today.

The first approach has been used by a few American authors, and they base their arguments on the fact that the American patent law is based on a constitutional provision authorizing Congress "to promote the progress of science and the useful arts," by assuring authors and inventors the exclusive right to their writings and discoveries for limited periods of time. Melman answers the question whether the American patent system today fulfills its constitutional purpose by saying: "On balance, based upon the study of selected typical industrial and non-profit laboratories, the answer is 'No.'"[92] Hamilton, a staunch critic of the abuses of patent monopolies, holding that the transformation of the patent from the purpose of furthering the progress of technology to becoming a dominantly acquisitive or defensive weapon has no foundation in the constitutional provision authorizing Congress to legislate in patent matters, says: "The public purpose is lasting; its realization has to be altered to changing circumstances."[93]

Most authors use the second approach menioned above, i.e. inquiring into whether the patent system today is fulfilling a useful role. The suggestions of these authors may be distinguished into three types: (1) arguments for a decrease or abolishment of the exclusive power to exploit inventions; (2) suggestions to substitute a system of straight awards for the patent system; and (3) propositions to substitute a

[92] Melman, *op. cit.*, p. 62. This report has been criticized because it allegedly lays too much emphasis on large industries and laboratories and too little on individual inventors. See, for instance, R. Carr, "Our Patent System Works – A Reply to the Melman-report," *J.P.O.S.*, 42: 295–323, May, 1960.

[93] Hamilton, *op. cit.*, p. 153.

system of limited applicability for the present system, or simply abolish it.

1. A system of general licenses

There is no doubt that present-day circumstances in the technological field raise the question of the appropriateness of giving any and all inventors the power of exclusive exploitation. The fact that the emphasis of the patent system has largely shifted from being an incentive to inventive activity to supporting innovation, together with the practice of using patents to stifle competition instead of stimulating it, has brought forward a number of proposals aimed at limiting the discretionary power of the patentee. Such suggestions are generally expressed by economists and vigorously refuted by patent lawyers.[94] At present the only principal derogation of the exclusive right of patentees, which is allowed by the majority of patent laws, with the notable exception of the United States, is the issuance of compulsory licenses in cases in which the patentee has not satisfactorily exploited the invention after a number of years.[95] The remedy of compulsory licenses, which in its practical application is aimed at foreigners, has been used only rarely. Some authors maintain that the mere possibility of applying a compulsory license is a sufficient deterrent against abuses of the monopoly power and therefore contend that abuses are very rare. Others, however, object to the principle of monopoly power itself inherent in a patent grant.

This opinion is the result of various contemporary practices of a re-

[94] Among the exceptions is H. R. Wilmot, Australian Patent Commissioner who has said: "If the experience of the Australian Patent Office is any indication ... then I am inclined to doubt whether we have advanced with the times. That the principle of allowing a limited monopoly to an inventor is almost universally accepted cannot be denied. That it was effective at the time at which the principle was originated seems justified by its results. But whether the principle holds true in modern economic conditions is, I think, open to doubt ... The manner of processing of at least some patents leads one to doubt whether the system, as one feature of the general economic set-up, completely serves today its original purpose." "The Patent System Today," *Souvenir – Indian Patent Centenary 1856–1956* (Calcutta: Patent Office, 1956), p. 37.

[95] Though American lawyers often claim that the absence of a compulsory license clause has made their patent system particularly beneficial, others point out that, since the clause is principally aimed at foreigners, the American trade protectionism may have served the same purpose of forcing foreign patentees to exploit their inventions locally. In addition, an American law of 1910, amended in 1918, goes much further than the traditional compulsory license system in derogation of the exclusive rights of patentees in certain cases. According to this law, anyone who is engaged in producing for the government may use any patented invention, without the consent of the owner and without even negotiating with him, the terms of compensation to be settled in court. See Whittlesey, *op. cit.*, p. 83.

strictive nature employed by industry. One suggestion is that after a few years of exclusive control, the patentee should be obliged to license any willing licensee upon the payment of royalties.[96] A suggestion that goes still further would have the patentee obliged at any time and against royalties to license his patents. This was one of the recommendations contained in the final report of the Temporary National Economic Committee set up in 1941 to inquire into the power structure of American Industry. This Committee recommended that

> Any future patent [should be] available for use by anyone who may desire its use and who is willing to pay a fair price for the privilege in order to eliminate the use of patents in ways inimical to the public policy inherent in the patent laws.[97]

The authors who have suggested the introduction of a general system of compulsory licenses have done so when they have criticized the restrictive policies of patent-pools. One of them has suggested as one possible remedy that of regarding patents in each important industry as affected with a public interest, forcing such pools to admit any new member willing to pay royalties for the use of such patents.[98] The chief objection raised against a system of general compulsory licensing is that it would have a negative effect on the incentive of the patent system, not so much the incentive to invent as the incentive to develop and introduce inventions. Another objection sometimes made is that the prohibition of closed patent pools would lessen the incentive to exchange patent rights. The difficulties and sometimes impossibility for a single firm to work its patents without the cooperation of outside patents seems to weaken this argument.[99] Some authors, admitting the danger of large patent aggregations, maintain that abuses arising from such situations ought to be treated by anti-trust legislation.[100] Criticizing such contentions, Vaughan points out the insecurity and possible inconsistency in relying on anti-trust legislation and judical interpretation. In addition, says this author, "any action, if at all, comes after the exercise of monopoly and restraint of trade."[101]

[96] See W. Röpke, *Die Gesellschaftskrisis der Gegenwart* (Zürich: Rentsch, 1942), pp. 389–90.

[97] Temporary National Economic Committee, Final Report and Recommendations, S. Doc. No. 35, 77 Cong., 1 sess., p. 36 (1941), quoted by F. Neumeyer, "Compulsory Licensing of Patents under some Non-American Systems," *U.S. Senate, Committee on the Judiciary, Study No. 19 of the Subcommittee on Patents, Trademarks and Copyrights* (Washington: Government Printing Office, 1959), p. 2.

[98] F. L. Vaughan, "International Cartels – Discussion," *A.E.R.*, 36(I): 781, May ,1946.

[99] Penrose, *op. cit.*, p. 196.

[100] Walleser, *op. cit.*, p. 47; Frost, *op. cit.*, p. 75 is of the opinion that the problem of abuses by large patent-holders "is now minimized through application of the anti-trust laws."

[101] Vaughan, *op. cit.*, p. 780. The author makes another point in favor of a general com-

As mentioned above, no principal changes of the patent system have been adopted anywhere. Several authors point to the trend in both theory and practice which might indicate the future establishment of a system in which the monopoly power of the patent is changed to a right to receive royalties. Neumeyer, commenting on conflicts in the United States between patent agreements and anti-trust law, finds that, generally speaking, "in a choice between these two means of promoting progress, free competition and patents, the preservation of competition generally carries greater weight." The author concludes that in a conflict between patent agreements and free competition the latter ought to, as in the United States, be given greater importance and a greater measure of protection, for he says:

> The risk that future technical research and development shall be rendered more difficult through the abolishment of patent restrictions seems less menacing than the risk that technical progress and the growth of industry and commerce shall be rendered more difficult.[102]

2. *A general reward system*

The idea of substituting a system of government bonuses for the patent system is not new. Indeed, at the time of the promulgation of the first American patent law, Alexander Hamilton, "great champion of industry," is said to have favored a system "in which inventors would be paid a federal award for worthwhile discoveries, and all inventions

pulsory license system. Such a system would favor smaller patent holders [whose protection is so cherished by patent advocates!]. For under a policy of general licensing, "the relative importance of the patents of large corporations would decrease to the extent that a more certain reward would stimulate independent inventors ....

Certainly of reward would arouse and sustain inventive activity more than the present uncertainty. Payment of royalty, rather than litigation and other uncertainties would be the price of admission to an industry, and therefore would permit the effective and maximum use of inventions."

[102] Neumeyer, *Patent* ..., p. 86, [translated from Swedish]. A colloquium on industrial property rights and the Common Market, of which *La propriété industrielle et le Marché Commun – Aspects économiques* (Paris: Dunod, 1966), quoted above, contains the papers submitted, seems to reflect the beginning of an objective dialogue between lawyers and economists, in which the former do not automatically reject the idea that contemporary economic and technological development may make changes of certain features of traditional patent law desirable. This apprehension is conveyed in the concluding remarks by G. Finniss when he says, p. 190: "En ce qui concerne la propriété industrielle et le droit de la concurrence, est-ce que le droit de la propriété industrielle ne fait pas payer un prix trop élevé, qui est un prix payé par les entraves portées à la concurrence?" and again on p. 191: "Il est important ... de voir si ce brevet d'invention dans sa structure juridique actuelle ... doit être maintenu. Autrement dit, si ce qu'il apporte comme instrument d'incitation au développement de la recherche doit être payé d'un prix qui est peut-être trop élevé dans d'autres domaines."

thrown open to encourage the free growth of industry."[103] Similar suggestions were proposed during the patent controversy. The chief objection was that such a system might give rise to arbitrariness and corruption. Similar reasons are sometimes given today for rejecting such a system.

From what has been shown in this chapter, the present system could hardly be more arbitrary. A more reasonable objection is the one made by Akerman. One could well imagine a system in which the government would give awards in terms of the economic value of the invention, says this author, if particular reasons did not require that in principle, the right of the patentee be of an exclusive nature. The special reasons are connected with the exploitation of patented inventions, for, Akerman maintains, no patentee could be induced to work his invention if he could not count on profiting from such exploitation, and that this would not be the case if his competitors were able to similarly exploit the invention.[104] In view of the fact that today the costs at the inventing stage are often merely a fraction of the costs of innovation – typically representing less than ten percent of total innovative costs – it would seem difficult to assess the amount of the award for an invention before it has been commercialized. On the other hand, any non-automatic system like the present one, would offer a range of discretion to evaluate each case on its merits and would be particularly capable of supporting individuals and small enterprises.[105]

3. *Substitution of general for special awards or abolishment*

Though complete abolishment of the patent system has rarely been proposed,[106] several authors are of the opinion that a system that discriminates between "innovations ... which may result from the normal course of vigorous inter-firm competition in existing markets" and "costly research contemplating major technological breakthroughs" might be advantageous. "The existence of these two broad classes of inventive activity," says Markhan, "suggests the advisability of a dual

[103] "War and Peace and the Patent System," p. 103. "Oddly enough," continues the article, "the only country in the world today that has adopted anything approaching the Hamilton System is Soviet Russia."

[104] Akerman, *op. cit.*, pp. 375–76.

[105] See Börlin, *op. cit.*, p. 64.

[106] Though, for instance, Röpke, *op. cit.*, p. 390, n. 96 *supra*, after suggesting the establishment of a general system of compulsory licenses, says that he goes as far as assering that a complete abolition of the patent system would be preferable, at least in the big industrial countries; Plant, *op. cit.*, and Melman, *op. cit.*, p. 54, are probably of the same opinion.

patent system ... Such a dual system would no doubt more nearly equate the marginal social costs of both classes of inventive activity with their corresponding social rewards."[107] Others suggest that only for exceptional circumstances would special incentives for inventive and innovative activity be necessary.[108]

The trouble for all those who argue for a change in the existing system is the lack of both experience and any scientifically based demonstration to prove the net benefit of any other system of remuneration and incentive. This, however, is equally true for those who argue for the retention of the present patent system.[109] "Those who apparently accept the system as it presently exists, "says Markham, "lean heavily on the logical appeal of the proposition that patent protection is necessary to induce inventive activity and the requisite investment to exploit it commercially." He continues with the following statement:

> Few economists who subscribe to this view regard the patent system as an unmixed blessing and some approve its retention only because no superior substitute has yet been offered. It is emphasized, however, that this position finds its principal support in the intuitive appeal of the a priori logic of the case rather than in any empirical proof of the premises on which the case rests.[110]

This dilemma is suggested in the concluding words of Machlup's report, when he says:

> If we did not have a patent system, it would be irresponsible, on the basis of our present knowledge of its economic consequences to recommend instituting one. But since we have had a patent system for a long time, it would be irresposible, on the basis of our present knowledge to recommend abolishing it.[111]

[107] Markham, *op. cit.*, p. 602.

[108] Machlup, "An Economic Review ...," p. 16; and Plant, *op. cit.*, p. 43.

[109] Thus when Roubier, *op. cit.*, Vol. I, p. 4, after mentioning the possibility of government rewards, says: "L'Expérience prouve que ces stimulants sont loin d'avoir la même portée," it is difficult to see what experience the author refers to; L. Robbins, *The Economic Bases of Class Conflict and Other Essays in Political Economy*, (London: Macmillan, 1939) pp. 74–75, qualifying the patent system in its present form as a "highly artificial creation emerging from a process of legislation in which the role of pressure groups and muddled thinking has been unfortunately only too prominent" says that "no convincing argument has yet been put forward to show that the abolition of the present system and the substitution of a 'licence of right' system, whereby, after a very short period, anyone might use a patent, on paying a licence fee to the inventor, would be less unjust to inventors or diminish the flow of invention."

[110] Markham, *op. cit.*, p. 598.

[111] Machlup, "An Economic Review ..." p. 80; "This last statement" adds the author, "refers to a country such as the United States of America – not to a small country and not to a predominantly non-industrial country, where a different weight of argument might well suggest another conclusion."

CHAPTER III

THE DEVELOPMENT OF AN INTERNATIONAL PATENT SYSTEM

During the third quarter of the nineteenth century it was recognized that patent protection limited by national boundaries was an obstacle to the expansion of international economic relations. In addition, many were of the opinion that justice demanded that an inventor be protected not only within his own country but in all countries. With these considerations in mind, the Paris Union for the International Protection of Industrial Property was to be created. The present chapter will examine the evolution of the rules that govern the exploitation of patents, contained in the text on which the relations among Union members in patent matters are based. It will also briefly mention other multilateral agreements regulating international cooperation in patent matters.

A. THE CLIMATE RIPE FOR AN INTERNATIONAL ORDER

Towards the middle of last century industrialization in several European countries, and to a lesser extent in the United States, had developed to such a point, that the potential gains from foreign trade in industrial goods became increasingly significant. Another spur to the rapid growth of foreign trade was the success of the free-trade movement in that period.

By this time most industrial countries had adopted patent laws. These laws protected national inventors and national industry but gave little protection to foreigners.[1] This was one of the major points of criticism during the patent controversy. National patent laws acted like tariffs, effectively shutting out foreign competition, and such laws

[1] "Foreigners" in connection with patent legislation generally means non-resident foreigners. Consequently the term "nationals" includes all residents.

were incompatible with the trend in commercial policy towards freer trade.

The little international cooperation in patent matters that did exist was contained in bilateral commercial treaties. The inclusion of patent provisions in such treaties, usually concluded for short periods of time, made patent rights acquired under them precarious. Even when countries managed to maintain a patent cooperation it was strictly bilateral, and such agreements could not lead to the establishment of unified rules.

During the ten years preceding the establishment of the Paris Union in 1883, there are three principal events during which the groundwork for the future convention was prepared: (1) the Vienna Exhibition of 1873; (2) the Paris Exhibition of 1878; and (3) an international conference on industrial property in Paris 1880.

1. The Vienna Exhibition of 1873

During the International Exhibition of Vienna in 1873 it became known, that several countries were unwilling to participate unless they received some protection for their products. Even if the exhibitors were to get patents in the country holding the exhibition, they would not be much helped because of the stringent working requirements in that country.[2] This prompted the Austro-Hungarian Government to sponsor the first international conference on patents that same year. Besides economic considerations, which were making an international order in patent matters necessary, there was also a strong opinion favoring the recognition of the patentee's "natural right to protection." The existence of such a right was affirmed in one resolution.[3] Of more practical interest was another resolution, which recommended compulsory licensing of patents in cases in which the public interest should require it.[4] Many participants believed that revocation of the patent grant for non-working, which was the rule of most national patent laws at the time, among the member States of an international union, would be too onerous on the patentee. Thus the Vienna conference

[2] See S. P. Ladas, *The International Protection of Industrial Property* (Cambridge: Harvard University Press, 1930), p. 73.

[3] *Ibid.*

[4] "This principle was not again to be accepted by an international conference for 50 years but the anti-patent movement ... had created such an awareness of the possible monopolistic and restrictive effects of the patent system." E. T. Penrose, *The Economics of the International Patent System* (Baltimore: Johns Hopkins, 1951), p. 47.

recommended that non-working in one country should not lead to revocation if the patent had been worked somewhere else, and if the citizens of the country in question were able to obtain licenses.[5,6]

2. *The Paris Exhibition of 1878*

During the Universal Exhibition of Paris in 1878 the French Government called an international congress to discuss patent matters. In contrast to the Vienna conference, where there were no French participants, this time the French point of view dominated, which may explain some differences in the opinions expressed at the two meetings. In the very first debate, and despite some opposition, a proposition was adopted laying down the natural property theory of inventors as a justification for the patent institution, which bears the imprint of French patent doctrine.[7]

One of the resolutions adopted by the congress admitted revoking a patent grant, if the patented invention was not exploited locally. It may seem strange that after upholding the patentee's right in the most extreme terms, the congress rejected compulsory licensing in favor of outright revocation. This was however a direct consequence of the natural property theory. While compulsory licensing only aided other private groups and constituted a violation of the right of property, revocation was an expropriation which was acceptable, if it was undertaken in the public interest.[8,9]

[5] "L'Obligation d'exploiter les brevets d'invention," *P.I.*, 40: 66, April, 1924.

[6] The Vienna Congress did not lead to any immediate results, though it set up a committee, in the name of which a program for further action was submitted to the French Government in 1877. Cf. *Union Internationale pour la Protection de la Propriété Industrielle*; *Mémoire publié par le Bureau International pour la Protection de la Propriété Industrielle à l'occasion de cinquantenaire.* (Bern: Bureau International de l'Union, 1933) p. 18.

[7] Penrose, *op. cit.*, pp. 50–51.

[8] *Ibid.*, pp. 51–52.

[9] One opponent to compulsory working requirements said that: "En fait c'étaient surtout les pays à industrie encore peu développée qui avaient inscrit dans leur loi l'obligation d'exploiter, croyant servir à son développement, ce'en quoi leur espoir avait été deçu." "L'Obligation d'exploiter ...," p. 66, continuing: "La législation des Etats Unis l'avait d'abord imposée aux étrangers, et elle l'a ensuite supprimée, sans que l'essor de l'industrie nationale en ait souffert. La législation anglaise ignore l'obligation d'exploiter; son industrie n'en a pas souffert d'avantage." In the case of the United States it might be recalled that one of the principal aims of instituting a patent system was to acquire foreign inventions, though neither through obtaining licenses nor through compulsory working requirements, but simply through the "importation" of foreign inventions by local manufacturers. It has also been held that for reasons such as the size of the market and still more, because of its tariff-policy (cf. *supra*, Chapter II, n. 95) compulsory working requirements would have been superfluous. In the case of Great Britain, as long as she was the industrial leader, there was no need to compel foreign patentees to exploit their inventions locally. Since she was by far the most industrialized country, foreign patentees would, in fact, often choose to establish

The question whether or not a country and especially an industrially less developed country would help its industrial development by compelling patentees to exploit their inventions locally was ro remain one of the most diputed points at successive conferences.

Another resolution voted by the Paris Congress of 1878 concerned the importation of articles made under a patent. The text of this resolution, which was eventually incorporated in the Convention of 1883 (Article 5, paragraph 1) and remained virtually unchanged through all later revision conferences, stated that importation of patented articles ought not to be prohibited. According to Penrose, this resolution was directed especially against France, which had a rule prohibiting such importation, in her legislation.[10] One participant, opposed to the resolution, said that inventors ought to compensate the industry of the patent-granting country by working their inventions locally.[11] The congress created a permanent commission, whose task it was to work out a draft agreement for an international union for the protection of industrial property. A first draft was circulated in 1879, and a year later a new conference was called in Paris.

3. The Paris Conference 1880[12]

At this conference a project was adopted, which was finally agreed upon almost without changes and signed three years later, marking the birth of the Paris Union for the International Protection of Industrial Property (hereafter referred to as the Union). The debate at this con-

themselves there. When towards the end of the last century some countries began to rival and even overtake Great Britain as industrial powers, a compulsory working clause was introduced. (Patent Act of 1907). For the cases of both the United States and Great Britain, see E. Dame, *Die volkswirtschaftliche Bedeutung des Ausführungszwanges im Patentwesen* (Berlin: Verlag Chemie, 1929), pp. 16–17; 33–35.

[10] Penrose, *op. cit.*, p. 75; the author quotes a paragraph from the French report that was the basis for the discussions which said in part: "The exclusive right that is granted to a patentee can only be legitimately recognized on condition that he effectively works his invention and that it is thus made to profit the country in which he has obtained his patent." (p. 76). This clearly exposes the inconsistency that has always marked the relation between the theories on "natural" or "inherent" rights in inventions and the practical application of patent laws.

[11] "Les inventeurs doivent récompenser par leur production l'industrie du pays, qui leur accorde un monopole momentané ... La délivrance d'un brevet doit entrainer un avantage correlatif pour l'industrie nationale." "L'Obligation d'exploiter ...," p. 66.

[12] Whereas the two previous conferences (Vienna, 1873, and Paris, 1878) had been unofficial, the Paris conference of 1880 had only official delegates. The following nineteen States were represented: Argentina, Austria-Hungary, Belgium, Brazil, France, Great Britain, Guatemala, Italy, Luxemburg, the Netherlands, Portugal, Russia, El Salvador, Sweden-Norway, Switzerland, Turkey, United States, Uruguay and Venezuela. *Actes de la Conférence de Paris 1880*, pp. 6–7.

ference on the question of compulsory working provides a good illustration of the different points of view on this problem. Compulsory working has often been compared to protectionist tariffs. The Swiss delegate, observing that his country, being a free-trader, did not, like her neighbors, shield her national industry by high tariffs, said that the use of a compulsory working requirement would therefore be the only weapon for the use of which she reserved her right in her future patent legislation.[13] The reason against a compulsory working clause, and also to a lesser extent against compulsory licensing, have always been that they are too onerous on the patentee, and that such clauses do not serve a real purpose, for, it is held that, if the conditions in a country are favorable to production of the invention, the patentee will undertake it, whereas in cases in which the circumstances are unfavorable, local production will only result in higher prices and be harmful to consumers. The Belgian delegate, reasoning along these lines, simply suggested that a patentee ought not to be required to work his invention in more than one Union country.[14] Several countries, who favored this principle – while thinking in terms of their nationals abroad – were, however, less prepared to let foreign patentees use their local patents as mere protection for their exports. This dilemma was well illustrated by the Italian delegate, who said that he recognized the good grounds for the proposal from a general point of view, but declared that he was nevertheless obliged to maintain his amendment (permitting compulsory working) *in the interest of his country.*[15] The text of what was to become Article 5 of the Convention of 1883 was finally adopted.

B. THE PARIS CONVENTION FOR THE INTERNATIONAL PROTECTION OF INDUSTRIAL PROPERTY

Using the results of the Paris Conference of 1880 as a draft for an international convention for the international protection of industrial property, interested governments were again invited to a conference in Paris in 1883 for the purpose of finally signing the proposed document. After some deliberation among the nineteen delegations,[16] the

[13] *Ibid.*, p. 67.
[14] *Ibid.*, p. 57.
[15] *Ibid.*, p. 67; for the various views expressed, see "L'Obligation d'exploiter . . .," p. 67.
[16] Argentina, Belgium, Brazil, France, Great Britain, Guatemala, Italy, Luxemburg, the Netherlands, Portugal, Rumania, Russia, El Salvador, Serbia, Spain, Sweden-Norway, Switzerland, United States, and Uruguay. *Actes de la Conférence de Paris* 1883, pp. 6–7.

draft project was adopted with slight changes. The text of the Convention was signed by eleven States, and within the additional time allowed for original signatures three more countries adhered.[17] The Convention entered into force in July of the following year.

1. *The basic rules of procedure*

The fundamental rules of procedure on which the Union was founded, and which still remain the guiding principles, concern: (a) membership (b) revision of the Convention, and (c) voting procedures.

a. Membership.

According to Article 16 any country is entitled to membership upon a unilateral declaration of intent. A new member can adhere only to the latest revised text.

b. Revision of the Convention.

Article 14 states that periodic diplomatic conferences shall be held for the purpose of revising the original text. In the beginning such conferences were held at frequent intervals, but it was quickly recognized, that longer periods of time were necessary between revision conferences to allow for sufficient time for preparation.

c. Voting procedures.

The greatest obstacle to any amendment was to be the rule requiring unanimous consent. Though this rule is not codified, it is an established practice of the Union. While it was less of a burden at a time when the members of the Union were few and formed a fairly homogenous group, the power of any single State to block a proposed amendment was to become increasingly important as the number of Member States grew and as a diversity of interests manifested itself.

2. *The basic substantive rules of the Convention*

There are two fundamental substantive rules on which the Convention has been based from the beginning: (a) the principle of national treatment, and (b) the right of priority.

[17] The fourteen original members of the Paris Union were: Belgium, Brazil, Ecuador, France, Great Britain, Guatemala, Italy, the Netherlands, Portugal, El Salvador, Serbia, Spain, Switzerland, and Tunisia. Three States soon left the Union: Ecuador (1886), El Salvador (1887), and Guatemala (1895).

a. National treatment.

According to the text of Article 2, national treatment is extended to the citizens of all Member States. Article 3 also extends such treatment to non-nationals of Member States, who are either residents of a Member State or have an industrial or commercial establishment on its territory. The principle of national treatment, together with the right of any country to become a member on its unilateral decision, also meant that nationals of Member States, that had no national patent law, would be granted patent rights in other Member States.[18]

b. Right of priority.

The aim of the contracting parties was to lessen the differences that existed between national patent laws. One approach to this end was to introduce certain minimum standards for national laws. Another and complementary approach was the creation of unionist rules. The first and still most important rule of the latter type is the one that concerns priority (Article 4). Originally patentees benefiting from the Convention, who had filed a patent application in one Member State, were given a priority right of six months during which they could file an application for a patent grant in any Member State without the risk of having third parties do it before them. The present priority period is 12 months.[19]

3. *Other original rules of the Convention concerning patents*[20]

The provisions of Article 5 (1), ruling out the forfeiture of patent rights on the sole ground that articles made under a patent are being imported by the patentee, is significant in two respects. It was the first minimum standard which the Paris Union managed to impose on national patent laws. It further marked the first successful step in the continuous efforts to attenuate the effects of compulsory working clauses con-

[18] This was the case, for instance, of the Netherlands until 1910 and Switzerland until 1887. Since the Lisbon Conference (1958), however, a country is expected to be able to give effect to the rules of the Convention by national legislation. [Article 17, (2)].

[19] A particular paragraph of Article 4 concerning the rights of third parties led to lengthy discussions and various interpretations at several successive revision conferences. It was finally established at London in 1934 that such rights could only exist prior to the date of the first filing of a patent application when such a date was used to claim priority at a subsequent filing in another country. Such rights are subject to national legislation.

[20] The Convention from the beginning also contained rules on industrial designs, trademarks and trade names, to which utility models, service marks, indications of source as well as rules for the repression of unfair competition were added later. None of these other areas of interest to the Union will be treated.

tained in most national laws. A second paragraph of Article 5 stated that a patentee remained under the obligation to exploit his patent according to the laws of each particular State. Article 11 contained provisions to extend temporary protection to inventions exhibited at international exhibitions. According to Article 12, Member States undertook to set up national patent offices for the publication of patents. Article 13 established an International Bureau of the Union for the Protection of Industrial Property (hereafter referred to as the Bureau) to act as a permanent secretariat. The Bureau was placed under the supervision of the Swiss Government.[21] The right of Member States to conclude special arrangements for the protection of industrial property, insofar as such arrangements did not contravene any provisions of the Convention, was recognized in Article 15. Finally, Article 17 contained an obligation for Member States to adopt the measures necessary to give effect to the provisions of the Convention with as little delay as possible.

C. REVISION CONFERENCES

As mentioned above, the following examination of the evolution of the Convention will deal exclusively with the rules concerning the exploitation of patents. Such rules are contained in Article 5 and prescribe the limits of the extent to which national laws may require patentees to exploit their inventions, and the types of sanctions allowed to enforce such requirements.[22] Although certain other rules of the Convention, such as those that define the administrative measures that a country may impose on foreigners and rules concerning the right of third parties, may have a certain economic impact, the measures concerning the exploitation of patented inventions allowed under the Convention remain by far the most important features of the Convention in terms of their economic significance.[23]

[21] In 1893, a joint Bureau was established for the Paris Union and the Berne Union for the Protection of Literary and Artistic Works, under the name of Bureaux Internationaux Réunis pour la Protection de la Propriété Industrielle, (B.I.R.P.I.). For the recently decided reorganization of the Paris Union and its Secretariat, and for the creation of a World Intellectual Property Organization, (W.I.P.O.), see pp. 258–65.

[22] In an appendix to the chapter (pp. 106–08) appear the English translations of Article V, and texts related thereto, of the various conventional texts as published by BIRPI in *Manual of Industrial Property Conventions*, Geneva, 1966.

[23] Considering that the two basic material principles of the Convention, i.e., the principle of national treatment and priority, have remained unchanged, the evolution of the original Article 5 constitutes the most important element of the history of the Union, as far as patents are concerned. In the words of C. Akerman, *L'Obligation d'exploiter et la license obligatoire en*

The texts of the first two revision conferences are of little interest since neither of them was ratified. The principal question at the first of these two, held in Rome in 1886, was the continuation of the efforts against compulsory working requirements. When discussion on this point was resumed at the second conference, held in Madrid in 1890, the suggestion was made that compulsory licensing be substituted for compulsory working as the most equitable method of conciliating the interests of individuals and those of society.

1. The Revision Conference of Brussels, 1897–1900[24,25]

At this conference the Belgian proposal, made in 1880, for a total ban on revocation for non-working when a patent was being worked in one member country, was repeated, but it was again rejected, this time by a majority of the delegates.[26] The Bureau, taking note of the difficulties created by the unanimity rule, which had led to the non-ratification of two previous revision texts, for the first time (as far as patents are concerned) introduced a proposal for the creation of a restricted union to which countries could adhere, which agreed to adopt a rule by which the sanction of revocation for non-working would be replaced by compulsory licensing. The general opinion, however, was not in favor of restricted unions in patent matters. As no agreement could be reached on any of the major proposals when the conference met in 1897, and in order not to have to close the conference without any tangible results, it was adjourned for the time being. Three years later, Belgium, having in the meantime conferred with the governments of some countries, which had opposed some amendments in 1897, recalled the conference and agreements were reached on several points.

The Bureau, having dropped its proposal for a restricted union, now suggested a clause prohibiting the revocation of a patent for non-

matière de brevet d'invention (Paris: Sirey, 1936), p. 57: "On pourrait dire que l'historique de l'article 5 'est dans un certain sens l'historique de l'Union elle-même'." For a similar view, see Ladas, *op. cit.*, p. 327.

[24] At the beginning of the conference, membership stood at sixteen, the following countries being new members: Denmark, the Dominican Republic, Norway, Sweden and the United States. The following non-member countries participated: Austria-Hungary, Chile, Ecuador, Germany, Japan, Luxemburg, Mexico, and Turkey, of which Japan became a member during the conference. *Actes de la Conférence de Bruxelles* (1897–1900), pp. 20, 129, 363–66.

[25] In the following references to the official records of the revision conferences, "*Actes*" will signify the documents concerning the particular conference being analyzed.

[26] The United States, supporting the proposal and invoking its own liberal patent law, proposed the introduction of reciprocity, which was, however, rejected by all other Member States. *Actes*, pp. 95, 304–05.

working before the lapse of three years from the date of application, with the further qualification that revocation would only be allowed in cases in which the patentee could not justify his inaction. Unsuccessful efforts to license was suggested as justification. Though agreement on this last point could not be reached, the clause as such was accepted, leaving it to each country to decide what constituted justification.[27]

The insertion of this clause may raise two questions: could other sanctions be used before the end of the three-year period, and could revocation be used as a sanction at any time in cases in which the patentee misused his monopoly power other than by non-working? Akerman has answered the first question in the negative, which seems reasonable in view of the fact that forfeiture was the only sanction mentioned in the debates.[28] The fact that causes for sanctions other than non-working were not mentioned may for the same reason be taken to indicate that revocation for whatever reason was prohibited for three years; such an extensive interpretation does not seem reasonable. The question is of some interest since a later revision conference (The Hague, 1925) introduced the concept of "abuse" of the patentee's monopoly power. Akerman, devoting much effort to show that the evolution of the Convention, and in particular Article 5, marks an increased awareness of the importance of society's interests, sees in the introduction of the wider concept of the abuse of monopoly power the major indication and support for his thesis. While a closer examination of this point will be made later, it is here merely suggested that the more plausible interpretation of the new clause must be that no limitation was imposed on sanctions that might apply, according to national laws, for other causes.[29]

Despite the fact that the principle of unanimity in theory gives an equally important voice to each member, it is obvious that economically more powerful States can wield considerable influence at times. This was shown in a particular form at the Brussels conference. Both Germany and Austria, neither of which was yet a member, had made it clearly known that, while they were prepared to join the Union, their adherence depended on the adoption of certain amendments, of which the limitation of the sancion of revocation was the most important. From the deliberations it is evident that the decisions taken were

[27] The clause appeared in Article 3 bis of a Final Protocol.
[28] Akerman, *op. cit.*, p. 110.
[29] *Cf. infra*, footnote 33 and pp. 81–82.

strongly influenced by the desirability to accomodate these countries.[30,31]

2. *The Revision Conference of Washington 1911*[32]

In view of the strong opposition of many countries to the abolition of revocation, the Bureau now proposed the following addition to Article 5: while the sanction of revocation should in principle be replaced by compulsory licensing, each country should retain the right to demand that consumers be adequately supplied, and that licenses be given on reasonable terms if asked for, at the risk of revocation; the use of this power should, however, be limited to cases in which parties immediately concerned, i.e., consumers and producers, had complained of not being able to either buy goods or obtain licenses; and the three-year rule limiting the use of revocation should be retained in any case. The Bureau proposal also contained the suggestion that countries, not willing to accept the new proposal, should be able to continue applying the existing provisions.

This latter suggestion would have introduced what is known as the "reservation system," which had been adopted for instance by the Berne Union. As had been the case at Brussels when the suggestion of a restricted union was made, now also a strong opposition against splitting the unity of the rules of the Convention manifested itself.

In their counter-proposals, several countries rejected the Bureau's proposal, which largely substituted compulsory licensing for compulsory working, on the grounds that their national laws were not in agreement with such a provision. The British proposal is particularly interesting in view of the fact that Britain had been a co-sponsor in 1880 of

30 For Germany's position, see *Actes*, pp. 168–70, 179, 317–18, and for its influence on the conference, see *Actes de la Conférence de Washington*, p. 284; for Austria's position, see *Actes*, p. 321. For more details on this point, see *Union Internationale* . . ., pp. 69, 73.

31 Among other changes concerning patents were the extension of the priority period from six to twelve months (Article 4); the rule that prior exploitation by the patentee does not invalidate the date of first patent application as the basis for claiming priority rights (Article 4); and the establishment of the principle of "independence of patents" granted in different countries, whether members or not (Article 4 bis).

32 At the conference membership stood at 22. The following five States had joined since the previous conference: Austria, Cuba, Germany, Hungary and Mexico. *Actes*, p. 25. The following non-members were represented: Bolivia, Canada, Chile, Colombia, Costa Rica, Ecuador, Greece, Haiti, Honduras, Liberia, Nicaragua, Panama, Paraguay, Persia, Peru, Russia, El Salvador, Siam and Turkey. *Actes*, pp. 159–70. The large number of Latin American countries represented among the non-members, of which only Haiti has since adhered, was probably due to the fact that most of these countries had created a Pan-American patent convention the previous year. On this matter, see *infra*, pp. 102–03. No country is bound by the Washington text.

the Belgian proposal to abolish the sanction of revocation for non-working completely. The British change of mind on this point was due to the introduction of compulsory working in a Patent Act amendment in 1907.[33]

The Bureau, in proposing the new Article 5, evidently had in mind the new English patent law. Referring to new circumstances which had appeared in some countries since the Brussels Conference, the Bureau said that, in order to avoid a regression from the progress already achieved, new provisions tending to conciliate the "legitimate rights" of inventors and the "requirements of public interest" might be desirable. Though reference to "public interest" has always been invoked, both to defend and reject proposed changes, the Bureau, for the above-mentioned reason, seems to have gone further in stressing the public interest at Washington than at any other conference, even with due consideration for the second point mentioned below. The new proposal concerning Article 5 was based on the following ideas according to the Bureau: (1) it is necessary to give the industry of every country the possibility of utilizing any invention on a footing of equality with all other countries protecting that invention; (2) any intentional bias must be prevented from operating either in favor of the inventor against the public interest or against the inventor in favor of any particular interest; and (3) certain countries apparently wish to retain the faculty to take the necessary measures assuring the introduction either of new industries likely to benefit their economies or of products demanded by their consumers.[34] It must of course be recognized that, though in general the interests of society and of individual patentees, as far as working provisions are concerned, are supposed to be in opposition, this may not always be so. Besides the opinion that there are no differences between the two groups of interests,[35] this seems to be the case parti-

[33] The British counter-proposal contained a point of particular interest, in view of what has been said earlier concerning the cases in which the three-year period during which revocation was not allowed, was applicable (*Cf. supra, p.* 74). It was pointed out that the Bureau proposal had omitted the words "for non-working" thereby giving the impression that by this omission Article 5 should be considered to extend to other causes for revocation. Great Britain suggested (*Actes*, p. 106) and the Bureau accepted (*Actes*, p. 228) the insertion of a phrase expressly stating that no patent could be revoked, during the first three years, for the sole reason of non-working or insufficient working. See also, "L'Obligation d'exploiter ...," pp. 73–74. This clearly supports the contention (*Cf. supra* p. 81–82). that the three-year limitation on the use of revocation, introduced at Brussels, was limited to the case of non-working. Further support for such an interpretation is the wording of the clause according to which revocation is not allowed in cases in which the patentee justifies his *inaction*.

[34] Actes, p. 48.

[35] See Ch. S. Oppenheim, "The Public Interest in Legal Protection of Industrial and Intellectual Property," *J.P.O.S.*, 32: 903–35, December, 1950, p. 907, who says: "No one

cularly of large industrial countries with a large or major portion of their patent grants given to its own nationals, and whose nationals hold significant numbers of patents in other countries.

A German proposal to the Conference suggested the substitution of compulsory licensing for revocation as a sanction for non-working, to be used after the three-year period. A number of countries opposed the proposal – Austria, France, Great Britain, the Netherlands and Spain. The position of France is particularly interesting. Far from basing itself on the principles of "inherent rights of inventors," the French rejection of this proposal stated, in fact, that the working obligation had its rationale in the economic necessity of feeding the national industry of the patent-granting country with the discoveries and inventions there patented.[36] Similar positions were taken by other countries in later conferences. This debate clearly indicates the existence of conflicting interests between inventors and society. The fact that only certain countries, and sometimes not the same ones, took such positions from conference to conference, further indicates the existence of differences of interest among countries in the matter of the international protection of patents.

After the German proposal was rejected, the general opinion was in favor of retaining the *status quo*. Thus, at the Washington Conference no change was made that affected the manner in which a patentee could be obliged to exploit his patent by national law. On the whole, only minor changes concerning patents were agreed upon.[37]

3. *The Revision Conference of The Hague 1925*[38]

At this conference the contents of Article 5 were changed in the following respects: in paragraph 2 the essential change was the substitution

would quarrel with advocacy of the protection of the public interest. The difficulty is that the term 'public interest' has been used by restrictionists as though it were something apart from and adverse to the private interest."

[36] *Actes*, p. 282, continuing: "que la France n'était pas en principe hostile à l'idée de tempérer le régime de l'obligation d'exploiter, mais que des études approfondies n'avaient fait entrevoir aucun moyen de nature à réaliser ce but; que d'après les expériences faites sous le système de la licence obligatoire en Grande Bretagne, en Suède et en Mexique, ce système était mauvais et inadmissible."

[37] Changes in the wording appeared in Articles 1, 2 and 4; Article 16 bis expressly mentions the right of countries to adhere to, as well as repudiate, the Convention on behalf of their colonies; and the text of Article 3 bis of the Final Protocol was inserted in Article 5 (2).

[38] At the Hague Conference, membership stood at 37 with the adherence of the following countries: Australia, Bulgaria, Canada, Czechoslovakia, Danzig, Estonia, Finland, Greece, Ireland, Latvia, Luxemburg, Morocco, Poland, Rumania, Turkey, and Yugoslavia (Serbia had been a member); in addition France had adhered on behalf of Lebanon and Syria. *Actes*, p. 27; the following non-member States were represented: Argentina, Colombia,

of the concept of "abuses which might result from the exclusive rights conferred by the patent" for that of "non-working"; a paragraph 3 was inserted, in which the idea of compulsory licenses was introduced for the first time. The paragraph stated that measures to prevent abuses "shall not entail forfeiture unless the grant of compulsory licenses is insufficient to prevent such abuses"; and finally a fourth paragraph was created essentially containing the second part of paragraph 2 of the Washington text, but with the following changes: the three-year period would start from the date of the patent grant rather than from the filing date of the patent application, and the patentee could exonerate himself by proving "the existence of legitimate excuses" rather than "by justifying his inaction."

This text gave rise to several, sometimes conflicting, interpretations. In order to suggest the most valid interpretation, the various propositions and opinions expressed at the conference will be examined as well as comments made on them afterwards.

The proposal of the Bureau suggested the deletion of compulsory working provisions, replacing them with provisions for compulsory licenses after the three-year period, in countries that wanted to prevent an invention from not being worked locally. The Bureau motivated this proposal with the fact that membership was now considerable and that the maintenance of compulsory working clauses in all but one of the Member States (the exception being the United States) was not rational, since if the patentee does not work his invention in a country it is generally because he can work it more profitably in another country, in which case the consumer will pay less.[39]

Later the Bureau added the following particular argument (which has been echoed by several authors commenting on this conference):

"The obligation for the foreign patentee to manufacture in the country may lead to the establishment of a foreign industry towards which the local manufacturers would not be favorable."[40]

Egypt, Guatemala, Hedjaz, Haiti, Liberia, Panama, Peru, El Salvador, San Marino, Siam, South Africa, and Venezuela. *Actes*, pp. 371 ff. Three countries, Brazil, the Dominican Republic and Poland, remain bound by the Hague text of the Convention as of January 1, 1969.

39 It is recognized, however, that this may not always be so. Saying that there remains one serious inconvenience in the abolition of compulsory working requirements, the Bureau proposal states (*Actes*, p. 235): "Certains producteurs nationaux peuvent se rencontrer, qui seraient prêts à exploiter le champ que le breveté étranger laisse en friche." The question of whether the patentee's choice of where to produce can be taken as an objective test of what is most advantageous from the point of view of society either in general or in particular for less developed countries, will be treated in Part II, Chapter II.

40 *Ibid.* [translation from French]; Ladas, *op. cit.*, p. 323, after stating that inventors cannot be expected to work their inventions in many countries and that the inventor himself

Although this latter argument must be seen in the context of the climate of strong economic nationalism that reigned after the First World War, it is of interest today in the case of developing countries whose very objective it is to attract foreign investment in industrial manufacturing.

Several countries objected to the suggestion to abolish any working requirements completely, which was raised this time by the United States. Spain, opposing the proposal, observed that if the abolishment of any working requirement may be favorable to the large, industrialized countries, assuring them complete control of export markets, such a measure would prejudice the interests of less industrialized countries by transforming the patent monopoly into a trading monopoly inimical to the development of local industry.[41]

Three countries (Japan, Poland and Yoguslavia) were also opposed to the abolition of the sancion of revocation for non-working and proposed the maintenance of the *status quo*. All three countries gave essentially the same arguments. The Polish declaration may be taken as an example. The refusal to abolish revocation was based on the fact that the Polish industry was far from being as developed as those of the great Western Powers and that the government had the duty to protect and assure the development of local industry. Therefore, it could not agree to let Polish industry be stifled by the importation of patent-

is the best judge of where conditions are most favorable for production, i.e., where costs are lowest, resulting in cheaper goods for the consumers, later (p. 333) states that "the compulsory working provisions cause the installation of foreign industries in the country, movements of capital and foreign investments, the effects of all of which may be far-reaching." This author also uses the following argument plainly contradicting his above-quoted statements, saying (p. 333) that in the case of a foreign industry being established through compulsory working requirements "the country will lose the customs duties it would collect on the importation of the new products from foreign countries, and competition in the national industry will be more severe, as the products manufactured in the country will be free of transportation expenses and customs duties." The argument that the consumer will pay less for imported goods contradicts the one saying that local production will cause tougher competition because of lower prices. A similar opinion is expressed in the article "L'Obligation d'exploiter ...," p. 120, which says that in the case of local exploitation by foreigners "l'industrie nationale se trouvera en présence de concurrents d'autant plus redoutables que la protection des droits de douane ne jouera plus à leur encontre." Thus in the same breath as one proposes the abolition of working obligations in the name of efficient resource allocation, one suggests that the obligation to work runs counter to protectionist measures tending to obstruct such efficient allocation; E. Dame, *op. cit.*, pp. 46–52 makes a distinction between industrial and non-industrial countries. Though she recognizes the advantages which the implantation of a foreign industry can have in promoting the local economy, the author is of the opinion that the increased competition would be harmful to the local industry, concluding (p. 52): "Wegen diesen grossen Nachteilen für die ***Industriestaaten*** [italics added] ist der Ausführungszwang nicht mehr als ein Mittel zum Einplanzung neuer Industriezweige und zur Schulung von Arbeitern zu verwenden."

[41] *Actes*, p. 432.

protected products. The most significant argument, considering that these countries were then comparable to the developing countries of today, and one that was made by all three, purported to indicate that compulsory licenses were not always a reliable remedy because of the difficulties of finding local licensees.[42]

As it appeared impossible to reach agreement on the abolishment of revocation, the President of the second subcommittee on patents wondered if anyhow, it would not be possible to work out a compromise text, "taking into account the understandable apprehension, that the suggestion has created within certain delegations."[43]

A compromise proposal, introduced by Great Britain and the United States, was adopted and became paragraphs two, three and four of Article 5. The sanction of revocation was maintained but was not to be used unless "the grant of compulsory licenses is insufficient to prevent such abuses" [Article 5 (3)]. Diverging opinions have been expressed on the problem of whether an actual grant of a compulsory license had to precede revocation, or whether direct revocation could take place (still only after three years), if a compulsory license was considered insufficient.[44]

The drafting committee, in its comments on the new text of Article 5, observed, that it laid down the principle of abolishing revocation and provided the means of compulsory licenses to oblige the patentee to work his patent or to sanction his inaction. It added, however, that the article even permitted the application of revocation if the compulsory license is not sufficient "in fact." The expression "in fact" would seem to indicate that actual proof of insufficiency was necessary before a patent could be revoked. Ladas apparently agrees with this point of view when he says that "only in case such a license

[42] *Actes*, p. 433.

[43] "Qui pourrait tenir compte des craintes, sans doute légitimes, qu'a fait naître la proposition chez certains délégations." *Ibid.*

[44] M. Plaisant, *Traité de droit conventionnel international concernant la propriété industrielle* (Paris: Sirey, 1949) pp. 129–30, 137, interprets the results of the Hague Conference as being a complete abolition of the earlier power to revoke patents. In view of the fact that this author was both a delegate at the Conference and a member of the second subcommittee, his interpretation would seem to be authoritative. In support of his interpretation Plaisant alleges that the American delegation had threatened to withdraw from the Union in case their proposal for the abolition of revocation were not accepted. Not only does the text of the new Article 5 contradict Plaisant's interpretation, but also the American delegation took pains to disperse any doubts about their alleged threat to leave the Union by saying (*Actes*, p. 414): "La Délégation américaine tient à préciser que sa proposition ne constitue ni un *ultimatum* ni une menace de la part de son Gouvernement de se rétirer de la Convention d'Union. Elle a tenu à exposer très sincèrement les vues de son Gouvernement sans avoir l'intention de dicter en quoi que ce soit à la Conférence ce qui doit ou ne doit pas être fait."

does not prevent the abuse of the exclusive right granted to the patentee, his patent may be forfeited."[45] The corollary to such an interpretation would imply that a country lacking a compulsory license system – it may have previously relied exclusively on revocation to sanction non-working – would suddenly be deprived of any sanction at all.[46] This would neither be a logical result of the gradual evolution of the Convention nor take account of the adamant opposition of certain countries to the abolishment of revocation.[47]

There is one interpretation that can be effectively defended, and which would agree with all the authors, who have maintained that the introduction of compulsory licenses in the Convention was merely a recognition of the *principle* of substituting compulsory licenses for revocation. It has been proposed by Ackerman.[48] He observes that the Bureau's interpretation of the new rules permitted member countries to take any measures deemed necessary to assure local exploitation. Referring to the categoric refusal of some countries to abolish revocation, he therefore concludes that each country is free to decide, given their economic and social conditions, whether the granting of compulsory licenses will be insufficient, and whether therefore only a revocation will effectively eliminate abuses of the patent monopoly.[49]

The important innovation at the Hague, in the text of Article 5, is the substitution of the concept of "the abuses which might result from

[45] Ladas, *op. cit.*, p. 98; See however *Ibid.*, p. 341, where Ladas does not exclude the "less liberal solution."

[46] Casalonga recognizes this outcome of his interpretation. Cf. A. Casalonga, "Forfeiture of Patents for Non-Working," *J.P.O.S.*, 33: 720–23, October, 1951.

[47] "Il serait ... contraire à la logique juridique de soutenir que, par l'introduction dans l'ordre juridique interne de la Convention de La Haye, dont l'article 5 devait réglementer le passage d'une époque d'intrasigeance absolue à une époque de semi-liberté ... on a voulu instaurer, *pendant* cette période de transition un régime de liberté complète, dépourvu de toute obligation ou sanction." Akerman, *op. cit.*, pp. 141–42.

[48] ... "L'Article 5 de la Convention de La Haye n'a apportée, par lui-même, aucun changement au régime existant dans un pays quelconque de l'Union au moment de son entrée en vigeur dans ce pays.

Il ne constitue qu'un *affirmation de principe* et un progrès 'moral' en tant que le système des licences obligatoires est officiellement reconnu ..." Akerman, *op. cit.*, p. 142. For a similar opinion, cf. M. Plaisant and F. Jacq, *Le nouveau régime international de la propriété industrielle* (Paris: Sirey, 1927) pp. 70–71, and the Bureau Proposal to the London Conference, *Actes de la Conférence de Londres* [1934] p. 174. The authors who have interpreted the Hague revision to mean that it completely abolished revocation (Plaisant) or that a compulsory licence would actually have to be proved insufficient before revocation was permitted (Casalonga), have supported their interpretations by pointing out that the Anglo-American proposal was supposed to be a compromise and that the Americans would never agreed to a mere moral obligation to refrain from revoking patents. It will be suggested below, however, that the Americans may have been "compensated" by the new restrictions introduced into the Convention through the concept of "abuse of monopoly power."

[49] Akerman, *op. cit.*, p. 141.

the exclusive rights conferred by the patent" for that of "non-working." The concept of "abuse of monopoly power" was introduced by the Anglo-American compromise proposal and was clearly inspired by the British Patent Act.[50] The phrase "for example, failure to work" was inserted at the request of one delegation, in order to make it clear that non-working might constitute such an abuse.[51] As far as non-exploitation is concerned, the new text has been interpreted to mean that such inaction in itself is not liable to sanctions, and sanctions are allowed only if it is considered an abuse of the patentee's monopoly power.[52]

Since until 1925 the Convention had only regulated the obligation to work and its sanctions, Akerman believes that the introduction of the wider concept of "abuse of monopoly power" into the Convention was a step increasing the powers of society in its efforts to prevent harmful practices due to patent monopolies and contrary to the public interest, by giving it wider powers of control than it had had before.[53]

Although prior to 1925, the Convention text had only dealt with non-working, this did not mean that other actions by a patentee deemed harmful by society could not have been subject to sanctions by virtue of a national law. The only plausible explanation for the fact that the Convention text treated only sanctions against non-working is that it did not regulate other abuses, leaving the Union countries free to legislate on the matter. From what has been suggested above, with reference to the Brussels Conference, on the non-applicability of the three-year grace period to sanctions for causes other than non-working, and, moreover, taking into consideration the British proposal during the Washington Conference to expressly make non-working the only case in which the period was applicable,[54] the obvious conclusion seems to be that the introduction of the concept of "abuse of monopoly power" was, in fact, a further curtailment of society's right to control the use made of the monopoly power that a patent gives its holder.[55,56]

[50] This was acknowledged by the President of the second sub-committee. *Actes*, p. 434.

[51] *Ibid.*, p. 519.

[52] Ladas, *op. cit.*, p. 339; *Union Internationale* ..., pp. 112–13.

[53] Akerman, *op. cit.*, pp. 144–146.

[54] Cf. *supra*, n. 33.

[55] For the opposite point of view, see F. Ostertag, "Exposé introductif de questions à l'ordre du jour du Congrès de l'AIPPI, Rome, 1928," *P.I.*, 44: 178–83, August, 1928, p. 179, who says: "Le texte *actuel* [Hague text] permet aux pays contractants, contrairement au texte primitif de la Convention, d'introduire des restrictions au droit exclusif du breveté non seulement en cas de non-exploitation, mais encore dans d'autres cas ... où il y a abus de monopole ..."

[56] The authors who have interpreted the new text of Article 5 as far as sanctions are concerned as more than a statement of principle and moral obligation (Cf. n. 44 and n. 48 *supra*) supported such arguments by observing that the text was supposed to be a compro-

The third and final modification of Article 5 changed the starting date of the three-year period from that of the patent application to that of the patent grant. It appears that there was little opposition to this change. It meant a substantially greater protection for the patentee against sanctions especially in countries that used the examination system.[57]

Of the three changes introduced in Article 5 at the Hague, the introduction of the concept of compulsory licenses would certainly have the most long term influence, even though initially it may have had less practical value. The appearance of the concept of "abuse of monopoly power," which now included among other causes the only previously, regulated cause for sanction – non-working – must be considered a gain for the patentee, as must also the third change prolonging the period during which sanctions could not be taken.[58] Thus there seems little justification for the opinion that the new Article 5, as revised at the

mise between the countries proposing far-reaching changes and those opposed to modification. With the interpretation suggested above (p. 81), the former countries would be left with the sole advance of the incorporation of a "moral" obligation into the Convention. When the American delegation, during a session of the Conference, sitting as a committee of the whole, commented on the amendments to Article 5 saying in part (*Actes*, p. 576) that "lesdits amendements à La Convention sont appréciés à leur juste valeur par la Délégation des Etats-Unis qui les considère comme des concessions réelles," it appears unlikely that it had in mind the mere "moral" value of the recognition of compulsory licenses. Instead, it can be held that the curtailment of sanctions for abuses other than non-exploitation – which, it has been suggested, was the real significance of the introduction of the "abuse of monopoly power" concept into the Convention – belonged to the real concessions of which the American delegation spoke. Some authors, seeing the introduction of this concept as a concession to the interests of society (as against those of the patentee), have directly linked its inclusion in Article 5 to the "compromise" solution proposed by the United States and Great Britain. (For instance, Akerman, *op. cit.*, 146 et *passim*, and *Union Internationale*, pp. 112–13). The logic for such a conclusion seems dubious. It is hardly possible that out of a compromise between those who wanted less interference in the freedom of patentees and those who wanted to retain *status quo* would come new, more extensive powers for society to control the activities of patentees.

[57] Akerman, *op. cit.*, p. 80. It is sometimes said that patentees in countries that have pre-examination systems do not start exploiting their inventions before they are granted a patent. Therefore, their effective protection would be only the three-year period. This contention would seem contradicted, however, by the arguments presented at the Lisbon Conference (1958) that supported a longer period of protection for patentees in non-examination countries to equalize conditions for patentees under the two systems. See the Bureau Proposal at Lisbon and comments by one delegation at that Conference. *Actes de la Conférence de Lisbonne* [1958], pp. 392, 395.

[58] The position of patentees was further improved to the extent that the individual countries interpreted the text to include all possible action against patentees. At the Lisbon Conference (1958), several delegations stated that their laws were based on such an interpretation.

Hague, took account of any increased awareness of the interests of society (as opposed to those of the patentee).[59,60]

4. The Revision Conference of London 1934[61]

At this conference only paragraph 4 was amended, but the change was important. Whereas the text of paragraph 4 in its earlier version contained the expression "the patent may not be subjected to such measures before the expiration of three years," the new text provided that "an application for a compulsory license may not be made before the expiration of three years." A second sentence was added, reading: "No proceedings for the forfeiture or revocation of a patent may be instituted before the expiration of two years from the grant of the first compulsory license."

The Bureau suggested one change of Article 5. The proposed amendment, aimed at the abolition of the sanction of revocation for non-working, would mean a revision of paragraph 3. The draft amendment for a new paragraph 3 read: "These measures may forsee *the compulsory license as a sanction for non-working but not the revocation of the patent grant.*"[62] The Bureau after affirming that according to the Hague text, the countries that had opposed the abolition of revocation, fearing that the importation of patented products would retard their industrial development, were still free to maintain that compulsory licenses were not sufficient to avert the disadvantages of non-working, nevertheless

[59] That is, if one does not use "interest of society" to mean the interests of the foreign patentee's own country. A member of the American delegation expressed this opinion. See *Actes*, p. 575. Though from the beginning, the principal goal of the Union was to secure the rights and interests of patentees, never was it claimed that "interest of society" referred to the country of the foreign patentee!

[60] How little impact the requirements of national interests have made, especially as argued by several less industrialized countries, is apparent in the following comment on the Hague Conference. Observing that non-exploitation may only be sanctioned if it is considered an abuse and that revocation was only a subsidiary sanction, it is said that: "Néanmoins, le danger subsiste que les pays pauvres en industrie utilisent l'obligation d'exploiter, non seulement pour introduire chez eux des objets brevetés, dans la mesure où ils en ont besoin, mais encore pour attirer sur leur territoire de nouvelles industries sans tenir compte de la question de savoir si ces dernières seront viables." *Union Internationale* . . ., p. 113.

[61] At the London Conference membership stood at forty, the following two States having adhered since the Hague Conference: Lichtenstein and New Zealand. *Actes*, pp. 9–10. The following non-members were represented: Bolivia, Chile, Colombia, Egypt, Ecuador, Guatemala, Iraq, Lithuania, Nicaragua, Peru, Siam, and Venezuela. *Actes*, p. 311 ff. The following twenty-four States are still bound by the London text of the Convention (as of January 1, 1969): Australia, Austria, Canada, Ceylon, Denmark, Finland, Greece, the Holy See, Iceland, Indonesia, Lebanon, Lichstenstein, Luxemburg, the Netherlands, New Zealand, Portugal, San Marino, Spain, Sweden, Syrian Arab Republic, Tunesia, Turkey, U.A.R. and Vietnam.

[62] [translated from French] *Actes*. p. 261.

maintained that it was difficult to admit that an abuse of the monopoly power exists, when the patentee is prepared "to satisfy all needs of the local market."[63] Although one may take issue with the assertion that the patentee is prepared to "satisfy all needs of the local market" – in a monopoly market the meaning of satisfaction of consumers is by definition far removed from the general significance of that term – as well as his professed readiness to license, there is another fundamental consideration that may invalidate the statement. As several countries observed at the Hague and would do again at this conference, the sanction of compulsory licenses may not be effective because of the difficulty to find licensees.[64] It is possible that less industrialized countries are primarily concerned less with the abuse on the part of the foreign patentee than with the ability of the patent system to meet the particular requirements of industrialization of developing countries. On the other hand, to the extent that certain sanctions for non-working are in reality ineffective, this might encourage abuse.

Three counter-proposals submitted by Member States are of particular interest. A Mexican suggestion for a new paragraph 3 would keep compulsory licensing but not the sanction of revocation. Instead a country would be able to sanction non-working with a "reasonable reduction" of the duration of the patent.[65] The Polish delegation proposed an amendment of the existing paragraph 3 containing the rule, that non-working should not be considered an abuse in the case where the demand of the local market did not justify local production. In motivating its standpoint, the Polish delegation referred to its declaration at the Hague,[66] and stated that the Polish Government must support its industry, and that it could not accept importation of patented products in the cases in which it was proved that the costs of local production would be covered by national demand. It concluded that Poland, *in order to prevent abuses detrimental to its local industry, could not accept the abolition of revocation.*[67] The significance of this approach is that it tries to solve the problem of the case in which the

[63] "... à satisfaire à tout les besoins du marché indigène." *Actes.* p. 174.

[64] It is obvious that this point is not taken into consideration in the following comment by the Bureau: "Lorsque ni le breveté étranger ni l'industriel indigène n'osent entreprendre l'exploitation dans le pays ... on ne saurait reprocher au breveté un abus de son droit exclusif, puisque l'inefficacité de son offre d'accorder des licenses aux industriels du pays constitue précisément la justification de son inaction." *Actes*, p. 175.

[65] *Ibid.*, p. 262.

[66] *Supra*, pp. 79–80.

[67] *Actes*, pp. 262–63. Czechoslovakia, Spain and Yugoslavia took the same position. *Ibid.*

foreign patentee and the national authorities do not evaluate the possibilities for local production in the same way.

The Czechoslovakian delegation, in a general commentary on the Bureau proposals, declared, that the changes suggested were evidently based on" the desire to satisfy the multiple claims of modern international commerce," and that it was certain, "that the proposals of the Bureau were likely to considerably improve the position of patentes internationally." Nevertheless," it continued:

> One must not lose sight of the fact that this improvement entails a weakening of the economic position of nationals to the advantage of foreigners. Given the proportion that exists between the manufacturing and trade of small countries such as Czechoslovakia, on the one hand, and foreign competition, on the other hand, it is to be feared that the advantages will far from compensate for the disadvantages to the national economy, if the Bureau programme was adopted.[68]

The Czeck delegation then declared that already the changes brought about at the Hague had come to lie heavily on the Czechoslovakian manufacturers and merchants. Therefore their government had to examine the Bureau proposal with the utmost care and oppose any reform, which might bring further disadvantages to its nationals. For these economic reasons the Czechoslovakian delegation proposed some amendments to the Bureau proposal.[69] The specific proposal concerning Article 5 submitted by Czechoslovakia did not go beyond amending the existing paragraph 3 in the manner suggested by the Polish delegation.[70]

A compromise proposal was worked out that left paragraph 3 unchanged and introduced a revision of paragraph 4, according to which the sanction of revocation would be kept, but under the condition that it could be invoked only two years after a compulsory license had been granted. In committee this compromise was accepted by the majority,[71] and during the session of the Conference sitting as a committee of the whole only Japan did not vote in favor of it.[72] The new paragraph 4 of Article 5 was finally adopted in plenary session without discussion.[73]

Even though the only textual change in Article 5 at the London Conference appeared in its fourth paragraph, it also had repercussions

[68] [translated from French] *Ibid.*, p. 245.
[69] *Ibid.*, pp. 245–46.
[70] *Ibid.*, p. 263.
[71] Eighteen in favor, seven opposed (Brazil, Syria-Lebanon, France, Italy, Japan, Morocco, Tunisia) with five abstentions (Belgium, Cuba, Danzig, Mexico, Poland). *Ibid.*, p. 379.
[72] *Ibid.*, p. 459.
[73] *Ibid.*, p. 515.

on the preceding paragraph. Whereas the third paragraph in its Hague version only constituted an affirmation of a theoretical principle, described as a "moral commitment," that revocation should not be resorted to unless a compulsory license was insufficient, the London version of paragraph 3, in virtue of the second sentence of paragraph 4, constituted a "unionist rule", i.e., compulsory for all its members.

The greater awareness of the interests of society (in opposition to those of patentees) which, according to Akerman, was manifest at the Hague Conference, would logically also have to have been present at the London Conference. Just as no indication of such an influence could be found in the results of the first of these conferences, the same seems to be true for the second, unless one does not mean, that since the protection of patentees was not reinforced even further, the interests of society prevailed.[74]

5. *The Revision Conference of Lisbon 1958*[75]

The revision of Article 5 at Lisbon left only its first paragraph unchanged. Paragraph 2, which recognized the right of Member States to take the necessary legislative measures to prevent abuses, now stated that this right was limited to taking measures "providing for the grant of compulsory licenses." In the first part of paragraph 3, the words "is insufficient", indicating the cases in which revocation was allowed, were replaced by "would not have been sufficient." The former second sentence of the fourth paragraph was inserted as a new, second part of paragraph 3. In the new paragraph 4, the introductory words "In any case" were deleted. Furthermore, the application of "grace" periods,

[74] Among other changes concerning patents, the reservation of the rights of third parties was finally eliminated. Plaisant, *op. cit.*, pp. 99, 101, commenting on this point, said: "La réserve du droit des tiers apparaît comme un élément étranger introduit dans le corps organique de la Convention d'Union.

. . . .

Le devoir des juristes est justement de construire un monument des lois et des traités qui offre aux inventeurs ... leur plein expansion. C'est pourquoi le droit de priorité ne peut être qu'absolu: la réserve des tiers apparaît comme héresie, une lacune dans un édifice logique."

[75] At the Lisbon Conference membership stood at forty-seven, a net increase of five since the London Conference. The new members were: Ceylon, Haiti, Indonesia, Israel, Federation of Rhodesia-Nyasaland (Rhodesia and Malawi have since become separate members), Monaco, South Africa, U.A.R., and Vietnam while the following "left" the Union: Palestine, Danzig, Estonia, Latvia. The following non-members were represented: Argentina, Ecuador, Iraq, Iran, Liberia, Panama, El Salvador, Saudi Arabia, U.S.S.R., the Vatican, Venezuela. Out of seventy-nine Member States (as of January 1, 1969) fifty-two are bound by the Lisbon text.

during which no compulsory licenses could be granted, was expressly limited to cases of non-working or insufficient working. A certain adjustment concerning the length of such periods was made. Finally a new phrase was added stating that compulsory licenses should be non-exclusive and non-transferable.

A Turkish proposal to the Conference may be significant, for it shows an increased awareness of the particular position of less industrialized countries. It is also important because it contains the first suggestion to reduce the period during which the patentee is protected against sanctions for non-working.[76] Observing that during every revision conference, including Lisbon, the period of time mentioned in Article 5 (A) had been extended, and referring to what Poland and other countries had said on this question at London, the Turkish proposal said, in part, that the present proposal, in creating an effective monopoly, would fortify the position of the very advanced industrialized countries, which was the reason why countries with less satisfactory economic conditions would maintain their refusal to accept the proposed text.[77] The Turkish proposal continues by arguing for a reduction of this period. Considering the present rhythm of growth of new technology if would be advisable to decide on a very short period for many inventions or else the advantages of the compulsory license will be lost.[78]
It further pointed out that although it is possible to limit the initial freedom of importation by means of restrictions, this cannot possibly help these countries during the specified period of time. The Turkish delegation therefore concludes that the proposed text would create conditions tending to widen the gap between the more and the less industrialized countries, and that unless the period during which sanctions cannot be applied, according to the existing rule, was reduced, Turkey would have to take internal measures to gurantee, such a reduction.[79]

As at all previous revision conferences the proposal to abolish revocation as a sanction for non-working, raised by the Bureau, was opposed

[76] Brazil seems to have had the same intention when it proposed that compulsory licenses be granted "pour l'exploitation de brevets si leur concessionnaire ou concessionnaires ne l'ont pas fait dans le délai établi par le Code de la propriété industrielle," a period which in the case of Brazil was, and still is, two years. *Actes.*, p. 918.

[77] *Actes.*, p. 404.

[78] *Ibid.*, continuing: "Les Etats industrialisés, sans être exposés à des sérieuses difficultés, ont bénéficié grandement de la possibilité de monopole que leurs brevets pourraient créer. Donc, les Etats moins industrialisés que les autres, n'auront-ils jamais le droit de bénéficier de ces avantages?"

[79] *Actes.* p. 404.

by several countries. Among these were Brazil, Iraq and Yugoslavia. According to their experience, the threat of compulsory licenses – especially in the case of developing countries – was insufficient as a remedy against non-working. The patentee often could not find a local manufacturer able to exploit the patent.[80]

It is interesting to note that Austria and Italy also opposed the move to abolish revocation. The Austrian delegation declared that it could not support the proposal since" such a measure would risk to delay the working of patents in small countries," while the Italian delegation was of the opinion that one could not entirely abandon the system of revocation "without prejudicing the industrial development of the country."[81]

In these two cases the stage of economic development was not mentioned. Instead a difference between larger and smaller countries was suggested; this idea stems from the fact that the percentage of nationals holding patents is generally lower in smaller countries.[82]

When paragraph 4 was discussed, the question of whether or not the patentee should benefit from the "grace" period in all cases of abuse, or merely in the case of non-working and insufficient working, was definitely settled. According to the London text the benefit of this delay in pronouncing sanctions was applicable to all cases of abuse. At Lisbon, however, an almost unanimous opinion held that the patentee should benefit from this delay only in cases of non-working and insufficient working.

The drafting committee, set forth the motivations for proposing a text which with only one change, became the new paragraphs 2, 3 and 4 of Article 5A.

In paragraph 2 the expression "each contracting country shall have the right to take the necessary legislative measures" was replaced by "each country of the Union shall have the right to take legislative measures providing for the grant of compulsory licenses," in order to make it clear that the primary sanction should be compulsory licenses.

Paragraph 3 was to contain the existing text of paragraph 3 of the London text (saying that a patent cannot be revoked unless the grant of a compulsory license is insufficient), plus the second sentence of para-

[80] *Ibid.*, pp. 411; 413.

[81] [translated from French] *Ibid.*, p. 412.

[82] In a vote on the proposal to abolish revocation for non-working nineteen delegations supported the proposal, five delegations opposed it (Brazil, Italy, Mexico, Spain, and Yugoslavia) and four abstained (Australia, Austria, Canada and Hungary.) *Actes*, p. 417.

graph 4 of the London text (revocation can only take place two years after the first compulsory license). In its motivation for the proposed paragraph 3 the Report of the drafting committee said in part, that, in the unanimous opinion of the Committee, revocation could not constitute a primary sanction against non-working (defaut d'exploitation) [sic] but could only be applied once the granting of a compulsory license had proved itself ineffective.[83] Though the drafting committee speaks of "non-working" there is no doubt that what is meant is abuse in general.[84] It might seem that the unanimous opinion of the drafting committee, and the insertion of the second sentence of paragraph 4 of the London text in the new paragraph 3, would definitely settle the matter of the interpretation of that latter paragraph. But first of all the drafting committee consisted of only six countries, five of which had voted for the abolition of revocation in the case of non-working and all of which were highly industrialized countries.[85] More important, however, is the fact that the one change which the text, submitted by the drafting committee, underwent before being adopted by the committee of the whole was that the words "would be insufficient (ne suffirait pas) appearing in the sentence "Forfeiture of the patent shall not be prescribed except in cases in which the grant of compulsory licenses would be insufficient" were replaced by "would not have been sufficient" (n'aurait pas suffi).[86] This change in wording would seem to leave open the possibility of interpreting paragraph 3 to the effect that revocation can also be resorted to in cases in which a compulsory license is supposed to be insufficient *if it were tried*.

[83] *Actes*, pp. 419–20.

[84] When the Conference sitting as a committee of the whole adopted the text of the Report, it was stated that "l'alinéa 3 a pour objet de disposer que la déchéance du brevet n'est jamais une sanction directe, qu'elle ne peut intervenir que si une licence obligatoire déjà accordée s'est revelée insuffisante, et après un certain délai après l'octroi de cette première licence obligatoire." Committee of the Whole, Report by the Second Committee, stenographic records, p. 89. The fact that there is a printing error is further borne out by the fact that the quotation made above from the report of the drafting committee appears under a subheading of the Report, entitled: "Sur la licence obligatoire pour abus du droit exclusif" (Part II of the Report), while provisions specifically concerning non-working appear under the heading: "Licence obligatoire pour défaut d'exploitation" (Part III of Report).

[85] Canada, France, Japan, the Netherlands, Sweden, Switzerland.

[86] Actes, p. 424–25; for the English text of the drafting committee report, see Doc. 171A (unpublished working document for the Lisbon Conference obtained from BIRPI); Though at the second plenary session, when the text of Article 5A was adopted, the English text is referred to as Doc. 287 (*Actes.*, p. 100, reading: "Revocation of the patent shall not be provided for in cases where the granting of compulsory licenses was not sufficient ...") said document appears to base its translation on an earlier text. The *Manual of Convention Texts*, using the expression "would not have been sufficient" is the only translation published and must be considered the official version. [At the Lisbon Conference, French was still the only official language and the English translations were merely working documents.]

As for paragraph 4, finally, the report of the drafting committee said that, despite the opinion expressed by certain delegations that the "grace" period should be provided for all cases of abuse, the committee, with the support of all members, limited the application of the period before which no compulsory license can be granted to the cases of non-working and insufficient working. Finally, the drafting committee suggested that this period should be either three years from the grant of the patent (the formula of the London text) or four years from the date of the patent application, as a compromise between *status quo* and the Bureau proposal. With the one change in paragraph 3, mentioned above, the text submitted by the drafting committee was adopted by the Committe of the whole[87] and later by the Conference without discussion.[88]

How is one to interpret Article 5A as it emerged from the Lisbon revision Conference? Paragraph 2 raises no problem. From the text itself it is clear that the sanction of compulsory license has been made the primary sanction. This is equally clear from the proposals submitted to the Conference and opinions expressed during it. Paragraph 3, however, as shown above, raises the question of whether and to what extent the principle of the previous paragraph is attenuated. The drafting committee evidently intended to limit the possibility of revoking patents to cases in which a compulsory license had, in fact, proved itself insufficient. But, for the reasons explained previously, the final wording of this paragraph appears to lead to the possible interpretation that, in fact, it constitutes a concession to the interests of those countries, that maintained steadfastly during the Conference that the threat of compulsory licenses was often insufficient to avoid abuses or to remedy them.[89] As paragraph 4 expressly limits itself to cases of non-working and insufficient working, this interpretation of paragraph 3 would mean that a country, upon judging that a compulsory license would not be sufficient to prevent or rectify a certain abuse of the

[87] Thirty-two votes in favor and seven abstentions (Brazil, Cuba, Dominican Republic, Indonesia, Mexico, South Africa, and Spain). *Actes.*, pp. 424–25.

[88] *Ibid.*, pp. 100–01.

[89] If it was a concession to certain countries, it should anyhow be remembered that it is so only in the sense of maintaining the *status quo*. If the more restrictive interpretation of paragraph 3 were maintained, i.e., the intention of the drafting committee that a compulsory license would have to be proved insufficient, what would be the solution for the case in which no licensee could be found? A possible interpretation of paragraph 3 would be that its first and second parts combined would, in the cases in which a compulsory license "would not have been sufficient" permit revocation two years after the first possible date of granting such a license.

monopoly power of the patentee, could directly declare a patent forfeited in all cases save those regulated specifically by paragraph 4. No author commenting on the Lisbon text has, however, mentioned such an interpretation.[90]

As for paragraph 4 two changes are evident. The first is that the only abuses now benefiting from a "grace" period before compulsory licenses may be imposed are non-working or insufficient working, whereas earlier all abuses, and, according to the interpretation of some countries, even grounds other than abuses by the patentee, such as cases involving particular public interests, were subject to the provisions of paragraph 4. Thus, there is one tangible change in favor of the interests of society. The second change amounted to a possible prolongation of the grace period. Though its effect was only to benefit patentees in countries that had pre-examination systems, it confirms the contention that the period of effective protection for the patentee might be not only the specified period but also the time between the application for and the granting of a patent.[91]

D. SOME CHARACTERISTICS OF THE EVOLUTION OF THE PARIS UNION

As a complement to the foregoing examination of the evolution of the rules concerning the exploitation of patented inventions through the various revision conferences, the evolution of the Paris Union will be here examined briefly from the following angles: (1) the influence wielded by new members; (2) collective (social) vs. individual (private) interests; and (3) legal vs. economic motives.

1. The influence wielded by new members

The growth of membership of the Union has been large, especially during the last decade. In fact, between 1883 and 1958 membership increased from eleven to forty-seven, and between 1958 and 1967 al-

[90] R. Plaisant, commenting specifically on paragraph 3 of the Lisbon text says: "L'alinéa 3 indique, en effet, que la décheance ne peut être prononcée qu'après la concession effective d'une licence obligatoire et la constatation de l'insuffisance de celle-ci. Il semble que telle était bien l'intention des négociateurs; mais il faut constater que le texte n'est pas encore d'une parfaite clarté." R. Plaisant, "L'Evolution des Conventions de Propriété Intellectuelle," *Les Unions Internationales 1883–1963* (Geneva: BIRPI, 1962) p. 104.

[91] Cf. Bureau proposal, *Actes.*, p. 392, and an interpretation in this sense by a delegation, *Ibid.*, p. 395.

most as much again, standing at seventy-nine in July 1969.[92] When considering the possible impact of new members on the Union, two questions arise: (a) has the influence wielded by new members affected the original policy of the Union, i.e., the general aims for which the Convention was set up, and (b) has the large increase in membership influenced the procedures under which the Convention may be revised.

a. Influence on the policy of the Union

The countries that originally created the Union constituted, with few exceptions, a homogeneous group of fairly industrialized countries. It is true that the group of original members contained a few countries which, with contemporary nomenclature, would have been labeled "developing" or "less industrialized" countries.[93] At the time, however, the idea that such countries formed a special category, with needs and requirements basically different from those of more advanced countries, was absent. Clearly the aim of the original members and of those industrial countries, which had all become members by the beginning of the twentieth century, was that of pursuing a policy directed at consolidating and strengthening the protection of inventors.

The increase in membership in the present century has almost completely consisted in what we today know as developing countries, on the one hand, and socialist countries, on the other hand. The fact that some countries belonging to the former group have since reached the status of industrialized countries does not alter the fact that at the time of adhesion to the Union they were underdeveloped countries. Although, with the exception of the U.S.S.R., all countries of the latter group were members of the Union before becoming socialist, at that time they could be classified as underdeveloped or less industrialized countries.

Thus two other groups have been added to the original group of

[92] The large majority of the new members since 1958 had belonged to the Union as colonies though in that capacity they merely constituted Union territory with no active part in the work of the Union.

[93] S. P. Ladas, "The Fundamental Bases of the International Protection of Industrial Property," *P.I.*, 70: annex, April, 1954 [original text of "Les bases fondamentales de la protection internationale de la propriété industrielle," *P.I.*, 70: 93–97, April, 1954] p. 1, replying to the view that the Convention "... was an instrument adopted by the large colonial powers possessing the privilege of an advanced industrialization ..." (S. Pretnar, "The International Protection of Industrial Property and the Different Stages of Economic Development of the States,") observes that among the eleven original members were Brazil, Guatemala, Portugal, El Salvador, Serbia and Spain. Of these, however, Guatemala and El Salvador soon left the Union (*supra* n. 17) and Serbia had no national patent law until 1918.

members, with interests more or less diverging from those of the latter group of industrialized countries. In order to establish whether and to what extent these new members have influenced the original policy aims of the Union, it is necessary to find out whether these groups of countries have been identified as representing particular interests.

The easier of the two groups to identify is the one that consists of the socialist countries, because it contains only a few countries, and because the existence of the group as such is of recent origin. As mentioned above, with the exception of the U.S.S.R., all socialist countries that are members of the Union – Bulgaria, Hungary, Poland, Rumania, Czechoslovakia, Yugoslavia[94] adhered to it before the Second World War. Roubier, commenting on the list of Union members in 1951 and observing that the most important non-member was Russia, said: "It is useless to hope that under its present economic system, it will become a member," and continuing, he said of other socialist countries that:

> Even countries of this region which are still members (Czechoslovakia, Poland, Hungary, Rumania, Bulgaria) will naturally end up by leaving the Union, as their economy is more and more sovietized, for in this régime the very basis of the law of industrial property disappears along with economic freedom.[95]

The fact that not only have these latter countries remained within the Union, but also that the U.S.S.R. has since become a member, suggests that some change has taken place. Although a certain evolution within the socialist countries has occurred with regard to their economic institutions, the socialist base of their economy remains. Therefore it would appear that the principal change, that the adherence of these countries implies, lies with the Union itself. Besides the fact that these countries are still members, one can only turn to the debates of the latest revision conference (i.e., Lisbon 1958) to see whether any distinguishable differences appeared between these countries as a group and other member countries. As far as patents are concerned at least, there seems to have been no such principal divergence. One commentator of that conference, in fact, has said that "the Iron-curtain countries generally were not difficult to deal with ... they were more cooperative and liberal than some western countries."[96] And yet, the application of the same conventional text to two diametrically opposed economic

[94] The German Democratic Republic considers itself a member, but the question remains unsettled.

[95] P. Roubier, "The Law of the Union for the Protection of Industrial Property," *Journal du Droit International*, 78: 1049, No. 4, 1951.

[96] Ladas, "The Lisbon Conference ...," p. 1294.

systems, must lead to conflicts of interests, whether or not they are acknowledged.[97]

Although the Convention has never expressly stipulated that a member must have a patent law at all, once such laws exist, member countries are bound to legislate in accordance with the latest conventional text to which they have adhered. A further step seems to have been taken at Lisbon with the introduction of the amendment to Article 17. That article, in its second part stipulates, in fact, that a country at the time of ratification of a new text is required to amend its law in conformity with the Union rules upon the adhesion to such a text.[98] With one exception, all the socialist countries mentioned by Roubier have ratified or (in the case of the U.S.S.R.) adhered to the Lisbon text.[99] Thus it would seem that considerations of expediency in its efforts to attain universal membership have led the Union to an elastic interpretation of some of the principles of the Convention.

The classification of countries as less industrialized or developing may be less precise than the classification of socialist countries. Though the principles of such a classification today are generally recognized in matters concerning economic and social policies, this was not so prior to the Second World War. Nevertheless, from the study of various revision conferences it is clear, that certain countries have motivated their standpoint by considerations of economic underdevelopment.[100]

97 "Chacun de ces systèmes a une conception diamétralement opposée à celle de l'autre en ce qui concerne la violation du droit exclusif sur une invention protégée, surtout s'il s'agit d'une violation en raison de la non-exploitation. Tandis que, dans les pays à ordre social économique privé, la non-exploitation est considérée un abus, dans les Etats socialistes une exploitation de l'invention à titre privé est une action directement contraire à l'ordre publique." S. Pretnar, "La notion d'intérêt public et la Convention d'Union," [Offprint from] *Mélanges Marcel Plaisant* (Paris: Sirey, 1960) pp. 9–10.
Mélanges Marcel Plaisant (Paris: Sirey, 1960) pp. 9–10.

98 Article 17(2) "It is understood that at the time an instrument of ratification or accession is deposited on behalf of a country, such country will be in a position under its domestic law to give effect to the provisions of this Convention." For the intention behind the revised article 17, see Ladas, "The Lisbon Conference ...," pp. 1312–1313.

99 Though all these countries, in their national laws for the protection of inventions, provide for a choice between "inventors' certificates" and patents, for obvious reasons, the traditional type of patent protection in these countries must have a very different significance from such protection in private enterprise economies. For more on this question. *infra*, pp. 242–44.

100 See, at the Hague: Spain, *supra*, p. 79; London: Poland, *supra*. pp. 85–86, and Czechoslovakia, *supra*., p. 86; at Lisbon: Turkey, *supra*., p. 88, and Brazil, Iraq and Yugoslavia, *supra*., p. 89; see also the cases in which extensions of the liberty of patentees have been opposed from the point of view of "smallness" rather than the "underdeveloped" character of the economy: at London: Czechoslovakia, *supra*., p. 86 and at Lisbon: Austria and Italy, *supra*., p. 89.

The question as to what extent such countries have been recognized as having interests and requirements different from the industrialized countries is less clear.[101] In the debates of the revision conferences and the proposals presented by the Bureau, certain references are made to these countries. Though some of these seem to imply that a less industrialized country may have certain particular interests, they usually discard the opinions expressed by the countries in question on the ground that those countries can either not be considered as less industrialized, or that the situation of such countries does not require special treatment.[102] With the distinct exception of Pretnar, and, in a more general sense, Penrose and Kronstein, no author seems to have considered that less developed countries merit special treatment. When, for instance, the question of compulsory licensing has been treated, its justification as a protectionist measure is mentioned for the period immediately following the foundation of the Paris Union, but is now held to be a great obstacle. Akerman contends that while the obligation to work may have been appropriate in the circumstances and necessary in the beginning of the era of industrialization, its usefulness has since disappeared.[103] The author maintains that, while the obligation to work might have appeared reasonable when only the interests of a particular country were considered and the interests of the inventor were neglected, it became an insupportable burden for the inventor and incompatible with an effective international system with the increasing economic interdependence between countries.[104]

Thus, although several countries at various revision conferences have made their special interests known, there is no instance, with the possible exception of the Lisbon Conference, where any special requirements of these countries have positively influenced changes of the conventio-

[101] S. P. Ladas, "The Revision of the Paris Convention," *I.C.C. Brochure, No. 206*, Paris, 1959, pp. 17–18, recognizes the existence of such interests, saying that "there have developed at the present time far sharper differences of view between strongly industrialized countries and economically underdeveloped countries, so that compromise solutions on proposed amendments of the convention were much more difficult to reach."

[102] The Bureau proposal to the London Conference recognized the existence of differences of interests between countries at different stages of economic development, but it is clear from the text that the Bureau was mainly interested in the problems created by this situation for the industrialized countries. The proposal says in part: "L'Union englobe des pays dont le développement industriel diffère profondément et qui ont des notions et des besoins très différents en ce qui concerne la protection de la propriété industrielle. On comprend dès lors que les pays fortement industrialisés envisagent comme absolument contraire à tout progrès le fait que les pays beaucoup moins développés peuvent empêcher toute amélioration de la Convention." *Actes de la Convention de Londres 1934*, p. 165.

[103] Akerman, *op. cit.*, p. 152.

[104] *Ibid.*, pp. 334–35.

nal text. This is clearly seen from the fact that at all the conferences, again with the possible exception of the latest, their efforts have resulted in the so-called compromise texts, which meant that their influence merely asserted itself in the negative sense of slowing down the "progress" of the Convention.

Until the beginning of the nineteen sixties, in fact, no particular efforts seem to have been made to bring underdeveloped countries into the Union. Although these countries have certainly been welcome into the Union, it was not until 1961 that suddenly the Union, through its Secretariat (BIRPI), began its present concern with the particular positions of these countries. Roubier, commenting on the absence of many Asian countries in the Union, said (1951) that "we can hardly count any longer on the continent of Asia, at least in so far as concerns those countries dominated by the ancient civilizations ... for these countries are still little adapted to our industrial economy."[105] In 1958, the Director of BIRPI at the time, Jacques Secretan, in an opening speech at the Lisbon Conference, said in part:

> In order that a country may usefully adhere to the Paris Union it should already possess a developed industry ... It would not be desirable that its interests were dealt with through majority votes [sic] of a world organization grouping nations with too widely diverging interests.[106]

When these opinions are compared with those expressed only a few years later, it is obvious that the policy towards underdeveloped countries has undergone a significant change, or, rather perhaps, that such a policy has been instituted since. Whether the recognition of the particular requirements of less developed countries has also led to a change of policy concerning the development of the Convention is doubtful. Though some developments such as that of Article 5A (3) may indicate this, other signs rather give the impression that, while encouraging these countries to join the Union, the efforts are instead directed at convincing these countries, that the present rules of the Convention are beneficial to all countries.

b. Influence on revision procedures

Whether or not particular considerations are now made in the interests of less developed countries, it is obvious that the existence of groups of countries within the Union with such different outlooks and requirements, as the industrialized and developing countries, must influence

[105] Roubier, *op. cit.*, p. 1049.
[106] [translated from French] *Actes de la Conférence de Lisbonne, 1958*, pp. 89–90.

the activities of the Union and the development of the Convention. The rule of the Convention that has made the split in basic interests most apparent is the one requiring unanimous consent to any revision. Objections against the alternatives to the unanimity rule, suggested at various occasions, – such as the "reservation system", the creation of "restricted unions" or majority voting procedures – have been that, while such alternatives may be politically expedient, they would shatter the unity of national legislations, the achievement of which is one of the fundamental goals of the Union. At the London Conference, the Bureau proposal contained a reference to this problem. After stating that the number of countries opposed to the unanimity rule had steadily increased, the Bureau analyzed the situation where the different stages of economic development made some countries resist changes considered highly desirable by other countries. The Bureau, however, then points out the criticism which can be raised against a system of majority vote. If the minority countries do not adhere to the majority opinion, this will create a situation in which different conventional texts are in force among various members, which in fact would lead to the existence of several restricted unions. In addition, the Bureau proposal observed, since non-ratification concerns the whole text, the result may be that other amendments, in themselves desirable and acceptable, would not come into force.[107]

The efficient working and development of an agreement, in which any change is conditioned by the need for unanimous consent, requires a basic community of interests. Such a community of interests did exist, or was at least presumed to exist, when the Paris Union was founded. It was then thought that such disagreements that might arise would be only those of degree, and it was thought that by prudently restraining the most "progressive" members through compromise solutions, the hesitations of other members would subside. Today, however, such a community of interests does not exist. In fact, despite the unanimity rule, the evolution has reached a point where a large group of countries has not ratified the latest text and a few countries not even the preceding one. Thus, the particular objection to a majority rule, mentioned

[107] *Actes de la Conférence de Londres*, p. 165. A number of majority vote systems have been suggested. The most interesting is that suggested by Ladas, *The International Protection* ..., p. 814. According to Ladas, industrialized and underdeveloped countries should from separate groups and a three-fourths majority would be required of each for any amendment. Though written in 1930, it is strikingly similar to the system used by the Trade and Development Board of UNCTAD.

by the Bureau at the London Conference, is less valid today. The contemporary situation has also led to the point, predicted by the Bureau and used as an argument against restricted unions, where a country, because of strong opposition to a particular rule in a new text, cannot benefit from the text at all.

2. *Social vs. private interests*

Though at various revision conferences less industrialized countries have opposed proposed changes in the name of the interests of society, it is uncertain to what extent the evolution of the Convention in general has been influenced by collective interests, when such interests have been considered contrary to the interests of patentees. Akerman, who has treated this aspect, maintains that an increased awareness of the interests of the community has had a real influence on the formation of the Convention.[108]

Except for the theory that inventions were the private property of their authors, which never was applied in practice, the dual interests of inventors and society have always been considered the proper foundation of national patent systems. While it has sometimes been held that the two interests are congruent, the great majority of authors, and all legislators, recognize potential conflicts of interests. When the Paris Union was founded almost every country obliged the patentee to work his invention, the usual sanction being forfeiture. As it was realized that the patentee's right would be severely impeded by maintaining the obligation to work in all Union countries, the primary goal of the Union was the strengthening of the patentee's position, and the ultimate goal was the complete abolition of any obligation to work the patent. It was soon evident that the attainment of the latter goal lay in the distant future, and the intermediate objective became that of substituting compulsory licensing for revocation, as a sanction for non-working. Even this goal is not yet accomplished. The pursuance of these two objectives, together with that of generally strengthening the protection of patentees, have been the motives for proposed and realized changes in the Convention. To what degree then has any collective interest been present? It may have shown itself either in the form of objections to proposed changes or by itself being the basis for such proposals. It is suggested that while the first alternative may be found

[108] Akerman, *op. cit.*, pp. 152–53 *et passim*. See, however, *supra*, p. 82.

at all revision conferences, the latter form, but for insignificant exceptions, is only found at the latest revision conference.

At Lisbon (1958) the changes of the Convention show the first instance in which considerations of public interest have *positively* changed the Convention: the concession to those countries which have argued that compulsory licenses may not be adequate, – allowing for the interpretation made of Article 5 A (3)[109] – and that which restricts the use of the three-year period of immunity to the sole case of non-working or insufficient working.[110]

What would be the reason for this, as it seems, rather sudden positive concern for the interests of society? The concession to less industrialized countries (if such it is) in Article 5A (3) would be the result of their increasing representation in the Union and, perhaps even more, present-day recognition of, and preoccupation with, the particular problems and requirements of these countries. As for the concession to social interests in general, as seen in the more restrictive application of immunity periods, it is clearly a question of greater awareness of possible harmful practices of patentees. Although it was already well-known in 1934, that patents were often used to create restrictive business agreements, the policy towards such practices has greatly changed since before the Second World War.

3. Legal vs. economic motives

National patent systems have always been based on a combination of legal and economic considerations. This was true even at the time of the first American and French patent laws. For all the stress laid on the legal considerations, such as the natural property theory, it was clear that what really mattered were considerations of the economic impact of patents. The impossibility of treating the patent institution as an almost exclusively legal domain would seem even more apparent on the international level. – And yet, with some notable exceptions, this has been the usual approach. Just as an appeal was often made to legal justifications in national debates, to promote the patent system, the same approach has often been used concerning the international patent

[109] *Supra*, pp. 91–92.

[110] The definite interpretation of the question of the relationship between paragraphs 2 and 3 and paragraph 4 meant a further concession to the extent that some countries had interpreted it as regulating the granting of compulsory licenses also for actions on other grounds then abuse of the patent monopoly. Cf. "Die Lissabonner Konferenz zur Revision der Pariser Verbandsübereinkunft," 61: 57–113, February, 1959. p. 71.

system. – This is illustrated by the cases in which national economic interests have found themselves in conflict with proclaimed legal principles. Three cases from the history of the Convention may be recalled to illustrate this. Great Britain, which in 1880 supported the suggestion for a complete abolishment of any obligation to work a patent in more than one country, did not find it in her national interest, in 1911, to even substitute compulsory licensing for revocation.[111] Great Britain had formerly been ranged with some other countries, notably the United States, as representing the progressive forces, whose "enlightened" policy was made an example for others to follow. To what extent such a legalistic position might have served as a cover for economic interests is indicated by the sudden turn-about. Great Britain had been the leading industrial nation in the world until the last decade of the nineteenth century. As such there was little risk that patentees would not work their inventions locally. Towards the turn of the century Great Britain was no longer the uncontested industrial leader but had to meet the rivalry of both Germany and the United States. At that point Great Britain found it in her national interest to forego the "internationalist" approach, when it no longer corresponded with her own interests. This might be well to remember today when the opposition of less developed countries against too independent a position for the patentee is often met with charges that they are too nationalistic and protectionist in outlook and not enough receptive to the virtues of "internationalism." Another example of the strength of legal motivations for patent grants is provided by the French position, also at the Washington Conference.[112] Having been the country, par excellence, sponsoring the legal rights of the patentee, France, in 1911, did not find it in her national interest even to support the abolition of revocation. A third example is illuminating for the outcome of the conflict with professed legal principles and national economic interests. Italy was one of the countries opposing the abolition of the obligation to work in 1880. She said, in fact, that although supporting the principle, she had to oppose such a move in the interests of her own country.[113]

These considerations put in doubt a statement such as the one Ladas makes, when he criticizes Pretnar's contention that the successive revision conferences have strengthened the position of highly industrialized countries, maintaining that:

[111] *Supra*, p. 75–76.
[112] *Supra*, pp. 77.
[113] *Supra*, p. 69.

> The successive revisions of Article 5 of the Convention were motivated by the consideration whether the compulsory working of patents was a sound legal principle or not, and not by any desire to strengthen monopolies.[114]

While it is true that certain rules of the Convention may seem to be entirely legal problems, it must be concluded that such is not the case for the rules concerned with regulating the exploitation of patented inventions. One author emphasizes this point when, saying that while certain questions[115] have been solved on the basis of legal considerations, the regulation of the obligation to work is dependent upon economic-political factors, he continues:

> However desirable it would be, from the point of view of the inventor-patentee that he acquired a legal protection through the Convention comprising a uniform, organically united regulation in the various countries . . . he is here often confronted with the economic policy of the particular country, putting the whole question into a wider context, in close relation to the customs policy of that country.[116]

E. OTHER INTERNATIONAL PATENT AGREEMENTS

Outside the Paris Union there exist a number of international agreements, all of which are of a much more limited scope. These agreements are multilateral and bilateral. The latter exist between some industrialized countries concerning working requirements, which are limited through such agreements to one of the countries,[117] and between some industrialized countries and non-members of the Paris Union concerning reciprocal treatment in patent matters.

Of the multilateral agreements, which exist among some American States, some European States and some Affrican States respectively, it is only the former which constitutes a parallel arrangement to that of the Paris Union.

1. Patent cooperation among American States

The various efforts to achieve a regional union for the protection of industrial property among American States has clearly been influenced by the creation of the Paris Union. The first Inter-American congress

[114] Ladas, "The Fundamental Bases . . ." p. 2.

[115] One example mentioned is the question of abolishing "the right of third parties" which was, however, resisted by some less developed countries on economic grounds.

[116] B. Godenhielm, *Utländsk och internationell patenträtt* (Stockholm: Institutet för utländsk rätt, 1953) p. 29. [translated from Swedish].

[117] Such agreements are expressly allowed by the Paris Convention. Cf. *supra*, p. 72.

to deal with patent cooperation was that of Montevideo in 1889. It resulted in a convention adhered to by five South American States.[118] All later efforts were undertaken within the Pan American Union. The first Pan American Conference, at Washington (1896), suggested that all members join the Montevideo Convention, but the second such conference did not support that suggestion. It was held in Mexico City (1902) and instead created another convention, ratified by eight countries.[119] The third Pan American Conference, meeting in Rio de Janeiro (1906), created a new convention adhered to by nine States.[120] This convention was finally superceded in 1910 when, at the fourth Pan American Conference meeting in Buenos Aires, the latest American Convention on patent rights was created. This Convention, signed by all (21) Member States of the Pan American Union excent Bolivia, was ratified by thirteen States [121] and is presently in force among fourteen States. [122] The Conventions prior to that of Buenos Aires differ little from the latter, and they have all been inspired by the Paris Convention.[123]

Though the Buenos Aires Convention remains in force and is the sole basis for patent relations among most of the adhering States, and notably between most of its Latin American members and the United States, it has never achieved full regional membership. Inquiring into the causes of this failure Ladas asks, if the answer is to be found in the fact "that the United States, a manufacturing country, has interests that conflict with those of Latin America, which produces only raw materials?"[124]

[118] Argentina, Brazil, Paraguay, Peru and Uruguay. This Convention remains in force only between Argentina and Peru, the other States having adhered to later conventions. Ladas, *The International Protection* ... p. 762.

[119] Chile, Costa Rica, Cuba, Dominican Republic, Guatemala, Honduras, Nicaragua and El Salvador. Though A. Troller, *Die mehrseitigen völkerrechtlichen Verträge im internationalen gewerblichen Rechtsschutz und Urheberrecht* (Basel, Verlag für Recht und Gesellschaft, 1965), p. 28, states that those countries are still bound by this Convention; according to Ladas, *The International Protection* ..., p. 762, the convention has been superseded by later agreements. The latter opinion is supported by the fact that all countries later adhered to other conventions.

[120] Brazil, Chile, Costa Rica, Ecuador, Guatemala, Honduras, Nicaragua, Panama, and El Salvador.

[121] Brazil, Costa Rica, Dominican Republic, Ecuador, Guatemala, Haiti, Honduras, Nicaragua, Panama, Paraguay, United States, and Uruguay.

[122] The thirteen original States plus Bolivia. The following States are also members of the Paris Union: Brazil, Cuba, Dominican Republic, Haiti, United States, Uruguay.

[123] Cf. P. G. de Medina y Sobrado, *Naturaleza juridica de la propiedad industrial y protección a los inventores en el derecho internacional y en el interno* [Havana (chez l'auteur), 1949] pp. 181–89.

[124] Ladas, *The International Protection* ..., p. 765; Or, the author continues, "is it the lack of long preparations and continuity of study of the questions involved in the protection

2. *European patent cooperation*

The various European efforts to achieve closer cooperation in patent matters, outside the Paris Union, have taken two forms. The most far-reaching is the one aiming at the unification of national patent laws. The other approach is that of making agreements to unify certain particular rules and procedures.

Projects according to the former approach are in process between the members of the European Common Market and among the Scandinavian countries. Within the former group of countries the initiative to harmonize and unify their national laws on industrial property was taken in 1959, and a draft convention was published in 1962. Though the Common Market project aims at the creation of a "European" patent, valid also for countries outside the group of six, the question of outside membership seems not to be settled yet,[125] nor the question of the accessability of non-nationals of the Common Market countries.[126] Efforts to promulgate a common patent law among the four Scandinavian countries are of long standing. The current draft convention is now only awaiting ratification by the respective parliaments.

The second form of European cooperation on patent matters has been initiated, with one exception, within the Council of Europe. So far three Conventions dealing with particular questions have been concluded.[127] Outside the Council of Europe, the so-called Hague Agreement was made in 1947 creating an international patent office. This agreement was made with the object of giving national patent offices the possibility to have novelty claims examined by a central international organization. Since a revision of the agreement in 1961 it is also empowered to undertake research into the "state of the arts". Furthermore,

of industrial property?," or again, "is it ... the failure to interest those countries sufficiently in the advantages of a common international regulation of the subject of industrial property?' Though many Latin American countries today are far from mere "raw material producers" [this was written in 1930] the wide differences of stages of economic development still seem to provide the most plausible explanation.

[125] Two alternatives have been suggested: either full membership with unconditional acceptance of all rules including the jurisdiction of the planned European patent court, or associate membership.

[126] The article in the draft concerning this problem (Article 5) gives two alternatives: one admitting any person unconditionally and the other with a more restricted application. The latter alternative would seem to be in conflict with Article 15 of the Paris Union.

[127] European Convention Relating to the Formalities Required for Patent Applications 1953); 2. European Convention on the International Classification of Patents for Inventions, (1954); 3. European Convention on the Unification of Certain Points of Substantive Law on Patents for Inventions (1963).

any person subject to the Paris Convention is now entitled to employ the services of the Hague Institute.

3. African patent cooperation

An agreement among the twelve States, members of the African and Malagasy Organization for Economic Cooperation, O.A.M.C.E. was signed in 1962 and entered into force in 1964.[128] The agreement, which is the only one of its kind, concerns the institution of a single patent territory with a central patent office. The main reason for this agreement was to remedy the uncertain situation in the field of industrial property rights after the accession to independence of the former French colonies. Prior to 1958, they had formed a single unionist territory. In order to preserve the advantages of such a régime, and to avoid the administrative burden of having national patent systems and administrations in each country, an agreement was made to form one patent territory, by which one single patent application is all that is required. In this agreement the members undertake to become members of the Paris Union and the agreement is open to all African States which are members of the Paris Union.

[128] Members are: Cameroon, Central African Republic, Congo Brazzaville, Chad, Dahomey Gabon, Ivory Coast, Malagasy, Niger, Senegal, Upper Volta, and Mauritania. Togo joined the group in 1967.

APPENDIX

Texts relating to provisions concerning working obligations and sanctions against non-working and other abuses of the patent monopoly in the various Convention Texts:

Paris 1883:

Article 5

(1) "The importation by the patentee into the country where the patent has been granted of articles manufactured in any of the States of the Union shall not entail forfeiture of the patent.

(2) "Nevertheless, the patentee shall remain under the obligation to exploit his patent in accordance with the laws of the country into which he introduces the patented articles."

Brussels 1900:

Article 5

(1) (identical to previous text)

(2) (identical to previous text)

"Final Protocol"

3bis "The patentee in each country shall not forfeit his patent for non-working until after a minimum period of three years from the filing of the application in the country in question and in case he cannot justify his inaction."

Washington 1911:

Article 5

(1) "The importation by the patentee into the country where the patent has been granted of articles manufactured in any of the

countries of the Union shall not entail forfeiture of the patent.

(2) "Nevertheless, the patentee shall remain under the obligation to exploit his patent in accordance with the laws of the country into which he introduces the patented articles, but with the restriction that the patent may not be forfeited for non-working in one of the countries of the Union until after a period of three years of the date of filing the application in that country and only in case the patentee cannot justify his inaction."

The Hague 1925:

Article 5

(1) (identical to previous text)

(2) "Nevertheless, each contracting country shall have the right to take the necessary legislative measures to prevent the abuses which might result from the exclusive rights conferred by the patent, for example, failure to work.

(3) "These measures shall not provide for forfeiture of the patent unless the grant of compulsory licenses is insufficient to prevent such abuses.

(4) "In any case, the patent may not be subjected to such measures before the expiration of at least three years from the date of grant, or if the patentee proves the existence of legitimate excuses."

London 1934:

Article 5A.

(1) "The importation by the patentee into the country where the patent has been granted of objects manufactured in any of the countries of the Union shall not entail forfeiture of the patent.

(2) "Nevertheless, each of the countries of the Union shall have the right to take the necessary legislative measures to prevent the abuses which might result from the exercise of the exclusive rights conferred by the patent, for example, failure to work.

(3) "These measures will only provide for the revocation of the patent if the granting of compulsory licenses shall not suffice to prevent these abuses.

(4) "In any case an application for the grant of a compulsory license may not be granted before the expiration of three years

from the date of the grant of the patent, and this license may be granted only if the patentee fails to justify himself by legitimate reasons. No proceedings for the forfeiture or revocation of a patent may be instituted before the expiration of two years from the grant of the first compulsory license."

Lisbon 1958:

Article 5A.

(1) (identical to previous text)

(2) "Each country of the Union shall have the right to take legislative measures providing for the grant of compulsory licenses to prevent the abuses which might result from the exclusive rights conferred by the patent, for example, failure to work.

(3) "Forfeiture of the patent shall not be prescribed except in cases where the grant of compulsory licenses would not have been sufficient to prevent such abuses. No prodeecing for the forfeiture or revocation of a patent may be instituted before the expiration of two years from the grant of the first compulsory license.

(4) "An application for a compulsory license may not be made on the ground of failure to work or insufficient working before the expiration of a period of four years from the filing of the patent application or three years from the date of the grant of the patent whichever period last expires; it shall be refused if the patentee justifies his inaction by legitimate reasons. Such a compulsory license shall be non-exclusive and shall not be transferable even in the form of the grant of a sublicense, except with that part of the enterprise or goodwill using such a license."

PART II

THE EFFECT OF THE INTERNATIONAL PATENT SYSTEM ON DEVELOPING COUNTRIES AND POSSIBLE CHANGES OF THE SYSTEM FOR THEIR BENEFIT

In view of the large and growing number of developing countries that have become members of the Paris Union,[1] it might seem unwarranted to question the importance and general usefulness of the international patent system to this particular category of countries. On the other hand, it is also possible that, for various reasons, membership may be considered by some of these countries merely the least disadvantageous solution under the present system. This then by no means excludes the possibility of finding a more satisfactory system for supplying the developing countries with legally protected technology and knowhow.

The driving force behind the endeavor of developing countries to obtain the transfer of technology from industrialized countries, is their desire and intention for rapid industrialization. No longer content to abide by the rules of comparative advantage according to the "classical theory" of international trade, they are consciously planning today to reorganize their economies. In order to escape the precarious position of raw material producers and exporters of semi-manufactured goods, the developing countries intend to broaden their economic base, including the setting-up of industrial activities, even if such activities will temporarily put these countries in a position of comparative disadvantage vis-à-vis established industries in developed countries.

Such policies have important implications for the movement of technology. According to the traditional theory of international trade, technology would spread from the industrialized to the unindustrialized countries if certain basic industries were set up in the latter, along the lines of comparative advantage. Whatever the merits of this theory – and doubts have often been raised as to the effectiveness of the "spread effect" that such industries are supposed to have on the rest of the local

[1] 40 Member States out of 83, as of January 1, 1969, belong to this category according to the classification chosen (cf. *infra*, p. 113).

economy – the developing countries are no longer willing to rely on such an autonomous system for the importation of foreign technology. Hence, there is an urgent need from the point of view of developing countries to increase the transfer of technology for the benefit of their economies. To the extent that it is possible to attract additional foreign investment, it is one way of increasing the inflow of foreign technology.

Though private foreign investment can certainly often play a very useful role, there are cases where this channel may be both too costly and of limited scope.

Because the whole development process implies efforts for a more or less balanced growth, private benefits on which investors calculate will sometimes not match the prospective social benefits underlying the planning by local authorities. – Such discrepancies between private and social benefits will also be shown to invalidate the traditional thesis of patent theorists, according to which the patentee will generally exploit his invention locally whenever such exploitation would be more favorable to the country, instead of importing the patented product.–

Before going into a detailed analysis of these and other points relevant to the effects on the developing countries of the international patent system and possible alternative arrangements, a chapter will be devoted to establishing the position of various developing countries with respect to national and international patent legislation; their position with respect to the latter will show which countries are directly affected by that system.

CHAPTER I

THE STATUS OF DEVELOPING COUNTRIES IN PATENT MATTERS

As the present thesis is concerned with the principles involved in the application of the Paris Convention to developing countries, rather than with any quantitative measurement of the effects thereof, the problem of selecting the countries referred to as developing is not of decisive importance. For the present purpose, the ninety-seven countries belonging to Economic Class II, according to the system adopted by the United Nations Statistical Office, have been chosen to represent this category.[2] Whatever classification is used, it must be recognized that such a grouping of countries is only an approximation. At one end of the scale the most advanced of these countries may in several respects be compared to small industrial countries, whereas at the opposite end, some countries would appear at present to be little concerned with patents. – Although the purpose of the present thesis is limited to the study of international patent relations, a very brief summary will be made with regard to national patent legislations as far as working requirements are concerned. For the particular section on some aspects of national patent laws, it must be stressed that in arranging countries into various groups according to their specific rules on working requirements and sanctions for non-working, it is inevitable that some inaccuracies exist despite careful checking. Therefore the section on national patent laws ought to be seen as an illustration of various approaches without a claim of exactness in all details for all countries. –

[2] *Cf. Handbook of International Trade and Development Statistics 1969* (United Nations: New York, 1969).

A. COUNTRIES WITHOUT A NATIONAL PATENT LAW[3]

Of the ninety-seven countries there are eighteen that seem to have no national patent legislation.[4] There are furthermore seventeen countries, that for lack of their own patent laws, apply entirely or in part the patent laws of other countries.[5] Of these thirty-five States, seven are Union members. One of them has no patent law at all, and six retain certain relations with either the British or French patent system.

Though the Convention has never contained a formal obligation for member countries to possess national patent laws, the purpose of the Union would evidently be defeated, if member countries remained without patent legislation for more than a transitory period. This must be particularly so in the case of developing countries, which have little use for the possibility of obtaining patent protection for their citizens in other Union countries; their primary object in joining the Union must be to attract foreign technology by granting local patents to foreigners. Besides, after the Lisbon text came into force, it appears at least questionable whether a country can adhere to the Union or ratify that text without having a national patent law.[6]

B. COUNTRIES WITH NATIONAL PATENT LAWS, NON-MEMBERS OF THE UNION[7]

Out of fifty-six countries, that do not belong to the Union, twenty-nine possess national patent laws. Though most of them do not match the minimum requirements of the Convention, some of them do in all respects except for the Union priority rule. Nine countries have no provisions at all that require the local exploitation of patented inventions.Since all non-Union members generally seem to apply the principle of national

[3] *Manual for the Handling of Applications for Patents, Designs and Trademarks Throughout the World* (Amsterdam: Octrooibureau Los en Stigter, 1927,) brought up to date to March 1969.

[4] Afganistan, Burundi, Ethiopia, Indonesia, Muscat & Oman, Qatar, Rwanda, Saudi Arabia, Sudan, Thailand, Trucial Oman and Yemen; no information obtained for Bhutan, Maldive Islands, Mongolia, Sikkim, South Yemen and Western Samoa.

[5] In eleven of these countries British patents may be registered within three years of the original grant: Bahrain, Cyprus, Gambia, Ghana, Kenya, Malaysia, Nigeria, Sierra Leone, Somalia, Tanzania and Uganda; in two countries the French patent law of 1844 is supposed to be in force: Cambodia and Laos; in one country the present French patent law, is supposed to be applicable: Mali; in Burma, the Indian patent law, as of 1947, is applicable; and in Botswana and Lesotho South African patents may be registered.

[6] Cf. *supra*, p. 95, n. 98 for relevant text. Yet several countries in this category are members of the Union.

[7] *Manual* ...

treatment, these nine countries would merely have to respect the priority rule to fulfill the requirements of the Convention completely.[8] Five countries have working requirements and sanctions that are in complete agreement with the Convention.[9] In seven countries there are rules that require local exploitation after three years, which is in accord with the minimum norms of the Convention, but which differ from these to the extent that the sanction for non-working in these countries may be compulsory licensing or revocation,[10] and in two of them, the patent grant lapses automatically after three years.[11]

According to this classification, only eight countries remain that have national patent laws which differ substantially from the minimum standards of the Convention. Fife of these countries require that the patent be worked after two years, with either compulsory licenses as the only remedy[12] or a provision by which cancelation may be sought,[13] or by which the patent lapses automatically, if it is not worked within the prescribed period.[14] Finally, three countries require local exploitation within one year, one of which has the only sanction of compulsory licenses[15] while two prescribe the automatic lapse of the patent.[16]

Thus it would seem that of the fifty-six non-member countries, twenty-one have laws essentially compatible with the Convention, while the rest have either no such laws or substantially different ones.

C. COUNTRIES MEMBERS OF THE UNION[17]

The position of the forty-one countries that belong to the Paris Union will be briefly examined from three different points of view: (1) do the

[8] Barbados, Chile, Colombia, Congo (Kinshasa), Guyana, Jamaica, Nepal, El Salvador and Singapore. In Barbados and Guyana compulsory licenses may be granted under certain conditions and in El Salvador non-exploited patents may be expropriated. Information on the Nepalese patent law has been obtained from *Nepal Gazette*, Vol. XV, No. 14(A), August 30, 1965. This law has some peculiar features such as double fees for foreign patentees (which would be contrary to the Convention) and secret patent files! – For countries with relatively little indigenous inventive activity, the mere application of the priority rule would seem to raise no problems from an economic point of view.

[9] China (Taiwan), Guinea, Kuwait, Liberia, and Peru. In the cases of China and Guinea, no detailed information has been obtained, and their classification is based on the information that their patent laws are "similar" to those of Japan and France respectively.

[10] India, Jordan, Korea, Pakistan, and Paraguay. In the case of India, the Government may at any time open a patent to general licensing.

[11] Libya and Panama.

[12] Ecuador.

[13] Venezuela.

[14] Bolivia, Costa Rica and Iraq.

[15] Guatemala.

[16] Honduras, Nicaragua.

[17] *Manual* . . .

laws of these countries at least match the minimum norms of the Convention, as far as working requirements and sanctions for non-working are concerned, or are they less stringent?; (2) how many of these countries were formerly in the Union as colonies or other dependent territories?; and (3) which is the latest revised text to which these countries have adhered?

1. Working requirements and sanctions for non-working

It may be recalled that the norms of the Convention are the following: (1) no exploitation may be required before the expiration of a three-year period from the date of the patent grant or four years from the date of application whichever is longer; (2) at the end of such a period only compulsory licenses may be granted; and finally, (3) two years after the date of the compulsory license, the patent grant may be revoked. Whereas all countries are bound by the first provision, two countries, that have ratified neither the Lisbon nor the London text, are not bound by the second and third rule.[18]

Since seven member countries have no national patent laws of their own, there remain thirty-four countries obliged to respect the standards of the Convention. The kind of working requirements and the severity of the sanctions can be seen in the table opposite.

Though the minimum requirements of the Convention concerning the obligation to work seem the most favorable, or perhaps the least onerous, to developing countries, there are, in fact, only five countries out of thirty-four that apply such rules.[19] Five countries, while they do not provide for the granting of compulsory licenses, cancel patent grants upon request after five years. Though these countries do not avail themselves of the faculty to grant compulsory licenses and as a consequence have no means to influence the patentee to have his patent exploited already within three years, it would seem that, due to the conditions in developing countries, in reality, the threat of compulsory licenses is in any case often an ineffective inducement to patentees for working or finding licensees to work their inventions, and that only the threat of forfeiture may obtain such results or break the monopoly on the product in question.[20] More than half of the member countries, that have

[18] Brazil and the Dominican Republic.

[19] *Infra* n. 21 a), b) and c), though two countries apparently go below the minimum standard required namely Argentina and Brazil (for the latter, cf. n. 21h infine).

[20] *Infra* n. 21 d) and e). For the effectiveness of the sanction of compulsory licenses, cf. *infra*, pp. 147–48.

Working Requirements and Sanctions for Non-working in Thirty-four Developing Countries, Members of the Union[21]

Number of countries	Local exploitation required after:	Sanctions: Compulsory licenses after:	Sanctions: Cancellation after:
1 a)	2 years	—	2 years on demand
2 b)	3 years	3 years (alternatively)	3 years on demand
2 c)	3 years	3 years	"3+2" years on demand
3 d)	3 years	—	5 years on demand
2 e)	5 years	—	5 years on demand
19 f)	3 years	3 years	—
1 g)	—	(3 years)	—
2 h)	3 years	—	—
2 k)	—	—	—

a national patent law, apply the minimum requirements for compulsory working and compulsory licenses but do not resort to cancelling non-

[21] a) Argentina. – In the case of Argentina as well as in some other countries the requirements of "local exploitation" appear, in practice, to be considered fulfilled when licenses have been offered. The recent Brazilian Patent Law, however, provides an example where the requirements in this respect have been made more severe: "The continual and regular exploitation of the invention on an industrial scale adequate for the consumer requirements of the country whether through production carried out by the patentee or through the granting of licenses to third parties, shall be considered effective working." Article 63 of the Brazilian Industrial Property Code, Decree-Law No. 254, of February 28, 1967. Reported in *I.P.*, 7: 340, November, 1968. [translation by Birpi].

b) Brazil and Ceylon; while the former country, bound by the Hague text, is free to revoke patents after three years, Ceylon, bound by the London text, should observe a five-year period before resorting to revocation.

c) Israel and the U.A.R.

d) Cuba, Syria and Tunisia; it would seem that where a sanction can be applied only after five years, the obligation to work is effective after five rather than three years from the patent grant.

e) Dominican Republic and Iran.

f) Algeria, Malawi, Mexico, The Philippines, Uruguay, Zambia plus the thirteen members of OAMCE (Cf. *supra*, p. 105, n. 128).

g) Trinidad-Tobago. It is not clear when a compulsory license may be granted, though presumably after three years.

h) Lebanon and Morocco. Without sanctions for non-working the obligation to work would seem ineffective. [According to the United Nations Report, *The Role of Patents in the Transfer of Technology to Developing Countries* (New York: United Nations, 1964: Doc· E/3861/Rev. 1) Annex D both Lebanon and Morocco may revoke non-used patents the former after two years; the same provision is reported for Brazil.]

k) Haiti and Vietnam.

worked patents.[22] This, as will be explained in detail in the next chapter, would seem to relieve most of the pressure on a patentee, who initially was unwilling to work the patent locally, from supplying or trying to supply licenses.[23] Finally, four countries use neither the faculty of granting compulsory licenses nor that of cancelling non-exploited patents.[24]

Too much importance should not be given to the demonstrated differences between the most rigorous rules permitted in virtue of the Convention and those actually in force in the majority of the countries here examined. The complaints of developing countries of alleged harms caused them by the Convention have been countered by several authors, who have pointed out that most of these countries do not even have rules as rigorous as the Convention permits in contrast to many developed countries. It is a paradox, however, that while certain highly industrialized countries may not have to resort to the sanctions contained in their legislations, the use of such sanctions by developing countries may have little positive effect. Vojáček, commenting on a list of countries that did not have any sanctions to enforce local exploitation (a list which with the exception of the United States, contained a number of developing countries), has said:

> The facilities which the United States holds for the exploitation of inventions ... made it superfluous to exert pressure on inventors in this direction [i.e., to work patents], while in the remaining countries on this list the almost complete lack of such facilities ... made such a pressure futile.[25]

Another reason, why the details of national patent laws should not be given too much weight or significance, is the consideration that often differences exist between theory and practice in patent matters.[26]

2. *The position of dependent territories*

The position of colonies and other dependent territories was not clear at the time when the original Convention was signed. From the practice

[22] *Supra*, n. 21 f) and g).
[23] Cf. *infra*, pp. 148–49.
[24] *Supra*, n. 21h) and k).
[25] J. Vojáček, *A Survey of the Principal National Patent Systems*, (New York: Prentice Hall, 1936; supplemented in 1951 and 1956), p. 61; it is probably more than a coincidence that three of the five countries that follow the minimum requirements of the Convention (*Supra*, n. 21 a), b) and c)) are among the most developed of the developing countries.
[26] See for instance S. Habachy, "Protection of Trademarks and Patent Rights in the Middle East History, Geography and Economics," *Patent, Trademark and Copyright Journal of Research and Education*, 6: 348, No. 3, 1962.

followed by the Bureau of the Paris Union, two authors have drawn the conclusion, which seems borne out by the records, that a distinction was made between colonies and other dependencies of various states.[27] French colonies automatically constituted Union territory, while for English and Dutch colonies, considered more autonomous, a special declaration by the mother country was considered necessary. According to the same authors, membership for protectorates required an express stipulation to that effect in the treaty of protection.[28] In the latter case, the protectorate was not only a part of the Union territory but also became a member in its own right, though it was often represented by the protector State at the revision conferences.

At the time of the Washington Conference (1911), the situation was somewhat clarified by the creation of Article 16 bis. The text of this article was later modified at the Hague (1925) and at London (1934). According to the London revision (which was not changed at Lisbon), an express declaration by the mother country is necessary, in order that dependent territories may constitute Union territory. When the mother country declares that they shall constitute Union territory, it can also request that full membership be granted to dependencies, that have arrived at a certain degree of independence, such as Dominions, Protectorates and Mandated Territories.

The faculty to extend Union territory and, in certain cases, full membership status to colonies and other dependencies has been used particularly by France, and to a limited extent by Great Britain, Germany and Holland. In fact, twenty-seven of the forty-one developing countries at present members of the Paris Union were members before their independence, though with a few exceptions,[29] only in the limited capacity of constituting Union territory without full membership status.[30] In contrast, only four out of fifty-six developing countries, non-members of the Paris Union, constituted Union territory before

[27] M. Pelletier and E. Vidal-Naquet, *La Convention d'Union pour la protection de la propriété industrielle* (Paris: Larose, 1902), p. 25.

[28] *Ibid*, pp. 26–27.

[29] Lebanon, Morocco, Syria and Tunisia were given full membership status before their independance. Roubier "The law of the Union for the protection of industrial property," Journal du Droit International, 78: 737, No. 3, 1951.

[30] Of the twenty-seven countries, four were Union Members from the beginning (Lebanon, Morocco, Syria and Tunisia on whose behalf France had adhered); sixteen were French colonies or protectorates: Algeria, Cameroon, Central African Republic, Chad, Congo (Brazzaville), Gabon, Ivory Coast, Laos, Malagasy Republic, Mauritania, Niger, Senegal, Upper Volta, Vietnam, Dahomey and Togo; six countries formerly belonged as British dependencies: Ceylon, Israel (Palestine), Malawi, Tanzania, Trinidad-Tobago and Zambia; Indonesia formed part of Union territory before its independence from the Netherlands.

their independence.[31] Two more constituted such territory between 1905 and 1919.[32]

3. Ratification of later texts

As may be recalled from the chapter on the evolution of the Convention, at several revision conferences some of the opposition to proposed and sometimes implemented revisions of the previous text was made on the basis, that certain changes would be unfavorable to economically or industrially less developed States. The extent to which developing countries have, or have not, ratified later texts of the Convention may provide an indication of the measure of consent to or disagreement with the changes undertaken. Before looking at the various positions taken in this respect it must be stressed that the examination proposed can have only a limited value for several reasons.

First of all, only fifteen of the forty-one developing countries, presently members of the Paris Union, had become full members by the date at which the Lisbon text came into force. Although previously dependent territories, that had formed a part of the Union, were free to choose between a formal adherence and a mere "declaration of continuity," which meant that in the latter case the Convention text in force at the time of independence would continue to be applicable,[33] all former dependant territories, that have become full members after the Lisbon text came into force and had obtained their independence before that date, were from the beginning of their membership bound by the Lisbon text.[34] Thus only fifteen developing countries have had the opportunity to adhere to anything but the Convention in its present version. Secondly, the question of whether and to what extent later texts have meant less favorable conditions for developing countries further limits the significance of the examination suggested above. Even given the interpretation of the evolution of the Convention, as far as its article 5 is concerned, exposed in a previous chapter and according

[31] Cambodia, China (Taiwan), Guinea and Mali.

[32] Burundi and Rwanda.

[33] *The Effect of Independence on Treaties* (publ. under the auspices of the International Law Association; London, Stevens, 1965) pp. 244–245.

[34] There would appear to be fourteen States in this category: the thirteen States members of the OAMCE (Cf. *supra*, p. 105, n. 128) and Laos which obtained independence in 1960 and became full members after the coming into force of the Lisbon text (1962). At least in the case of Congo (Brazzaville) and the Ivory Coast "declarations of continuity" were made, which according to the source mentioned above (*supra*, n. 33) should have led to the application of the London text. The same is true for Laos which reportedly made a "declaration of continuity."

to which each successive revision, with the possible exception of the latest, made the position of economically less developed countries more onerous, there is no way to know, within the context of the present study, whether other rules of the Convention have followed the same pattern or not from the point of view of these countries. Of the fifteen countries, that joined the Union before the Lisbon text came into force, six countries have ratified this text after their adherence,[35] three have ratified the London text (1934) after their adherence,[36] and two have only ratified the Hague text (1925) since their adherence.[37] The remaining four countries have all adhered to the London text by which they are still bound.[38]

The basic difficulty in interpreting the significance of acts of adherence and ratification by developing countries is that so little is known about the underlying motives. Besides the official records of the revision conferences, summarizing the position of countries on various questions, little seems to have been written on the subject concerning either individual countries or the developing countries as a group.[39] For this reason, and in view of the wide variety in the records of these fifteen countries, little, if anything, can be deducted from the extent to which later texts were ratified. Although among the six countries that have ratified the latest text, one may be said to represent a border case in the division between developed and developing countries (Israel), and one is in the category of the most developed of the latter group (Mexico), four countries (Cuba, Haiti, Morocco and Iran) clearly belong to the group of developing countries. Of the seven countries bound by the London text, only two countries (Lebanon and Syria) have had the option as independent States not to accept that text.

Are there any criteria that could be used in the search for an answer as to why certain developing countries have joined the Union, while

[35] Cuba, Haiti, Iran, Israel, Mexico, and Morocco.

[36] Lebanon Syria and Tunisia. Although these countries were full members from the beginning of their attachment to the Union, they were clearly influenced by France prior to their independence, as shown by their voting records. See, for instance, the voting in the second subcommittee at the London Conference on the text of the new Article 5 (3).

[37] Brazil and the Dominican Republic.

[38] Ceylon, Indonesia, the U.A.R., and Vietnam.

[39] One notable exception is the official report by S. R. Ayyangar, *Report on the Revision of the Patents Law* (New Delhi: Government of India, 1959) where the author develops the reasons why India ought not to join the Paris Union. An article, previously quoted, by S. Pretnar, "The International Protection of Industrial Property and the Different Stages of Economic Development of the States," may indicate the reasons why some countries have either not adhered or abstained from ratifying later texts.

others have remained outside? The great number of countries and their widely differing economic situations, their various legal, political and cultural backgrounds, do not lend themselves to any generalizations on a group basis at least. Certain patterns are discernable, however, on a regional basis. The most conspicuous example of a group of non-members is that of sixteen Latin American countries (out of a total of twenty-four), as compared to the group of fifteen African countries (out of a total of thirty-eight). One immediate difference that stands out between these two groups of countries is that, while almost all members of the former group have been independent since the start of the Paris Union, the majority of the countries in the latter group has until quite recently been dependent upon and under the influence of some developed countries.[40]

Furthermore, the question of full membership for most African countries arose only lately, i.e., after their independence, and coincided with the growing interest of the Paris Union to achieve universal following by attracting developing countries. This does not mean, however, that the Latin American countries have not been urged at earlier times to join the Union. No other group of countries has been under heavier pressure to become part of the Union. Several authors have suggested that the failure of the large majority of these countries to become members was caused by the establishment of an Inter-American system.[41] According to this opinion then, the reason would be legal difficulties rather than economic. But Roubier, making the above-mentioned point, also holds that economic considerations may have been influential, saying:

> The fact that the countries of America which are the most industrialized (Canada and the United States) have become members ... should be noted and it is doubtless the very fact of the arrested development of the Latin American nations which has accounted for their slowness in becoming members.[42]

The same author, commenting on the lack of membership of many Asian countries, says that one cannot count on those countries to become members for the reason that "those countries are still little adapt-

[40] One suggestive difference of the influence of legal traditions in formerly dependent territories may be the fact that while among Union members there are twenty States formerly dependent on France and thirteen on Great Britain, among the non-members there are only four formerly dependent on France while there are some twenty-three formerly dependent on Great Britain.

[41] See, for instance, S. P. Ladas, *The International Protection of Industrial Property* (Cambridge: Harvard University Press, 1930), p. 808 and Roubier, *op. cit.*, pp. 1049–51.

[42] Roubier, *op. cit.*, p. 1051.

ed to our industrial economy."[43] It is important to observe that Roubier wrote the above-quoted article in 1950, when only eight of the forty-one developing countries, that are at present members of the Union, had joined it as independent States. It has been suggested earlier that since then, the above mentioned considerations have become less prominent and, furthermore, that it has increasingly become the policy of the Union to convince every country, whatever its stage of economic and industrial development, of the benefits of Union membership. What Ladas wrote in 1930 concerning the Latin American countries provides a good illustration of the present approach towards all non-member countries. The author, noting that many of the former countries are not interested in becoming members "in as much as they believe that they would assume many obligations in exchange for benefits of a meager character, in as much as they are not manufacturing countries," said that it was necessary to convince these countries of the advantages afforded them by the Union, and that the required propaganda efforts would seem to be the business of the Bureau as well as of the League of Nations.[44] As for the present drive by the Paris Union to enlist the developing countries, it might never have started, or at least reached its present extent, had it not been for the action of one developing country, member of the Union. For it was only after the Brazilian initiative during the 1961 session of the United Nations General Assembly, demanding study of, and remedial action for, some alleged inequities of the position of developing countries within the Union, that a series of efforts on various levels was started to make these countries join the Union. Another result of the Brazilian initiative was the Report by the Secretary General, *The Role of Patents in the Transfer of Technology to Developing Countries*[45] demanded by the resolution that followed the Brazilian initiative.[46] This report has often been cited as giving support for the contention that the present international patent system is well suited for the requirements of the less developed countries.[47] More than half of the developing countries, presently members of the Paris Union, have joined it since 1961.

[43] *Ibid.*, p. 1049.

[44] Ladas, *loc. cit.*; in a footnote the author refers to Bureau desiderata to the League of Nations, submitted in 1922, urging the latter organization to propagate in favor of the international patent system, the last sentence of which said: "Si ces appels, partant de Genève, étaient répétés, il serait difficile pour ces pays [non-members] de s'y soustraire à la longue." Cf. *P.I.*, 38: 20 January, 1923.

[45] United Nations Report, *op. cit.*

[46] General Assembly Resolution 1713 (XVI), January 8, 1962.

[47] For this Report see *infra*, pp. 75–83.

Instead of relying on social and economic indicators and relative stages of economic development to explain the increase in membership of the Paris Union, the coincidence of independence of a large number of States, and the increased activity of the Paris Union, as well as of other international organizations, to convince them of the benefits of membership, seem to offer a simpler explanation. The fact that most of these countries constituted Union territory prior to their independence may also provide a reason. In fact, of thirty-three former colonies and other dependencies that belonged to the Union in a passive capacity or in a few cases as full members, twenty-seven today make up two-thirds of all developing countries in the Union.[48] This would seem to indicate that, in many cases, economic cooperation or dependent status and affinity of legal traditions with the former mother country have been more important factors than for instance the country's state and evolution in the economic and technological fields.

[48] In contrast, only six States, formerly attached to the Union as dependent territories remain outside. *Supra*, n. 31, 32.

CHAPTER II

THE DIRECT EFFECTS OF THE INTERNATIONAL PATENT SYSTEM ON DEVELOPING COUNTRIES

The expression "The International Patent System" stands for the system that governs certain rules of patent legislation, and to which the members of the Paris Union have submitted themselves. The effects of this system are called "direct" when they derive from obligations under the Convention.[1] – A subsequent chapter will deal with some practices in international patent matters that are labelled "indirect" effects of the Convention in that they are not the necessary result of the conventional rules, although they are based on them. – Since the present chapter is concerned with the effects of obligations under the Convention, it follows that only the developing countries, that are members of the Union, are affected.

Patent-legislation, whether national or international, is based on the consideration of individual as well as of national interests. The fact that the interests of individuals sometimes conflict with those of the community has led to rules limiting the power of the former. Such conflicts arise in all countries that have a national patent legislation. On the international level such conflicts will arise between the patent-granting country and the foreign patentees. For the case in which a large majority of patents is granted to foreigners, as in the developing countries, most of the conflicts will arise between the national interests of these countries and those of foreign patentees.

The effects of the international patent system on developing countries may be analyzed within two different frames of reference. On the one hand, these effects can be examined using the traditional criteria to estimate costs and benefits from Union membership. Though such a

[1] Though a number of countries are bound by conventional texts preceding that of Lisbon, it will be used as the text of reference. The differences between the Lisbon text (1958) and the one immediately preceding, that of London (1934) are, in any case, minimal,as far as the rules on non-working are concerned. It may be recalled that only two developing countries are bound by the still earlier text of the Hague (1925).

calculation can never amount to more than a tentative evaluation of an over-all net effect, the criteria employed are fairly simple. The result of applying those criteria to the case of developing countries is, furthermore, so uncontrovertial, that nobody today recommends the adherence of these countries to the Union on the sole basis of the traditional motivations for joining the international patent system. The effects of the conventional rules on developing countries may, on the other hand, be analyzed with reference to their particular conditions and requirements in the context of policies for economic development and industrialization. This approach suggests itself by the frequent claim, that developing countries will benefit from Union membership particularly through an increased inflow of foreign technology. Judging the effects of the Convention from this second point of view presents problems of a quite different nature. The cost of granting patents to foreigners would have to be compared, not with the equivalent benefits of national patentees abroad, as in the classical case, but with the contribution of the foreign technology, secured through patent protection, to the economic and industrial development process of the developing countries. To single out one of the many different factors that contribute to that process is neither realistic nor possible. Still, by comparing the conventional rules concerning the working of patented inventions and the sanctions against non-working with the conditions characteristic of developing countries, one may judge the relative effectiveness of the international patent system as a vehicle for the transfer of technology to these countries.

Both these approaches will be used below. The contents of the present chapter will be arranged in the following manner: section A will contain a brief analysis of the position of the developing countries in terms of traditional cost/benefit criteria; section B will deal with the alleged particular benefits of Union membership to these countries; a detailed examination of the compatibility of the conventional rules with the conditions and requirements of developing countries will be made in section C; and, finally, section D will deal with some questions of principle, that have been raised in the application of the rules of the convention to developing countries.

A. SIGNIFICANCE OF THE CONVENTION IN TERMS OF TRADITIONAL CRITERIA

The principal motivation of the countries that founded the Paris Union was to extend the patent protection of their nationals over an area covering the territories of other Member States. The purely national patent systems, confined within the boundaries of each country, were seen as effective barriers to the international exchange of goods manufactured on the basis of patented technology – barriers comparable in their effect to protective tariffs. By obtaining patent protection for its nationals abroad, a member country could assure itself a valuable protection for its export markets.

1. Economic considerations: the costs and benefits resulting from international patent protection

In an attempt to evaluate the balance of costs and benefits that are the consequence of an international extension of patent protection, there are a number of factors involved in addition to the mere increase of certain costs and gains inherent in any national patent system. They may be classified into three groups: (a) protection in export markets and the price of patent protected imports, (b) the rate of invention in export industries, and (c) the availability of patented inventions and unpatented knowhow.

a. Protection in export markets and the price of patent protected imports

It is undeniable that the protection of the interests of national patentees in foreign markets, considered as the chief economic benefit of the Convention, may be of great value. This will be true especially for those countries, whose citizens acquire more patents abroad than their countries grant to foreigners. In order that a country be able to benefit on this particular count, it obviously has to have inventor-patentees, who want such protection. Save for a small number of large and relatively advanced developing countries, this is rarely the case. The increase in the price of imports, due to the fact that the products or the processes by which they have been produced are patent protected, is clearly the cost of granting patents to foreigners. This cost may be offset, wholly, partly, or not at all, according to the extent to which a particular country itself exports products that have patent protection abroad. The additional income secured by having patent protection for exports allows the exporting country to import more goods in exchange for their exports, than they would otherwise have obtained, i.e., the terms of trade of the exporting country are improved. The effect on the importing country is the reverse. These respective movements in the terms of trade will mean an increase in the real income for the exporting country at the expense of the importing country. In other words, a transfer of real resources (purchasing power) will have taken place. A net gain on this particular count can only accrue to large exporters of industrial goods, who export more patent protected goods than they import.[2]

The discrepancy in the total amount of costs and benefits for any one country from the working of the international patent system has always been recognized as the inevitable price to be paid for having an international order in the patent field. Whether it has been realized how much some countries have to pay is less certain and for the following reasons: (1) it is not possible to quantify the gains and losses of a country from the operation of the international patent system; (2) there are no means to measure the added welfare to the world as a whole from the wider use of technology to which the system is supposed to contribute; and (3) there is a lack of tools with which to estimate the incentive effects of the international patent system on inventive and innovative activities of export industries.[3]

At the various Revision Conferences, countries were aware of the fact that benefits from the international patent system were not shared equally among all members. The opposition to rules extending the liberty of patentees was usually motivated by a country's relative backwardness in terms of economic development.[4] These countries, which usually formed a small minority at any conference prior to that of Lisbon in 1958, objected to the extension of the liberty of patentees on the grounds that their own developing economy would not permit them to reap any benefits for their own nationals but merely would lead to greater advantages for foreign patentees locally. The standard answer was that such inconvenience was only temporary, and that the rules established for the international cooperation in patent matters were

[2] Countries in this category need not be large industrial exporters in an absolute sense; small, highly industrialized countries exporting a high content of industrial goods, while importing relatively more raw materials, would also belong to this category.

[3] E. T. Penrose, *The Economics of the International Patent System* (Baltimore: Johns Hopkins, 1951) p. 96.

[4] Though at one stage also countries like France and Great Britain invoked reasons of national economic interest to oppose more liberal rules for patentees. Cf. *supra*, pp. 75–77.

never intended to result in strict reciprocity in terms of benefits among countries at any point of time, but that countries would inevitably experience varying degrees of advantages and disadvantages over time. In the specific cases it was often said that it was only a question of time before these countries would reach parity with the more industrialized countries.

Though this has happened in a few cases, it is a deceptive basis for policy for two reasons. Nothing indicates that, in general, the development of less industrialized countries will diminish the relative technological preponderance of the large industrialized countries. Secondly, despite the phenomenal rise in research expenditures today, the increase in the number of original patents is fairly small. According to an analysis by the German Patent Office, the rise in the number of patent applications in that country is almost entirely due to a rise in the number of applications by foreigners: "With certain modification this ... will probably apply to other countries as well."[5]

b. The rate of invention in export industries

The operation of the international patent system may increase the rate of invention, from the point of view of a Member State, in two ways: the country's exporting industries may receive an added incentive from receiving protection in its foreign markets; and a foreign industry, exporting to the Member State in question, may increase its rate of invention when receiving protection in its export market. Though a case may be made supporting the contention that a country with a limited home-market may be influenced by the possibility of obtaining foreign patent protection,[6] developing countries, possibly with a very few exceptions, do not have the resources to benefit from such facilities. Although it is sometimes suggested that one of the benefits of the wider protection given patentees through the international patent system is the additional incentive to foreign inventive activity, this was never a principal consideration, in any case, when the system was instituted. The extension of patent protection to foreigners was not based on an

[5] K. Haertel, "Crisis of National Patent Systems and Necessity for International Solutions, *Creative Ferment in World Patent Systems, Conference of the National Association of Manufacturers, June 1965*. (New York: N.A.M., 1965, pp. 12–22) p. 15. Nevertheless, the idea that the non-equal benefits from the international patent system is merely a temporary phenomenon is often suggested, and the moment when they will disappear held out as something for the developing countries to look forward to. Cf., for instance, S. Habachy, "Protection of Trademarks and Patent Rights in the Middle East History, Geography and Economics," *Patent, Trademark and Copyright Journal of Research and Education*, 6: 355, No. 3, 1962.

[6] See Penrose, *op. cit.*, pp. 117–20.

expectation that such protection would benefit the local economy. On the contrary, patent protection was only given to foreigners on the assumption that its costs would at least be balanced by the benefits derived from comparable protection for the country's own citizens abroad. It is at least questionable whether in general the mere extension of patent protection to foreigners will benefit the patent granting country economically through an added incentive to the export industries of foreign countries. Penrose lists two possible gains for a country participating in the international patent system: those received from granting patents to foreigners, which may stimulate introduction of inventions in export industries selling to the patent granting country, and, those from receiving patent protection for its own nationals abroad, which may stimulate local inventiveness or at any rate provide monopoly positions in foreign markets. Of the gain derived from granting patents to foreigners, the author says that it can probably be dismissed as unimportant.[7] If the incentive to export industries can, in general, be dismissed as unimportant, such incentives would appear wholly insignificant for export industries, that have been granted patent protection in one additional developing country. For developing countries, with little if any inventive activity, this incentive is bound to have little practical impact. As these countries are heavily dependent upon exports there is certainly a case for promoting exports, but there would seem to be other measures, adaptable to particular cases, that would be more efficient.

Despite this conclusion for the general case, there may exist a particular case for developing countries. The requirements of these countries sometimes call for a technology especially adjusted to the conditions of the local economy. It might then be argued that the extension of patent protection provides an incentive to foreign inventors to supply such particular technology. However, if in general the incentive to foreign inventive activity from patent protection in developing countries is considered unimportant, it must be even less significant as an incentive to solve technological problems of more limited application. The generally small export markets of developing countries would seem to exert little influence on decisions allocating research resources in industrialized countries. Furthermore, and besides questioning the effectiveness of the incentive to foreign inventors to work in fields of particular interest to developing countries, the actual volume of demand for such special technology may anyway not warrant the costs

[7] *Ibid.*, p. 113.

of a general as compared to a special incentive system. Without denying the existence of particular cases in which separate technologies may be needed by industrialized and developing countries, it would seem that for such "dynamic" technology as is generally protected by patents, these instances form a negligible part of the total patent protected technology required by these countries.[8]

c. The availability of patents and unpatented knowhow

The supply of patented inventions and related unpatented knowhow is of singular importance to developing countries. The extent to which the international patent system increases the availability of patented inventions and related knowhow is also the most complicated problem in calculating the costs and benefits to be derived from the system. Traditionally it was said that the international patent system made foreign inventions available, through the disclosure appearing in the patent application, at the end of the period of protection. Though this argument is still made today, it must be of little significance particularly for the developing countries. As it has been concluded, that these countries have nothing to gain from the point of view of protection for its exports and will lose to the extent that the protection of imports raises the price of such products and that furthermore, the incentive effect on the inventive activity in export industries, both at home and abroad, is presumed to be negligible, the only possible benefit to these countries from the international patent system must come from the introduction of foreign technology into the local economy at the time that patent protection is granted to the foreign patentee. To assess the potential of the present international patent system in this respect requires an approach that examines the adequacy and effectiveness of the traditional patent system – originally intended as a support for local inventiveness – to provide a vehicle for the introduction of foreign technology. The capacity of the international patent system in this respect will be analyzed below in sections B and C. Here it may merely be observed, that the proposition that the traditional international

[8] Rather than need a separate technology, the developing countries may sometimes need to adapt existing inventions to local conditions; such innovative activity would probably be undertaken locally. During the deliberations of the Model Law Committee (an event sponsored by the Paris Union Secretariat to work out a patent law text to serve as a guideline for developing countries) it was suggested, that it might be advantageous for developing countries to provide an incentive for such innovative activity serving local conditions by granting patents for improvements of patented inventions, although such improvements might not meet the usual test of patentability. The suggestion was not adopted. *Model Law for Developing Countries on Inventions* (Geneva: BIRPI, 1965), p. 19. See further *infra*, pp. 203–04.

patent system constitutes an adequate or even optimal instrument for the transfer of technology to developing countries contains the apparently unlikely supposition that the same rules, that through the long evolution of the Paris Convention have been tailored to the needs of protecting the exports of industrialized countries, may be of particular usefulness to developing countries in their quest for foreign technology; in other words, that the granting of patent protection to foreigners, which was traditionally seen as the cost of acquiring equivalent protection abroad for the citizens of a member country, may under the same rules, constitute the principal and only benefit for one category of member countries.

2. *Legal considerations*

During the establishment and the first few decades of the Paris Union, legal considerations were sometimes mentioned along the lines that such arguments appeared, especially in France, during most of the nineteenth century. It was then held that the patentee's right to recognition and protection – according to the thesis that the inventor had an "inherent" property right in his invention or his patent – did not stop at the borders of his country, but that it was the duty of all countries to protect him. Such arguments, which were often of doubtful sincerity on the national level, have probably had little practical influence on the evolution of the Convention. The overwhelming economic significance of both national and international patent protection has always been recognized. Implicit references to legal considerations are nevertheless often contained in recommendations made to the developing countries to join the Union. The standard terminology describing the type of protection these countries are urged to extend to foreign patentees is "adequate." Evidently, "adequate," from the point of view of those advocating adherence to the Union, includes at least the minimum requirements of the Convention. As far as legal consideraations are concerned, and given the extremely one-sided relationship in the granting of patent protection, that prevails between industrialized and developing countries, there is no reason why the latter countries should be expected to pay a price merely for the sake of "internationalism."

3. *National vs. individual interests*

As has been amply illustrated in Chapters I and II of Part I, national patent legislation is a compromise between the interests of the individual and those of society. It was suggested above that this conflict of interests also exists on the international level, though in this case, the potential conflict exists between society and the foreign individuals who are granted local patent protection. However, this is not all. Whereas on the national level the authorities will strive for maximum benefits for society from the granting of patents, whether to citizens or foreigners, in the form of access to and exploitation of the patented technology, the same authorities will usually side with its nationals, when the latter obtain patent protection abroad. In other words, the conflict of interests between individuals and society on the national level will change into an identity of interests between the individuals of one country and the authorities of that country against the national interests of the country granting the patent. Though such conflicts of interests between individuals and their countries on the one hand, and the authorities of the patent granting country on the other hand, may cancel out in cases where the respective countries are of more or less equal strength in terms of patents granted to their nationals abroad, the situation will be quite different for countries with little or no patent protection for their citizens in other countries. This situation is of course the case of at least the large majority of developing countries that are members of the Paris Union. These countries not only have to resist pressures from individuals, when the interests of the latter are in conflict with those of society, but in addition may have to resist pressures from foreign countries as well. These conflicts of interests between countries, which the international extension of patent protection entails, will be particularly accute between industrial and developing countries. It is this situation that has led some authors to question whether the same system can apply to countries of fundamentally different strength. A negative answer to this question has been given notably by S. Pretnar.[9] It was suggested above that the national interests in patent protection abroad may be more or less balanced among countries of equal strength. The case will be quite different between industrial and developing countries. Yet not every author is prepared to recognize this situation.

[9] S. Pretnar, "The International Protection of Industrial Property and the Different Stages of Economic Development of the States," [translation supplied by BIRPI of "La protection internationale de la propriété industrielle et les différents stades de développement économique des Etats," *P.I.*, 69: 213–21, December, 1953] 10 pp. [BIRPI library].

Ladas, in particular, refutes the contention of Pretnar. According to him, "certainly the Convention deals with interests and claims but these are of private persons or entities and not of the states."[10] This fundamental difference of opinion is due to the fact that, while Pretnar takes into account the ulterior economic repercusions on national economies from granting patent rights, Ladas limits himself to the exclusive consideration of the protection to individuals accorded by the Convention.[11] This approach fails to take into account both the very real economic interest of society in patent legislation on the national level and the extension of such interest through the international system, an extension which has manifestly been the major objective of the creation of the international patent system. The untenability of Ladas' approach in the present context is well illustrated by his reply to Pretnar's contention, that the same rules cannot successfully apply to countries of fundamentally different strength, when he says:

> It is not seen why treating an American inventor . . . in Greece as a Greek citizen and doing the same thing in Germany are two different things and that this principle is hard on Greece because it is a weak country economically. This does not increase the economic power of the United States on Greece.[12]

One further case of a conflict of interests would seem of particular significance to developing countries. Though a country takes a negative attitude towards (further) extension of international patent protection because of an unfavorable trading position in the field of patented exports vs. imports, private interests (the importers of such products and local licensees) may take an opposite position, for the reason that they

[10] S. P. Ladas, "The Fundamental Bases of the International Protection of Industrial Property," *P.I.*, 70: annex, 4 pp., April, 1954. [original text of "Les bases fondamentales de la protection internationale de la propriété industrielle," *P.I.*, 70: 93–97, April, 1954.]

[11] "The end of law is to recognize and satisfy the greatest number of claims, demands and interests possible with the least sacrifice of any. If this is the end of law in the national field, the same is the end of an international convention in the international field. The international convention is not merely a contract between the individual countries . . . It is based on the sheer fact that those persons [entitled to the benefits from the Convention] operate across the boundaries of the individual states and that recognition and protection of their interests involve the legislation of countries other than the country of which they are nationals." *Ibid.*

[12] *Ibid.*, p. 2. An example of the inability (or unwillingness) of this author to consider the national economic interests involved and the differences in strength between industrialized and developing countries is provided by a comment on another contention by Pretnar, to the effect that not only have the successive revisions conferences achieved an ever larger protection for patentees but that the decrease in the effective life-length of an invention, i.e., the period during which it may be advantegously exploited, further increases the detrimental effects of unexploited patents. "This argument," says Ladas "proves too much. If the *real* life of a patent is only five years, then why so much exitement about the obligation of working, and how is it that the so-called economically weak countries are suffering from these monopolies." *Ibid.*, p. 3.

are only concerned with private, and not with social, costs and gains. Though this category may be less significant because it is less powerful, it will still play a role through the pressure exerted by national interest groups as well as by private international organizations with local representation.[13]

B. SIGNIFICANCE OF THE CONVENTION ACCORDING TO SPECIAL CONSIDERATIONS

The foregoing analysis showed that according to those criteria, that have traditionally been used to measure gains and costs resulting from the extension of patent protection internationally, the developing countries were on all counts at a disadvantage. Not only do they stand to lose from the fact that their little developed industrial economies do not permit them to exploit the potential advantages of a mutual extension of national patent protection; moreover, there is the general consideration, that the weak economic structure of the developing countries makes them vulnerable to pressure from various interests and, to that extent, places them in a still more onerous position within the international patent system.

As was previously observed, the claimed benefits for the developing countries from the operation of the international patent system, are most often stated, not with reference to the traditional criteria, but with reference to considerations, that are said to meet the special requirements of these countries. The two most frequently mentioned considerations for developing countries are (1) what may be called the "transfer of technology" argument and (2) the "incentive to foreign investors" argument.

1. Transfer of technology

The ability of the international patent systen to secure the transfer of patent protected technology to the less developed countries is today generally referred to, to convince these countries of the advantages of joining the Union.

The "transfer of technology" argument did not appear as an original motive for the international extension of patent protection neither in general, nor in particular for the case of developing countries. Though it is true that the members of the Union from the very beginning have

[13] For the activities of two such organizations, see *infra*, pp. 210–18.

demanded that certain remedies be allowed against the non-exploitation of patents, such safeguards were not motivated primarily by a desire to use the international patent system as a means to acquire foreign technology, but in order to limit the harmful effects of granting patents to foreigners. Though the opposition of a few countries has, at various revision conferences, helped to slow down the evolution towards greater liberty of patentees, nevertheless, all the ensuing "compromises" have in fact resulted in some measure of greater liberty.

a. The disclosure thesis

It has already been shown that the "disclosure thesis" in the context of national patent legislation can be criticized on both theoretical and practical grounds.[14] But whatever the merits of this motivation for granting original patents, i.e., on the national level, the argument is untenable for granting patents by virtue of the priority rule. As a patent description is made public already in its country of origin, there is no need from the point of view of disclosure to repeat such publication in other countries. Yet the argument is sometimes suggested as also valid in the international context. Ladas, commenting on the reasons why some countries have opposed changes of Article 5 of the Convention says that one of two reasons is what the author calls "the juristic theory" according to which society in exchange for a limited monopoly grant demanded that the invention be made available by being worked in the country granting the protection. According to Ladas, however, "the exclusive privilege is granted to an inventor in exchange not for working his invention but for disclosing it immediately and fully to the public."[15] This author has also invoked the argument when he specifically refers to developing countries. Replying to a charge by Pretnar, that in economically weak countries foreigners obtain patents and by not working them cause a detriment to national industry and to local labor, Ladas states that:

> Even if the patentee should not be willing to grant licenses, the maintenance of his patent does not involve a detriment to local industry. The exclusive privilege granted to an inventor is in exchange not for his working the invention but of disclosing it wholly to the public.[16]

[14] Cf. *supra*, pp. 36–37.

[15] S. P. Ladas, *The International Protection of Industrial Property* (Cambridge: Harvard University Press, 1930), pp. 329–31; the force of this argument is reduced however, when at another point (p. 332) the author says, "It is only rarely that the printed description of a patent conveys sufficient information to enable a new process to be commonly worked."

Whatever support this disclosure argument may have in the context of national patent protection, it cannot really be expected that countries, whose only benefit from the international patent system may come from granting patents to foreigners, should be content to do it on the basis of the disclosure agrument.

b. Patent grants to foreigners may restrict local industry

One often used argument to refute the charge that patents granted to foreigners, and that are not being worked locally, are detrimental to local industry, holds that a patent monopoly is not like a monopoly in the traditional sense of the word. According to this argument – which has long been both asserted and refuted on the level of national patent legislation[17] a patent monopoly does not deprive the public of anything it had before, since the grant of patent protection only concerns hithertho unknown inventions, which add to, rather than subtract from, the amount of available goods. Besides forbidding the public to copy the most rational way of doing a certain thing, which is the most easily recognizable price to be paid for the patent system, it also stops the exploitation of independently made identical inventions. There are, furthermore, two other restrictive effects, that may be particularly severe for developing countries. Firstly, when a foreigner takes out a patent to protect an export market and refuses to either license or exploit the invention locally himself, despite the fact that conditions may exist for such exploitation, then the country is obliged not only to pay "what is under the theory of the patent system, the legitimate reward to the inventor but suffers in addition because it could have used its own resources more efficiently had the invention been available."[18]

[16] Ladas, "The Fundamental Bases ...," pp. 2–3; "By such disclosure," continues the author, "through the patent application, the scientific and technical public of the particular country is stimulated to find an alternative solution of the problem which will not be tributary to the patent."

[17] Cf. *Supra.* pp. 45–46.

[18] Penrose, *op. cit.*, p. 106; "If new technology or new products developed in other countries could be economically used or produced domestically and yet cannot be used or produced there because the domestic patents are held by foreign firms who refuse either to license them or to work them, the domestic economy suffers in several possible ways: Either 1) the production of some products is entirely prevented and they must therefore be imported at higher costs; 2) inferior qualities are produced without the use of the patented inventions, while superior qualities must be imported; 3) the same quality of product is produced by different, unpatented processes which involve less economic use of the factors of production available and hence production at higher cost." *Ibid.*, pp. 106–07. – It may be observed that the concern in the present context is with the effects of protecting foreign patentees under the present system and not with the incentive effect of patent-protection on foreign inventors. The latter effect has anyhow previously been assumed to be negligable in the case of any one developing country.

Though it is often said that in the case in which conditions exist for local exploitation, there will be no restrictions on industry, for either the patentee in such a case will himself exploit the invention or he will be prepared to license such exploitation,[19] there are obviously cases in which this is not so. For one thing, the fact that, with one exception, all industrial countries have rules concerning compulsory licensing seems to disprove such an assertion. For developing countries there will, in addition, be a series of special considerations due to their particular conditions and economic development policies. Suffice it here to turn again to Penrose for a succinct observation in this respect. The author, considering the argument that a foreign firm would produce locally if such production were cheaper than elsewhere, since their profits would be greater, says that:

> This statement from the field of theory must of course have a *ceteris paribus* clause attached to it.
>
> A foreign firm may face or fear discrimination at the hands of the domestic authorities – for example possible expropriation once the plant is established, discriminatory taxation, special difficulties in raising capital in the domestic market ... Hence for many reasons foreign firms may consider it less advantageous ... while domestic firms, who do not have the same choice ... would find it advantageous to produce the product in competition with imports.[20]

Secondly, it is often said that forfeiture of a patent is a pure loss to the economy, whether the country is highly industrialized or just developing, because no one would dare to exploit the invention for the risk that competitors would do the same and thus extinguish the profits to be derived.[21] This argument, which is based on one of the fundamental motivations for patents at the time of the introduction of the contem-

[19] Ladas, *Propiedad Industrial* ..., p. 5, makes this point saying that "a patent does not restrict industry. A person who applies for a patent will be interested in its local exploitation. Such a person will either establish an industry in the new country to exploit his patent or he will license a local firm to manufacture the product or utilize the patented process." [translated from Spanish].

[20] Penrose, *op. cit.*, pp. 107–08.

[21] Coupled with this assertion is always the one that holds that revocation is also an unfair provision against the patentee, because he cannot be expected to work his invention in every country that grants him protection. Though this proposition is generally admitted as realistic because the benefits to be derived from not obliging patentees to work their inventions everywhere is supposed to be distributed among all countries, it is quite another question, whether countries, whose exclusive benefit from the international patent system would be the effective introduction of the invention into the local economy, can be expected in "fairness" to the patentee, to protect his interests beyond the situation where the economy may benefit from the foreign technology.

porary patent institution, is neither possible to prove nor to disprove.[22] However, the following considerations would seem to question this argument. It is a fact that while the pace of technological development is increasing at a phenomenal speed, the number of original patents granted has been increasing at a much slower rate for a number of years, indicating that a decreasing part of total new technology is patent protected. Why then, one may ask, should one particular part of technology be supposed dependent on a specific protection, while non-patented technology is both produced and spread without such protection. Furthermore, the fact that advocates of the international patent system, particularly in connection with arguments urging developing countries to join, very often evoke the possibility of "pirating" in case "adequate" patent protection is not provided,[23] also seems to put the argument in question.

There is, in addition, a particular case in which a country may stand to gain or at least will not lose from revoking a patent for non-working. For although, particularly in a developing country, the invention may not be exploited locally for lack of the right conditions, there is always the possibility that cheaper imports may be available.[24]

2. *Incentive to foreign investments*

An argument related to the one that the international patent system favors the flow of technology to developing countries, is the one that holds, that adherence to the system will favorably influence the flow of foreign investments. While this argument is supported by all those who argue for the adherence of developing countries to the Paris Union, and

[22] Originally the argument concerned the incentive of patent protection to inventive activity; later, when the relative costs of innovation – the stage of development after an invention has been patented – increased, it has been used to assert that the patentee would not risk his capital if he were not assured of the exclusive rights of exploitation. See, for instance, H. Rondon de Sanso, "The Effect of Patent Protection on the National Economy of a Developing Country," *I.P.*, 4: 116, May, 1965; and Ladas, *Propiedad Industrial* ..., p. 6; for the opposite view, see Penrose, *op. cit.*, p. 100, who supports her contention by referring to "innumerable instances of international 'piracy'" which were also the chief complaints against countries with "inadequate" or no patent protection in the last century.

[23] Habachy, *op. cit.*, p. 366.

[24] When such a possibility is admitted by those who urge developing countries to join the Paris Union, revocation is also labelled unfair to the patentee, for "it may discourage the inventor from importing products made under the patent because he would fear unfair competition," and dangerous for the importing country as "it may encourage foreign manufacturers to import counterfeited goods of inferior standard and quality." Ladas, "The Fundamental Bases ...," pp. 2: 3. If a patent is revoked it is hardly correct to talk about "unfair competition" or "counterfeit goods." A price difference will not necessarily be the result of inferior quality but will often be due to the monopoly position of the patentee.

in view of their great need for foreign investments may have a strong appeal for those countries, the argument is rarely put in the context of the conditions of developing countries. Whereas the argument, that adherence to the international patent system will be influential on foreign investment decisions, cannot be either proved or disproved factually, there are reasons to doubt whether such adherence has, to any significant extent, helped to increase foreign investment in developing countries above what it would have been in the absence of patent protection according to the rules of the Convention.

First of all, in trying to reasonably assess the contention that membership in the Paris Union, guaranteeing certain standards of patent protection to foreigners, has any important bearing on foreign investment decisions, the elusive concept of "investment climate" must be considered. Although that concept lacks clear definition, it is generally thought of as including a number of more or less interrelated factors all of which influence the non-economic prospects, i.e., the non-business risks, for foreign investment. Economic, political and legal conditions are all important, and it is only the sum total of these various factors, that will finally influence the decision of whather or not to undertake a particular investment.

If the legal framework for conducting investments in a given country reads like a copy of the legislation of an industrialized country, but either or both of economic and political conditions make an investment hazardous, the fact that the country has signed the Paris Convention will hardly influence any investment decision favorably. It is probably not an overgeneralization to suggest that for developing countries the two latter groups of factors, i.e., economic and political, are more often deficient from the investor's point of view. Thus, only in the case in which neither economic nor political conditions pose any significant non-business risks for the venture would the legal conditions be of primary importance. The fact, that this is much more the situation in developed than in developing countries suggests, that the argument has been carried over from the sphere of developed to that of the developing countries without adjustment. One author, suggesting that the proposition that effective patent protection is a *sine qua non* condition for foreign investments is lacking in documentation, says:

As a matter of fact, investors contemplating overseas investment apparently are not influenced very much in their decisions by the nature of the patent protection available to them. Numerous surveys of the factors obstructing or encouraging overseas investment fail to turn up so much as serious mention of the question of patent protection.[25]

A second reason for believing that a system of general patent protection is in itself of little significance as an incentive to foreign investment in developing countries is the fact, that the conditions upon which investment decisions are traditionally based are often, in the case of these countries, influenced by deliberate actions of the authorities in pursuance of a policy for economic development. Some such aspects will be treated in the following section of this chapter. Suffice it here to suggest that a developing country, often following a particular policy designed to promote certain high priority developments through deliberate economic and legal incentives might do likewise, when it wishes to promote the introduction of desirable technology without incurring the costs of sponsoring a generalized system of far-reaching protection to foreign patentees.

Finally, when advocates of the international patent system stress the need for an "adequate" patent system, this implies a system containing at least the minimum requirements of the Paris Convention and membership in the Paris Union. But besides such patent legislation as is compatible with the Paris Convention, there exist other means to attract foreign investments and the introduction of foreign technology. Either there may be national patent laws or else other systems of incentives and guarantees, that would not be conditioned by any fixed and generalized standards, but might be made flexible and selective.[26]

[25] R. Vernon, "The International Patent System and Foreign Policy," *U.S. Senate Committee on the Judiciary, Study No. 5 of the Subcommittee on Patents, Trademarks and Copyrights* (Washington: Government Printing Office, 1958), p. 16.

[26] For suggestions on this point, see Penrose, *op. cit.*, p. 143, and Vernon, *op. cit.*, pp. 12–13. The experience of India in this respect is described by M. J. Kust, "Industrial Property Rights," *Foreign Enterprise in India; Laws and Policies* (Durham: University of North Carolina Press, 1964) p. 419: "The scheme of industrial licensing and approval of foreign collaboration ... is more important than the laws and policies on patents in facilitating and regulating the flow of technical knowhow and assistance to India. ... Nevertheless, patent law and policy has to facilitate this process; hence it must conform to the economic development laws and policies of the country." India has not become a member of the Paris Union. The reasons are set out in the Report by Ayyangar, *op. cit.* One observation of this Report (p. 118) is that the Convention "... in so far as the articles relate to patents for inventions [is] suited more to the industrially advanced than to the underdeveloped countries."

C. THE EFFECTIVENESS OF THE INTERNATIONAL PATENT SYSTEM AS A VEHICLE FOR THE TRANSFER OF TECHNOLOGY TO DEVELOPING COUNTRIES

From the previous sections of this chapter one would conclude, that the international patent system may benefit developing countries only as it promotes the flow of foreign technology to these countries. The following section will examine the appropriateness of the international patent system in this respect.

1. Allocation of patent exploitation according to the traditional theory and the objectives of policies for economic development

The extension of patent protection to foreigners has two different types of cost-effects. The first is that costs to society of granting patents in general are merely increased, and the second is that new types of costs are incurred. To the first group belong the costs of monopolies that are created when exclusive rights are granted. The effect of such a grant is in principle the same whether patents are held by nationals or foreigners, provided the inventions are exploited locally. To the second type of costs belongs that which may arise, when the foreign patentee works his invention abroad, although it could have been exploited locally.

Since developing countries extend patent protection to foreigners not in order to get reciprocal benefits abroad but to encourage the inflow of foreign technology, the first type of cost mentioned above is of little concern to them. This leaves the second type of cost to be dealt with, i.e., the disadvantages that might be incurred in cases in which the patented invention is not worked locally but abroad, supplying the home market via exports.

a. The traditional theory on the allocation of patent exploitation

According to traditional theory, however, no real costs were involved in these latter cases. It was said that whenever the patentee would find it economically advantageous to work his invention locally, he would do so. In the opposite case, i.e., when costs of production were lower abroad, it was held that it would be more economical, along the lines of the theory of comparative costs, for the patent granting country to import the patented products. The underlying premises upon which this argument was and is based, are a high degree of economic liberalism, full employment of resources and free trade.

Despite the high-sounding phrases of the "rights of inventors" during the several conferences which led to the establishment of the original Convention, the text of that Convention contained only one restriction on national patent legislation. Patents to foreigners were not to be revoked for the sole reason that patented products were being imported. Though at this stage, a few of the most developed countries wanted to abolish any obligation on the foreign patentee, most countries opposed such proposals. The simple reason was that several of the original members of the Paris Union were at that time at more or less the same stage of economic development as are the developing countries today. These countries, arguing from the point of view of national interest, insisted that their only benefit from granting patents to foreigners would be if the latter could be compelled to exploit their inventions locally.[27]

The steady increase in the effective protection of patentees since the founding of the Paris Union has been variously supported by claims that patentees need such protection in order to perfect and commercialize their inventions, and by the argument that it is not possible for the patentee to work his invention in every country. Though these various arguments have often been presented in the name of the interests of individual patentees, the fact that the countries that have most actively supported the changes (and argued for further extensions of the protection of patentees) are generally also those whose nationals make up a large portion of "foreign patentees" in third countries, illustrates the national interest of certain countries for such extended protection.

In practice, the theory that patents granted to foreigners will benefit a country either through importation of patented products (if production costs are lower abroad), which would not be imported and available unless protection were granted, or through local exploitation by the patentee or a local licensee, has never been strictly adhered to by any country at all times. Many countries have implicitly recognized the shortcomings of this theory at various times by insisting on the retention of certain working requirements. A small number of countries have been opposed to any deletion in existing requirements. The argument upon which the latter have invariably based their position has been

[27] "The theory that all patents should be worked within the country that granted them arose when encouragement of industrialization was the chief aim of the patent system. ... The purpose was the immediate establishment of a new industry ... The question was not one of 'rights of inventors' but of industrial development." Penrose, *op. cit.*, pp. 137–38. For a similar opinion, see, C. Akerman, *L'Obligation d'exploiter et la licence obligatoire en matière de brevet d'invention* (Paris: Sirey, 1936), pp. 333–34.

that due to their inferior economic development they have not only benefited less by having few nationals obtaining patent protection abroad but have also had to pay more by granting protection to foreign export industries. The efforts of these countries and the force of their arguments have had far less impact before 1945 than they are likely to have today.

b. Inapplicability of the traditional theory in the case of developing countries.

For two principal reasons the traditional theory on the allocation of patent exploitation must be considered, at least partly, inoperable: (i) from the point of view of national interest because the traditional theory of comparative costs is often not compatible with policies for economic development, and (ii) from the point of view of private interest because the particular conditions may often lead to a difference in evaluation of the feasability of local exploitation between the foreign patentee and the local entrepreneur.

(i) It is generally recognized today that developing countries, that pursue a policy aimed at industrial development, cannot rely solely on the profit-incentive of private business. Scarcity of resources calls for selectivity in their allocation. The choice of investment projects must not only favor long-run viability over possibly short-run unprofitability, but such choices must also be made with a view to their impact on total economic activity. On both counts the profitability of investment projects will be calculated in terms of social costs and benefits which will often diverge from such a calculation made in terms of private costs and benefits. Thus the "infant industry" argument, wellknown from the sphere of foreign trade theory as a justification for temporary tariff protection, may also be used to defend the requirement that an invention be worked in the developing country despite the patentee's unwillingness to do so. The authors who recognize the particular position of developing countries in this respect have argued either that these countries ought not to be in the Paris Union or at least made clear the disadvantages of membership.

Ayyangar has developed, at length, the reasons why India ought to remain outside the Paris Union. This author, talking in terms of any developing country, says:

> No doubt the imported product might be cheaper, but even if the cost of the article manufactured in the country might be considerably higher, it might in the long run prove an advantage to the national economy.[28]

[28] Ayyangar, *op. cit.*, p. 14.

The author, after giving some examples of the possible gains of local exploitation despite higher costs,[29] concludes:

If therefore the problem is viewed as one of balancing gains and losses to the economy of each nation, it does not need much argument to show that the costs to an underdeveloped country far exceed any possible gains.[30]

(ii) The traditional theory that holds that the patentee would exploit his invention locally in his own interest, whenever economic reasons indicated that this would produce cheaper goods, has never been wholly accepted. But whatever the value of this theory in general, its application must be severely limited in the case of developing countries. While, according to the theory in question, the patentee relies only on the evaluation of normal business risks, many non-business risks will have to be taken into account in the case of developing countries.[31] It would seem that those who do not recognize the relevance of calculations based on social as opposed to private costs and benefits could hardly deny the possibility of divergences between private interests of nationals and foreigners. If a comparison of business prospects should ba valid, all other determinants must be equal. For to maintain that the test is still valid when non-business conditions are not equal would be to acquiesce to the fact that developing countries are made to pay a higher price because of the very fact of their underdevelopment.

2. *"Spontaneous" local exploitation*

The introduction of foreign technology into the local economy may come about either "spontaneously" or (possibly) under the pressure of the threat or implementation of sanctions. The case in which the foreign patentee on his own initiative either exploits the invention himself or gives licenses to interested parties raises no particular problems. In

[29] "(1) the saving of foreign exchange, (2) the absorbtion of surplus labor, (3) the utilization of the country's scientific and technical talent, (4) the utilization of indigenous material ..., (5) the increase in technical knowledge ..., (6) the utilization of by-products ... and (7) greater security, particularly in emergencies, and economic independance ..." *Ibid.*; For a comparable enumeration, see Akerman, *op. cit.* pp. 331–33; and M. Börlin, *Die volkswirtschaftliche Problematik der Patentgesetzgebung unter besonderer Berücksichtigung des Schweitzerischen Verhältnisse* (Zürich: Polygraphischer Verlag, 1954, pp. 167–69).

[30] Ayyangar, *loc. cit.*; Cf. Börlin, *op. cit.*, pp. 180–81.

[31] Even disregarding non-business risks, a case could be made for compelling the patentee to work his invention locally despite higher costs of production. For though there may be lower costs of production abroad, the size of the export market may induce the patentee to charge a higher price than he could in the case of local exploitation where lower prices might be necessary in order to recuperate his investment.

such cases the incentive of the patent grant has had the desirable effect from the point of view of the developing country in that it has led to the effective transfer of foreign technology. In this case, there is therefore no reason to contest the usefulness of awards in the form of patent monopolies.[32] It might even be argued that such cases would warrant even stronger protection along the lines of specific investment incentives which are often found in developing countries. – In any case, the fact that developing countries see only one instance in which the costs of granting patents may be justified, would seem to be an invitation to consider the substitution of a system of special incentives or at least one of differentiation for the present one of general incentives.

That local exploitation or "spontaneous" licensing is not undertaken in all cases in which from the point of view of national interest such exploitation would appear advantageous is illustrated by the existence of various sanctions in almost every patent law. It is not surprising that such cases should be all the more frequent in developing countries. The blame cannot, of course, rest with the patentee, whose only guideline is his own potential profit.[33] In cases in which the patentee is not prepared to undertake local exploitation himself although such exploitation would be advantageous from the point of view of its expected social benefits, there is still the possibility that the patentee may offer licenses to local entrepreneurs. Such a course of action, however, will often be barred for lack of potential licensees.

3. *Working obligations and sanctions for non-working*

Despite incessant efforts by several countries to abolish or at least reduce the obligations put on patentees for the local exploitation of their inventions, both the obligation to license an invention and that of being "obliged" to work it himself remain permissible according to the Convention. The sanction in the former case is that of compulsory licenses and for the latter, that of revoking the patent grant. That a number of developed countries have been among those objecting to the abolishment of sanctions, in particular that of compulsory licenses,

[32] Though a powerful patentee might be able to extract undue advantages from a weak and underdeveloped country in the form of excessive royalty payments, etc., still the main justification for the patent grant has been fulfilled.

[33] "The reason why private foreign investment does not and will not flow to underdeveloped countries in substantial quantities is easily understandable. The private investor looks for security and profitability in his investment; he is not concerned with the social consequencies of his actions." B.K. Nehru [Indian Ambassador to Washington] "Foreign Aid and Technical Assistance," *International Studies*, 5: 366–76, No. 4, 1964., p. 367.

indicates that in general there may be justification to retain them. For developing countries, whose only real benefit from the operation of the international patent system is the effective transfer of foreign technology in the form of local exploitation of patent protected inventions, effective sanctions are clearly called for. Arguments against the use of sanctions have generally mentioned sanctions in terms of means to punish a patentee, and it has then been suggested that, if and when there is no "fault" on the part of the patentee, it would be unjust to employ sanctions. For developing countries, however, the fact that a patent is not being worked locally will often not be imputable to any "fault" or abuse on the part of the patentee. Nevertheless, since a patent granted by a developing country and not worked locally is potentially always a burden to the local economy, sanctions against non-working are simply measures to reduce such costs. This point of view has been expressed concerning compulsory licensing by Akerman, who says:

> The compulsory license no longer represents a mere negative limitation of the rights of the patentee; it has acquired a positive function in that it serves to satisfy the interests of society independently of any abuse on the part of the patentee.[34]

Ayyangar agreeing with this opinion and applying the principle to the conditions of developing countries, says:

> These provisions though they might undoubtedly operate to counteract cases of deliberate ,,abuse" must, on the other hand, be viewed as a necessary adjustment of the patent system to the demands of an underdeveloped economy.[35]

Having established the justification, from the point of view of developing countries, for employing sanctions against non-working, the effectiveness of such sanctions as allowed by the Convention remains to be analyzed.

a. The effectiveness of compulsory licenses

When the effectiveness of this sanction is discussed it is usually pointed out that the records of national patent statistics show that, in fact, very few compulsory licenses are sought and even fewer are granted. The conclusion then drawn is that the major effect of this sanction is the inducement it gives for voluntary agreements in case the patentee does not himself exploit his invention. Such voluntary agreements, whether "spontaneous" or induced, are of course preferable, since the active

[34] [translated from French] Akerman, *op. cit.*, pp. 311–12.
[35] Ayyangar, *op. cit.*, p. 60.

cooperation of the patentee is usually required to supply the licensee with the additional unpatented knowhow often required for the effective exploitation of a patented invention.

When developing countries are urged to join the Paris Union the fact that they may grant compulsory licenses is stressed as particularly beneficial for the effective transfer of foreign technology. These countries, however, have often objected that the effectiveness of a compulsory license sanction is doubtful both as an inducement to conclude voluntary agreements and as a remedy against non-working. The reason in both cases is that it will often be impossible to find local entrepreneurs able to demand such a license. When this is the case, it is obvious that the pressure on the patentee to avoid being subjected to granting such licenses will disappear.[36] And even for the case in which a potential licensee may exist, the fact that he will almost invariably be dependent upon the patentee for additional knowhow will reduce the force of a compulsory licensing provision both as an inducement to conclude voluntary agreements and as a remedy against non-working.[37]

b. The effectiveness of compulsory working requirements.

The ultimate sanction against non-working has always been the revocation of the patent grant. That many countries have always objected to its abolition, despite incessant efforts by certain countries to abolish revocation as a sanction for non-working, would seem to contradict the often made statement that the forfeiture of a patent is a "pure loss" to the economy. This sanction, like the previous one, may have two effects. On the one hand, it may induce the foreign patentee to work his invention locally; on the other hand, it will extinguish the patent monopoly. The inducement effect of a compulsory working requirement is uncertain. For, as Penrose says:

> In spite of the name ... compulsory working provisions cannot *compel* foreigners to work their patents. ... If domestic producers cannot use his invention, he will not fear their competition very much and certainly won't go to the trouble of producing under what are, to him, unprofitable conditions, in order to maintain his patent.[38]

[36] Though compulsory license provisions are today said to be particularly appropriate for developing countries, it is interesting to note what Ladas said in this respect in 1954. Answering the charge by Pretnar that the faculty to grant compulsory licenses does not provide protection for developing countries against the economic expansion of the industrialized countries, Ladas said: "The truth of the matter is that the working obligation for patents may conceivably be alleged to be of interest to only highly industrialized countries, because only in such countries there is found sufficiently developed industry to use the new inventions..." Ladas, "The Fundamental Bases ..." p. 3.

[37] Cf. *infra*, p. 177 and quotation from United Nations Report.

[38] Penrose, *op. cit.*, p. 151.

On the other hand, the patentee, interested in protecting his export market, may fear, if not local competition, then the potential competition of foreign producers, should his patent be revoked. Under such circumstances, compulsory working requirements may force a foreign exporting firm holding the patent to establish a branch plant in the country.[39] Most developing countries today provide too unimportant export markets for the foreign patentee. This may change when, and if, the various efforts towards regional integration materialize, and if the countries in such groups either plan the localization of certain industries or if they, like the twelve members of the African and Malagasy Organization for Economic Cooperation, institute a common patent system and a common patent territory.

In contrast to the uncertain curative effect of the threat of revocation, the actual revocation of the patent will at least reduce the monopoly power of the patentee. To what extent such an action will be beneficial to the local economy will depend upon whether imports of the same or similar products can be obtained from other sources. Such an action would at any rate, never increase the costs of the patent system.

Thus it may be concluded that a compulsory license provision by itself will be of doubtful value for developing countries and, in any case, be of less assistance than to developed countries. Such a provision, backed up by the ultimate threat of revocation, would seem to acquire more force, though its ability to provoke local exploitation is probably, still negligible. The only definite result that can be obtained through sanctions against non-working is the abolition of the patent monopoly. The effectiveness of sanctions is further reduced by the delays that have to be observed before their implementation. Thus a patentee enjoys absolute protection during the three years following the patent grant, though the effective period of absolute control may be much longer.[40] To the extent that the sanction of compulsory licensing is ineffective, the initial period of protection for the patentee will be extended for another two years.

[39] *Ibid.* The author considers, however, (p. 156) that such effects of compulsory working provisions are likely to appear only under very special conditions.

[40] One author, observing that, in practice, a compulsory license cannot be obtained for five or six years after the deposit of a patent application and that two more years have to lapse before the patent may be revoked, concludes that "at the present rate of technical progress, most patented inventions are superceded long before the shortest of these periods has expired." Pretnar, "The International Protection ...," p. 9.

D. THE APPLICATION OF THE CONVENTION TO COUNTRIES OF FUNDAMENTALLY DIFFERENT STRENGTH

Besides criticizing certain particular features of the Convention as they affect developing countries, the international patent system may be, and has been, criticized in more general terms: can the rules of the Convention be expected to be reciprocally beneficial to both highly industrialized and developing countries, or will the application of the same rules to the two groups of countries tend to preserve or even increase the hegemony of the industrialized countries?

The new awareness of the problems facing the developing countries, that manifested itself after 1945, and the realization that the solution of these problems was a matter of concern to the whole world, led several writers on the subject to question the appropriateness for developing countries of the existing machinery for international cooperation in various fields. This was true also in the case of the system of international patent protection. One author, writing in 1948, severely criticized what he considered the inequities of the international patent system for developing countries, stating that:

> The Convention – and the practices developed under it – are basic to the whole structure of the pre-World War II policy of restriction of economic development in the less industrialized countries and monopolization or cartelization in the more industrialized ones.[41]

This opinion has been much criticized also by authors who have otherwise indicated that developing countries do not participate to a comparable extent in the benefits of the system. – The author quoted above mentions two things as being "basic" to "a policy of restriction of economic development": the Convention itself and the practices developed under it, the latter of which will be examined in the next chapter. – What the author is saying is only that the legal framework of the international patent system has facilitated the economic expansion of the industrialized countries to the detriment of developing countries, not that the Convention was necessarily created for that purpose. Penrose, refuting the above quoted statement as "nonsense" maintains that only to the extent that the views of the industrialized countries had prevailed over those of the non-industrialized countries the Convention would be an "exploitary" arrangement. Penrose, nevertheless, admits the existence of one possible exception, which would seem to support

[41] H. Kronstein, "A Reevaluation of the International Patent Convention," [1948] *Law and Economic Power, Selected Essays* (Karlsruhe: C. F. Müller, 1962) p. 358.

the charge that the Convention has served to restrict developing countries, when she says that "it is difficult to see where this has been the case in any important matter with the possible exception of the extension of the period in which compulsory licenses cannot be granted."[42] Since it is precisely the rules concerning obligations to work and their sanctions, that are disadvantageous to developing countries, their evolution forms, in any case, a considerable "exception." It is on the basis of the evolution of these rules that Pretnar contends, that the working of the Convention today favors the industrialized over the developing countries. Comparing the days when the Convention was originally signed with contemporary conditions, Pretnar observes that in the place of a few highly industrialized States exercising control over vast territories serving as markets, a number of new States exist today, that are endeavoring to develop their industrial potential and promote their own economic progress. Since the evolution of the Convention has meant an ever increasing measure of protection of the export markets of the industrialized countries, Pretnar concludes that:

> By virtue of this article 5, the Paris Convention, instead of being an instrument in the service of the general development of the economy (as it is where highly industrialized countries are concerned) may become the contrary: a retrograde instrument. This is clearly so in the case of the relations between highly industrialized countries and those that are not.[43]

Against the charge that the original rules of the Convention were determined by a small group of industrial countries, and that the whole evolution of the Convention has since been determined by these same countries, two points are usually made: that, in fact, there were several underdeveloped countries among the fourteen original members, and that the rule of unanimity provides an equal power of decision for each member. Though it is true that eight out of fourteen original members may be characterized as underdeveloped, it is also a fact that three of them soon left the Union, that a fourth was a French protectorate and that one other country had no national patent law.[44] As for the effect of the unanimity rule, the latter has not hindered the "progressive" evolution of the Convention – it merely slowed it down –; and it may be remembered that opposition often came from developed countries as well. The principle of unanimous consent has been of little value to the developing countries at present members of the

42 Penrose, *op. cit.*, p. 210.
43 Pretnar, "The International Protection ...," p. 8.
44 Cf. *supra*, p. 93, n. 93.

Paris Union, since all but very few of them have become members after the essential features of the existing rules were shaped at the London Conference (1934).

The strongest argument in support of the contention that the Convention does not give a reciprocal share to all members of the benefits accruing from the international cooperation in patent matters, holds that while the rules of the Convention secure equal treatment in legal terms, the vast discrepancies among its members in terms of economic and technological strength result in the unequal distribution of benefits. Commenting upon the disinclination of India to join the Union, one author observes that:

> Like so many international agreements of this type, the differing economic positions of the industrialized and underdeveloped countries, does not afford the reciprocity required to make the convention fair and equitable to both types of countries. Such a treaty is frequently a one-way street with all the benefits running to the industrialized countries. An underdeveloped country becomes a member only to its economic detriment.[45]

It is clear, according to Pretnar, that only a technically very highly developed country is capable of exploiting foreign inventions, and that it will itself seek markets for its own inventions only in equally highly developed countries. Comparing the cases of Germany and Yugoslavia, which under the Convention are "legally on a footing of equality", Pretnar finds that the application of the Convention has produced totally different results in the two countries. "In view of the possibilities offered under the terms of the Paris Convention to the countries that are rich both in capital and in invention" the same author states:

> The Convention may be described as the instrument that allows the economic expansion of the countries that are highly developed technically and economically.
>
> Thus to accord the same legal treatment whatever the de facto position may be, is, in practice, to sanction inequality.[46]

[45] Kust, *op. cit.*, p. 428; Cf. Penrose, *op. cit.*, p. 115.

[46] Pretnar, "The International Protection ...," p. 5. "Sooner or later," the author concludes his article, (p. 10) "the Convention will have to be completely recast. This Union which has, since its foundation, so greatly contributed to the development of the world economy, must now aim at the equalization of the economic conditions prevailing in the various countries." See, however, Ladas, "The Fundamental Bases ...," p. 4, who, analyzing the significance of the Convention exclusively from the point of view of individuals, asserts that contrary to the criticism by Pretnar, "the Convention has been one of the finest pieces of international legislation regulating our world and ensuring equality of treatment in large and small countries alike."

CHAPTER III

INDIRECT EFFECTS OF THE INTERNATIONAL PATENT SYSTEM

The results of certain practices in patent matters which, while they do not follow from the obligations under the Paris Convention, are greatly facilitated by its existence, are called "indirect effects." The most important source of such effects is the cartel agreement that relies on the enforcement of patent rights for its basic "legal" structure.

Whereas in the preceding chapter only the position of the developing countries that are members of the Paris Union was directly at cause, there is for the present examination less need to distinguish between members and non-members of the Union.

A. INTERNATIONAL CARTELS

Before examining cartel agreements specifically based on patent agreements and some of their effects on developing countries, it may be useful to consider some of the general features of cartels. Cartels in general are an older phenomenon than the particular cartel practices based on industrial property rights.

1. *International cartels in general*[1]

Although most authors on the subject of cartels prefer their own definitions, they all agree on the essence of such agreements, as it has been formulated by one author: "A cartel is an association of independent enterprises in the same or similar line of business which exists for the purpose of exercising some sort of control over competition."[2] If one inserts "in two or more countries" after "independent enterprises" one

[1] Although the effects of national cartels may resemble those of international cartels, their total effects in the present context are likely to be much smaller.

[2] R. Whittlesey, *National Interest and International Cartels* (New York: MacMillan, 1946), p. 1.

arrives at a definition of cartels binding enterprises across national boundaries.

Cartels, although they existed at an earlier date, did not become a subject of much interest and debate until the inter-war period for several reasons. The most important are without doubt the factors that gave rise to cartels based on the exchange of technology, but other factors were also present. The task of reconstruction after the First World War was, from the industry point of view, facilitated by the regulation of competition, and again, following the 1929 depression, the same arguments were in favor of such cooperation. Another factor was the belief that economic rivalry among nations had been one of the main causes of the war. This gave rise to the idea that some form of international cartel agreements, regulating competition and expanding trade in an orderly fashion, would diminish friction among States and so serve to promote peace. Evidently such support for cartels was eagerly seized upon by many industries.[3] A League of Nations Committee in 1934 also expressed approval of what was called "industrial ententes" as being beneficial to world peace and security.[4]

International cartel agreements were also set up to overcome the restrictions to international trade created by government measures, such as tariffs, quotas, export subsidies and exchange controls, which were introduced with increasing frequency during the thirties in support of the national economy. The cartel device was "one means of doing business in foreign countries despite government prohibitions."[5] The main feature of such industrial cartels were the reservation of home markets and the division of markets in other countries.

The impact on international trade of this cartelization of industry between the world wars is difficult to assess. A study by the United States Department of Justice in 1939 enumerated 179 international cartels.[6] According to the League of Nations official statistics at least 32 percent of all international trade was under some form of "market control."[7]

[3] A large number of cartel agreements between French and German firms in particular were officially sponsored in the 1920's.

[4] League of Nations: *International Cartels* (United Nations Archives, 1948, II, D. 2).

[5] R. Opie, "A Critical Appraisal of the International Cartel," *International Cartels and Private Trade Agreements, America's Place in the World Economy* [eds. A. J. Zurcher, R. Page] (New York: New York University, Institute on Postwar Reconstruction, Conferences, Fourth Series, 1945) p. 128.

[6] F. Machlup, "The Nature of the International Cartel Problem," *A Cartel Policy for the United Nations* [ed. C. D. Edwards,] (New York: Columbia University Press, 1945) pp. 10–11.

[7] *Ibid.* p. 11. See also, R. Terrill, "The American Trade Proposals: Restrictive Business Practices," *The Department of State Bulletin*, March 24, 1946, p. 455.

During and immediately after the Second World War the earlier implicit support of or complacency towards cartels drastically changed. Instead, an almost complete mistrust of the alleged virtues of cartels and condemnation of their restrictive influence on international trade, were manifested.[8]

C. D. Edwards, writing in 1945, said, that "there is a widespread recognition among the United Nations that the international cartel pattern which prevailed between the two world wars should not be permitted to renew itself in the coming peace."[9] The author names two principal developments responsible for the widespread concern about international cartels. Besides the revelations during the war of the extension of cartel practices, there was the hope that "the economic part of the coming peace may be founded upon full employment and upon liberal principles of international trade."[10] These principles were contained in the Atlantic Charter of 1943 and to some extent were to be incorporated into the United Nations Charter (article 55). The thinking behind this new, severe condemnation of international cartels has been expressed in the following terms:

> In the aggregate, the private restrictions of international cartels are comparable in breath and severity to the restrictions imposed by government; but whereas governmental restrictions however harmful to the world economy, are at least supposed to serve the interest of a national group and are to some extent responsive to the opinion of the people in that group, private cartel restrictions are not designed to serve any public interest ... To attack governmental trade barriers and leave private trade barriers untouched would be illogical and ineffective.[11]

During these years all the traditional arguments for cartels were revived by those who were defending such practices in court actions, Congressional Hearings and other fora. The major arguments were the following: (a) that cartels promote efficiency of production; (b) that cartels reduce business fluctuations; and (c) that cartels check un-economic competition.

[8] See, for instance, C. D. Edwards, *Maintaining Competition; Requisites of a Governmental Policy* (New York: McGraw Hill, 1949).

[9] C. D. Edwards, "America's Postwar Policy toward International Cartels," *International Cartels and Private Trade Agreements, America's Place in the World Economy* [eds. A. J. Zurcher, R. Page] (New York: New York University, Institute on Postwar Reconstruction, Conferences, Fourth Series, 1945) p. 101.

[10] These principles were incorporated into the Atlantic Charter, where the United Nations endeavored "to further the enjoyment by all states, great or small ... of access, on equal terms, to the trade and to the raw materials of the world which are needed for their economic prosperity." *Ibid.*, pp. 103–04.

[11] *Ibid.*, p. 106.

(a) It was said that by pooling certain technical services, by allocating different types of production to different members of a cartel – thus obtaining economics of scale, by giving each market to the closest producer – thus reducing transportation costs, and by preventing "unwise" investments, higher efficiency and lower costs of production would result. While the pooling of technical services (collection of trade statistics, etc.) does not restrict competition, the other propositions clearly do.[12] The general criticism against the "efficiency" argument is that, in order to form a cartel, it is necessay to include a large part of the existing productive capacity, which means that the high cost producers will also be included – this is implicit in the "stability argument" below – thereby retarding their elimination. In addition, the cartel's policy of preventing competition and maintaining prices enables its members to avoid passing on eventual benefits to the public.[13]

(b) The most heavily stressed argument is probably that cartels reduce business fluctuations. It has also led some authors to assert that cartels are a product of depression or economic instability.[14] The general argument is that in making prices and output conform to a predetermined plan, fluctuations are avoided and stability promoted. According to Edwards, however, "cartels probably enhance rather than decrease other types of instability both in their own industry and in the economic system as a whole."[15]

(c) The argument that cartels check uneconomic competition has been called the "maladjusted industry" argument by Machlup.[16] The idea is that cartels reduce fluctuations by controlling "excessive" competition. But whereas it might be a good policy to control the decline of prices in a depression, the cartel's policy of maintaining prices will only reduce incentives for firms to shift into other activities, and thus prolong rather than overcome the "maladjustment."[17]

In a summary of criticism of alleged beneficial effects of cartels, Edwards categorically states that "there is no satisfactory evidence

[12] The criterium for opposing new ventures was that such investments were considered "unwise" when they would have a negative effect on the values and properties of previous investments. Cf. Edwards, "American Postwar Policy ...," pp. 107–09.

[13] *Ibid.*, p. 109.

[14] See Opie, *op. cit.*, pp. 127–31; for a refutation, see Machlup, *op. cit.*, p. 21.

[15] Edwards, *op. cit.*, p. 110; see also Whittlesey, *op. cit.*, p. 29.

[16] Machlup, *op. cit.*, p. 17.

[17] Edwards, *op. cit.*, pp. 112–13.

that cartel restrictions are capable of performing valuable economic services."[18]

Thus all the "traditional" arguments in support of cartel agreements have been convincingly refuted. The qualification "traditional" is used to separate the arguments mentioned above from another one, more or less closely connected with cartels based upon the exchange of patents. The latter argument holds that the technological cooperation among enterprises, which is often a major feature of a cartel, would not be possible outside the cartel, and that without such cooperation technical, and hence economic, progress could not be sustained at its present level.

2. *International cartels based on patent agreements*

Beginning in the 1920's, a particular type of cartel agreements appeared, usually known as licensing agreements or patent pools depending upon their structure. Although the International Patent Convention, without which patent cartels, if not completely hindered, would at least have been severely hampered, has been in existence since the 1880's, there are several reasons why the patent cartel did not develop until this time.[19] The 1920's saw revolutionary changes in inventive and innovative industry, making such activities a major component of industrial activities in many fields. Large laboratories were set up employing teams of scientists to carry out research and development programs on a sustained basis under corporate control. These developments generally increased the speed of technological progress, leading to an increasingly complicated and diversified technology, making it more and more desirable and profitable for the firms in an industry to exchange their research results. According to R. Terrill, "the technical agreement is not therefore an alien development, intruding into an otherwise unchanged world; rather it is a response above all to recent technological circumstances of industry."[20]

The exchange of technology across national boundaries was also a

[18] *Ibid.*, p. 114.

[19] Although the exchange of technological information including patents was not unknown earlier, it is generally assumed that only in the 1920's did such exchange begin to provide both the legal basis for cartel agreements and sometimes its principal raison d'être. Cf. E. Hexner, *International Cartels* (Chapel Hill: University of North Carolina Press, 1946) p. 71 ff.; the first major analysis on the subject of cartels and patent rights appears to have been H. Isay, *Die Patentgemeinschaft im Dienst des Kartellgedankens* (Leipzig: J. Bensheimer, 1923).

[20] R. Terrill, "Cartels and the International Exchange of Technology," *A.E.R.*, 36: 750, May, 1946.

way of carrying out international trade despite protectionist trade measures, particularly during the 1930's.

The main emphasis in the following will be on the aspects of international patent cartels that relate directly to the exchange of patents and other technological knowledge. It is certainly true that such cartels have also applied the forms of coooperation described previously. In such cases patent rights merely facilitate the operation of traditional cartel agreements. – Some cases as these will be examined below as they affect developing countries. – The essential difference between patent cartels and other industrial cartels have been described in the following way:

> The traditional cartel agreement, on the one hand, seeks *directly* to eliminate or reduce competition in vendable commodities; the technical agreement, on the other hand, attempts the same result *indirectly* by reducing to an agreed system of control the requisite technical information embodied in production or design.[21]

The reason for choosing the exchange of patent rights as the "legal" basis for an international cartel is that in this way arrangements under the cartel are easily enforcible, because the property rights obtained in various countries can be enforced.[22]

A cartel may be anything from a single company selling patent licenses under restrictive conditions, to a group of companies sharing not only patent rights but also the technical knowhow connected to patents and even the results of future inventions and other technical knowledge.[23] The foremost reason why patent cartels became a favored device for restrictive business practices also indicates the difficulties facing the authorities. While in general they were inclined to combat all efforts to restrict competition both nationally and internationally, where such restrictions are not legally sanctioned as in the case of simple patent monopolies, "the fear of losing the advantages of the interchange of technical information," according to Penrose, "has been responsible for a general hesitancy to condemn outright the international patent cartel."[24] It is said that firms will not grant licenses, pool

[21] *Ibid.* p. 746; see also M. E. Massel, "Evolving Needs for the Protection of Industrial and Intellectual Property: An Economist's View," *IDEA*, 9: 37, Conference No., 1965.

[22] Cf. Machlup, *op. cit.*, p. 8; Whittlesey, *op. cit.*, p. 80. A reason for basing cartel agreements on patent rights is also that other agreements have often been challenged by anti-trust legislation. Several authors have suggested that ninety percent of all cartel agreements between the United States firms and foreigners are in the form of patent cartels. See, for instance, Mason, *op. cit.*, p. 49.

[23] For various types of "patent cartels" see Isay, *op. cit.*, p. 12 ff and F. Neumeyer, "Die Rolle von Patenten in internationalen Kartellen," *Wirtschaft und Recht*, 4: 222–27, No. 3, 1953.

[24] E. T. Penrose, *The Economics of the International Patent System* (Baltimore: Johns Hopkins, 1951), p. 193.

their research results and make their secret knowhow available, unless they can ensure certain limitations on competition, especially in their home markets. Such safeguards, it is claimed, can only be assured by appropriate provisions in the license agreements.

3. Contemporary prevalence of industrial cartels

According to one author previously quoted, the cartels that existed in the inter-war period were mainly the result of the economic climate that existed at the time.[25] To judge from this opinion it would seem that the post-war period, with its general and sustained prosperity and sincere moves toward the liberalization of international trade, ought to have afforded much less incentive to the formation of international cartels. It is probable, however, that the existence of cartels is more due to the opportunities that may exist for forming such cartels than to any other reason.[26] The strong opinion against industrial cartels after the last war may have made it more difficult, at least for cartels that do not rely upon the exchange of patent rights, to continue.

As industrial cartels in general have been much criticized in the post-war period, actions taken to check cartel practices may indicate the prevalence of cartels. In general, the opinion is that national actions are not adequate to cope with international cartels. In some instances, however, and notably in the United States, actions on the national level have resulted in the break-up of such agreements. As was mentioned previously, the resolution to curb inequitable trade practices and to liberalize international trade in the post-war period was set down in the Atlantic Charter and, in a diluted form, in the United Nations Charter. More important were the efforts to regulate international trade practices set down in Chapter V of the Havana Charter, which was, however, never ratified. In 1951, an Ad Hoc Committee on restrictive business practices was created by the Economic and Social Council of the United Nations.[27] The Resolution instructed the Committee to obtain information on restrictive business practices affecting international trade. It further recommended the United Nations to cooperate in preventing such practices from obstructing international trade and economic cooperation. Finally, it instructed the Secretary General

[25] Opie, *op. cit.*, p. 131.
[26] In support of this thesis, cf. Hexner, *op. cit.*, p. 171.
[27] ECOSOC Res. 375 (XIII) of September 13, 1951.

to make a report and recommendations for the implementation of proposals to be submitted by the Committee. In 1953, the Ad Hoc Committee submitted two documents, entitled: "Analysis of Governmental Measures Relating to Restrictive Business Practices" and "Report of the Ad Hoc Committee on Restrictive Business Practices to the Economic and Social Council."[28] Finally, in May 1953, the Secretary General notified the Council that due to shortage of time, he was not yet prepared to submit the required report on means to implement the Committee's proposals.[29] The next initiative within the United Nations came in 1968 at the second United Nations Conference of Trade and Development (New Delhi).[30]

B. HOW CARTELS AFFECT DEVELOPING COUNTRIES IN PARTICULAR

After having mentioned briefly and in general terms the restrictive influences associated with cartel agreements, some of these effects, which may be of particular importance to less developed countries, will be examined in more detail below. The following four effects will be treated: the influence of international cartels as they (1) restrict trade, (2) restrict investment in new industries, (3) limit the spread of technology, and (4) restrict the use and development of new (future) technology. Whereas the last two effects are completely linked to the purpose of technological exchange, the first two, resulting from the division and control of markets, may appear more loosely connected with the exchange of technology. The practices leading to such market control are, however, always defended as constituting an inevitable corollary to technical cooperation among firms. It should be emphasized that the division of the present section into four paragraphs is somewhat arbitrary as the effects of cartel practices are often due to more than one of the aspects enumerated.

These effects of cartels are of course not limited to developing countries, but because of their economic and technological underdevelopment, these countries will be more adversely affected. With rare exceptions, enterprises of developing countries do not participate in international cartels. Hence, these countries cannot offset the social costs of cartels by the private benefits accruing to individual cartel members.

[28] Documents E/2379 and E/2380 of March 30, 1953.
[29] Document E/2443 of May 26, 1953.
[30] *Infra*, pp. 192–93, 195–96.

1. *Restrictions on international trade*

International trade may be restricted in several ways. It is always the result of a limitation on competition, either actual or potential. One particular case in developing countries is when a license is obtained from a foreign firm with the condition that the product may not be exported. Such a restriction is particularly severe for most developing countries which, because of their limited home markets, often have to plan for exports to obtain sufficient demand to achieve an efficient operation of their industries. The more general case of cartel practices is the one in which several firms cooperate. The restriction on trade may result either from an explicit agreement to divide markets among the particular firms, in which case it is possible for outsiders to obstruct the aims of the cartel, or the restriction on trade may result from a monopoly on the relevant technology, in which case outsiders are effectively barred. When these two restrictions are combined, the strongest possible formula for regulating international trade is obtained. Competition from outside the cartel is effectively checked and competition among cartel members eliminated. Such a degree of control over total competition can only be achieved through cartel agreements that are based upon the sharing of technology. This easily explains the popularity of patent cartels. As will be seen below, patent cartels often contain agreements not only to share existing technology but also the exclusive sharing of future inventions and other knowhow. Agreements in the latter direction may often be of even greater value for the cohesion of the cartel policy.

By far the most common and, at least as far as international trade is concerned, the most important restriction stemming from cartel agreements is the one that divides markets among cartel members. One author has estimated that only ten to fifteen percent of all technical agreements between the United States and foreign nationals do not contain market sharing provisions and there is little reason to suppose that the same is not the case for such international agreements in general.[31]

The territorial allocation of markets has two aspects. The first object of such allocation is usually to reserve the home market of each cartel member for himself. This aspect is exclusively a problem for the industrialized countries, and does not concern the developing countries. What does concern them, however, is the second part of most market

[31] Terrill, "Cartels . . .," p. 746.

allocation agreements according to which the remaining international market is divided among the members of the cartel. Just as the allocation of home markets is based on the systematic assignment of all patent rights in the respective markets, regardless of who made the invention or first sought the patent, this same procedure will be employed whenever possible in other markets also. Here a theoretical distinction may exist between members and non-members of the Paris Union to the extent that the latter do not offer the same facilities to foreigners for obtaining patents. However, even when patent rights are not the basis for allocation of the market in developing countries, the commercial and technological strength of the cartel, in combination with the weak industrial position of developing countries, will usually be sufficient to ensure the effectiveness of an agreement not to compete.

The developing country will thus be submitted to the monopolistic control of the cartel member that has been assigned its market, or as it is sometimes called, within whose "area of influence" it lies. The partition of world markets has often been done on an area basis rather than for particular countries. – So, for instance have United States corporations often insisted that Latin America lies within their sphere of interest. – The monopolistic position of the cartel member will be the greater and the more secure the less likelihood there is for outside competition. This leads the enterprise not only to stave off competition from outside exporters but also to oppose the establishment of local competition.

2. *Restrictions on investments*

One alleged benefit of industrial cartels is their policy to check investments which are not considered "economic." As has been pointed out above, however,[32] the prevention of "unwise" investments means that the established concerns oppose new ventures, when such investments are considered to have a negative influence on the values of previous investments. A developing country, that wishes to encourage the establishment of a new industry, and which often bases its calculations on the long-run prospects of such a venture and on its over-all effects on the national economy, will have to contend with the opposition of the cartel. The occasions in which such a new venture, facing at least short-term net losses from the point of view of private costs and benefits, will not constitute an "unwise" investment in the eyes of the cartel are

[32] Cf. *Supra*, n. 12.

certain to be rare. And even where conditions in the country would appear favorable to an independent entrepreneur, it is difficult to see in what circumstances the appearance of a competing firm would be considered "wise" by the cartel.

Besides the practice of cartels for allocating markets among its members and opposing the establishment of local competitors, there is another type of international restrictive arrangement, that has gained increasing importance with the spread of industrialization to developing countries. This is the exploitation of new areas by companies in which the parties to the cartel participate jointly with various shares. According to two authors, an almost indespensable corollary to such agreements is the exchange of patents coupled with cross-licensing.[33] Though such arrangements, which, according to Neumeyer are frequent,[34] are defended on the grounds that such ventures mean the sharing of financiel and other risks, they vastly increase the monopolistic power over the local market, and it is difficult to imagine that the "defense" cited above would really hold if the cartel members were forced to compete. Such joint operations by cartels are less likely to be set up for the purpose of a single country than for a region. The now dissolved agreements between Du Pont de Nemours and I.C.I., for example, provided for the operation of a jointly-owned company in Latin America where there is certainly room for more than one company.

To counter the charge that the Paris Convention has led to "restrictions of the economic development in less industrialized countries and monopolization or cartelization in the more industrialized ones,"[35] Penrose observes that:

> It has never been argued that the Convention has prevented national actions although it has been stated that because the same measures must be taken against domestic patentees as are taken against international patentees, some countries have been loathe to apply any measures at all.[36]

This is a surprising statement from an author, who repeatedly argues that developing countries have nothing to gain from joining the Paris Union, and who must be aware of the opposition put up by a few coun-

[33] W. Friedmann and P. Verloren van Themaat, "International Cartels and Combines," *Anti-trust Laws, A Comparative Symposium* [ed. W. Friedmann,] (Toronto: Carswell, 1956), p. 471.

[34] Neumeyer, *op. cit.*, p. 227.

[35] Kronstein, "A Re-evaluation of the International Patent Convention," *Law and Economic Power, Selected Essays* (Karlsruhe: C. F. Müller, 1962), p. 358. Cf. supra, p. 150.

[36] Penrose, *op. cit.*, pp. 210–11.

tries at almost every revision conference against further protection for patentees. The Convention certainly prevents national action by the minimum requirements prescribed for the protection of patentees, and it is precisely because of such limitations on the powers of national patent authorities that many countries, and notably India, remain outside the Paris Union. Penrose concludes her above-quoted statement by saying that "the Convention is 'basic' to the development of restrictive practices in a much lesser degree than the laws permitting the granting of patents are 'basic' to them."[37]

If it can be agreed that the degree of protection enjoyed by patentees influences their possibilities to abuse the patent, then it must follow that the countries, that have national patent laws, and that are bound to observe certain minimum standards in the protection of foreign patentees through an international convention, are at a disadvantage compared to countries, that are free to legislate according to local conditions. Hence, to maintain that national patent laws by themselves are more "basic" to the development of restrictive practices than the Convention, would only be true – in more than a purely theoretical sense – if the Convention had had the influence of lowering the protection enjoyed by patentes, or at least had not had the opposite influence. But it is a fact, that the Convention has considerably influenced national patent laws in the direction of increasing the protection of patentees. Relatively few countries that are members of the Paris Union have, in fact, higher minimum standards than those prescribed by the Union.

Since the above-quoted statements by Penrose were made (1951), there has admittedly been a change in the Convention to the effect that national authorities are now (through ratification of the Lisbon text) allowed to take immediate action against abuses if non-working is not the only reason. Though this provision may help countries to take action against individual patentees, their power to influence cartels is questionable. For one thing, a cartel may not have to resort to obtaining local patents in order to impose its market control, and to that extent the position of developing countries, whether they are members of the Paris Union or not, does not differ. And if one or several locally obtained patents would be revoked for abusing the monopoly power, the combined financial and technological strength of the cartel members is more likely to help maintain the monopolistic control of the cartel.

[37] *Ibid.*, p. 211.

3. Restrictions on the spread of technology

The two types of restrictions so far discussed are rarely thought to be an indespensable part of an agreement between industrial firms for the interchange of technology (except by spokesmen for such firms). With some generalization, they may be described as devices resorted to because the means for doing so already exist, i.e., the legal basis of patent ownership. Thus, if such practices are not deemed vital or even beneficial to the international exchange of technology, they could be discontinued without fear of a decrease in such exchange.[38] For the two remaining types of restrictions by patent cartels – restrictions on the spread of existing technology and restrictions on the development and use of future technology – the situation is less clear. That firms participating in an interchange of technological knowledge should insist on some limitations on its use may appear justified. The question is whether some authors do not recognize such assertions too readily. Mason, after making some suggestions for international action against cartels, the effect of which, according to the author, would be limited, says:

> Furthermore . . . the highly desirable exchange of research results and technical knowhow between nationals in different countries may involve a considerable limitation on competition among them not only in their own but in third countries. This will have to be accepted along with the benefits of the technical interchange.[39]

Before enumerating various restrictions on the spread of technology, the contents of the technology exchanged should be defined. There is patented technology and there is unpatentable and unpatented technology. It is generally recognized that a large portion of modern technology is not patented and that the technology described in patent applications is often insufficient to exploit the invention efficiently, and that, therefore, additional knowhow is necessary. It is the quantity of secret technology exchanged that makes many authors hesitant to condemn certain practices of cartels, presuming that such exchange would be impeded if severe restrictions were put on cartels.

The basic effect of the policies of a patent cartel on the spread of technology is that the total technology of the members of the cartel is kept for the exclusive benefit of the cartel. As a cartel member is often

[38] A possible exception would be the reservation of home markets which in the present context is of no interest.

[39] Mason, *op. cit.*, pp. 89–90.

prevented, by contractual obligation, from sub-licensing any outside company, the latter is effectively denied the possibility to acquire any knowledge within the "domain" of a cartel.[40] This is of course a serious limitation on the claim that the patent system provides a mechanism for the transfer of technology; and it must be especially serious for a country that has no part of any cartelized industry and, thus, may be absolutely prevented from acquiring certain technological knowledge for its local industry. It must be equally evident that the 'exclusive sharing of patents and' 'secret" technology is contrary to the underlying objective of the patent law.[41] But not only is the total technology held by the cartel members contained within the cartel, but often the use of such technology is further restricted among the cartel members. A certain technology, applicable to various more or less closely related fields, is allocated to the firms participating in the cartel agreement with limitations on the use that any one firm may make of it.[42]

A frequent complaint against powerful patentees is that they withhold certain patented inventions from being used, thus abusing their monopoly power. This claim has either been outrightly denied or else it has been said that the power conferred by the patent grant includes the prerogative to withhold any patented invention from exploitation. From the patentee's point of view, the rationale for such behavior may be that the introduction of certain inventions would entail the scrapping of existing investments bringing a net loss to the company. Though no conclusive evidence seems ever to have been produced that patented inventions have been suppressed for economic reasons, the belief is widely held that such is the case.[43] It is evident that such practices, if employed by a cartel exercising a large measure of control on competition, could be successfully implemented.

There is no doubt that the exchange of technological knowledge

[40] Another clause designed to limit the importance of technology outside the "domain" of the cartel is the one that prohibits members of the cartel from acquiring licenses from third parties, in order to avoid that any cartel member becomes dependent on "outside" technology.

[41] See Whittlesey, *op. cit.*, pp. 81–82.

[42] See Document E/2379, paragraph 15 (*supra*, n. 28); Terrill, "Cartels ...," p. 747.

[43] "The main basis for assuming that the suppression of technology does take place in the international sphere are the large number of national statutes providing for remedial action if a local patent is not exploited." Doc. E/2379, paragraph 37 (supra, n. 28). As the various quotas (sales, market, etc.) of each cartel member are fixed on the actual size of operations, cartels are likely to support high-cost, inefficient producers. There may therefore be reason to believe that the introduction of certain technology may be withheld or delayed. Cf. Whittlesey, *op. cit.*, pp. 25–26.

which takes place among cartel members is of benefit not only to the limited group of producers but to the economy as a whole. In estimating the net benefit of such exchange, however, two questions ought to be answered. Firstly, what are the effects on the economy of the restrictions connected with such exchange? One restriction on economic activity that is likely to take place as a consequence of cartel agreements is a diminuation of the output and exchange of goods. Whether such a decrease in the total output of goods is balanced by a possibly higher exchange of technology, may not be possible to answer in general. It would appear likely, however, that in the case of developing countries, a decrease in the exchange of goods will not be offset by any increase in the supply of technology. Secondly, to what extent, if any, would such exchange decrease, if the accompanying restrictions were abolished? When the appropriateness of the patent institution to contemporary circumstances has been questioned, it has sometimes been held that, whereas larger firms would be able to carry on their activities even in the absence of a patent system, smaller firms and newcomers would be severely handicapped.[44] In the case of patent cartels it appears unlikely that such arrangements serve and are beneficial to this latter category. On the contrary, patent cartels are generally set up by corporations that are already large and dominant, often with the objective of squeezing out smaller competitors and newcomers. The discrepancy between the alleged need for patent protection and the benefits reaped from the system of general patent protection (i.e., smaller vs. larger firms) is undeniably increased in the case of patent cartels, to the detriment of those who are said to particularly need such protection. If it can be assumed that a large company would be able to continue its research and development activities in the absence of a patent system and, furthermore, that the exchange of technology between such companies is mutually beneficial, is it not plausible that such exchange would continue even if some accessory restrictions of patent cartels were eliminated? It is not intended here to try to answer these questions, but simply to stress their importance and their relationship to the system of international patent protection, allegedly of particular benefit to developing countries as a vehicle for the transfer of technology.

[44] Cf. *Supra*, pp. 49–50.

4. *Restrictions on the use and development of future technology*

Frequently the members of a patent cartel not only limit the use and application of existing technology but also agree to the exclusive use by the cartel members of their future research results. An American author has suggested that such stipulations are probably contained in more than half of all patent agreements between American and foreign parties.[45] By agreeing to the exclusive control of future inventions, the purpose of the patent system, of conferring limited monopoly rights to stimulate competition, may be suspended indefinitely. An accompanying purpose of the patent system is also likely to be frustrated, namely the incentive effect on inventive activity.[46] A particular feature of some patent pooling agreements seems to contradict the purposes of the patent system to an even greater extent. This consists in an agreement among the members of a patent cartel for each firm to specialize in one particular field. Each company receives for its exclusive use any patent relating to its particular field and assigns, in its turn, all its own patents and other technology relative to the other fields of specialization to the other members of the cartel. One author, commenting on such a division of research activities, suggests that such methods are artifical and against the nature of scientific research, and continues:

> One may ... fear that important inventions – which, as experience so far has shown, often appear as by-products in one area and become applicable in quite a *different* area – remain unexploited, since neither inventors nor the company, considering the agreement for specialized production, are interested in further development of such inventions.[47]

[45] Terrill, "Cartels ...," p. 747. "Among those agreements" the author continuous, "that provide the principal technical 'linkages' between the national economies of the world it is probable that all include this particular feature." *Ibid.*, pp. 747–48.

[46] An American author, who has made several studies of American industries, has made the following conclusion on cross-licensing of future patents: "I believe ... not only that it is important for small and medium-sized firms to be encouraged to develop research but that competition among the large patent-holders in an industry should be fostered. Hence I doubt that cross-licensing of *future* patents should ever be permitted." W. R. Maclaurin, "Patents and Technical Progress – A Study of Television," *The Journal of Political Economy*, 58: 157, Nr. 2, 1950. Isay, *op. cit.*, pp. 15–16, though very favorable to patent cartels in general, recognizes that in this respect, they may turn the objective of patent legislation of promoting inventiveness into the contrary.

[47] F. Neumeyer, *Patent, reflexioner kring patent-institutionens uppkomst, utveckling och*

C. POSSIBLE REMEDIAL ACTIONS

The effects of certain cartel practices described above concern all countries. The justification for emphasizing their effects on developing countries lies in the fact that these countries will experience relatively less of the benefits of patent cartels and relatively more of the disadvantages from such arrangements.

The restrictive effects of such agreements, especially on the spread and development of technology, further impedes the efficacy of the international patent system as a vehicle for the transfer of technology to developing countries.

What are the possibilities to remedy the negative effects of international industrial agreements based on patent rights? Before enumerating some proposals often made to that end, the possibility to take remedial actions offered by the rules of the Convention may be examined, and their practical consequences assessed. Before the latest revision conference, no measures were allowed against patentees, who abused their patent rights whether by non-working or any other practices, before the expiration of three years from the patent grant. With the latest revision of the Convention (Lisbon 1958) however, the earlier rules concerning non-interference with the rights of patentees for certain periods now only relate to non-working, whereas sanctions (compulsory licenses and, after a two-year period, revocation) against other abuses may be taken directly. Besides the fact that many countries have not ratified the latest text, the practical importance of such sanctions against powerful cartels are doubtful. In the case of developing countries the effect of such sanctions is probably small. It was suggested above that international cartels would often not need to acquire patents in these countries in order to exercise their influence, and to that extent their effects do not vary whether or not the particular country is a member of the Paris Union.

It is often asserted that, in general, measures by national authorities are not sufficient to deal with international cartels. The two efforts made so far for international cooperation in this respect (the Havana Charter, Chapter V, and the draft convention of the Ad Hoc Committee of the ECOSOC) have both remained unimplemented. Two authors, concluding that it seems unlikely that any general international agreement affecting international cartels and other restrictive practices will

ställning i vår tid. [Studier och Debatt, Vol. IV 1958] (Stockholm: Studieförbundet Näringsliv och Samhälle, 1958) p. 82. [translated from Swedish].

be adopted in the forseeable future, mention the possibility of concluding bilateral conventions.[48]

Besides the solution that would lie in an international convention, another approach that is usually mentioned, in order to overcome the restrictive effects of private agreements, is that with the expansion of government-sponsored research, such research agencies could allow the free dissemination of technology to all interested parties.[49] Such a solution would amount to no more than what on the national level is known as "open" patent pools meaning that any firm may join it. As such arrangements exist within several industries, it is not seen why a similar solution on the international level would not in the long run be advantageous for all parties involved.

[48] Friedmann, Verloren van Themaat, *op. cit.*, p. 507.
[49] See Mason, *op. cit.*, p. 53; Hexner, *op. cit.*, p. 175; Terrill, "Cartels ...," p. 754.

CHAPTER IV

THE POSITIONS OF VARIOUS INTERNATIONAL ORGANIZATIONS

As the result of a Brazilian initiative, a resolution was adopted by the *United Nations General Assembly* in 1962 concerning patents and developing countries.[1] This move by Brazil set off the current debate on patents and developing countries both within and outside the United Nations.

The principal organization outside the United Nations with an interest in international patent relations is the *Paris Union*, acting between its revision conferences through its Secretariat (BIRPI) and, since 1961, also through its Permanent Committee. In addition to these two intergovernmental organizations there are two private international organizations with a particular concern for the subject: the *International Chamber of Commerce* through its *Committee on the International Protection of Industrial Property* and the *International Association for the Protection of Industrial Property*.

The present chapter will examine the evolution of the question of international patent protection and developing countries within each of these four organizations. It is hardly necessary to stress the close interrelation among the actions of the various organizations on the subject; this will become abundantly clear when they are described separately. What may be emphasized here, although it will be dealt with in more detail later, is that the actions of these various organizations inevitably reflect the particular purposes and interests for which each organization stands. It is obvious that the more specialized an organization is as to its objectives, the narrower will be the considerations upon which its opinions are based; far from being a pejorative judgement, this is simply a realization that the opinions and decisions of any organization reflect goals and priorities for which each organization represents its members.

[1] G. A. Res. 1713 (XVI) January 8, 1962.

The first organization to be examined is the United Nations and the various bodies of that organization, which since 1961 have considered the problems of international patent protection and developing countries. This order is convenient since the question was initially dealt with by this organization, and because the background knowledge of the activities within the United Nations will explain the activities and reactions within the other organizations.

A. THE UNITED NATIONS

1. The "Brazilian resolution"

In November 1961, Brazil introduced a draft resolution, in the Second Committee of the General Assembly, entitled *The Role of Patents in the Transfer of Technology to Underdeveloped Countries*.[2] In a number of preambular paragraphs several critical references to the working of the international patent system were made: access to technical knowledge is limited by the system; patents are taken out by foreigners without the intention of local exploitation; license agreements often contain harmful restrictive provisions; and royalty payments constitute a heavy burden on the balance of payments, which might be further aggravated by imports of patented products carrying artificially high prices. Besides some introductory paragraphs referring to earlier actions and recommendations in the fields of technical assistance, only one paragraph of the preamble of the draft resolution would remain in the text of the resolution as finally adopted:

> *Affirming* that it is in the best interest of all countries that the international patent system should be applied in such a way as to reconcile the legitimate claims of patent holders with the needs and requirements of the economic development of underdeveloped countries.[3]

The operative part of the original draft resolution called for a report by the Secretary General, containing: (1) a survey of national patent legislation with emphasis on the treatment of foreign patentees; (2) a study of the effects of royalties paid to foreigners on the balance of payments

[2] Doc. A/C.2/L.565, November 8, 1961.

[3] Preambular paragraph six of the original draft resolution. The only change made in its final version was that the phrase "applied in such a way as to reconcile the legitimate claims of patent holders with the needs and requirements of the economic development of underdeveloped countries" was replaced by "applied in such a way as to take wholly into account the special needs and requirements of the economic development of underdeveloped countries as well as the legitimate claims of patentees." (part of preambular paragraph six of final text, *supra*, n. 1).

of developing countries; (3) a preliminary analysis of patent legislation in developing countries in the light of economic development objectives; (4) an indication of the possibility of revising legislation to serve economic development objectives; and (5) "a recommendation on the advisability to hold an international conference with the aim to adjust the existing patent conventions to the needs of developing countries."[4]

This Brazilian initiative met strong opposition both inside and outside the United Nations. It was seen as a threat to existing international conventions on patents and also to the hitherto unchallenged position of the Paris Union.[5] Introducing its draft resolution the Brazilian delegation, after pointing out the changes that have taken place in the technological evolution, which, having been local and empirical, had become universal and scientific, and where the lone inventor had been replaced by teamwork and socially organized research, said in part:

> Man could invent whatever he wished provided adequate material conditions were available .... Much of the technological backwardness in many countries today could be remedied if the pertinent political decisions were adopted.[6]

The criticism of the text of the draft resolution, as voiced by several delegations, emphasized three things: that abuses to which the patent system might give rise ought to be remedied through national legislation; that the existing machinery of the Paris Union was highly sufficient to deal with any questions concerning its field of activity and that countries not yet members ought to accede to it; and that particularly for developing countries unpatented or unpatentable technology was of greater importance than patented inventions.[7] A number of amend-

[4] The operative part of the original draft resolution also suggested that States, in making or revising their patent laws, should consider both national economic requirements and the rights of patentees, should eliminate abuses, etc., "without interfering with the rights of industrial property recognized by international law." The implication that general international law recognizes certain standards of protection – apart from the minimum standard of protection of aliens – is questionable.

[5] Cf. T. Hesser, "Det immatriella rättsskyddet och u-länderna," *NIR*, 34: 156, 1965; the fact that Brazil is a Member of the Union seems to show that the draft resolution was directly aimed at the Union.

[6] General Assembly, Official Records, Sixteenth Session, Second Committee, 778th Meeting, December 7, 1961.

[7] See, in particular, General Assembly, Official Records, Sixteenth Session, Second Committee, 779th, 781st, 786th and 789th Meetings. One Delegate (New Zealand), at the 779th Meeting, agreeing that there were both advantages and disadvantages of patent protection for economic development, said, in part: "Internationally the patent system was governed by the Paris Union, which, although it might attempt to protect inventors rather than assist the underdeveloped countries, nonetheless contained a clause providing for its own revision"; another Delegate (Holland), at the 779th Meeting, objected to the calling of an international

ments were proposed which, besides deleting preambular paragraphs containing negative references to the international patent system, were designed to soften the wording of the operative text. The most important amendment, and the only one over which serious disagreement developed, was a proposed addition to operative paragraph 1(d), requesting the Secretary General for "a recommendation on the advisability of holding an international conference in order to examine the problems regarding the granting, protection and use of patents, taking into consideration the provisions of existing international conventions and the special needs of developing countries," reading: "and utilizaing the existing machinery of the International Union for the Protection of Industrial Property."[8] This amendment, aimed at securing the position of the Paris Union in any future developments which might result from the resolution, was passed by the majority of a single vote.[9] The text as a whole was then passed by the Second Committee by fifty votes to none with ten abstentions and later by the General Assembly unanimously.

A comparison of the operative texts of the original draft resolution and the text contained in the General Assembly Resolution shows that the latter, besides calling on the Paris Union secretariat to collaborate with the Secretary General, avoids the implication in the original text of a possible need to change existing international agreements. Thus, the opponents of the Brazilian initiative had managed a subtle turn of the problem away from arrangements regulating international patent protection and onto measures to be taken by the developing countries on the national level to get optimum results from the international patent system.

conference, saying in part: "An international conference would duplicate the existing perfectly effective procedure for the revision of the international patent system ... Throughout its some eighty years of existance, the International Bureau of the Union had taken into account the interests of the developing countries ...

... the sponsors of the draft resolution appeared to be setting 'the interests of patentees' in opposition to 'the needs and peculiarities' of the economies of the underdeveloped countries. In so doing, they did less than justice to the economic value of the patent system, the fundamental purpose of which was to encourage research and exchange of technological discoveries." – Since the object of developing countries in joining is primarily, neither to "encourage research" nor to "exchange technological discoveries," but to obtain such technology in one-way transactions, it seems justified to question whether the traditional system is optimally adapted to their needs.

[8] Doc. A/C.2/L.627.

[9] Twenty-one votes to twenty with 25 abstentions. Doc. A/5056, p. 77.

2. *Interim report by the Secretary General*

In April, 1963, the United Nations Secretariat presented an interim report, entitled: *Transfer and Adaptation of Technology – Patents and the Economies of Underdeveloped Countries.*[10] The interim report, covering only a part of the area to be included in the final report, was severely critisized, and it did not become the basis for any deliberations within the United Nations.[11]

This interim report did not suggest any general conclusions on the questions posed by the General Assembly Resolution, and it did not provide an answer as to whether an international conference ought to be called or not.

3. *The Final Report*

In March, 1964, the final report by the Secretary General, entitled: *The Role of Patents in the Transfer of Technology to Developing Countries,* was published.[12] The Report consists of two parts plus a number of annexes. Part I, *Major Characteristics of Patent Systems,* takes up almost three-quarters of the space. It is descriptive in character and is of minor interest in the present context. The second part of the Report, *The Effects of Patents on the Economies of Underdeveloped Countries,* considers three points: (1) the role of patents in the actual transfer of technology; (2) the role of patents in relation to imports of patented products or goods produced under patented processes, and (3) the role of patents in improving the process of invention and innovation through the indigenous technology of developing countries themselves. The

[10] The report was submitted to the Committee for Industrial Development at its Third Session. Doc. E/C.5/35, April 30, 1963.

[11] "The advice to cooperate with BIRPI was certainly well-founded. To start with, the United Nations Secretariat tried to work alone but the result was what could have been expected. Its first report [1963], was materially deficient and was exposed to a crushing criticism from BIRPI." [translated from Swedish] Hesser, *op. cit.*, p. 157.

[12] Doc. E/3861/Rev. 1, March, 1964. The Report was based on the following written material:

(1) replies by fifty-three countries to a questionnaire (text and answers reproduced in annexes B and C of the Report); forty-eight of these replies had been submitted for the interim report.

(2) a survey of patent legislations in thirty-four countries by BIRPI (reported in annex D); such a survey of thirty-six countries had been submitted for the interim report.

(3) a study of patent legislation in ten countries by the I.C.C. and the I.A.P.I.P.; the study was submitted already for the interim report.

(4) information contained in official reports on patent law revision from a few countries.

present examination of the second part of the Report will be limited to the first two points.[13]

The patent system will affect developing countries not only through the actual transfer of technology but also through imports of patented products and products produced by patented processes. Another possible influence of patents mentioned (par. 245) is that their protection in developing countries may be an "essential inducement or precondition" for research and development in the industrialized countries. After examination (pars. 282–84), the validity of this argument is termed "doubtful." In this context, it is further said (par. 283) that:

> Even insofar as patent protection in the underdeveloped countries were thought to have a discernable effect in promoting research and development in the supplying countries, it would have to be questioned whether it is to the interest of the world economy that the poorer countries should be expected by way of higher prices for their imports to contribute to the recoupment of research expenditures in the richer countries.

a. *The role of patents in the actuel transfer of technology*[14]

While, according the Report, there is not necessarily a difference be-

[13] Chapter VI of Part II, *Patents and Development of Indigenous Technology: Patents to Domestic Inventors and Innovators*, certainly would warrant some attention. Since its subject matter is not central in the present context, some of the points made will merely be indicated. The Report does not definitely pronounce itself in favor of the traditional patent system. Several arguments both in favor and against the patent system are questionable and at least in one case appear contradictory. (1) After enumerating a series of possible incentives of which the patent system is "not necessarily the most important," (par. 298), the Report makes the following point against monetary or other awards to inventors: "... such rewards ... for new processes which do not apply to priority fields within a country's development plan may be expensive without commensurate benefits to an economy." (par. 299) – If there was one major point in favor of selective rewards as opposed to a general reward system for developing countries, it would certainly be the ability of the former system to direct inventiveness to priority fields. –

(2) Two arguments in favor of granting patents are said to be the following (par. 300): that the discouragement and limitation on imitation and competition (recognized as a drawback in developed countries) may not be a drawback at early stages of development, where national plans may often only permit a single enterprise in various sectors; and, that patents stimulate the search for alternative processes, i.e. "inventing around." – While thus on the one hand minimizing the harmful effects of the monopoly grant for the reason that a country's scarcity of resources will often not permit "duplicate" enterprises, on the other hand, the "inventing around" argument, which must precisely for the reason of scarcity of resources be especially costly to developing countries, is said to favor the patent system. –

(3) Stressing the fact of scarce research resources the Report says (par. 302) that care must be taken so that the patent system does not divert these limited resources to applied technical research "to the exclusion of more urgent and more important problems" and (par. 304) that it is not used "to retard and block local production," and that "in spheres of production vital to the national interest ... limitations on patentability or ... the scope of the patent grant ... are natural, as is evidenced by the presence of such limitations in the legislation of many countries." – The fact that many countries have such provisions does not lessen the theoretical ambiguity involved. (Cf. *Supra*, pp. 39–40) The weakness of this last argument would seem to be particularly striking in the case of developing countries.

[14] Full title of Chapter IV: *The Role of Patents in the Actual Transfer of Technology: Production of Patented Products and Use of Patented Processes Within the Developing Country* (par. 248–76).

tween the interests of the foreign patentee and those of the developing country, as long as the latter is content to import the products instead of the technique, the government of a developing country, "using a set of cost and benefit calculations different from the private profit-cost calculation of the foreign patentee, may conclude that it would be desirable to have the patented product produced in the country."

> It is this problem [of the divergence between social and private cost/benefit calculations] which is at the heart of the difficulty and controversy concerning the effect of a patent system on underdeveloped countries, as far as products or processes are concerned which could be worked in these countries.[15]

After evaluating the likely need for additional knowhow for effective local exploitation of a patented invention and the possible sources from which to obtain it, the Report (pars. 251–53) arrives at the conclusion that the cooperation of the foreign patentee is generally needed for the successful transfer of patented technology. Analyzing the reasons why the foreign patentee and the government of the developing country respectively may or may not want local production, the Report arrives at the following policy implications:

> Obviously, if an underdeveloped country wants to have the foreign patentee's knowledge, management knowhow or capital, and cannot obtain it as readily anywhere else, it must meet his price and conditions if it wants to induce him to come.[16]

In an analysis of the conditions for and the effectiveness of the rules that compel the patentee to work his invention locally or license it, the Report starts with the fundamental observation that a foreign patentee, unwillingly induced to produce in a developing country by the threat of a compulsory license or revocation, will tend to limit his operation and his commitments to the minimum required to avoid the consequences of the loss of patent protection and to justify his investment. Therefore, the Report continues:

> The threat of compulsory licensing will be effective only to the extent that patented knowledge is the total external knowledge required for national operation or where the other necessary knowledge can be obtained in the open market.[17]

[15] Par. 248.

[16] par. 261. Implicitly recognizing that non-business risks may be important, and saying (*ibid.*) that "patent protection ... may or may not have a high place among ... profitable conditions and guarantees which he [the patentee] expects" the Report assumes that in many cases patent protection could be replaced by other forms of guarantees, adding, however, that "even where such alternatives exist, patent protection may well be a cheaper and more effective way of giving the foreign patentee what it needs to attract him." (*Ibid.*)

[17] par. 264; in order that the compulsory license be effective, it could have been added,

In addition to the strong bargaining position of the foreign patentee in the above-named respect, the Report points out that for several reasons, which are quite outside the limited field of patents, the foreign patentee will have a very strong position in negotiating license conditions.[18]

Whereas the text of the draft resolution, as originally introduced by Brazil, requested, among other things, "a study of the effects of royalties paid for the use of patents in the balance of payments of underdeveloped countries," the text as finally adopted replaced this by the much broader question of "a study of the effects of patents on the economy of underdeveloped countries."[19]

The importance of distinguishing between the two approaches is recognized by the Report. While the former inquiry would lead to an examination of the cost of importing technology, i.e., royalties, and increased costs of importing goods due to patent protection, (termed "invisible royalties") only an over-all examination of the impact of patents on the economy can also deal with the social costs to a developing country of not utilizing inventions though they could advantageously be put to use in the local economy. "In this respect [i.e. social costs of non-working]" the Report states (par. 275) that "those who criticize the patent system from the point of view of economic development of underdeveloped countries have sound grounds for believing and pointing out that a serious problem exists." This division between actually transferred and non-transferred technology characterizes the conclusions of the Report as far as the chapter now being treated is concerned:

> There is reason to believe that in spite of license fees and royalties the underdeveloped countries derive net benefits from the transfer of the patented knowledge. The more serious burden is not visible in specific transactions and balance of payments accounts. Rather, it must be deduced by economic analysis. It relates mainly to those cases where the patented technology is not in fact transferred.[20]

it is also necessary that there exist potential licensees "willing and able" [as the Report puts it in another passage (par. 254)] "to give the necessary commitments – in itself not always easy in underdeveloped countries."

[18] "His [the foreign patentee's] knowledge of the necessary non-patented technology, his management knowhow, his access to necessary components, capital or markets and the possession of his protected brand name will usually give the foreign patentee a very strong position in negotiating the conditions of the license even if his position as a patent holder should be weakened by the pressure of compulsory licensing ... It must be realized that the royalty paid will be only one dimension of the total bargain in which the foreign patentee might be involved."

[19] Operative paragraphs 1(b) and 1(a) of the two texts respectively.

[20] Par. 276; "This burden" the Report continues (*Ibid.*) "could be estimated only as a result of detailed studies of specific countries and industries. Such studies do not seem to have

b. Foreign Patents without transfer of technology[21]

Chapter V of the Report starts with the observation that frequently a developing country will not (yet) be interested in introducing a patented product or process for local exploitation, continuing (par. 277): "... where this is clearly the case, patent protection in underdeveloped countries will not usually be sought, since the benefits would not justify the efforts and the costs involved." – This statement implies that patent protection generally is sought in developing countries only when there are conditions for local exploitation. If this were true, then the often-made charge that patent-protection is used to protect export markets would be unfounded. – The policy implications for such a case can be, and have been, differently interpreted. On the one hand it can be argued, that if a country does not need the technology embodied in a certain patent, there can be no harm in granting the patent and collecting the fees. On the other hand, since the technology in question is not going to be used locally, the country has no interest in granting patent protection, the only effect of which will be to restrict the potential competition among foreign suppliers. Before examining the two arguments, the Report stresses (pars. 279–80) the difficulty in deciding whether or not a developing country will need a certain technology within a twenty-year period. Such a differentiation in the granting of patent protection would, according to the Report, mean that if patents were refused to the inventors and owners of such new processes, on the grounds that the process concerned would only be imported and not applied within the country, this might delay the subsequent introduction of the new technology when the economy had sufficiently matured.

This point is not convincing. If there is no local requirement for the technology embodied in a particular invention, it is difficult to see the point of granting a patent to guard against the possibility that it will be needed during its term of protection. Generally, it does not appear probable that a country could have an interest in starting local production later, considering that the products in question would have been produced and sold the world over for several years. For the exceptional case, patents of confirmation may be granted, as the Report also points out (par. 281).

Two possible advantages for developing countries from granting

been carried out and they would in any case involve a good deal of non-measurable judgement."

[21] Full title of Chapter V: *Foreign Patents without Transfer of Technology: Import of Patented Products and Processes* (pars. 277–95).

patent protection for inventions that are not locally worked are, according to the Report (par. 284), "the possible – though doubtful – encouragement of research and development in the supplying countries"[22] and the fact that "the import of today is the local manufacture of tomorrow." In support of the latter argument, it is stated (par. 284) that:

> Once the foreign patentee has been allowed to build up a patent protected export market, he may then be more easily induced to undertake or license local manufacture as the next step. Historically, the process of import-substitution has certainly played an important part in the modernization and diversification of products in underdeveloped countries.

It seems unrealistic to assume that a foreigner having built up an export market would voluntarily relinquish it for local production or the collecting of license fees. Furthermore, and though it is true that import-substitution is a feature of the process of economic development, the import-substitution that takes place probably occurs in spite of rather than with the support of the foreign exporters. In addition it is also questionable whether such import substitution will take place, in the case of patented technology, within the effective term of protection of a patented invention, which will often be in a field of advanced technology.

As for the disadvantages in granting patent protection for inventions that will become available merely through imported goods, the Report observes (par. 285) that if the negative conclusions concerning the lack of influence of patent protection in developing countries on research in developed countries is correct, "the argument against granting patent protection for imported products gains in force." The weight of this conclusion is tempered, however, by the following observations, that: (1) although there is an assumption that the absence of patent protection means lower prices, there is no empirical evidence; (2) free competition between potential suppliers might anyway be precluded due to patents and other market factors in the supplier countries; and (3) interchangeable patented products, where there is no "cashing-in" on the patent protection through an inflated price to the consumer,

[22] Cf. *supra*, pp. 129–31; the Report (par. 283) asserts that, on the one hand, frequently the markets of developing countries will be so marginal as not to influence research in the industrialized countries. "In such cases," it is observed within parentheses, "patents in underdeveloped countries will usually not be applied for." – To say that the prospect of patent protection in developing countries will not be an incentive to research in industrialized countries, is definitely not equivalent to saying that it will not pay a patentee to seek protection there.

probably figures very importantly in the imports of developing countries. – If, in general, monopoly control in a market leads to higher prices, there seems to be reason to believe that the same is true in the case of patent monopolies, since there would be no reason to submit to the costs of seeking patent protection, unless the prospective patentee expected to "cash in."

In the final part of Chapter V, the Report considers the *Combined Effects on the Balance of Payments*, that is, the net benefit to developing countries of protecting patents on imported goods.

The cost and benefits are difficult to measure quantitatively and to compare with each other. In particular the effect of higher prices specifically due to patent protection is almost impossible to disentangle from higher prices due to such factors as exclusive know how, trade secrets, restrictive practices, or the dominant market position of the supplier, all of which are intrinsically unrelated to the patent system.[23]

This is an important statement in the Report as its underlying idea appears as the essence of its final conclusions. In the present context, however, this argument seems besides the point. For the "higher price" is not higher in comparison with some standard of fair price which would rule if developing countries were not underdeveloped. The "higher price" can be higher only in relation to the price that would have ruled if there were no patent protection. – After all, the present concern is with the effect of patent protected imports in developing countries, not with the effect on these countries of being underdeveloped. – Following the above quotation, the authors of the Report continue: (par. 291):

Since patents are thus only one of the features which may bring about higher prices, the question arises whether measures directly affecting price levels or general anti-trust legislation are not an administratively more feasible technique of coping with the problem than legislation devoted specifically to the patent system.

As the Report does not elaborate on this point, though it mentions, in its conclusions (par. 307, 310), the possibility for both industrialized and developing countries to counter "misuses" of the patent system through antitrust legislation, it is difficult to see how higher prices due to patent protection on imported goods can be dealt with without changing the patent system. If the developing countries are recommend-

[23] Par. 291. Whether (or to what extent) these "other factors" are really "intrinsically unrelated" to the patent system is questionable. That "restrictive practices" may be closely related to patents has been shown previously, and such practices may be the principal reason for "the dominant market position of the supplier." Though "trade secrets" and "exclusive knowhow" are not patentable, their inclusion in patent licensing agreements may give them the same position as if they were patented.

ed to accept the principles of the present international patent system, it seems unlikely that they could influence patent practices in developed countries through antitrust laws or rules against restrictive business practices. Furthermore, higher prices that are simply due to patent protection do not amount to "misuses" of the patent system. When the traditional system of international protection is urged on developing countries, which can neither calculate benefits on the traditional basis of reciprocal protection in foreign markets, nor expect any benefits from importing patent protected goods, many arguments have been used to convince them that it is still in the best interest of developing countries to adhere to the established system. But the fact that higher prices due to patent protection is not the only burden of being underdeveloped is not a convincing argument for acquiescing in the present system.

The subject of legal equality vs. economic and technological inequality is raised once in the Report. Refuting the argument that developing countries, on the basis of reciprocity, ought also to issue patents for inventions, that are not being worked locally, the authors state (par. 295): "This argument is weak from the economic standpoint, particularly for countries in earlier stages of development. In their cases reciprocal treatment of patentees is a somewhat unreal concept, in the absence of technological equality", continuing:

> Generally speaking in trade relations among unequal partners, the principle of non-reciprocity is becoming more and more accepted. In the case of patents perhaps even more than in trade generally, formal reciprocity amounts to actual non-reciprocity.

These reflections, however, found no expression in the final conclusions of the Report. The much-quoted final paragraph (311) of these conclusions, reads:

> In the final analysis, the question of patents must be seen – and dealt with – in the broader context of facilitating the transfer of patented and unpatented technology to the developing countries, and enhancing the ability of the latter to adopt and use such foreign technology in the implementation of their development programmes.

The Report has been very favorably received. The manner in which it fails to make any definite conclusions as far as the patent system itself is concerned has certainly helped to satisfy different points of view. Every comment on the Report – from whatever point of view – has praised it as a highly objective document. The fact that the question of patents still remains with various United Nations bodies indicates, however, that the Report did not satisfy all points of view to an equal extent.[24] While the Report has analyzed the system of patent protection as such, it has generally been seen as an implicit endorsement of the Paris Convention in the sense that, in contrast to the Brazilian draft resolution, the Report exclusively emphasizes measures that can be taken on the national level as far as patent legislation is concerned. The greatest satisfaction conveyed by the Secretary General's Report to those uncompromisingly defending the existing international system was the answer given to the question concerning the advisability of holding an international conference. Referring to that question, the Report says that "no views on this question have been expressed by any Governments in their replies to the Secretary General's inquiry."[25]

4. Further treatment of the question of patents and the transfer of technology

a. The Committee for Industrial Development, March 1964

The first United Nations body to which the final Report was submitted was the Committee for Industrial Development at its Fourth Session.

[24] All commentators emphasize the conclusion that "the system is on balance likely to be beneficial provided effective safeguards against abuses exist." See, for instance, K. Lachmann, "The Role of Industrial Property in the Dissemination of Technical Information in the World Context – A United Nations View," *IDEA*, 9: 183, Conference No., 1965, who also says, "Here [concerning safeguards] the study suggests a number of possible approaches which have since found their way into the Model Law ...:

The need for compulsory licensing and working provisions which will assure that foreign inventions protected by patents are actually worked in the country itself, whenever it would be economically sound to do so ..." – Such provisions cannot "assure" anything; it may be noted that the Model Law contains no provision for the revocation of patents. See also, "The Role of Industrial Patents in the Transfer of Technology to Developing Countries," *Industrial Research News*, 1: 28, No. 1, 1966. The authors of *Patentschutz und Entwicklungsländer, Dokumente und Materialen, Max Planck-Institut für ausländisches und internationales Patent-, Urheber- und Wettbewerbsrecht, Vol. XV* (Köln: Carl Heymans Verlag, 1966), interpret the Report more extensively when commenting on Part I concerning national patent laws and provisions against abuses, they state that: "Ein vernuftig gestaltetes Patentsystem vermeidet daher per se die Gefahren, auf die Bolivien [co-sponsor] und Brasilien in dem von ihnen vorgelegten Entschliessungsentwurf hinweisen sollen glaubten."

[25] Report, Summary and Conclusions, p. 7; without discounting the successful influence of various pressure groups in turning the preoccupation of the Report away from the international patent system and towards national action (after the 1963 interim report, BIRPI enlisted the support of its members which through their criticism undoubtedly influenced the final Report. Cf. Hesser, *op. cit.*, p. 157.) – it may be observed that while most information necessary to produce the Report and in general to fulfill the requirements of G. A. Res. 1713 (XVI), was solicited through a questionnaire (Annex B of the Report), and while the letter of transmittal of the questionnaire enumerated all points contained in the G.A. Resolution when referring itself to that document, it specifically only asked for answers to the questionnaire. Since this questionnaire contained all questions raised by the G.A. Resolution *save* that one concerning the desirability of holding an international conference, it certainly conveyed the impression that this latter question had been dropped.

No discussion of substantial issues took place. In the Committee's report of this session, the Secretary General's conclusion, that the convening of a conference would not be useful, is noted.[26] It is also reported that delegations making statements with reference to the Report expressed their satisfaction with it and general agreement with its conclusions. One delegation, however, speaking for developing countries in more advanced stages of economic development, said that these countries could benefit more readily from the latest technological developments, provided access to this technology was not hampered by obsolete patent provisions. Other delegations, stressing the benefits of the patent system to developing countries, expressed the hope that "the abuses which might have crept into the system would soon disappear."[27]

b. The United Nations Conference on Trade and Development (UNCTAD), March-June, 1964

The question of *The Role of Patents in the Transfer of Technology to Developing Countries* was dealt with by the Third Committee (financing of trade and invisibles). The Yugoslavian delegate, in introducing a draft recommendation that would later be adopted with only a few changes, said among other things, that:

> The report [by the Secretary General] showed unequivocally that there were various obstacles which rendered transfer difficult ... Those obstacles could not be overcome through action by the developing countries only, particularly because the prevailing system of industrial property had, to a certain extent, unfavorable effects in that it placed the holders of exclusive rights in a strong position which was further enhanced by the fact that unpatented technology could as a rule only be used in conjunction with patented technology.[28]

In the ensuing debate, the draft recommendation was in general favorably received, though some reservations were made concerning its third paragraph, which called for competent international bodies

[26] *The Role of Patents in the Transfer of Technology*, pars. 59–64, of Doc. E/C.5/65.

[27] How can, it may be asked, abuses due to or at least aggraved by unequal economic and technological power be expected to "disappear" if the solution to the problems facing developing countries are left completely within the bounds of the traditional patent system and its established organization?

[28] Doc. E/Conf. 46/C.3/S.R.44, p. 2. [co-sponsors were Ethiopia, Indonesia, the U.A.R., and (after revision) Pakistan and Rumania.] A note submitted by BIRPI to the conference – Doc. E/Conf. 46/141 – put a different emphasis on the Report. Since, according to BIRPI, from the Report it would seem to follow that the problems of developing countries in connection with patents are mainly problems to be solved by "appropriate legislative and administrative measures" on the national level, probably the best practical measure of the conference would be to invite BIRPI to continue its technical assistance to developing countries. (pars. 12–13).

to explore the possibilities for adopting legislation concerning the transfer of technology.[29] The third paragraph of the revised draft resolution may warrant special attention:

Competent international bodies, including the United Nations bodies and the Bureau of the International Union for the Protection of Industrial Property, should explore possibilities for adaptation of legislation concerning the transfer of technology to developing contries including the possibility of concluding appropriate international agreements in this field.[30]

This revised text was adopted in the Third Committee by eighty-three votes to none and four abstentions and later unanimously by the Conference.[31]

c. The Economic and Social Council, Thirty-seventh Session, July 1964

One of the agenda items was the *Role of Patents in the Transfer of Technology to Underdeveloped Countries*. In the discussions of Committee VI differences of interpretation of, or emphasis on, the problems and their solutions, especially as they appear in the Report, were clearly noticeable. While delegates of the developed countries emphasized the conclusion of the Report, that the calling of an international conference would not be helpful and stressed the opinion of the appropriateness of national legislative administrative measures to be taken by the developing countries, representatives of the latter took the position that international measures were needed.

The Secretariat, introducing the question and after referring to the negative conclusions of the Secretary General's Report concerning the holding of an international conference, said:

[29] The United Kingdom representative, for instance, said that "he was sure that the sponsors of the draft recommendation did not wish to imply any disagreement with that conclusion [of the Report concerning an international conference] by calling for re-negotiation of existing conventions." Doc. E/Conf. 46/C.3/SR.49, p. 9; the Director of BIRPI welcoming the measures proposed in the draft recommendation "wondered whether those measures could not be linked up more closely with the efforts of the International Union, which was the only intergovernmental organization specializing in that field." Doc. E/Conf. 46/C.3/SR.44 p. 5.

[30] Doc. E/Conf. 46/141. Vol. I, Part 3, Annex A.IV.26.

[31] The report of the Third Committee says, concerning paragraph three, that the sponsors of the revised draft resolution "felt that a re-negociation agreements on protection of industrial property might be desirable in the future," whereas some representatives of developed countries with market economies "could only accept the draft recommendations on the understanding that the 'possibility of concluding appropriate international agreements in this field' did not imply that the existing patent agreements should be renegociated." Doc. E/Conf. 46/141, Vol. I, Annex F, Report of III Committee, par. 354. – Since "existing patent agreements" i.e., mainly the Paris Convention, appear for all practical purposes perpetual under present circumstances, the limit to which the developed countries were prepared to go and the difference in interpretation of the UN Report, are well illustrated.

It [the Report] also expressed the view that it would not be helpful for the Secretariat to undertake further studies of the patent system or of the harmful effects which that system might have on the balance of payments of under-developed countries.[32]

Such an interpretation of the conclusions of the Report contrasted with those given by several developing countries and did not, in such a definite form at least, appear in the Report. When a draft resolution was proposed afterwards,[33] heavily stressing the role of BIRPI and requesting a close collaboration between it and the United Nations, with the understanding that the essential solution for the developing countries was to adopt "appropriate" legislation, and that BIRPI was best suited to assist them in that task, objections were raised by several developing countries. The Chilean delegate stated, that the effects of patents on the economy had not yet been established, and that it was necessary to find out the extent to which the present system might be harmful to developing countries. Noting that the Report had not reached any definite conclusions in these respects, the same delegate characterized the Report as "an important first step in a study of these problems."[34]

The original draft resolution was later withdrawn in favor of one submitted by a number of developing countries.[35] The first operative paragraph of that text called on the Secretary General, in cooperation with "competent international bodies," to explore possibilities for adapting legislation regulating the transfer of technology and providing for additional facilities for the transfer of technical documentation and knowhow. It resembled paragraphs three and four of the UNCTAD Recommendation, with the exception that "the possibility of concluding appropriate international agreements" was not mentioned. That possibility was however indirectly referred to in operative paragraph three, providing for the transmission of the Report to the General Assembly "for appropriate action in the light of the ... [UNCTAD Recommendation]."[36] The Resolution was adopted without dissent.[37]

[32] *Ibid.*, p. 4.

[33] Doc. E/AC.6/L.295; this draft was sponsored by the United Kingdom and Northern Ireland. After a revision, France became a co-sponsor.

[34] Doc. E/AC.6/SR.343, p. 4.

[35] Doc. E/AC.6/L.296. The sponsors were: Algeria, Chile, Czechoslovakia, Ecuador, India, Indonesia, Iraq, Mexico, U.A.R., Tanzania, and Yugoslavia.

[36] The delegates of France and Great Britain repeated their statements from the UNCTAD to the effect that the adoption of the UNCTAD Recommendation did not signify an intention to renegotiate existing legislation. Doc. E/AC.6/SR.344, pp. 4–5, 7. Cf. *supra*. n. 29.

[37] ECOSOC Res. 1013(XXXVII), July 22, 1964.

The submitting of the Secretary General's Report, the debates in the UNCTAD and ECOSOC and the respective texts voted at these meetings may be seen as the first stage in the evolution of the subject of patents and developing countries within the United Nations.[38] In the opinion of many developed countries, questions directly related to patents were thereafter to be handled essentially by BIRPI, while various United Nations bodies were to attend to the problems of overall assistance in the transfer of technology to developing countries. Although efforts to include a direct recommendation for the developing countries to join the Paris Union in the texts voted by UNCTAD and ECOSOC were unsuccessful, the position of the Paris Union had undoubtedly been strengthened since the "Brazilian Resolution" in early 1962. With the support of the industrialized countries, BIRPI had managed to establish the principle of cooperation between the United Nations and itself and to delete all negative references to the international patent system in various resolutions and recommendations. Thus the door was open to BIRPI for the continued exclusive control of the evolution of international patent relations.[39] That this was not to the liking of many developing countries had been shown at the UNCTAD and ECOSOC debates and would again become apparent at the Twentieth Session of the General Assembly.

d. The United Nations General Assembly, Twentieth Session, October-December, 1965

As in 1961, Brazil introduced a draft resolution *The Role of Patents in the Transfer of Technology to Developing Countries.*[40] This new initiative by Brazil demonstrates the difference of views between those who considered that the Report had settled the question of the transfer of technology, as far as patents are concerned, by recommending the

[38] Though the ECOSOC Resolution transmitted the Report "for appropriate action" to the Nineteenth Session of the General Assembly (1964), it was only brought up the following year. Meanwhile, the Advisory Committee on the Application of Science and Technology to Development considered the Report, at its Fourth Session (1965) and passed a resolution asking for an examination of "existing and possible measures for reducing the cost to developing countries of securing access to foreign patented and unpatented industrial technology." *Industrial Research News*, 1: 32, No. 1, 1966.

[39] Hesser, *op. cit.*, p. 157, commenting upon the efforts of BIRPI to influence the evolution of the questions raised by the "Brazilian Resolution" and finding that (after the UNCTAD and ECOSOC meetings) "the contemplated attack on the Paris Union had practically come to nothing," concluded that "there is reason to suppose that the United Nations will leave it to BIRPI to realize the desiderata made [in the ECOSOC Resolution]." [translated from Swedish].

[40] Doc. A/C.2/L.824, November 26, 1965. Co-sponsors were Austria, the Dominican Republic, Mexico and Peru.

developing countries to take legal and administrative measures on the national level, and those who considered the Report only as an initial and tentative study to be followed up by more detailed analysis. This latter point of view was put forward by the Yugoslavian delegate, who said that rather than studying the present patent system as such it was a question of analyzing its impact on the economy of developing countries. Referring to the Report and its emphasis on the difficulties facing developing countries as a result of their weak financial and technological situation, this delegate also said that:

> The time had therefore come to make a serious analysis of the prevailing patent system and to tackle more resolutely the study and establishment of an international machinery to improve the transfer of technology, chiefly for the benefit of the developing countries.[41]

The Brazilian resolution was, with minor changes, adopted unanimously by the General Assembly.[42] The most interesting part of that text is one of its preambular paragraphs which reads: "Considering that the existing international agreements and practices may not deal adequately with the problems arising in connection with the transfer of technological knowhow," and the part of operative paragraph three requesting the Secretary General to continue his studies of "the adequacy of existing national and international practices for the transfer of patented and unpatented technology to developing countries."

Despite the limited number of reservations voiced against the text of the resolution,[43] it must be assumed that differences of emphasis and interpretation remain, and that most industrialized countries will oppose any change in the existing international patent system as long as BIRPI retains exclusive control over international patent relations.

e. Further developments within the Economic and Social Council

At the Forty-second Session of ECOSOC[44] the Secretary-General, in

[41] General Assembly, Official Records, Twentieth Session, Second Committee, 999th Meeting, par. 25.

[42] General Assembly Resolution 2091(XX), December 20, 1965.

[43] The United States Delegate repeated what he, and other Delegates had said at earlier occasions to the effect that most patents being in private hands, there was little the Government could do to encourage direct transfer. In connection with operative par. 3, the United States Delegate doubted "whether, apart from information on the possibility of obtaining access to patents, the Secretary General could do much to secure the transfer to developing countries of privately- owned patented technology." *Ibid.*, par. 261; The French Delegate recalled that when the UNCTAD (Geneva, 1964) Recommendation A.IV.26 had been voted on "France had abstained on the ground that international agreements on that subject would be undesirable" adding that "his delegation's views on that subject had not changed." General Assembly, Official Records, Twentieth Session, Second Committee, 1000th Meeting, par. 23.

[44] March, 1967.

response to G. A. Res. 2091 (XX),[45] submitted a progress report: "Application of Science and Technology to Development."[46] The corresponding part of the above-mentioned resolution concerned an evaluation of the actual experience of developing countries regarding the effectiveness and cost of foreign patented and non-patented technology. Two specific, already initiated measures, were reported:

(1) the preparation of studies showing how technology has been transferred, within certain industries, from industrialized countries to a limited number of the more advanced of the developing countries; and

(2) studies undertaken parallel with those mentioned under (1) above, concerned specifically with the costs involved in the transfer of technology to developing countries. To provide material for this second series of studies the Secretary-General had circulated a questionnaire to all Member States[47] "to secure comprehensive information on all relevant measures and arrangements in effects or contemplated to ease the cost-burden of technological transfer to developing countries."

Two observations may be made concerning the above-mentioned studies, of which the second series is of more particular interest for the subject of the present study.

Though the text of the G. A. Res. 2091 (XX), not only mentioned the high costs of technology transfers to developing countries but also the adequacy of national and international agreements and practices in connection with such transfers[48], the studies mentioned limit themselves to what can be done to alleviate the costs to developing countries under present international agreements.[49] As a direct result of such a

[45] *Supra*, p. 188 and n. 42.

[46] Doc. E/4319, March 27, 1967.

[47] For the text of the questionnaire, see Doc. E/4319, Annex II.

[48] Cf. Preambule and operative par. 3 of G. A. Res. 2091(XX).

[49] The progress report of the Secretary General mentions, as examples of cost-reducing measures various forms of financial support for either the company transferring technology or that recieving it, measures that could be initiated by either "donor" country, "recipient" country, or by an international organization. (par. 21, E/4319).

A separate sector of inquiry to be included in the studies initiated by the Secretary-General, should be mentioned. This concerns inventions either already in the public domain or those having been made by public or non-profit organizations, or with the support of such bodies (*Ibid.*) The conclusion of international agreements for the dissemination of such technology on less onerous terms than those offered under the present international patent system has long been suggested by several authors. Cf. *supra*, p. 170.

One advantage from any such agreement would be to weaken the objection against changes in existing arrangements often raised by industrialized countries to the effect that patented inventions being private property, there is little a government can do to affect their limited inquiry, the only costs that may be treated by these studies are such arising from an actual transfer of technology, while the part of technology transfers under the present system termed "invisible royalties" will not be taken into account.[50]

At the Twenty-second Session of the General Assembly,[51] where the report of the Forty-second Session of ECOSOC was treated, no particular action was taken with regard to this agenda item.

At the Forty-fourth Session of ECOSOC[52] one resolution was passed at its 1529th plenary meeting, which is of particular interest for the present study. This resolution, "Transfer of Technology,"[53] dealt with the draft resolution presented at the second United Nations Conference on Trade and Development (New Dehli, February-March, 1968) which was passed on by the latter's plenary session for further consideration by the Trade and Development Board at its Seventh Session, due in August, 1968.[54]

The resolution passed by the Council notes that the requested new organ had met opposition on the grounds that it would be doing parallel work with already existing organs and organizations. The Council resolution, therefore, requests the U.N. Secretary-General to prepare a study for submission to the Forth-fifth Session of the Council, showing to what extent the area of work foreseen for the suggested new organ, by the UNCTAD draft resolution, was already being carried out by existing organizations.

At the Forty-fifth Session of ECOSOC[55] (July-November, 1968, Geneva) the report requested of the Secretary-General at its previous Session [Res. 1312 (XLIV)] was submitted.[56] It contains extracts from the terms of references and work programs of various United Nations bodies concerned with the transfer of technology, including an annex describing the activities of BIRPI. No recommendation was given whether or not the new organ requested in the UNCTAD draft resolution was desirable.

transfer. Cf. *supra*, p. 188, n. 43. This same objection would again be raised at the New Dehli Conference (UNCTAD II) by representatives of "developed market economy countries" Cf. Doc. TD/81/Add. 1, par. 4.

[50] The term "invisible royalties" was coined by the Secretary-General in his report "The Role of Patents in the Transfer of Technology to Developing Countries" to design the cost-increase of imports due to patent protection. Cf. *supra*, p. 178ff.

[51] September–December, 1967.

[52] May, 1968.

[53] Res. 1312(XLIV), May 31, 1968.

[54] Doc. TD/II/W.G.1/L.4/Rev. 1; see further below.

[55] July–November; 1968.

[56] Doc. E/4552, July 18, 1968.

At its 1560th plenary meeting, the Council passed a resolution, "Arrangements for the transfer of operative technology to developing countries,"[57] requesting the United Nations Secretary-General, in consultation with the UNCTAD Secretary-General and appropriate organizations within and outside the United Nations, to submit a report to the Forty-sixth Session of the Council, "outlining the means by which the scope of present and contemplated activities [concerning the transfer of technology to developing countries] could be more clearly defined, strengthened and coordinated."

This resolution also requested the Trade and Development Board to take into account the views of the Council, "including the desirability of defering any final action, until it has had an opportunity to consider the further report and the comments made thereon by the Council at its Forty-sixth Session."

At the Twenty-third Session of the General Assembly,[58] where the report of the Forty-forth Session of ECOSOC was treated, no action was taken with regard to item 6 on the Council's agenda.

f. *United Nations Conference on Trade and Development (as a permanent organ of the General Assembly).*

Since a permanent organ of the General Assembly was set up on the basis of the first United Nations Conference on Trade and Development, the question of patents in connection with transfer of technology to developing countries, has remained with the Committee concerned with the financing of trade and invisibles. Between periodic conferences – the second to take place in New Delhi, February-March, 1968 – the committees prepare for the subsequent conference, reporting to the Trade and Development Board, a permanent organ of the Conference.

At the Fourth Session of the Trade and Development Board (July, 1966) a review of the implementation of the recommendations of the Conference (UNCTAD I) was made. After reviewing Rec. A. IV. 26, it was said with regard to patent legislation:

> Legislation on inventions has received much international attention in recent years, and model laws on patents and knowhow have been drafted for the developing countries. ... But the patent laws [of developed countries] often date back to the nineteenth century and need to be adapted to the requirements of modern technology and to take account of increasing governmental responsibility for national economic policy, especially in the initial stages of development. Thus,

[57] Res. 1361(XLV), August 2, 1968.
[58] September–December; 1968.

while important efforts are being made for the promotion of patent-legislation in developing countries, little attention seems to have been given to the need for corresponding adjustments in industrialized countries.[59]

The Trade and Development Board, at its Fifth Session (July, 1967) included the question of transfer of technology under item IX of the provisional agenda,[60] for the New Delhi Conference.

g. The Second United Nations Conference on Trade and Development (UNCTAD II) and further developments within the Trade and Development Board.

In preparation for the Second United Nations Conference on Trade and Development, a large number of developing countries met in Algiers in the automn of 1967 to establish unified positions on many of the topics appearing on the provisional agenda for the New Dehli Conference. The outcome of this meeting was a "position paper" known as the "Charter of Algiers."[61]

This document contains two paragraphs relating to agenda item IX, as far as the transfer of technology is concerned. The first paragraph illustrates the continued concern of developing countries for the adequacy of the international patent system, with emphasis on the necessity for these countries being able to export products made with acquired technology:

The developed countries should encourage the transfer of knowledge and technology to developing countries by permitting the use of industrial patents on the best possible terms which will enable products manufactured in developing countries to compete effectively in world markes;[62]

[59] Doc. TD/B/Add. 2, July 20, 1966, par. 91 (partly); that despite the "important efforts" that have been made to promote patent-legislation in developing countries (including the Model Law on Inventions for Developing Countries by BIRPI) all countries are not satisfied, may be seen from a suggestion made at the meeting of the Committee on Trade and Invisibles (April, 1967), that the Economic and Social Council "should initiate the preparation of 'basic texts' on various economic subjects, including industrial property." *I.P.*, 7: 53, February, 1968.

[60] P. Loby, "Les pays riches ont fait un premier pas en faveur du commerce international des pays en voie de développement," *Le Monde Diplomatique*, October, 1967, p. 14, commenting upon the Fifth Session of the Trade and Development Board, says on the provisional agenda: "Cet ordre du jour est sans surprise, si ce n'est l'inclusion *in extremis*, à la demande des pays en voie de développement, du 'transfer des techniques, y compris les tours de main et les brevets' ... L'inscription de cette question à l'ordre du jour répond au désir du secrétaire général [UNCTAD] ... de combattre la disparité technologique croissante entre le monde industrialisé et le 'tiers monde'. Elle s'est heurtée aux réserves des pays développées, qui craignent que l'activité de la [UNCTAD] ... ne doublonne [sic], dans ce domaine, avec celle d'autres organismes internationaux dépendant de l'O.N.U."

[61] Doc. A/C.2/237; this text is also included as an annex in Vol. I of the Official Records of the Second United Nations Conference on Trade and Development.

[62] *Ibid.*, Part II, F. 1, (a).

The second paragraph mentioned above is particularly interesting for the importance it pays to the ellimination of restrictive business practices connected with the transfer of industrial property. Such practices, previously referred to in this study as "Indirect Effects of the International Patent System,"[63] had until then received little attention in debates and in the several recommendations and resolutions passed by United Nations bodies. The treatment of this topic at the subsequent Conference in New Delhi was certainly promted by the following passage in the Charter of Algiers:

They [the developed countries] should also promote the ellimination of restrictive practices, relating to market distribution and price-fixing, which are imposed by enterprises in developed countries in granting licenses for the use of patents and trademarks in developing countries;[64]

In preparation for the New Delhi Conference, the UNCTAD Secretariat requested a study by an independant research unit, in connection with item IX of the provisional agenda, entitled "Trends and Problems in World Trade and Development." The research unit was asked to review the methods of transferring technology and to try and access the costs to the developing countries. Though the second part of this request appeared very difficult to meet for lack of statistics, the study nevertheless produced a very interesting document.[65]

The major part of the study is taken up by the successful experience of Japan in applying foreign technology. While briefly enumerating a number of different (and complementary) ways in which technology can be transferred, the study concerns itself mainly with the transfer of technology through licensing, patent and knowhow agreements.

If one should single out the two most important points in Japanese experience, made in this study, with relevancy for developing countries today, they are these: the preponderant role played by the government both as an initiator of transfer agreements in the early stages of development and as a permanent "watch-dog" over the compatability of specific transfer agreements with the economic development policy of the country; and secondly, the necessity for the development of indigenous technological research activities, the necessity of which follows from the finding that foreign firms are more interested in trans-

[63] *Supra*, pp. 153–70.

[64] Part II, F. 1 (b) of Doc. A/C. 2/237 (supra, n. 61).

[65] "Trends and Problems in World Trade and Development" Study prepared by C. H. G. Oldham, C. Freeman and E. Turkcan, Science Policy research Unit of the University of Sussex, United Kingdom, Doc. TD/28/Supp. 1, November 10, 1967, 26 p.

ferring parts of their technology if the domestic firms have something to offer in exchange.[66]

Without impairing the value of this document, it may be observed, that the direct experience of Japan must be of less value to all but the very large developing countries, as resourceful as Japan, and thus, offering equally interesting markets for foreign industries.[67]

In an opening speech at the New Delhi Conference, the United Nations Under-Secretary General for Economic and Social Affairs, Mr. Ph. de Seynes, treated the whole spectrum of international technology transfers, reviewing some past developments and outlining desirable future directions of international economic relations to increase the transfer of technology to developing countries.[68]

With special reference to the role of patents and the Secretary-General's report on that subject, Mr. de Seynes said:

The patent system can be of great benefit in the industrialization of the less developed countries, provided that they are able to protect themselves against the abuses often inherent in the monopoly position created by the patent. Many countries simply do not have the knowhow or personnel to examine applications with these criteria in view. Consequently many patents are issued without justification and impose unfair restrictions on imports and production.[69]

Working Group I, alloted among other items that of transfer of technology, spent only two sessions on that question, for lack of time.[70] A draft resolution "Transfer of Technology, Including Knowhow and Patents" was submitted by four developing countries.[71]

The principal novelty in this draft resolution was the suggestion that the Trade and Development Board should consider establishing a Committee on Science and Technology to review the work so far done by various United Nations bodies, and present proposals for unified action.[72]

[66] *Ibid.*, par. 65.

[67] For some observations on Japanese experience, *infra*, pp. 238–39.

[68] Doc. TD/misc. 41, February 6, 1968, 12 p.

[69] *Ibid.*, p. 5. Though at first sight this statement appears to say merely that an insufficiency of administrative resources within local patent offices may hinder developing countries from avoiding abuses of the patent system, its last sentence, mentioning unjustified patent grants that impose restrictions on imports and production, could be interpreted to mean that only patents leading to local production should, in principle, be seen as justified from the point of view of developing countries.

[70] For the report of Working Group I on this question, see Chapter II of TD/81/Add. 1, March 17, 1968.

[71] Doc. TD/II/W.G.I/L.4/Rev. 1, submitted by Brazil, Chile, India, and Pakistan (also in United Nations Conference on Trade and Development, Second Session, Proceedings, Vol. I – Report and Annexes, p. 388).

[72] The draft resolution contained a large number of suggestions for the work of the pro-

For lack of time to consider the draft resolution, its text was attached to the Group's report to the plenary meeting of the Conference "for such action as may be deemed appropriate."

In the plenary session of the Conference, the same objection against this draft resolution were made by several industrialized countries, as had already been made during the deliberations of Working Group I. Those who objected to establishing the committee, proposed in the draft resolution, maintained that such an organ would merely involve a doubling of functions with already existing organs and lead to unnecessary expenses and spread even thinner the small group of experts on the subjects involved.

Since no agreement on the wording of the draft resolution could be reached, it was finally decided merely to refer the text of the draft resolution to the Seventh Session of the Trade and Development Board, due in September, 1968.[73]

The Second Committee of the New Delhi Conference, dealing with questions concerning manufactured and semi-manufactured exports of developing countries, had before it a draft resolution, submitted by Brazil, regarding the effects of restrictive business practices on the export potential of developing countries.[74] Considering that export-hindering restrictive business practices are all the more harmful to developing countries, "since they rely to a large extent on the transfer of patents, knowhow and capital from enterprises of developed countries"[75] and referring to the previously quoted paragraph of the Charter of Algiers concerning restrictive business practices,[76] the draft resolution requested the UNCTAD Secretariat to prepare a study on restrictive business practices. The requested study should also suggest means to establish an international machinery to deal with such practices. The text finally recommends the (UNCTAD) Committee on

posed committee, among which may be noted the recommendation that the committee "study the effects of existing international legislation for the protection of industrial property on the economic development of developing countries"; [I(v)] and that the Committee review the implementation of the recommendations to developed countries to encourage patentees "to refrain from imposing in the transfer agreements any undue restrictions on the exports by the developing countries of the resultant products"; [II.A(iii)] and "to refrain from imposing such conditions on the supply of plant and machinery and on the transfer of technical processes as would retard the development of indigenous manufacture and technology"; [II.A(iv)] It may also be observed that the draft recommendation in its first preambular paragraph opened by "*reaffirming* the recommendations contained in annex A.IV.26 to the Final Act adopted at its first session," (Cf. *supra*, pp. 184–85).

[73] See *infra*, p. 196.

[74] Doc. TD/II/C.2/L.7, March 9, 1968.

[75] Preambular, par. 3.

[76] *Supra*, p. 193.

Manufactures at its Third Session, at which the requested report should be submitted, to give special consideration to actions that could be taken to limit and abolish restrictive business practices as they affect the exports of developing countries.

As had been the case with the previously mentioned draft resolution, this one was also referred to the Trade and Development Board for further action, without a final vote by the Conference.

The Trade and Development Board, at its Seventh Session[76a] treated the draft resolution referred to it by the plenary meeting of the New Delhi Conference, concerning "Transfer of Technology, Including Knowhow and Patents."[77]

The suggestion contained therein, to set up an intergovernmental committee to examine the over-all question of the transfer of technology, met the same objections from the developed countries as at the Conference and the (subsequent) Forty-fifth Session of the ECOSOC.[78] The basic objection, voiced by many of these countries, was that the work of the proposed committee was already being carried out by various organs and organizations.

A draft resolution, presented by some developed countries, wanted to defer any action by the Board until after the report of the United Nations Secretary-General, requested at the Forty-fifth Session of ECOSOC and to be presented at the Forty-sixth Session of the Council[79], could be considered by the Board. This draft was rejected, after all developed countries had voted for it (18), all developing countries against it (22), while the socialist countries abstained (6).

Instead, a draft resolution, submitted by the developing countries, was passed by the Board[80] with the votes devided on the same lines as above, asking the UNCTAD Secretary-General, when cooperating with the United Nations Secretary-General in making the report requested by the Forty-fifth session of ECOSOC, that:

> He [UNCTAD Secretary-General] should take into consideration the fact that the existing institutional arrangements are not adapted in this respect [to promote the economic development of developing countries] to the requirements of the developing countries and to emphasize the role that UNCTAD might play in the field of transfer of technology in accordance with the objectives of the organization.

[76a] September 1968.
[77] *Supra*, p. 194.
[78] *Supra* 195 and 190 respectively.
[79] *Supra*, p. 191.
[80] Res. 48(VII), September 21, 1968.

In its last paragraph this resolution said that final action should be taken by the Board at its session following the Forty-sixth Session of the ECOSOC.

h. United Nations Industrial Development Organization (UNIDO)

One of the tasks of this organ, established in late 1966, will lie in:

> Proposing, in cooperation with the international bodies or intergovernmental regional organizations concerned with industrial property, measures for the improvement of the international system of industrial property, with a view to accelerating the transfer of technical knowhow to developing countries and to strengthening the role of patents consistent with national interests as an incentive to industrial innovations.[81]

Before the text of the functions of UNIDO was adopted, and after initial strong disinclination from the General Assembly Committee, an amendment was adopted – fifty votes to nine with forty abstentions – to insert the words "in cooperation with the international bodies or intergovernmental regional organizations concerned with industrial property."[82]

At its First Session (April, 1967) no special action was taken with regard to transfer of technology to developing countries. At an "International Symposium on Industrial Development" arranged by UNIDO (Athens, December, 1967) one recommendation was adopted calling upon UNIDO, in collaboration with other national and international organizations, to study present industrial property arrangements, having regard to the special situations and problems of the developing countries.[83] At the Second Session of the Industrial Development Board (May, 1968), the Board approved the UNIDO work program for 1968–69, including "assistance to developing countries in the field of patents" with the "cooperation and participation of the United Nations Department of Economic and Social Affairs, of BIRPI, and of other interested agencies."[84]

[81] Par. 2(a)(x) of the regulation of the functions of UNIDO, Doc.: G.A. Res. 2152 (XXI) November 17, 1966.

[82] Cf. doc.: A/C.2/L.868; thus whatever may come out of this new United Nations organ, it will be done in cooperation with BIRPI and other interested international organizations. "This amendment ... should put it beyond doubt that BIRPI will be asked to cooperate on any implementation of this paragraph." – "Cooperation between the United Nations and BIRPI in 1966," *I.P.*, 6: 46–48, February, 1967, p. 47.

[83] ID/11, United Nations; New York, 1969, par. 122.

[84] ID/B/41, May, 1968.

B. THE ACTIVITIES OF BIRPI

Although it is sometimes claimed that the Paris Union and its Secretariat have always been preoccupied with the particular interests of developing countries, the sudden intensification during the last few years of activities designed to assist these countries in matters of patent legislation, and to interest them in joining the Paris Union, certainly indicate a change of attitude. Though signs of a mounting conflict of interests between industrialized and developing countries were visible during the Lisbon Conference, it was only the appearance of the Brazilian initiative in late 1961 that stimulated the present activities of BIRPI for the benefit of developing countries.[85]

The preoccupations of BIRPI have taken two directions. One has been to influence the evolution of the question of patent rights within the various United Nations bodies, acting both directly and through its members. Its other field of activity has consisted in initiating various projects of assistance for the benefit of developing countries. These latter activities have served to give added weight to BIRPI's contention that, being the only intergovernmental organization specialized in the field of patents, it ought to be recognized as well qualified to lead the evolution also in the case of developing countries.[86]

1. BIRPI's influence on the work of various United Nations bodies

The idea behind the Brazilian action was apparently that the United Nations should study the question of patents of particular interest to developing countries, whereafter an international conference should be convened under its auspices, as had been the case under somewhat similar circumstances in the field of international copyright protection. As was shown above, the industrialized countries managed, not only to delete all negative references to the international patent system

[85] Hesser, *op. cit.*, p. 155. In the words of the Director of BIRPI: "Whatever the merits of this resolution and wherever it may lead to, it had at least the effect of causing action in the Paris Union. This Bureau wholly realizes that there are other intergovernmental organizations which may deal with matters of international cooperation in the field of industrial property, and that countries outside our Union may also have thoughts about the way in which industrial property should or should not be protected." Doc. I.A.P.I.P. Annual Report 1963: II, p. 16.

[86] A third preoccupation within the Paris Union and its Secretariat during the last decade, and one which may have important repercussions on the position of developing countries within the international patent cooperation, has been the question of reorganization. These plans and their recently decided implementation will be discussed in Chapter VI, Cf. *infra*, pp. 258–65.

in the final text of the General Assembly Resolution but also, to insert by a majority of one vote, a clause requesting the Secretary General to carry out the study in consultation with BIRPI.

In conformity with the terms of the General Assembly Resolution [1713 (XVI)] underlying the Report, the Secretary General solicited the cooperation of BIRPI, among other organizations. The extent to which BIRPI assisted the Secretary General is not known.[87] It may be deduced, however, from the difference in the reception of the interim report and the Final Report, that the support lent by BIRPI to the Report increased considerably between the two publications.[88]

At the First United Nations Conference on Trade and Development in 1964, BIRPI submitted a note[89], and its Director made one intervention in Committee III.[90] Both these statements, as well as a similarly worded intervention made by BIRPI at the ECOSOC session in July 1964,[91] suggested that the close cooperation between BIRPI and the United Nations should be reaffirmed since, according to the Report, the problems of developing countries were mainly such that they could be solved by national legislation. Though in the respective recommendation and resolution passed on these two occasions, as well as in the General Assembly Resolution 2091 (XX) of December, 1965, the cooperation between the United Nations and BIRPI was reaffirmed, all three texts raise the possibility of adapting existing rules and practices concerning the transfer of industrial technology. BIRPI so far has shown little inclination to assist in such a project.

Although it might have been premature to conclude, as was done by some writers in 1964, that BIRPI from then on would direct the further evolution of the question – its Director at several occasions

[87] In the introduction of the Report, it is merely mentioned that BIRPI was asked to prepare the survey of national patent legislation which appears in Annex D; according to a BIRPI representative, "it had assisted the United Nations Secretariat in preparing the report .... In particular the synoptic table [Annex D] ... was based on the analysis of national patent legislation carried out by the Bureau ..." Doc. E/AC.6/SR.341, p. 5; a reference to BIRPI's part in the making of the Report is contained in a speech by the chairman of the I.C.C. *Commission on the International Protection of Industrial Property Rights*, where, after drawing particular attention to the value of the Report and the satisfactory nature of its conclusions, tribute is paid to BIRPI and its Director as well as to a United Nations expert, "for their part in the drafting of this remarkable report." Doc. ICC. 450/254, April 30, 1964, p. 2; the fact that the written material underlying the Report had been submitted, almost in full, already for the interim report (cf. *supra*, n. 12) suggests the influence of additional outside opinions on the drafting of the Final Report.

[88] See also Hesser, *op. cit.*, p. 157.

[89] Doc. E/Conf. 46/141, April 10, 1964.

[90] Doc. E/Conf.46/C.3/SR.44, pp. 3–5.

[91] Doc. E/A.C.6/SR.341, pp. 5–6.

stressed his opinion that "the battle had not finally been won"[92] – it is nevertheless true that the Paris Union Secretariat had managed in a few years time to regain much of the initiative and control over the further evolution of the questions raised by the "Brazilian resolution" in 1961. It seems plausible to believe that, as long as there is no appearent challenge to the position of the Paris Union, BIRPI will be more interested in converting the developing countries to the existing system of international patent protection than in the adaptation of its rules to the needs of these countries.

2. *BIRPI's activities for the benefit of developing countries*

In its various activities designed to assist developing countries, BIRPI has taken three lines of action: it has initiated apprenticeship schemes for the benefit of patent officials of developing countries; it has sponsored several regional seminars on industrial property; and it has invited representatives of developing countries to participate in the work of expert committees dealing with industrial property problems of special concern to these countries.[93] Of the first field of activity, trainee schemes, no more will be said. As for the second – regional seminars – the published material concerning them is limited to general and uncontroversial reports and the texts of various resolutions voted at each occasion. Three such regional seminars have been held: an African seminar in 1963,[94] a Latin American seminar in 1964,[95] and an Asian seminar in 1966.[96]

Within the third field of activity, two events concerning patents have so far taken place. In 1963, a *Committee of Experts* was convened by BIRPI to study industrial property problems of less developed countries. One result of this conference was the calling of another *Committee of Experts* in 1964 to work out a Model Law for developing countries on patents for inventions.

[92] Doc. I.C.C. 450/254, April 30, 1964, p. 2; for the same observation, see Doc. I.C.C. 450/260, September 24, 1964, p. 4.

[93] A recent BIRPI project designed to simplify the patenting of any given invention in a number of countries, may bring benefits also to developing countries, *which are Members of the Paris Union*. This is the BIRPI *Plan for a Patent Cooperation Treaty* (PCT). A first draft was published in September, 1967, and a second one in July, 1968. The latest development until January, 1969, was a meeting of a Committee of Experts in December, 1968. A Final Report of that meeting with a detailed account on each paragraph of the planned treaty, was published in the January 6, 1969 issue of the *Official Gazette* of the United States Patent Office.

[94] Reported in *I.P.*, 2: 190–92, September, 1963.

[95] Reported in *I.P.*, 3: 164–68, July, 1964.

[96] Reported in *I.P.*, 5: 54–57, March, 1966.

In the 1963 meeting,[97] in which ten countries participated,[98] the topics discussed concerned adherence to the Paris Union, the question of whether model laws should be prepared and various forms of assistance by BIRPI to developing countries.[99] The Committee recommended that developing countries "should establish legislation and an administration appropriate to their needs in the field of industrial property," and that "so far as they are not members of the Paris Union, should consider the possibility of adhering to that Union, taking into account the advantages of such an adhesion." It was further recommended that BIRPI should draft a model law on patents and institute programs of technical assistance for member countries.[100]

a. The Model Law for Developing Countries on Inventions

Having worked out a draft model law on patents, as recommended by the 1963 committee, BIRPI invited, in 1964, representatives from sixty-nine developing countries to participate in a Model Law Committee.[101] Twenty-two countries meeting under the auspices of BIRPI constituted the Model Law Committee.[102] Of the twenty-two participants nine were members of the Paris Union (and three more have since joined it).

The Model Law is intended to be a model for the legislation in developing countries – not a draft for a uniform law.[103] The text, established by the Committee, consists of three parts. The first, by far the largest, concerns patents. It contains fifty-two articles, encompassing all major

97 Reported in *I.P.*, 2: 234–39, November, 1963.

98 Six of the participating countries were developing countries; three were at the time Members of the Union (Brazil, Iran and Tanganyika) and three were outside it (Algeria, Colombia and Venezuela) the first of which has since become a Union Member.

99 Introducing the question of Union Membership, the Director of BIRPI outlined some of its disadvantages and advantages. Among the former was mentioned the seemingly disproportionate number of patents granted to foreigners. "However," assured the BIRPI Director, "this phenomenon has not prevented industrial development of countries such as Switzerland and the Netherlands, which were themselves quite recently less industrially developed countries." *I.P.*, 2: 237, November, 1963. It is also reported (p. 238) that one delegate, pointing out the advantages of membership, said that "it must also be remembered that fiscal revenues will be increased ... [through fees for filing and maintaining patents]."!

100 For the text of the resolution see *Model Law for Developing Countries on Inventions* (Geneva: BIRPI, 1965), p. 11, n. 1.

101 The sixty-nine countries were chosen from those "which at the United Nations Conference on Trade and Development [UNCTAD, Geneva, 1964] considered themselves developing." *Ibid.*, p. 11.; among the latter group of countries twelve African States – the members of O.A.M.C.E. – were not invited, having recently adopted a uniform patent law. *Ibid.*, p. 11, n. 3.

102 Some developed countries and international organizations sent observers. Among the latter were representatives for the United Nations, the I.C.C., and the I.A.P.I.P.; Doc. I.C.C. 450/262, December 15, 1964, p. 1.

103 *Model Law* ..., p. 12.

rules appearing in national patent laws. A second part deals with the legal protection of knowhow in five articles.[104] A third part, covered in two articles, treats procedural questions. In addition, there are two addenda (Annexes A and B) containing possible provisions concerning so-called patents of introduction and authors' certificates, covered in five and six articles respectively.

A commentary is provided parallel with the sections of the law itself. It is explicative and sometimes provides information concerning alternative solutions to specific problems suggested in the Committee. Since the draft model law, which BIRPI submitted to the Committee, has not been published, and as the commentary does not specify the positions taken by various delegates and observers, it is not possible to know the extent to which the individual rules and the draft as a whole were approved by the participants in the Model Law Committee. Nevertheless, two sources indicate that in general the United Nations observers were critical on several points. The authors of an I.C.C. Memorandum on the work of the Model Law Committee state in this connection that:

> It should be noted that the observers for the United Nations took the most critical view of the project in the sense that it did not go far enough to satisfy the assumed interests of developing countries and they made many suggestions for more restrictive provisions of patentees' rights. *These observers felt they were bound to take their position by virtue of this year's resolutions of UNCTAD and ECOSOC.*[105]

The Model Law Committee did not raise the question of the usefulness of patent protection but worked on the assumption, that such protection was generally useful to developing countries.[106]

In essence, the Model Law is no more than a document containing, in general, the minimum requirements of the Paris Convention.[107] One,

[104] Though existing patent laws generally do not contain special provisions concerning the protection of knowhow, the Committee agreed that the insertion of such provisions would be "useful and desirable" in view of the special interest that the supply of knowhow has for developing countries. *Ibid.*, p. 75.

[105] italics added. *Model Patent Law – Memorandum on the Geneva Meeting of the Committee of Experts*, submitted by S. P. Ladas and P. J. Pointet, Doc. I.C.C. 450/262, December 15, 1964, p. 3.

[106] This assumption was based on the views expressed by the 1963 Committee of Experts and on the contents of the Report (by the U.N. Secretary General), *Model Patent Law ...*, p. 12.

[107] Certain sections go beyond purely legal questions. This is the case, for instance, with section thirty-two on *License Contracts Involving payments Abroad*, which admits the screening of such contracts by a Government agency. To have such a practice "approved" by BIRPI may be of psychological value. Its Director, saying that its inclusion" seemed to be the inevitable price ... if one wishes to have an effective patent protection for foreigners in a developing country" adds, however, the observation that "it is, in essence, not very different from the foreign exchange control measures which are or have been known in almost all the

and probably the major, reason for sponsoring the Model Law was quite understandably the desire, from the point of view of BIRPI, to dissuade developing countries from adopting more "radical" patent laws. This is clearly admitted by the Director of BIRPI when he says:

> If it [the Model Law] is not to the liking of everybody, the critics should be asked to compare the results with what would happen if all developing nations were to legislate sooner or later on patents *without any guidance or under political or economic pressure from various states.*[108]

In specific cases where there appears to be good grounds to argue for special rules for developing countries, there is a strong impression, that the decisive test of the appropriatenes of suggested rules or modifications of rules was their compatibility with the existing conventional rules. Some instances in which special rules may be appropriate for developing countries – and were suggested during the Model Law Committee meeting – are the following.

i. Patentability of adaptations to local conditions

One condition generally required for an invention in order to be patentable is that it represents a certain measure of inventiveness, i.e., a certain advance on prior technology. The same is also true for improvements on earlier patents for inventions, which may be patented if they fulfill certain standards of inventiveness. In the latter case, most patent laws allow the holder of an improvement patent to be granted, if necessary, a compulsory license for the original patented invention. That such improvement patents may be of particular interest to developing countries, in encouraging local innovators to adapt foreign technology to local conditions, is evident and was recognized by the Committee.[109] A suggestion by, among others, the United Nations observers,[110] that it might be advantageous for developing countries to grant patents for local innovations of foreign inventions, even though they may lack the generally required measure of inventiveness, was, however, rejected. And yet, the case for rewarding such innovations of foreign inventions, which might not be applicable without adjustment, would seem to be in the interest of developing countries. Such a special rule on improvement patents would not only encourage local innova-

countries of the world." G. H. C. Bodenhausen, "A Model Patent Law for Developing Nations," *Creative Ferment in World Patent Systems; Conference of the National Association of Manufacturers, June, 1965* (New York: N.A.M., 1965) p. 27.

108 Italics added, *Ibid.*, p. 29.

109 *Model Law* . . ., p. 19.

110 Bodenhausen, *op. cit.*, pp. 25–26.

tors but might also allow them to obtain a compulsory license from the holder of the "original" patent.

ii. Local vs. world-wide novelty

Another requirement for an invention to be patentable is, that it should not have been previously available to the public. Most national patent laws require what is known as world-wide or universal novelty. Though the majority of the Committee members favored this requirement, the minority was of the opinion that a system of local novelty might be preferable for countries in the early stages of economic development. The result was that while in the text of the law (section two) the standard mentioned is world-wide novelty, the commentary admits the possibility of replacing it by a requirement of local novelty.[111] A factor in favor of requiring merely local novelty would be that it would increase the number of patents in the country, which in its turn might encourage the introduction of new industries. The general argument against recognizing mere local novelty would appear less weighty in the case of developing countries, the major potential benefit to these countries from the international patent system being the importation of technology. According to that argument, the granting of patents for inventions that are not new and perhaps not patented abroad would create obstacles in the international trade of the patent-granting country.

iii. Patents of introduction

The same argument favoring the requirement of mere local novelty for the incentive it would constitute to the one introducing the foreign technology, is also valid for the use of a special type of patent grant, known as a patent of introduction or patent of confirmation. This was also recognized by the Committee. Annex A of the Model Law contains a possible addendum to a national patent law with five articles regulating the grant of such patents of introduction. The rationale behind such a patent grant is to enable the protection of foreign technology which is being introduced after the priority period has run out. Certain rules suggested in Annex A would seem to limit the usefulness of such patents and some of the restrictions suggested on such patents seem to put in question the appropriateness of corresponding restrictions allowed on patent grants in general.

First of all, a patent of introduction may only be applied for by the

[111] *Model Law* ..., pp. 21–22.

foreign patentee. Thus the use of the special form of patents of introduction, as known for instance in Spanish law, and according to which anybody interested in and capable of introducing a foreign patented invention may be granted protection – provided, of course, that the foreign patentee has not availed himself of the priority rule to apply for a local patent – is precluded.[112]

Secondly, a patent of introduction may not be granted if the products produced under the patented process or involving the patented invention have been sold in the country. The fairly long period during which a foreign patentee cannot be restrained from importing patented products from abroad is sometimes defended, in the case of developing countries, by pointing out that the local market may not be prepared for local exploitation of a patent until it has been imported for some time and local demand justifies local production. This argument appears a fair one and provides an obvious case in which it should be advantageous for the local economy to grant protection even after the ordinary priority period has lapsed. Whether this point was discussed in the Model Law Committee is not known, but in any case, such a use of patents of introduction is expressly prohibited by the text.

Thirdly, the suggested duration of patents of introduction is only half of that of ordinary patents. The logic of this is difficult to understand in the case of developing countries. In the general case for the duration of patent grants, the commentary, admitting that the proposed twenty years may be longer that the average, motivates such a length, saying that:

> A relatively longer term of protection, however, seems to be justified in the case of developing countries. In fact, in the case of a developing country, the owner of the patent will generally need some time for studying the possibilities of working the patented invention in the countray. ... If ... the remaining term of protection of the patent would appear to be too short for lucrative exploitation, this circumstance might substantially diminish the attractiveness which a patent should have for industrial investments in the country.[113]

Where a duration of ten years is suggested for patents of introduction, it is said that, on the one hand, "a shorter term would be difficult to justify as the owner must be given a reasonable period of time to

[112] Does not the fact that only the original patentee may obtain a patent of introduction completely nullify the influence, in case world-wide novelty is required, which the existence of a possibility for a third person to take a patent would have in obliging the foreign patentee to apply for a patent grant within the priority period? Does not the suggested text (in connection, at least, with a requirement for more than local novelty) constitute, in fact, a mere prolongation of the ordinary priority period?

[113] *Model Law* ... p. 48.

exploit the invention in the country" but that on the other hand, "the exceptional nature of patents of introduction would hardly justify a much longer duration."[114] It is difficult to see what is so exceptional about patents of introduction, except that they seem to be particularly well suited in responding to the "particular needs and requirements" of developing countries.[115] If a local patent had not been applied for originally for the reason that its local exploitation was considered impossible, such a situation would seem to favor a substantial period of protection for someone still prepared to exploit it. Fourthly, and for the same reasons just given, the provision of nullity of patents of introduction for non-working – after two years – and the reasons in support of such a rule, raise the question as to whether the rules concerning working conditions for patents in general (mentioned below) are the most appropriate for developing countries. The commentary, motivating the rule, that a patent of introduction, if not locally exploited, may be declared null, states that:

> The reason for which a patent of introduction is granted is to encourage exploitation *in the country*. If this expectation is frustrated, the reason for the grant appears not to be justified and therefore the patent of introduction should be considered not to have been granted.[116]

It is not suggested that the two-year rule may not be a reasonable provision as such, but on the contrary, that it may be a reasonable provision in the case of all patent grants. In the introduction to the Model Law, entitled: "Guiding Principles of the Model Law," it is stated that: "Grant of patents is the traditional means of encouraging *inventive activity and the necessary investments for research and for the industrial exploitation of inventions*."[117] If it can be agreed, as has been suggested elsewhere, that the granting of patents to foreigners by developing countries constitutes no major incentive to foreign inventive activity, including the allocation of research funds, the one major function that remains is the incentive to local industrial exploitation of inventions. If this is so, there is little reason for these discrepancies between ordinary patents and patents of introduction.

[114] *Ibid.*, p. 84.

[115] Though it will probably be argued that a patent of introduction is not calculated to recuperate research costs, neither ought developing countries to pay for such research in general, nor is the possibility of such recuperation a significant incentive to the foreign inventor-patentee.

[116] *Ibid.*, p. 85.

[117] *Ibid.*, p. 17.

iv. Provisions for working requirements

Finally, the provisions of the Model Law concerning working requirements for patented inventions provide a case where it can be argued – and was argued in the Committee – that particular rules may be advantageous to developing countries. When a foreigner is granted patent protection, three different results are possible as far as local exploitation of the patented invention is concerned: local exploitation may come about voluntarily; it may be undertaken by means of a compulsory license; or no local exploitation takes place. The case in which an invention is exploited locally either by the patentee himself or by means of licensing a local manufacturer, whether induced or not by the possibilities to apply remedies against non-working, is evidently the most beneficial for any country, and need no further elaboration.

It is clear, however, that a number of patents granted to foreigners (whether the patent granting country is developed or not) will not be voluntarily worked. But whereas developed countries may often accept such a situation without further action – the reciprocal treatment of its own patentees abroad will more or less counterbalance the initial loss to the local economy – the developing countries, whose only major benefit from granting patents to foreigners will be an actual transfer of technology, will quite justifiably insist on the local application of the foreign technology. Therefore it is important that these countries have effective remedies in cases where the patentee is disinclined to allow local exploitation. This is also recognized in the Model Law:

> The special needs of developing countries are mainly served by the detailed provisions ... preventing the patent from degenerating into a means of controlling importation without contribution, through an obligation to exploit the invention *in the country,* to the development of national economy and industry.[118]

Despite various suggestions made in the Model Law Committee for allowing developing countries to also employ compulsory licensing procedures, in cases in which such procedures were not allowed by the Paris Convention, none of them were retained. Section 34, concerned with the general case of compulsory licenses, only takes up the minimum requirements of Article 5A(4) of the Convention. The reasons why none of the suggestions for increased powers to grant compulsory

[118] *Ibid.* In the introductory comment on the two sections concerning compulsory licenses (sections 34–35) it is also stressed (p. 58) that "adequate provisions for compulsory licenses are of exceptional importance for developing countries because such provisions constitute the best means to encourage the exploitation of patented inventions in the country itself and to avoid any economic or social drawbacks of the rights granted to the owner of the patent."

licenses were retained, the commentary explains, were that broader and vaguer compulsory license provisions might result in abuses. "This" it is said, (p. 58) "could lead to a general distrust of the value of patents in the country concerned, with the consequence that inventorship would not be encouraged and industrial investment in the country discouraged." This is the standard argument both against more stringent compulsory license provisions than those allowed by the Convention and against provisions for revoking non-worked patents (see below). Suffice it here to say that the "encouragement of inventorship" can conceivably only refer to local inventorship, in which case compulsory license provisions, primarily aimed at foreign patentees, will not need to be employed; and that the supposition that industrial investment in the country will be discouraged by certain types of compulsory license provisions is questionable. The only type of industrial investment with which a patent law is concerned is the one in which investments are made for the local exploitation of patented technology; when such investments are contemplated nothing need to be feared from compulsory license provisions.

Considering the traditional motivation for the three-year period before compulsory licenses may be granted – that the patentee will need that period to decide whether or not to undertake local production or to arrange for local licensing – one of the suggestions made in the Committee seems to merit special attention. It is described in the following words in the commentary:

> That compulsory licenses should be made available for non-working . . . whenever the owner of the patent has not filed with the Government (within 6 or 12 months after having been invited to do so) a concrete and satisfactory plan for starting the working of the invention within a stated period of time.[119]

Though no further details of this suggestion are given, this presumably refers to a case in which a local manufacturer would be prepared to take a license. In such a case, it is difficult to see how the foreign patentee could plead not to be ready to decide whether or not to exploit the patent himself.

The ultimate sanction against non-working has always been the revocation of the patent grant. Such a provision can serve two purposes. On the one hand, it may put pressure on the patentee to work his invention voluntarily or to cooperate with a compulsory licensee, and on the other hand, it will extinguish the import protection of the paten-

[119] *Ibid.*, p. 58.

tee in case of non-working. Insofar as the threat of revocation would result in the local working of the invention, it is a means to induce the patentee to cooperate in the transfer of technology. In the Model Law Committee suggestions were made to provide for possible revocation, which, it should be remembered, appears in many national patent laws and is allowed by the Convention. No such provision, however, appears in the Model Law.

There will always be cases in which a foreign patent is not being worked locally. The proportion of such cases to the total number of patents granted will, for reasons explained elsewhere,[120] tend to be greater in the developing countries. Despite the repeated reference to the importance for underdeveloped countries that patent grants do not become mere market protection for the foreign patentee-producer, the commentary states that the Committee's attitude was "negative" to any proposal to include a provision for revocation. This stand is explained in the following words:

> Although the lapse or revocation of unexploited patents may facilitate importation, these measures certainly do not encourage investments and industrialization, which may become, without the protection of a patent, even less attractive than before.[121]

Since a provision for revocation in case of non-working would, by definition, not affect cases where investments were made, which the patent grant is supposed to encourage, the motive quoted above is less than convincing. If the only major benefit to developing countries of granting patents to foreigners is the possibly ensuing transfer of technology and attraction of foreign investments connected with such exploitation, then clearly the patents which, for whatever reasons, the patentee has no intention to make available through a transfer of technology, should be revoked.

This fairly detailed examination of some questions of patent law and their treatment by the Model Law Committee, serves two purposes. The immediate one has been to substantiate the strong impression that, despite the repeatedly stated concern for the special and urgent needs of developing countries and their economic and industrial development, the decisive test as to the appropriateness of suggested patent

[120] Cf. *supra*, p. 138.

[121] *Ibid.* "Furthermore," it is said (p. 58), "such provisions would ... be too general ... Finally a system of automatic lapsing would be much too rigid, because the sometimes very valid reasons for non-working could not even enter into consideration." Whatever "valid" reasons there may be for non-working, they would seem to be so only from the point of view of the patentee.

law provisions was constantly whether or not such provisions were compatible with the existing rules of the Paris Convention. The second purpose has been to show the practical scope for concessions to developing countries within the existing organization of international patent protection. Despite the fact that only developing countries took part as delegates in the Model Law Committee, obviously the stand taken by BIRPI, backed by many developed countries and by the two private international organizations with special interests in the field, often had a decisive influence on the drafting of the Model Law.[122]

C. THE ACTIVITIES OF THE INTERNATIONAL CHAMBER OF COMMERCE

The International Chamber of Commerce, founded in 1921 and which has national affiliates in eighty countries,[123] is one of the most powerful and influential non-governmental organizations.[124] Its main objective is to work for the expansion of international commercial relations based on private enterprise; the expression "commercial relations" is understood in a large sense, including not only merchandise but also capital and services. Jean Meynaud observes that though in many cases the organization can work through private parties to obtain its objective, there are today numerous problems, the solutions of which depend entirely on government action, and that therefore an appeal to public authorities is one of its means of action.[125] An organization like the I.C.C., with a large number of affiliated national committees, is able to influence government policies both by means of its national representa-

[122] The close collaboration and identity of views will become apparent below. In an I.C.C. memorandum on the Model Law Committee (cf. *supra*, n. 105), it is said that while Dr. Bodenhausen supported the BIRPI draft, he also offered amendments suggested by the I.C.C. and I.A.P.I.P. "Because of this initiative of Dr. Bodenhausen," the authors of the memorandum continue, "the observers for these two organizations preferred not to intervene in the particular discussions since obviously it was better that desirable amendments be offered by BIRPI itself. The observers of the AIPPI and ICC intervened only to aid Dr. Bodenhausen whenever it was felt that he required assistance in support of the proper position." Doc. I.C.C. 450/262, December 15, 1964, p. 4.

[123] At the beginning of 1968 there were forty-two countries with national committees and thirty-eight more countries with individual members. I.C.C. "Aims, Action, Organization and Who's Who 1968/1969" Paris, 1968.

[124] "La chambre ... est organisée pour intervenir directement auprès des instances intergouvernementales. ... En même temps, la qualité des membres et la position qu'ils occupent dans l'économie de leur pays lui assurent une voie de pénétration efficace auprès des autorités nationales. Sous tous ces aspects, peu de groupes de pression internationaux peuvent lui être comparés." J. Meynaud, *Les groupes de pression internationaux.* (Lausanne: [chez l'auteur], 1961) p. 371.

[125] *Ibid.*, p. 67.

tives and its representatives to intergovernmental organizations. In the latter respect the I.C.C. has advisory status with several intergovernmental organizations, among them ECOSOC. The fact that the I.C.C., among several hundred non-governmental organizations that have advisory status with the ECOSOC, belongs to the exclusive group of ten with the highest status (group A) sufficiently demonstrates its powerful position.[126]

How can one estimate the influence of the I.C.C. on the actions of the United Nations and its various bodies? On the characterization of the relations between private international organizations and the United Nations Organization, Meynaud says, that in giving these organizations the attribute "pressure groups," one cannot but contribute to a more realistic view of the relationship between non-governmental organizations and the United Nations.[127]

In studying the actions taken and the opinions expressed by the I.C.C. in the field of industrial property and developing countries, the following considerations ought to be kept in mind: although an almost equal number of developed and developing countries have national affiliations with the organization, the preponderance of the former become apparent when the industrial power behind the various national associations is considered; even though the I.C.C. may have the backing of national committees or private individuals in developing countries for its actions, their interests are likely to be closer to the interests of individuals in developed countries than to the social and economic interests of their governments; while a curb on foreigners' patent rights in a country may be thought of as a trade liberalizing move within that country, from the international point of view, it is more likely to be seen as an attack on acquired rights; and finally, to the extent that the international patent system is thought of as favoring investments and the transfer of technology, a "weakening" of that system will be contrary to the aims of the I.C.C.

In the field of industrial property rights, the I.C.C acts mainly through a permanent *Commission for the International Protection of Industrial Property* which was established along with the I.C.C. in 1921.

[126] Not only can it send observers to the Council and its Committees; it may also submit written declarations, which are distributed to member governments of the United Nations as official documents, and orally expose its view in Committees. A special prerogative of organizations of category "A" is that they may, on special recommendation, present their views in the Council and suggest questions for its agenda. *Ibid.*, pp. 253–54.

[127] *Ibid.*, p. 256.

In the sudden outburst of activities within the United Nations, which followed upon the Brazilian initiative in late 1961, the International Chamber of Commerce was taken by as much surprise as the Secretariat of the Paris Union.[128] The reaction, however, was swift. Within two weeks of the introduction of the original Brazilian draft resolution in the General Assembly,[129] the I.C.C. Commission treated the question.[130] The Chairman, pointing out "the grave repercussions which such a resolution might have on the system for the protection of industrial property," said that:

> There were grounds to fear that the report requested ... might challenge hitherto unchallenged principles and adopt certain inaccuracies which under-lay the Brazilian point of view.[131]

Emphasizing that the sponsors of the draft resolution were endeavoring to win support from other delegations, the Chairman invited the Commission to draw up a statement designed to defend the patent system against the attacks made on it.[132] The gravity with which the I.C.C. regarded the situation also comes out in another statement made by an I.C.C. official who, after announcing that the permanent representative of the I.C.C. to the United Nations had already stated the I.C.C. point of view, said:

> It was now for the commission to finalize a text which the combined action of all the ICC organs could put up in opposition to the point of view which menaced the whole foundation of the system for the international protection of patents.[133]

[128] Though a report on the Lisbon Conference (previously quoted; cf. *supra*, p. 96, n. 101) shows the awareness of sharper differences between industrialized and developing countries, a document proposing a work programme for 1961/63 in nine major points fails to mention the problem of patents and the transfer of technology to developing countries. Doc. I.C.C. 450/209, September 26, 1961.

[129] The original draft resolution was submitted on November 8, 1961; its final version was passed by the Second Committee on December 9, and by the General Assembly on January 8, 1962.

[130] Doc. I.C.C. 450/212; Summary Records from November 23–24, 1961.

[131] *Ibid.*, p. 2.

[132] In view of the urgency of the matter, the I.C.C. Council had given prior approval of a statement to be drawn up by the Commission. An I.C.C. official confirmed that "in obedience to the I.C.C. mission to facilitating international trade without any restrictions, the I.C.C. Council and Executive Committee had given the Commission authority to act with all speed." *Ibid.* p. 3. – That one of the principal remedies sought by Brazil was the suppression of *trade restrictions* caused by non-worked patents never seems to have been considered!

[133] *Ibid.* Following this statement, the BIRPI representative, saying (*Ibid.*) that it would be a very good thing for the I.C.C. to take a position as a matter of urgency "regretted that a statement of this kind [i.e., the Brazilian draft resolution] had been drawn up at the very moment when the office of the Union was trying to persuade the new countries to join in the Paris Union."

Among the several interventions during the meeting there was one of special interest for its moderate stand. This intervention was made by the Yugoslavian delegate, who referred to "the complexities of the problems of industrial property in the new countries," and who made the point that "while the deliberations of the I.C.C. had always dealt with the legal aspects, the Brazilian resolution was more concerned with the economic repercussions."[134]

The result of the deliberation was, as recorded, that:

> It was understood that while seeking to show sympathy for the legitimate concerns of the new countries, the draftsmen frankly state the opinion of the I.C.C. for the enlightenment of all who sought it.[135]

The ensuing statement contained among other things, the following assertions: that "the prosperity and high standards of living of industrially developed countries are due, to a large extent, to the existence of a patent system"; that "the generally existing system of compulsory licensing avoids any abuse which might result from non-working of an invention in any country"; and that:

> The most advanced and equitable system of international patent rights taking account of the public interest in the use and working of foreigners' patents, is that secured by the international convention for the protection of industrial property.

The greatest threat to the established order from the Brazilian initiative was seen in the possible creation of a new machinery, through an international conference, for the regulation of international property rights. To counter such a threat, the statement, lauding the experience of the Paris Union, said that:

> At a revision conference countries have an opportunity to propose and discuss any amendments of the international regime of patents deemed desirable by them. It is submitted that this is the proper and proven method for finding appropriate solutions for any desired changes in the international system of patents.

Because of this, the statement concludes by urging all countries not yet parties to the Paris Convention to adhere to it and "to give by their law effective protection to inventors and patentees in order to ensure normal development of industry and trade on a world basis."[136]

The document scarcely shows a willingness or ability to understand the particular problems of developing countries. Besides the uncritical references to the causes of property in developed countries and the

[134] *Ibid.*
[135] *Ibid.*
[136] Doc. I.C.C. 450/210 Rev., November 24, 1961, pp. 1–2.

relevance of historical experience, the assertion that the compulsory license system is a cure-all for all countries and circumstances is sufficient proof. To call the Paris Convention "the most advanced and equitable system" is rather meaningless, when no other system of its scope exists or has been tried out. Finally, to call on the developing countries to ensure "normal development of industry and trade on a world basis" (does "normal" imply the rate and direction it has taken since the Paris Union was founded?) does not even show the promised "sympathy" for what is generally considered "legitimate concerns of the new countries."

To the question put above of how the influence of the I.C.C. on the activities of the United Nations could be measured, there exists, as far as the Brazilian initiative is concerned, I.C.C.'s own opinion on the matter. In a note from I.C.C. Headquarters it was said, with respect to the statement made "to serve as a basis for the steps it would be necessary to take both within the United Nations and with the governments of countries having a national committee," that:

> A highly satisfactory reception was accorded to the statement ... thanks in particular to the energetic action taken by the National Committees with the compentent authorities ....
> International Headquarters are pleased to inform the National Committees ... of the success it was possible to achieve by drawing their attention to the text of the Resolution as finally adopted by the General Assembly of the United Nations. ...[137]

In the preparation of the U.N. Report, the I.C.C. assisted by submitting reports from ten countries on their national patent laws. The Secretary General of the I.C.C., in a letter to the Secretary General of the United Nations, submitted some observations on the basis of these reports, saying in part, that "there is really no substantial difference in the general principles and general effects of the patent system in developed and underdeveloped countries." It is not surprising that the "general principles" were found to be substantially alike since all ten countries examined were members of the Paris Union.[138]

[137] Doc. I.C.C. 450/213, February 22, 1962, p. 1.

[138] Doc. I.C.C. 450/243, October 28, 1963, p. 1. If "general principles" merely refers to the principles of national treatment and priority then there are no differences between the industrialized and developing countries involved (five of each were examined). But if "general principles" should refer to the latest text of the Convention, there are clear differences. While the five industrialized countries had all ratified that text, only Mexico among the developing countries had done so, the latter having anyway the peculiarity of providing for the reduction of the term of non-worked patents. Of the other four countries, Israel and Morocco follow the Lisbon text though they have only ratified the London text of 1934, while Brazil and Ceylon follow the rules of the Hague text (though Ceylon has ratified that of London).

Referring to statistics showing total numbers of patents granted by various countries, the percentage of patents granted to foreigners, etc., and saying that these statistics show (a) a close connection between patents and industrial growth and (b) that there are large number of foreign-owned patents also in the highly industrialized countries, the conclusion is drawn, that the patent system has been and remains an important element in industrial development, and that the practice of developed countries of protecting foreign inventors is of great significance.[139]

These conclusions are thought to demonstrate the necessity for the developing countries to grant patents to foreigners. But when it is later said in the same document that, as very few patents are taken out in these countries, "the taking out of patents in developing countries, even though they are taken mostly or wholly by foreigners, is of minor effect, positive or negative, to the growth of industry in such countries," does this latter statement not contradict the implicit meaning of the conclusions quoted previously?[140]

The reason for the analysis of the various I.C.C. documents, quoted above, has been to show that the I.C.C., however progressive it may call itself in certain fields, can hardly be expected to substantially revise its past policies, when such a course would be considered detrimental (though it might be a short-sighted view) to its main sponsors.[141]

Over the years the patent question and developing countries has been on the agenda of the Commission at several occasions and the records show that there has been no change in the initial stand.

[139] *Ibid.*, p. 3.

[140] *Ibid.* It has been emphasized elsewhere that the effect of the patent system cannot be measured merely in terms of numbers of patented inventions, but that such effects include the use of that system to protect unpatented knowhow. This is recognized in a draft memorandum submitted to the Commission on "Modern Technology and Industrial Property," in the following words: "Owners of knowhow are more likely to enter into agreements communicating such knowhow if they can tie this up to patents to which the knowhow refers. Therefore developing countries should encourage the grant of patents if for no other reason that it encourages the communication of knowhow to patent licensees." I.C.C. Doc. 450/264, April 26, 1965, p. 8.

[141] Though at several occasions policy statements have been made seemingly showing an openminded approach to questions of changes and adaptations to new conditions, nothing has so far emerged in practice. In 1963, a review of a 1951 resolution on patent-licensing was called for; one of the reasons given for such a review was the "urgent claims of underdeveloped countries in their struggle for speedy industrialization and importation of technology and the present and prospective revisions of existing patent systems. It seems to me," the author of the memorandum concludes, "that this review calls for a pragmatic approach ... which seeks to resolve present and actual problems rather than build on ideological systems. If this means that we have to sacrifice to some extent the sacred cow of laissez faire in favor of certain controls and restrictions imposed by the facts of life, we should have the courage to say so." I.C.C. Doc. 450/245, November 7, 1963, p. 3. See also I.C.C. Doc. 450/264, April 26, 1965, p. 12.

D. THE ACTIVITIES OF THE INTERNATIONAL ASSOCIATION FOR THE PROTECTION OF INDUSTRIAL PROPERTY

The organization was founded in 1879. As its name implies, the work of the organization lies exclusively in the field of industrial property. It has national branch organizations in thirty countries and individual members in thirty-eight.[142] It was founded in close connection with the creation of the Paris Union, and its first task was to work for an increased membership of the Union. An international congress is convened every three years, and between its sessions business is handled by an Executive Committee. The organization has advisory status with the ECOSOC, category B. There is a close cooperation between the organization and the I.C.C. Commission through a joint commission. The fact that the chairman of the I.C.C. Commission is also the secretary general of the I.A.P.I.P. further indicates their close connections. Thus the success of opposing some features of the Brazilian draft resolution is shared by the I.C.C. and the I.A.P.I.P.[143]

A document submitted to an Executive Committee Meeting on September 25, 1961 (i.e., before the Brazilian draft resolution was introduced in the United Nations) says, in part, that:

> The diplomatic conference at Lisbon in 1958 has taught us a lesson which coupled with the development of technical and economic cooperation that has taken place in the last few years, imposes a change of attitude.[144]

Saying that "it is unrealistic to hope that the Paris Union may continue to serve as the only or even the main instrument for future legislative unification," the author of the report continues:

> I am convinced that we may already consider ourselves lucky if we succeed in upholding the fundamental principles of the Convention in the vast territory of the Union ... there is no longer room for spectacular improvements of industrial property protection in the Paris Union because the degree of industrial, technological and economic development differs widely among the numerous Union countries.[145]

Though the author quoted above had principally the problems of industrialized countries in mind, it is clear from the opinion expressed

[142] A.I.P.I.P. Annual Report 1968; nine developing countries (eight individual countries and O.A.M.C.E. as a group) have national associations and twenty have individual members.

[143] Mentioning the activities of its secretary general, S. P. Ladas (being thus also the chairman of the I.C.C. Commission) the Association's 1963 Annual Report says that "it is ... quite especially his achievement that the so-called 'Brazilian Resolution' ... was accepted in its final, moderate version." Doc. I.A.P.I.P. Annual Report 1963: I, p. 74.

[144] Doc. I.A.P.I.P. Annual Report 1961: II, p. 105.

[145] *Ibid.*

by the same author in 1963, where reference is made to his earlier report, that he also had the problems of developing countries in mind. Though a number of recommendations, submitted at the earlier occasion, had been followed, the author says, that "I am still concerned by this association's contribution to the future shape of the present rather outmoded industrial property system," continuing: "Apart from the severe criticism raised in studies by economists, there have recently been official proposals in various countries aiming at weakening or abolishing patent protection at least in certain specific fields of technology." In addition to these developments the author emphasizes the investigation conducted by the United Nations on the basis of the Brazilian initiative.[146]

Though the I.A.P.I.P. considers its main task to be connected with the legal aspects of industrial property, it has also taken upon itself to study the economic problems involved. In preparation for its congress in 1966, a program for preparatory studies to be made for the congress suggested, in 1964, that the following points, among others, under the agenda title "The industrial property in the developing countries," should be considered: "Is the industrial property helpful to the economic progress of developing countries?", and "Is it necessary for the protection of industrial property to be arranged so as to be adapted to the developing countries?"[147] That the former of the two questions would be answered in the affirmative must have been a foregone conclusion. In a summary of the country-reports on this item, it is said, in part, that:

It cannot be challenged that the protection of industrial property . . . is apt to promote the technical and economic progress of developing countries.

The experience of countries which have nowadays developed their industrialization demonstrates that the protection of industrial property has been an important factor in the development and progress of these countries.

On the second question, the summary is less definite:

There is no doubt that certain adjustments of traditional legislation are necessary to take into account the particular situation in the developing countries.

These adjustments, however, should not interfere with the basic principles underlying the protection of industrial property.[148]

146 Doc. I.A.P.I.P. Annual Report 1963: II pp. 88–90.
147 Doc. I.A.P.I.P. Annual Report 1964: II p. 133.
148 Doc. I.A.P.I.P. Annual Report 1966: I, p. 78.

Although the I.A.P.I.P. has at various occasions expressed concern over the possible threat to the existing order within the protection of industrial property rights, caused by forces opposing parts or the whole of the traditional patent system, and has been urged by its officers to consider the proper actions to take, it seems as if comparatively little interest has been given to these problems.[149] Since the I.C.C. is carrying on activities along these lines and the I.C.C./I.A.P.I.P. Joint Commission was established in order to avoid overlapping of activities, it may well be that the association deliberately has left the problems connected with patents and developing countries to the I.C.C. and BIRPI.

After examining the activities of the four organizations and their positions on the problems in question, it is clear that there is, on the one hand, the United Nations and its various bodies, and, on the other hand, BIRPI, the I.C.C. and the I.A.P.I.P., all three with no apparent differences of view among them. While the United Nations has striven to take a neutral position on questions directly concerning the international patent system and prefers to treat the question concerning the transfer of technology in the broader context of assistance to the economic development of the developing countries, the other three organizations have united their considerable power to influence the outcome of the issues in a way, that will safeguard the acquired rights of patentees, whether or not the actions of the latter have any positive value to the patent granting developing countries. The cautious and inconclusive opinions expressed by the United Nations – partly of course, as a result of the actions of the other organizations both directly and through its members – have facilitated interpretation of such opinions to suit those of the other organizations. The latter, while not opposed to the general idea of assistance to the developing countries, show by their repeated arguments drawn from the conditions of developed countries their inability, or at least unwillingness, to understand the predicaments of the developing countries.

[149] The determination of its future work program in 1966, shows this. Deciding to chose, by ballot, the four questions (out of fifteen suggested) to be included in that program, it turned out that the subject of "transfer of technology" only ranked no. 11, the last-placed subject being "protection of knowhow." Doc. A.I.P.I.P. Annual Report 1966: II, p. 51; however, at the annual Conference of Presidents, April, 1968, the Argentine Delegate proposed that the question of the connection between industrial property rights and the progress of developing countries, be included in the agenda for the June, 1969 Congress of Venice.

CHAPTER V

THE SCOPE FOR REMEDIES WITHIN THE EXISTING SYSTEM

Though the principal aim of the Paris Union since its founding has been to enlarge the field of activity of patentees, who are nationals or residents of its member countries, it has always been recognized that complete liberty for patentees in chosing where and under what conditions to exploit their inventions was not in the best interest of most countries. From the evolution of the Convention it can be seen, that the ideas on what type of restrictions ought to be allowed and their degree of severity have shifted both among countries and over time. In that context it can also be seen that divergences between countries arguing for less restrictions, and those who want to retain if not amplify existing restrictions, generally divided members in groups of more and less economically developed countries. Though this pattern was discernable at almost every revision conference, the conflict of interests between industrialized and developing countries became particularly evident at the 1958 Lisbon conference.

In order to estimate the potential benefits to be derived from a successful implementation of the available remedies it is necessary, not only to examine the effectiveness of such remedial actions as are allowed under the Convention but also, to the extent that they are successful, their total impact on the benefits to be derived from participation in the international patent system. The greater the need for safeguards for a particular country or group of countries, the more important will it be that the remedies available are effective. – Though this latter point is often admitted by stressing the importance of working provisions for developing countries, when it comes to the effectiveness and potential impact of available remedies, they are almost invariably discussed in terms of conditions of developed countries.

When certain effects of the international patent system have been criticized, it has sometimes been pointed out that a number of these countries, although they are members of the Paris Union, do not even apply, through their national legislations, the remedial provisions permitted by the Convention and applied by most developed countries.[1] The sometimes more lenient attitude of developing countries towards foreign patentees may be due to the supposition, that the existing rules are anyway unlikely to provide real remedies, and rather than to cause a deterrent effect on potential investors, which stringent working provisions are alleged to result in, they prefer, in that situation, to show a "liberal" attitude.

One of the most frequently emphasized advantages to developing countries (or any country for that matter) of belonging to the Paris Union is the possibility they have as members to obtain amendments to the Convention on subjects of particular interest to them.[2]

Thus, there exist two ways in which developing countries, that belong to the Paris Union, can seek to remedy certain effects of the Convention that are considered disadvantageous: directly, in accordance with existing substantive rules and indirectly, through revising the Convention. The probable practical value of these two means to remedy the effects of non-working and other abuses of patents will be examined below.[3]

A. POSSIBLE REMEDIES UNDER THE PRESENT SUBSTANTIVE RULES

The differences between the considerations upon which the Paris Convention was built, and those motivating today the adhesion of developing countries, have been emphasized previously. That the existance of these differences are generally recognized is demonstrated by the importance always attached to the availability of effective remedies (sanctions) against non-working and other abuses for the benefit of developing countries. What may be disputable, however, is the extent to which the presently available remedies are of real value to developing countries.

Though such provisions are generally referred to as sanctions, the

[1] See, for instance E. T. Penrose, *The Economics of the International Patent System* (Baltimore: Johns Hopkins, 1951), p. 210.

[2] See, for instance, S. P. Ladas, *Propiedad Industrial y Desarrollo Económico*, (Bogotá: Brigard y Hurrutia), p. 6.

[3] Since the possibilities and limitations of the present conventional rules concerning sanctions against non-working (and other abuses) have been analyzed previously, what follows below will be limited to stating the principles involved.

term remedy is deliberately used as being more appropriate, at least in the case of developing countries, to designate measures especially against non-working. While the term sanction naturally implies a corrective measure against a harmful situation imputable to the patentee, cases of non-exploitation are not necessarily the fault of the patentees.[4] Before examining the utility of remedies available for specific cases, the absence of any rule regulating the non-application of the patent system, or its restricted application for certain categories of inventions, should be mentioned.

1. The possibility to exclude or limit the application of the patent system for certain products and/or processes

No rule has so far been introduced into the Convention that prohibits derogations from the general application of the patent system.

The faculty to limit the application of the patent system has been used for two principal reasons. A country may wish to avoid that, during the initial stage of creating a new national industry, its activities are hampered through the granting of patents in that particular area, where the temporary advance of foreign industry may lead to foreign domination. Whatever its logical deficiency when compared to the general theory for granting patent protection, it is clear that any rational use of such an exception of patentability based on a sort of "infant industry" argument would, in the case of developing countries, amount to its application in a very wide range of industries and its practical effect would be to renounce the international patent system. Furthermore, the fact that the very lack of national technology and scientists is the primary motive for the developing countries to join the Paris Union, decidedly rules out any rational application of exemptions from patentability on this ground.

Another reason for exempting inventions in certain fields from patentability, or limiting the application of the general patent system in certain cases, concerns a number of varying situations, which may be grouped under the heading of inventions affecting a particular public interest. The areas where such restrictions on the patentability of inventions (either for products or processes or both) are most generally

[4] Though this idea was expressed some thirty years ago already (cf. *Supra*, p. 147) it is often being held today that for the case where the (foreign) patentee has offered licenses there are no grounds for further actions against him, implying thereby that the "sanctions" provided for in the Convention should only be employed to counter abuses over which the patentee can be held to have effective control.

applied, are foods and pharmaceuticals. – The questionable logic of such restrictions and the questions it raises concerning the general theory underlying patent protection have already been examined.[5] – The Model Law Committee, in an evident effort to counter demands for a more general lowering of the limits within which actions against non-worked patents could be taken, included a section according to which patents within particular areas could be attached with compulsory licenses, without any waiting period, upon government order. The text does not provide any limitation as to the categories of inventions that, according to this section, may, by decree, be opened to immediate grants of compulsory licenses. As the various demands for such provisions as revocation, free use of patents for governmental purposes and other limitations of the general application of the patent system, which were also raised in the Model Law Committee, have always been opposed, on the ground that too many exceptions would discourage foreign investments, the substitution of the type of provision suggested in the Model Law for a general lowering of the "automatic" protection of patentees, would seem preferable to the patentees only if the rule in question would be quite sparsely used.

2. *Remedies against non-working and other abuses of patents*

Though the remedial actions allowed under the Convention against the non-working and other abuses of the patent grant basically remain the same as before the last revision conference, the Lisbon conference introduced an important change as far as the required waiting periods are concerned. Whereas compulsory licenses in the case of non-working may be granted only three years after the grant of the patent (or four years after the date of application), such licenses may, according to the latest text, be granted without any waiting period in the case of abuses of the patent monopoly other than non-working. The rule that revocation may be ordered only two years after the date of the first compulsory license remains unchanged from the previous Convention text for both cases, although there seems to be room for interpreting the Lisbon text in the sense that a patent may be revoked immediately in the case of abuses if the granting of compulsory licenses *would not have been sufficient* to prevent them.[6] Though the text of the Convention does not provide for any criteria on what is to be considered "abuse of

[5] Cf. *Supra*, pp. 39–41.
[6] Cf. *Supra*, pp. 91–92.

the patent monopoly," it is clear from the deliberations at Lisbon on article 5A, that simple non-working of a patent does not necessarity constitute such au abuse. An abuse of the patent grant, besides non-working, may result from such practices as were mentioned in the chapter on "Indirect Effects of the International Patent System," that is, practices resulting from cartel agreements based on patent rights or from restrictive practices by a single dominant patentee. As actions on the national level against international cartel practices are often ineffective in the case of industrial countries, this must be even more so in developing countries, especially as, in the latter case, the cartel may not need to acquire or maintain local patent for their agreement to be effective. The principal practical interest to developing countries is the available remedies they may provide for against non-exploitation of patented inventions.

a. Compulsory licenses

The compulsory license is the most widely prescribed sanction against non-working, especially in industrialized countries. Only around half of all developing countries which have a national patent law, have provisions for compulsory licenses. This figure undoubtedly supports the contention that a number of developing countries do not avail themselves of the possible remedial actions permitted under the Convention. This fact must not lead to the conclusion, however, that the only action necessary for these countries would be to apply the provisions permitted, unless such provisions are likely to have either a preventive or a remedial effect capable of satisfying the needs and requirements of developing countries.

When the question of compulsory licenses is dealt with, the only difference mentioned between industrialized and developing countries is often that the conditions in the latter countries make the provision of compulsory licenses particularly important to them. When the probable effects of such provisions are discussed, this is almost invariably done in terms of the experience of developed countries. The fact, that in the latter countries only a very limited number of compulsory licenses is issued, is mentioned to show either that a country generally does not find it in its own interest to force the local exploitation of a patented invention, where the patentee has not found such exploitation worthwhile, or that the mere threat of a potential compulsory license makes the patentee willing to reach voluntary licensing agreements with local manufacturers. For this experience to be relevant to the developing countries, the presence of two related premises would be required, both of which will usually be lacking: that cases where the local authorities insisted on exploitation, when the patentee was neither working the invention himself nore licensing it, would be exceptions to the general rule; and that the preventive effect of a compulsory license clause was not impeded by the underdeveloped state of indigenous technology and the lack of local manufacturers able to apply an invention successfully, should it come to the point of granting a compulsory license.

Underlying the Convention is the idea that, in general, patentees ought to be allowed to chose where to manufacture in the interest of the international division of labor. As mentioned previously, however, the theory of comparative costs may not always be applicable in its traditional form for developing countries undertaking the task of creating whole new branches of industry. This fact, together with the "investment climate" complex, sufficiently illustrate the often wide separation between the interests of patentees and those of local authorities. As it has furthermore been repeatedly observed, that the only rational ground for developing countries to grant patents is that the inventions so protected be actually worked locally, it must follow, that the case where such local exploitation is desirable, despite the unwillingness of the patentee to cooperate, will be the general rule rather than the exception, thus invalidating the premise, implicit in the Convention, that in general the interests of patentees and the patent granting countries are parallel.

There is general agreement on the requirement of developing countries to have an effective system of remedies against non-working and other abuses. "The conclusions of the United Nations study," says Lachmann, "that the [patent] system is on balance likely to be beneficial is coupled with a provisio regarding safeguards against monopolistic abuses."[7] The disagreement starts only with the evaluation of what "safeguards" ought to be used and their effectiveness. It is generally recognized, as the U.N. Report repeatedly emphasizes, that the technology contained in a patent very seldom is sufficient to work the invention in an effective manner. The Report, as has been shown, in this respect makes a distinction between various cases, concluding that only in the rare circumstances, where the technology contained in the patent grant would suffice to effectively work the invention, would

[7] K. Lachmann, "The Role of Industrial Property in the Dissemination of Technical Information in the World Context – A United Nations View," *IDEA*, 9: 183, Conf. No. 1965.

the licensee normally be able to operate independently of the patentee. The probability that such cases occur under the conditions prevailing in developing countries is further diminished by their generally feeble technological base, often not even providing potential licensees. When the author, quoted above, therefore refers to the safeguards, mentioning "the need for compulsory licensing and working provisions which will assure that foreign inventions protected by patents are actually worked in the country itself,"[8] such effectiveness of compulsory license provisions may be automatically expected only for the rare case, where the technology conveyed by the patent is sufficient for its effective exploitation.[9] If no additional pressure is applied on the patentee, the latter will be inclined to cooperate with the grantee of a compulsory licensee only when the latter would anyhow be able to work the invention independently. In what is certainly the great majority of cases of non-worked patents, additional knowhow will be required, and in all these cases the mere existence of compulsory license provisions cannot "assure" anything.[10,11]

Thus is it seen that, in the majority of cases of non-worked patents, the lack of two essential premises underlying the present system for international patent protection makes the often-quoted experience of industrial countries not quite relevant to developing countries.

In the previously mentioned concession, that was evidently made by the Model Law Committee,[12] to counter suggestions for the inclusion of a revocation provision and other more radical measures, is included, besides the faculty to grant compulsury licenses without the normally required waiting period, the power to grant compulsory licenses for the importation of the products concerned.

[8] *Ibid.*

[9] Though Lachmann mentions "compulsory licensing and working provisions" which might include a provision for revocation, the fact that the author (p. 183) refers to the possible "safeguards" suggested by the Report as having since been included in the Model Law – which contains no provision for revocation – suggests that he merely considers provisions for compulsory licenses.

[10] Cf. *Supra*, p. 148

[11] To the extent that outside sources would be able to supply the required additional technology, the effectiveness of compulsory licensing would increase. The importance of such outside sources is recognized in various United Nations resolutions, where the creation of such supplies of technical knowledge is called for. Other considerations, however, would seem to limit the possible independence of the licensee from the patentee. Not only is much of the knowhow required for the effective working of an invention based on the personal experience of the patentee (-inventor), but the rapid technological evolution often requires a continuous flow of information from the licensor to the licensee.

[12] *Supra*, p. 222.

Though at first sight this faculty might seem a derogation of the Convention, it is evidently not considered so.[13]

A compulsory license provision can thus only be expected to provide an effective remedy in a limited number of cases as far as developing countries are concerned. In the majority of cases a more powerful remedy is required, which would either lead to the local working through the ultimate threat of the loss of the patent privilege or inhibit the negative effects of the market control exercised by the patentee.

b. Revocation of the patent grant

This sanction, which was contained in the original version of the Convention, has often been considered of particular utility to developing countries. This is attested by the fact, that only the action of some of these countries have permitted its retention in the present text. Of the some thirty-eight developing States, out of sixty-two having national patent systems, which have provisions for granting compulsory licenses, only ten also provide for the possible revocation of the patent grant, four of them being Union members. Another thirteen countries rely exclusively on revocation provisions as a preventive or remedial measure, five of which are members of the Paris Union.

According to the Convention, a revocation of a patent grant may not be carried out before the expiration of two years from the date at which compulsory licenses could be issued, or, in other words, not until after at least five years from the grant of the patent. Such a long waiting period may today considerably reduce the benefit, that a developing country could obtain by revoking a patent grant.

The above analysis demonstrates that the traditional rules of the Convention concerning remedial provisions in case of non-working, do not meet the requirements of developing countries. The "safeguarding," in an effective sense of that word, of their interests, is not compatible with the "adequate protection of inventors" in its conventional sense, and on the basis of which the Paris Convention was founded and has evolved.

[13] "Compulsory licenses may be granted even before this three-year waiting period and even for importation ... These provisions are compatible with the existing British Legislation." G. H. C. Bodenhausen, "A Model Patent Law for Developing Countries, "*Creative Ferment in World Patent Systems, Conference of the National Association of Manufacturers, June, 1965* (New York: N.A.M., 1965) p. 27. –

Though the provision in question may appear advantageous, it means in contrast to the free importation that could take place after revocation, a submission to a monopoly possibly resulting in higher prices; in addition, a compulsory license to import carries with it an obligation to pay the patentee "adequate royalties." *Model Law* ..., section forty.

B. REMEDIES THROUGH CHANGING THE RULES OF THE CONVENTION

When the advantages of Union membership are explained to developing countries today, one claimed advantage is that in their capacity as members they can activily participate in revision conferences seeking amendments that they deem particularly desirable for their own needs. The weakness of this argument is shown by the fact, that the most important feature conditioning the working of revision conferences is the unwritten rule requiring unanimity.

How has this unanimity principle helped or hindered the developing countries in the past, and how is it likely to affect their possibilities to influence future revisions? Undoubtedly it has meant a slower pace in the liberalization of rules on working requirements. At times, the opposition of a small number of countries, or even that of a single member, has inhibited the adoption of certain rules. On the other hand, it may be that the very existence of the requirement of unanimous consent has led to the exercise of pressure to convince certain opposing members. The possibilities for developing countries to effectively amend the Convention at a future Conference, with respect to their special requirements, depend among others on two related considerations: the traditional aim of the Paris Union and its Secretariat in the evolution of the international patent system, and the position taken by developed countries intent on safeguarding their own interests.

Since its beginnings, the principal aim of the Paris Union has been to achieve uniformity among national patent laws, especially of the rules concerning working requirements, and to render such rules more lenient to patentees. Whenever opposition to concrete proposals in the latter respect has appeared, so-called "compromise" clauses have usually been agreed upon, on the theory that the opposition would sooner or later come to agree with the opinions of the more "progressive" members. This understanding of the significance of compromises reached is illustrated by the alternative designation of such agreements, which have often been referred to as "textes transactionnels." Practically no member country has ever proposed limitations on already existing rights of patentees and, true to the original intentions of the founders of the Union, the compromises have led, albeit at a slower pace, to the uninterrupted evolution of greater liberty for patentees as far as provisions against non-working are concerned. Although this traditional pattern of the evolution of the system does not rule out a change of objectives or direction, it seems plausible to assume that under existing conditions such changes are not likely to come about.

Beside the unlikeliness that under present conditions the objectives and the direction of the evolution of the international patent system will change, a related consideration, that must be taken into account in evaluating the practical possibilities of developing countries to posetively change the present rules in their favor, is the position of developed countries on any concrete question. While it is not possible to know their positions at any future revision conference, they may be predicted on the basis of the opinions expressed so far relating to suggested changes in favor of developing countries. Judging from the position taken by most of these countries in the various United Nations bodies, and the opinions expressed by BIRPI and the private international organizations supporting the present system and warning of the alleged consequences of any derogations to existing rules, it appears extremely unlikely that, under present circumstances, the developed countries will agree to any proposal limiting the present protection of (their) patentees.[14]

On the basis of this examination, it must be concluded that despite frequent assurances implying the contrary, developing countries, members of the Paris Union, are unlikely to be able to achieve any significant changes in the existing international patent system through their participation in revision conferences, under present conditions.

[14] The typical position in this respect is illustrated by a reply of the BIRPI Director to a question posed by a participant in the Asian Seminar on Industrial Property (sponsored by BIRPI). On a question whether the provision of the Convention concerning compulsory licenses and forfeiture could not be made more flexible and liberal, the BIRPI Director said that "such an amendment to the Paris Convention would certainly fail to obtain unanimity" adding that in his personal opinion "any national law overstepping the limits established in the Paris Convention in this respect would so much weaken the patent system that it would have an adverse effect on the industrialization of any developing country." Asian Seminar on Industrial Property, Documents, pp. 120–21 [Papers prepared by BIRPI, for/and report of proceedings of, Asian Seminar on Industrial Property, Colombo, Ceylon, February 7–10, 1966.]

CHAPTER VI

POSSIBLE REMEDIES OUTSIDE THE PRESENT SYSTEM

The preceding chapters have shown some of the fundamental differences between industrialized and developing countries with respect both to their objectives in joining the international patent system and to the kinds of benefits each can derive from its working. It has been demonstrated that the rules concerning sanctions against non-working and (other) abuses can only rarely fulfill their objects in the case of developing countries. Though this situation alone would justify a reconsideration of the present rules as they apply to these countries, it may not appear to be a sufficient reason for the industrialized countries to re-evaluate the principles of the Convention. Of greater importance seems the finding that, though the very principle of reciprocity, on which the Convention is built, has little practical relevance for developing countries, these countries are nevertheless supposed to abide by rules under which only industrialized countries can wholly benefit. This latter finding hardly conforms to contemporary developments in the fields of international economic cooperation between industrialized and developing countries and the concern for the latters' rapid economic development.

Before examining the justifications and prospects for a more fruitful cooperation in patent matters between the two groups of countries, brief mention will be made of the only other (theoretical) alternative for solving some of the deficiencies of the present situation.

A. COOPERATION AMONG DEVELOPING COUNTRIES THEMSELVES

One possible "remedy," which will not be considered, is the abolishment of patent protection. Though the general survey of the patent institution has shown that doubts may exist as to the appropriateness and effectiveness of a general patent system today, as long as practically all the countries of the world grant patent protection, it would not be constructive for developing countries to abolish the system as such. No author has suggested such a course. Very often in the debate, and especially with the ardent defenders of the system, there is an all-or-nothing approach which serves to confuse what ought to be the real issue, namely an appraisal of the present system in terms of its marginal effects.[1]

There remains the solution that would involve the renunciation, on the part of the developing countries, of their participation in the present international patent system.[2] This would not necessarily mean an elimination of all patent relations between industrialized and developing countries. As the large majority of present non-members of the Paris Union accord equal protection to nationals and foreigners, the developing countries could, in the event of leaving the Paris Union, maintain the principle of national treatment but with more severe working requirements.

If the developing countries were to leave or remain outside the international patent system, they could, of course, set up an organization among themselves, creating a large patent territory and by way of a priority rule foster the exchange of technology between themselves, though the limited scope of such an exchange of technology must be recognized. The strength of a large group of developing countries might provide bargaining power for obtaining mutual concessions – also including priority treatment – between themselves and the industrialized countries, but it would leave the basic problem of the present imbalance between the two groups unsolved. The only practically possible approach to diminishing this imbalance will be for the developing countries to obtain unilateral concessions from the industrialized countries. This could only be obtained through cooperation between the two groups, not through competition. Thus, the developing countries should unite in a common effort to obtain such concessions, not by

[1] The same situation often prevails in the debate on the theory of patent protection in general. Once the conclusion is reached that some patent protection is likely to be beneficial, it is convenient to imply, however lacking in scientific approach, that the present rules of the system are as likely as any other to serve that purpose. A notable departure from this type of analysis is provided by F. Machlup: "An Economic Review of the Patent System," *U.S. Senate, Committee on the Judiciary, Study No. 15 of the Subcommittee on Patents, Trademarks and Copyrights* (Washington: Government Printing Office, 1958.)

[2] For such a suggestion, at least as far as developing countries in the early stages of industrialization are concerned, see E. T. Penrose, *The Economics of the International Patent System* (Baltimore: Johns Hopkins, 1951), pp. 221, 233.

seceding from the present system but by changing its rules. It has been repeatedly suggested in previous chapters that such changes are very unlikely to be implemented under present conditions, but there are means by which the present dominance of the Paris Union could be challenged, in which case this organization might become more amenable to changes.

B. BASIS AND JUSTIFICATION FOR PREFERENTIAL TREATMENT

When the rules of the Paris Convention were laid down, they were designed to achieve two fundamental aims: to overcome obstacles created by national boundaries for patentees through the formation of a union patent territory; and to unify certain basic rules of national patent laws. The rules designed to support the latter aim were the principle of unanimous consent to amendments, the rule prescribing unconditional ratification of new texts, and the rule for outside countries to accept the latest version of the Convention unconditionally on becoming members. These rules were considered the most likely to fulfill the aims of the Member States, but there was a price to be paid. The unanimity rule was certain to slow down the speed of the legislative evolution of the Convention. Furthermore, the principle of national treatment, coupled with the introduction of certain minimum standards of protection for patentees, were certain to be more advantageous to some countries than to others.[3] The countries opposed to measures ensuring greater freedom for patentees were nearly always less industrialized. In this respect, the situation has not changed today. However, the whole complex of problems connected with developing countries has changed fundamentally since 1945, both quantitatively and qualitatively; quantitatively in the sense that the world today is confronted with the insistent desire of every non-industrialized country to develop economically and technologically; qualitatively, in that the successful implementation of economic development in these countries is today regarded as much of a concern to the world as a whole as

[3] It has always been pointed out however, that the discrepancies in the amount of benefits to be derived by the various countries is only a temporary phenomenon. P. Roubier, "The Law of the Union for the Protection of Industrial Property," *Journal du Droit International*, p. 711, No. 3, 1951, has stated that it was wise of Member States to accept initially unequal benefits "for the very principles on which the Union was founded ... had sooner or later to bring about a complete equality of interests, *at least an equality before the law.*" [Italics added]

to the developing countries themselves. This situation has led to, and justifies, adaptation or redefinition of traditional theoretical concepts and arguments in support of these countries' economic development. Below, some indications of such a change of attitudes in the field of international economic relations will be examined, and its bearing on existing international patent arrangements suggested.

In the liberal, individualist society of the last century, the areas of government intervention were few and well-defined. One of its tasks was to ensure the equality of its citizens before the law. Once such equality was achieved, the individuals were left to themselves. From a small start of handing out token assistance to its most destitute citizens for purely humanitarian considerations, the idea came to be accepted, that it was not only the function of society to assist its less well off members, but also that the latter had certain rights to such assistance. Moreover, such assistance was not wholly disinterested on the part of society, for it was recognized, that the full potential of the well-being of society could only be realized, when all its citizens were ensured a certain minimum standard of living; and furthermore, that the higher that standard, the higher would be that of society as a whole. Later, the same pattern of thought and action was applied to regional development within countries. Though the philosophy underlying this evolution is today wholly accepted, it may be well to remember, that there was often fierce opposition from individuals, who saw their vested interests threatened.

An evolution along similar lines has started in the field of international relations.[4] International law, which until quite recently has been concerned merely with the regulation of diplomatic intercourse among States, now needs adjustment to meet the changes in the structure and scope of contemporary international relations. The need for such changes is due to two principal factors: the active participants in interstate relations are no longer a small group of Western nations but a much larger number of States representing different civilizations; and the ambit of international law has expanded from the mere regulation of diplomatic relations to a concern for matters of social and economic interest, particularly apparent in the vast field of pro-

[4] Cf. S. Pretnar, "More on the Legal Protection of Industrial Property," *P.I.*, 71, annex, p. 1, January, 1955 [translation supplied by BIRPI of "Nochmals zur Frage des gewerblichen Rechtsschutzes in der Struktur des heutigen Weltwirtschaft," BIRPI Library]; W. Röpke, "Die unentwickelten Länder als wirtschaftliches, soziales und gesellschaftliches Problem," Röpke et al., *Entwicklungsländer, Wahn und Wirklichkeit* (Zürich: Rentsch, 1961, pp. 11–82) pp. 14–17.

blems concerning international economic development.[5] While the classical system of international law, with its emphasis on the "sovereign equality" of States, was limited to a concern for legal equality, the contemporary scope of international relations makes it evident, that such legal equality, in the face of fundamental social and economic inequality, is an insufficient basis on which to build international cooperation.

This has been recognized to some extent in the field of international economic relations. Myrdal calls it a "false principle of equality" when it is argued, that developing countries should adhere to the same rules as do industrialized countries as far as trade restrictions are concerned. Against the idea that all nations are equal, and that the international community should be based on principles and rules that are applied to all, the same author says: "It is an ideal that they *should* be equal, but if, in fact, they are not, equal treatment becomes inequality."[6] Observing that this thought and the underlying basic facts are gradually being recognized by various international organizations, Myrdal concludes his argument by saying:

> My main point is that these [developing] countries are in a quite special situation as long as they have not caught up with the developed countries; for this reason a double standard of morality in international trade is rationally motivated.[7]

Such a concept is however far from being universally accepted. Though the various bodies of the United Nations are in several instances implementing policies to that effect, some other international organizations seem firmly entrenched in the traditional concept of legal equality among States.

During the 1964 UNCTAD Conference, the idea of preferential treatment for developing countries was brought up on several occasions. The extent of the concessions finally agreed upon in this respect is

[5] Cf. W. Friedmann, *The Changing Structure of International Law* (London: Stevens, 1964), and also M. Virally, "Vers un droit international du développement," *Annuaire Français de Droit International*, XI: 3–12, 1965.

[6] G. Myrdal, *An International Economy* (London: Routledge and Kegan Paul, 1956), p. 291; according to an Indian Government representative in G.A.T.T., quoted by Myrdal, *loc. cit.*, "equality of treatment is equitable only among equals."

[7] *Ibid.*, pp. 291–92; a similar opinion is expressed by A. A. Fatouros, "International Law and the Third World," *Virginia Law Review*, 50: 783–823, June, 1964. He argues for the rationality of a double standard, because "there is no inherent injustice in applying different tests of legality to actions taken by parties in significantly different situations. To the contrary," says Fatouros, "it would seem less than fair to apply precisely the same tests to the actions of the parties under such conditions." Since international law occasionally accepts the rationality of double standards, namely in the case of war, Fatouros suggests "that the existance, with respect to the third world, of a state of necessity akin to war, arising out of its attempt to achieve rapid economic development, should be recognized." (*Ibid.* p. 812)

unclear. Whereas one author has said, with regard to trade preferences, that "what UNCTAD adopted was a set of principles, which does not have general agreement,"[8] the Secretary General of that Conference, is reported to have stated that:

The most favored-nation principle is modified to include the granting of concessions by developed countries to developing countries without reciprocity and without extending them to other developed countries.[9]

One author points out that both statements are correct: insofar as the adoption of some provisions (with respect to manufacturers and semi-manufactures) are concerned, it is not clear whether the principle of preferential treatment was conceded by all delegations, whereas in the case of commodity trade, such a principle did have general consent.[10] Whatever the actual extent of trade categories where the principle of preferential treatment was generally agreed upon, the more important result of the UNCTAD 1964 is that the principle of non-reciprocity in favor of developing countries was accepted – the specific areas where it will be implemented depending on political considerations rather than legal principles – and that the argument of legal equality will not in the future play the decisive role it has played in the past. Though before and during the UNCTAD, the idea of preferential treatment may not have been accepted as a general principle for economic relations between developing and developed countries,[11] by the latter, there are signs that this position is changing.[12]

It would seem that, as far as the majority of international lawyers are concerned, the new ideas have won little recognition. W. C. Jenks sees two reasons for this: "the inertia which every legal system invariably opposes to every proposal for change," and "the inherent tenden-

[8] G. Weintraub, "After the United Nations Trade Conference: Lessons and Portents," *Foreign Affairs*, 43: 37–50, October, 1964, p. 45.

[9] R. Prebisch, quoted by E. Etra, "Time for a Change: The United Nations Conference on Trade and Development," *Revue Belge de Droit International*, 1: 50–67, No. 1, 1966, p. 65.

[10] *Ibid.*

[11] D. Cordovez, "The Making of UNCTAD: Institutional Background and Legislative History," *Journal of World Trade Law*, 1: 243–328, No. 3, 1967, states (pp. 243–44) that such a principle was agreed upon at the 1964 Conference, saying notably that the Conference "exploded the myth that all countries are economically equal and thus established the principle that a code of rules of international trade should reflect the existance of basic differences of economic and social organization, economic development and bargaining power."

[12] P. Loby, "Les pays riches ont fait un premier pas en faveur du commerce international des pays en voie de développement," *Le Monde Diplomatique*, October, 1967, p. 14, reporting from the fifth session of the UNCTAD Trade and Development Board (August-September), says that the principle of preferential treatment has at least been agreed upon; see also J. L Hess, "U.S. Shift on Trade Preferences Seen," *The International Herald Tribune*, October 6, 1967, p. 7, reporting from an O.E.C.D. meeting.

cy of every legal system to protect the vested interests with which it has become familiar."[13] Though this is neither unnatural nor in itself wrong, since the protection of acquired rights is an essential function of any legal system, the same author states that "no legal system can protect itself against revolution except by providing adequate scope for evolutionary change."[14] The implication of this latter point for international law, according to Jenks, is:

To achieve this result [the needed change of perspective] by a sufficiently evolutionary process to avoid impairing the authority of well-established law in a degree which would prejudice for an indefinite period the possibility of establishing an effective body of international law on a world wide basis.[15]

According to this train of thought, the present policies within the Paris Union, of trying to avoid any change in the basic rules for fear of an erosion of established law, might lead to the much graver situation where these rules would become completely disregarded. Or, in the words of Jenks, the lack of possibilities for evolution may lead to revolution.

The insufficiency of the principle of legal equality as a basis for cooperation between developed and developing countries, in the field of international patent protection, has rarely been criticized.[16] A notable exception is S. Pretnar, whose two articles have been previously referred to. After analyzing article 5 of the Paris Convention concerning minimum protection for patentees against working obligations, and observing that such protection has steadily been increased, Pretnar holds that while this article of the Convention has successfully served the development of the now industrialized countries, it may have the opposite effect on the developing countries because of the

[13] C. W. Jenks, *The Common Law of Mankind* (London: Stevens, 1958), p. 85.

[14] *Ibid.*, The author continues: "It is not the primary function of international law in the second half of the twentieth century to protect vested interests arising out of an international distribution of political and economic power which has irrevocably changed, but to adjust conflicting interests on a basis which contemporary opinion regards as sufficiently reasonable to be entitled to the organized support of a universal community."

[15] *Ibid.*, p. 87.

[16] R. Vernon, "The International Patent System and Foreign Policy," *U.S. Senate, Committee on the Judiciary Study No. 5 of the Subcommittee on Patents, Trademarks and Copyrights* (Washington: Government Printing Office, 1958), p. 34, states: "Where we are convinced that a mutual interest exists in having another nation grant exclusionary rights to foreigners through patent grants, we should have no hesitation in trying to persuade it to our own point of view. But we must always recognize the quite extraordinary nature of our demands ..." and with special reference to developing countries, the author continues: "These nations can hardly be expected to see the extreme grant of patent monopoly rights to foreigners as being unqualifiedly consistent with their own national aspirations. *A bridge between our conceptions and theirs in this regard will need a kind of understanding which we have so far rarely displayed in international patent negotiations.*" [italics added].

economic and technological inequality between the two groups of countries.[17] The author, tracing the history of the Paris Union to its origins, maintains that the Paris Convention was drawn up at a time when political, economic and technical conditions were totally different from what they are today. Asking whether the Paris Convention can meet the requirements of the present economic situation, and whether it can be reconciled with the tasks undertaken by the United Nations in the field of economic development, the author replies in the negative. Though the system of international protection of industrial property scarcely can retard the evolution of international relations "towards a new form of economic and progressive humanism" as manifested by the programs of assistance for the benefit of developing countries, "sooner or later," according to Pretnar, "the Convention will have to be completely recast." The author concludes by suggesting that the future role which the Paris Union ought to play is to aim at the equalization of the economic conditions in various countries.[18]

Though there have always been economic considerations underlying the granting of patent rights, the problems of international patent protection have almost invariably been dealt with by lawyers, who quite naturally have been preoccupied with the legal aspects of the protection of patentees. One of the most well-known authorities on patent law and the international patent system rejects Pretnar's above-quoted contention, saying that contrary to the charge that the Convention is disadvantageous to developing countries, "the Convention has been one of the finest pieces of international legislation regulating our world and ensuring equality of treatment in large and small countries alike."[19]

[17] S. Pretnar, "The International Protection of Industrual Property and the Different Stages of Economic Development of the States." [translation supplied by BIRPI of "La protection internationale de la propriété industrielle et les différents stades de développement économique des Etats," *P.I.*, 69: 213–21, December, 1953. BIRPI library].

[18] *Ibid.*, p. 10. Representatives of industrial countries frequently stress that most patents are in private hands, in order to show the limited power of their Governments to influence the transfer of patented technology. D. L. Ladd, "Industrial Property and the Iron Curtain Countries," *Address to the National Association of Manufacturers* (New York: N.A.M., 1964), p. 7, has said, however, that "we ... should begin to think of industrial property as more than a means of advancing private interests ... as an instrument for achievement of national policies – of assisting the newly developing countries ...

Perhaps the time has come for reassessment of national policy on exchange in patents, knowhow [and] technical data ...

... it is clear that industrial property can now become an important instrument in the service of national policy, including the dominant policy of advancing the cause of human welfare ..."

[19] S. P. Ladas, "The Fundamental Bases of the International Protection of Industrial Property," *P.I.*, 70: annex, April, 1954 [original text of "Les bases fondamentales de la protection internationale de la propriété industrielle," *P.I.*, 70: 93–97, April, 1954.] p. 4.

A recent development, which may well come to influence the views of industrialized countries on the problems of the technological discrepancy between them and the developing countries, and emphasize the irrelevancy of often made historical references, is the quite recent concern with the so-called technology gap among industrialized countries, which allegedly exists, basically between the United States and Western Europe. Whatever the precise reasons for this disparity, nobody today denies its existence.[20] The sheer difference of financial resources employed indicates that the present "gap" is unlikely to disappear unless both markets and resources for research and development are radically increased.[21] Lachmann emphasizes the connection between problems of developing countries and the present awareness of an existing technological discrepancy also among industrialized countries, when he says:

> Dealing with the transfer of industrial technology from one country to another one would ... take too narrow a view if one were to see this unequal relationship as existing only between the developed and the underdeveloped countries. It also exists, and in a potentially much more explosive form, between what one may call the industrial superpowers and all other advanced countries.[22]

The reasons which have led to this situation (need for more complex and costly research, for which only enterprises in the largest industrial countries have the facilities and the markets) may be expected to lead the "superpowers" continuously to increase their technological and their competitive advantages over other countries, which, regardless of their technical sophistication and inventive genius, lack the resources and the markets of these countries. The fact of this technological gap is already making itself felt in reactions by some countries "*which fear*,"

[20] Though one authority seems to belittle the question reportedly saying that differences exist not on the inventing and innovating stages but because innovations are not being properly exploited, making the differences between the United States and other industrialized countries "almost a marketing problem in most cases," – see C. Kurtis, "Technology Gap Laid to Lack of Promotion," *The International Herald Tribune*, June 29, 1967, p. 7 – others stress more farreaching reasons such as differences in emphasis on competition, in education, size of markets etc. Cf. "Technological Gap Is Upsetting Western Europe," *The New York Times International Edition*, March 14, 1967, pp. 1, 10, and "Pour rattraper son retard technologique, l'Europe s'engage dans la voie de la coopération," *Le Monde Diplomatique*, February, 1967, pp. 2–5. Cf also J-J. Servan-Schreiber *Le défi Americain* (Paris: Denöel, 1967).

[21] The difference in resources spent by the United States and Western Europe on research and development is usually put at between three and four hundred percent. Cf. "Technological Gap Is Upsetting Western Europe," *op. cit.*, p. 10 (*supra*, n. 20); "U.S. Widening Science Edge over Europe," *The International Herald Tribune*, October 9, 1967, p. 9.

[22] K. Lachmann, "The Role of Industrial Property in the Dissemination of Technical Information in the World Context – A United Nations View," *IDEA*, 9: 184, Conference No., 1965.

according to Lachmann, *"that foreign companies are using their advantages to preempt the domestic market and to discourage domestic research."*[23]

In view of these considerations, historical references, employed to convince developing countries that protection of foreign patentees will be mutually beneficial, appear rather dubious.

As far as patents are concerned it is obvious that the imbalance in resources employed in research and development will also result in a comparable discrepancy in terms of the numbers of patent protected inventions and royalties and other income derived from inventions patented abroad.[24] One author, studying the problem of patent relations within the Common Market, says that one of the reasons why such cooperation does not function well is because of the number of patents sought by foreigners, and notably United States nationals, within the Common Market.[25]

The example of Japanese industrial development with its, partly, very heavy reliance on foreign technology might be taken to indicate a successful use of the international patent system as far as patented and patent-connected technology is concerned. And certainly, the importance of foreign technology in the Japanese development is undisputa-

[23] *Ibid.*, p. 186. [italics added].

[24] In 1962, the countries of Western Europe spent five times more on acquring United States patented and licensed technology than the United States spent to acquire European technology, reportedly a "technological balance-of-payments deficit" of U.S. $ 200 million. That "deficit" today has been estimated at U.S. $ 1 billion. Cf. "Technological Gap is Upsetting Western Europe," *op. cit.*, p. 1, (*supra*, n. 20); a measure of the global net position has been given for the year 1957. In that year United States companies earned on the sale and licensing of patents abroad some U.S. $ 400 million, while spending a mere U.S. $ 20 million to acquire foreign technology, Cf. "Trading in Knowledge," *The Economist*, June 4, 1960, p. 1004; a more recent exposé of the proportions of receipts and payments for foreign technology for the world as a whole as well as for some large individual countries is contained in a document submitted to the second UNCTAD Conference (New Delhi, 1968): TD/28/Supp. 1, pp. 10–14.

[25] Comparing the disproportion of patents sought by United States citizens in the Common Market and by the citizens of the latter countries in the United States, the author adds: "Phénomène plus inquiétant, elle [cette disproportion] s'accentue." C. Neme, "Pénétration de produits sous marque ou licence et unification des marchés dans la C.E.E.," *La propriété industrielle et le marché commun, aspects économiques; Colloque université – industrie, 19–20 novembre, 1065, Lyon.* (Paris: Dunod, 1966), p. 131. Neme also indicates why it may be expected that the relatively more resourceful countries will continue to increase their technological power over other countries, saying (p. 131): "Les américains adoptent une politique de brevets d'autant plus dynamique que l'Etat membre [de la C.E.E.] a lui-même un comportement dynamique. Inversement l'attitude américaine conditionne la politique de chaque Etat membre; l'Allemagne puise une partie de son dynamisme dans l'afflux des brevets américains. Les deux phénomenes, à la fois cause et effet, se renforcent dans un processus cumulatif de progrès technologique ..."

ble. Many elements in the Japanese experience must therefore be of interest to developing countries today.[26]

The case of Japan must nevertheless be seen in its proper perspective, in order that superficial parallels are not too readily drawn.

In terms of most contemporary developing countries, Japan probably left their current stage forty to fifty years ago. The remarkable position of Japan today, it should also be born in mind, is the fruit of almost a century of very conscious governmental planning for economic and technological development and of important direct foreign investments since the beginning of the present century.

One of the most important features of Japanese development policies has been the role of its Government in controlling and regulating the acquisition of foreign technology and the terms on which it has been transferred.

It is unlikely that a developing country today, without the resources and thus potential markets of a country the size of Japan, could so effectively steer its development without the real support for its objectives and active cooperation of the technology-exporting countries.

C. THE CASE FOR A UNIVERSAL PATENT CONVENTION AND THE PRESENT DOMINANT POSITION OF THE PARIS UNION

If the concept of preferential treatment in favor of developing countries in the sphere of international economic relations is accepted to provide a more equitable position for these countries, and if the present rules of the Paris Convention run counter to such a concept, a change of these rules is justified. Since it has been concluded that for the developing countries simply to leave the Paris Union (or remain outside) would not solve any fundamental problem, the only realistic solution would be for an agreement on a universal system of patent cooperation with principles based on the needs of various groups of countries, *including* the acceptance of preferential treatment for developing countries. Such an organization would not only be in the interest of the latter countries, whether or not they are at present members of the Paris Union, but would also be in the *long-term interest* of the developed countries, for

[26] For a very interesting "case study of Japan" see a document submitted to the New Dehli Conference (UNCTAD II): TD/28/Supp. 1, pp. 15–36; for some specific features in the development of Japan, see the short and comprised outline in J-J. Servan-Schreiber, *Le defi americain*, (Paris: Denoël, 1967) pp. 299–305 ["Note sur l'expérience japonaise"].

the same reason that present-day economic assistance in general will increase future world prosperity. At present there is, however, one formidable obstacle to such an evolution, namely the opposition of existing organizations concerned with international patent protection.

It must be clear by now that unless the Paris Union would be confronted with a situation posing a threat to its present dominant position, it will hardly be inclined to change any of its basic principles in favor of the developing countries. Though the Union felt a sudden threat to its exclusive position when the question of patents was first brought before the United Nations in 1961, it quickly managed to reassert its position. Through support of its industrialized members, and not the least through backing by the International Chamber of Commerce, the attack on its hegemony was averted, and the role of the Paris Union in any new arrangements, which might result from the "Brazilian resolution," was established.

To the great satisfaction of those opposed to any changes, no suggestions in that direction were made in the Secretary General's Report. Still, the possibility remains that renewed actions outside the Union might endanger its exclusive position in the future. At least partly with this in mind, BIRPI promptly (after 1961) started several activities specifically aimed at the developing countries. Among them the much heralded Model Law was published. While seemingly a gesture to these countries, it was primarily designed to foreclose any debate on the appropriateness of the present rules of the Convention for the needs and requirements of the developing countries. That the real idea behind it was to stop other organizations from undertaking similar projects has been recognized at several occasions. According to the Director of BIRPI quoted previously, those inclined to critizise the Model Law should compare it with the result that might be expected in case developing countries would legislate on their own "without any guidance or under political or economic pressures from various sides."[27] Ladas, commenting on the Report, expresses himself with the same clarity, saying:

> The Bureau of Geneva has wisely and promptly intervened by undertaking to draft a Model Law ... thus preventing the doing of this job by persons or institutions who have little expertise on the subject and who would be motivated by political considerations.[28]

[27] G. H. C. Bodenhausen, "A Model Law for Developing Nations," *Creative Ferment in World Patent Systems, Conference of the National Association of Manufacturers, June, 1965* (New York: N.A.M., 1965), p. 29; Cf. *supra*, p. 203.

[28] I.A.P.I.P. Annual Report 1964: II, p. 211; a similar opinion is expressed by P. J. Pointet and A. Chavanne, "Réforme des structures administratives des BIRPI," *R.I.P.I.A.*, 74: 206, December, 1966.

The reference to other institutions is a clear address to the United Nations. The expressions "political and economic pressure" (Bodenhausen) and "political considerations" (Ladas) refer of course, to what might happen if the question were to be dealt with by that organization, whose aim is to bring about a greater measure of social and economic equality among all its members rather than to help enhance the economic power of industrial countries through the protection of their vested interests.

To put various possible solutions in opposition to each other for being based on "legal" and "political" considerations respectively, is correct only in a limited, static sense.[29] It illustrates the dichotomy of the present policies of BIRPI with regard to developing countries. While, on the one hand, BIRPI claims to be the organization most suited to look after the special interests and requirements of developing countries in the patent field, on the other hand, it seeks by all available means to stave off any changes in the established system. The role of law is certainly to provide guidelines and assure stability for the particular activity for which it has been designed. The specific rules will serve this purpose, however, only insofar as the considerations upon which, and the conditions for which, they were made remain unchanged. A decision to allow changes of established rules to fit new conditions is clearly of a political nature. When such a "political" decision is put in opposition to "legal" considerations, as in the present case, then the role of law is reduced to its partial function of preserving the established order.[30,31] The evolution of the rules within an existing legal system does not come about by itself. The existing rules may be more advantageous to some parties than to others, and opposition to any change by the former will be in proportion to their vested interests dependent on the maintenance of *status quo*. And the stronger the resistance to change, the stronger will have to be the determination of those parties interested in ensuring change. That BIRPI can advocate so strongly for the adherence of the developing countries and yet oppose any change of the established rules, shows the lack of sufficiently strong such determation on the part of developing countries. Once a

[29] The implicit assumption in the two quotations above, furthermore, that BIRPI is a non-political organization, can be criticized.

[30] The Australian delagate to the 37th Session of ECOSOC recognized the "stabilizing" effect of BIRPI on the existing order. Stressing the necessity for the transfer of technology to developing countries, he added that "the transfer must, however, take place on a legal basis, and no organization was better qualified than BIRPI to ensure the desired stability in that respect." Doc. E/AC.6/SR. 343, p. 7.

[31] Cf. *supra*, p. 235. and ref. to C. W. Jenks.

stronger cohesion among them would be created, it is probable that the Paris Union would feel obliged to reconsider its stand. It would then be politically expedient to adopt such an attitude to avert the risk of losing members and prospective members and its present dominant position in the field of international patent protection.

One example of the type of flexibility that might be expected, if there is sufficient political motivation for it, is illustrated by the recent adherence of the U.S.S.R., and the incorporation of the concept of authors' certificates into the Convention, on an equal footing with patents, for priority purposes.

In 1951, a recognized authority on the international patent system, P. Roubier, said it was "useless to hope" that under its present economic system, Russia would join the Paris Union, for "in this régime, the very basis of the law of industrial property disappears along with economic freedom."[32] Nevertheless, the Soviet Union did become a Union member in 1965. This clearly shows that when politically expedient, the Paris Union may be rather flexible. This was further underlined by the recent adoption of an amendment to the Convention concerning authors' certificates. This system, whereby the inventor assigns his invention to the Government, provides for a remuneration calculated as a percentage on savings made during one year from employing the invention.[33] A Study Group, treating this question within the Union, reached, among others, the conclusion that "there was no reason to consider the system of authors' certificates as contrary to the spirit and aims of the Paris Convention."[34] A Committee of Experts considered the question in 1965, and in the same year it was decided to propose to the Union Members that the granting of authors' certificates should be recognized as a basis for priority, when such certificates were issued by a country in which inventors, at their own discretion, may apply for either a patent or such a certificate.[35] A provision to that effect

[32] Cf. *supra*, p. 94.

[33] The remuneration consists of a fixed sum plus a percentage of calculated savings. The upper limit on total remuneration is twenty thousand rubles which would be paid out in the case of annual savings of one million rubles! *Instruction on Remuneration for Discoveries, Inventions and Technical Innovations*, (Moscow: The Scientific and Research Institute of Patent Information, 1965[?]), p. 45.

[34] BIRPI Doc. S/2, April 15, 1966, p. 8. [document prepared for the Intellectual Property Conference at Stockholm, 1967.]

[35] *Ibid.*, p. 11. At the above-mentioned 1965 meeting of a Committee of Experts, the U.S.S.R. participated as an observer. The Soviet participant announced during the meeting the adherence of his country to the Union, saying, in part, that "in joining the Paris Convention, the U.S.S.R. is sure that the problem of authors' certificates will be solved appropriately and correctly." *Ibid.*, p. 8.

was adopted as a partial revision of the Paris Convention at the Intellectual Property Conference of Stockholm in July, 1967.[36] Although the new text (article four) makes the recognition of authors' certificates conditioned upon the existence of a choice, for an applicant, between patents and such certificates, the practical importance of such a choice is doubtful. Though such a choice is provided for by the Soviet Statute,[37] the structure of the Soviet economy definitely does not favor a patentee trying to exploit his invention.[38] While two Russian authors compare the rights of the patentee in the U.S.S.R. to those in other countries and state notably that the Russian patentee has "the monopoly for the use of the patent ... in articles of local manufactures as weh as articles imported,"[39] it is a fact, at least, that the relative number of inventions protected by patents is insignificant. For 1962, one author has estimated that one percent of protected inventions in the U.S.S.R. were patented.[40] The same author also strongly advises foreigners against applying for patent protection for their inventions for a number of reasons.[41] It would therefore seem safe to suggest that Soviet patents are of doubtful value, and that the grant of certificates of authorship may be likened, in terms of a traditional patent system, to one where compulsory licensing takes place from the date of the grant[42] and in which, furthermore, *royalties are paid for only one year.*

The recognition of authors' certificates in the new Convention has created the peculiar situation that, while the developing countries are not supposed to deviate one iota from the established system, a whole group of countries is allowed to substitute, in practice, the entire system of the protection of industrial property for a mere reward system. Should then, it may be asked, the developing countries have to

[36] *I.P.*, 6: 217–18, September, 1967.

[37] Paragraph 4 of the Statute on Discoveries, Inventions and Technical Innovations of April 24, 1959, Cf. Y. I. Sviadosts, *Principes Généraux de la protection des inventions* (Moscow, 1966), p. 36.

[38] Cf. E. H. Ruf, "U.S. Patent Concepts v. U.S.S.R. Patent Concepts and Inventors' Certificates – A Comparison of Public Policies and Social Objectives," *J.P.O.S.*, 49: 15–37, January, 1967.

[39] M. Boguslavsky, I. Cherviakow, *Protection of Industrial Property in the U.S.S.R.* (Moscow: Novosti Press Agency Publishing House, 1966[?]), pp. 23–24.

[40] M. Hyams, *Russian Patent Law and Procedure* (London: Dervent Information Service, 1962), p. 2.

[41] *Ibid.*, p. 10. Besides the practical considerations, which must limit the usefulness of Sovjet patents, the law itself appears to discriminate *against* patentees. According to Article 48(h) of the Sovjet Statute (Cf. *supra*, n. 37) someone already holding a patent for one invention, may not enjoy all the privileges that the law normally envisages for holders of inventors' certificates. This is also pointed out by Ruf, *op. cit.*, pp. 19–20 [*supra*, n. 38].

[42] "Very broadly, the current Sovjet patent law is really more of a system of awards for workers who contribute usable ideas to the State." Ruf, *op. cit.*, p. 37. [*supra*, n. 38].

adopt a law and a system on the Soviet model in order to be granted preferential treatment?

The suggestion to include provisions for the grant of authors' certificates, as an alternative to patent grants, was made in the Model Law Committee. An addendum to that effect was included in the Model Law. In the commentary to that Law, it is emphasized, however, that such provisions "will rarely be very attractive to foreign investors."[43] On compensation to a holder of an author's certificate it is further said that he "has the right to receive adequate remuneration, commensurate with the extent of the exploitation of the invention."[44] If the terms "adequate" and "commensurate" are taken in their traditional sense, they clearly go far beyond the Soviet Statute.

Besides its activities for the benefit of developing countries, undertaken, partly at least, to strengthen the position of the Paris Union and averting "outside" actions and initiatives inimical to the organization, BIRPI has also promoted another scheme. This has been the creation of a new international organization for the protection of all rights at present protected under the Paris and the Berne Conventions. Such an organization was established at the Intellectual Property Conference of Stockholm in July, 1967. Before examining the creation of this new organization – World Intellectual Property Organization – a section will be devoted to an examination of the contemporary situation within the field of international copyright protection. Such an examination will not only indicate some of the reasons for the establishment of the new organization (W.I.P.O.) but also illustrate a case where an established organization, previously exclusive in its field, was effectively challenged from the outside.

D. THE CASE OF THE UNIVERSAL COPYRIGHT CONVENTION

An illustration of how competition between international organizations may effectively challenge the established rules in a certain field is provided by the developments in the field of international copyright protection since 1947. In that year the first initiative was taken by UNESCO which would result in the establishment of the Universal Copyright Convention in 1952. Prior to this date, the Berne Union for the Protection of Literary and Artistic Works had held a similar position in the field of international copyright protection to the one held

[43] *Model Law for Developing Countries on Inventions* (Geneva: BIRPI, 1964), p. 87.
[44] *Ibid.*, p. 89.

by the Paris Union in the field of industrial property protection. Though neither Union was wholly exclusive in its respective field – in both cases there exist Inter-American conventions – for all countries outside the American continent the Paris and Berne Unions represented the only choice.

The following analysis of some developments in the field of international copyright protection is not intended as a comparative analysis of the problems within the two Unions of particular interest to developing countries. Its justification lies in the illustration of possible beneficial effects for these countries from the creation of a competitive climate between organizations in a certain field. Nevertheless, it will be seen that traditional copyright protection raises some problems for developing countries which may in principle be compared to those existing in the patent field. This is one reason for chosing this particular field as an illustration. Another reason is the resemblance of the Paris and Berne Unions from both historical, structural and organizational points of view.

1. The Berne Union for the Protection of Literary and Artistic Works.[45]

The Berne Union was formed in 1886, establishing the Berne Convention, and signed by ten States. The original text has been revised at several occasions. The most recent revision took place at the Intellectual Property Conference of Stockholm in June-July 1967.[46] Since 1893, BIRPI serves as the common secretariat for the two Unions. Present membership[47] is fifty-nine of which twenty-six are developing countries.

One fundamental rule of the Convention provides for national treatment [Article 3(1,2)].[48] Another rule contains the principle of "automatic protection" meaning that no formalities are required to enjoy protection [Article 5(2)]. The Convention also contains the rule of in-

[45] The expression "literary and artistic works" embraces every production in the literary, scientific and artistic field, whatever may be its form of expression. Cf. "BIRPI – General Information," *BIRPI Publication No. 400 (E)* (Geneva: BIRPI, 1965), p. 22. Only two rules of substance will be mentioned below: the protection of an author's copyright in his original published work and the protection of translation rights to such works.

[46] Other revisions have been made in Berlin (1908), Rome (1928), and Brussels (1948); the Convention has also been "completed" in Paris (1896) and Berne (1914).

[47] January 7, 1969.

[48] Reference to articles is generally to those of the Stockholm text, which as of January 1, 1969, was not yet in force.

dependance of protection [Article 5(2)]. In contrast to the Paris Convention, however, a country providing for higher protection than that required by the Convention, need not extend protection farther than does the law of the country of origin in each case [Article 7(8)]. Among important rules there are also those saying that a country ratifying a text or adhering to the Union, must be in a position to fulfill the requirements of the Convention [Article 36(2)]; that a new member must accept the latest text (Article 34);[49] and that amendments require unanimity [Article 27(3)].

Two of the most important minimum standards established by the Berne Convention are those concerning the protection of authors' original works and their rights to the translations of such works. In the following, reference will be made to the rules of the Brussels (1948) text. Such changes as have taken place in the recent Stockholm text will be treated later, since they are due, at least to a large extent, to the creation of the Universal Copyright Convention, which came into being between the two latest revision conferences of the Berne Union.

The term of protection for authors is the lifetime of the author plus fifty years (Article 7). The principle of "lifetime plus fifty years" was introduced in the Berlin (1908) text, but as the rule was coupled with the possibility for exceptions, whenever domestic law provided a lesser term of protection, it was, in fact, reduced to a voluntary rule. This was maintained at the Rome revision (1928), and it was only at Brussels (1948) that the principle was made unconditional.[50]

The right to translation of the original work (Article 8) has always enjoyed the same protection as the right to the original work itself. Here, however, there exists a possibility to make an important exception. The subject of exceptions or reservations is the one important aspect on which the Paris and Berne Conventions differ in principle. Whereas, within the Paris Convention, exceptions and reservations were never admitted, the Berne Convention, as revised in Berlin (1908), allowed countries to replace any one of the new rules by those of the original text as "completed" in Berne (1896). The subsequent Rome revision (1928) limited the scope of possible reservations to the one rule

[49] Though not necessarily integrally. In the latest text presently in force (Brussels, 1948), Article 25(3) provides one possible exception concerning translation rights (cf. *infra*, p 247). In the Stockholm text that provision is retained in Article 30(2)(b); Article 7(7) of the latter text provides another exception (Cf. *infra*, n. 65 in fine); and finally there is in the Stockholm text an important innovation consisting in a "Protocol Regarding Developing Countries," Cf. *infra*, pp. 251–56.

[50] Of twenty-five developing countries, four are not bound by the Brussels text; of thirty-two developed countries, eleven are not bound by that text (as of January 1, 1969).

concerning the protection of translations into the national language(s) of the country where protection is sought. This rule was left unchanged in the Brussels text [Article 25(3)]. A country availing itself of this right would substitute a rule providing for the protection of translation rights during ten years [Article 5 of the original text as "completed" at Berne, 1896) for the rule of "lifetime plus fifty years." – The general applicability of reservations provided for by the Berlin text (1908) is of little significance, since only one country remains bound by that text.

The possibility to make reservations concerning translation rights has been motivated by the needs, especially of developing countries, to acquire foreign literature for educational and scientific purposes, and the onerous situation in which they might be placed if they would have to abide by the main principle of protection for the same length of time as for original works. Despite the apparent attractiveness of this provision, only two developing countries have used this option.[51]

2. *The Universal Copyright Convention*

At the Second Session of the General Conference of the United Nations Educational, Scientific and Cultural Organization (UNESCO) in 1947, the first steps were taken towards the Universal Copyright Convention. In the following year the UNESCO Copyright Division was established, and at the Sixth Session of the General Conference in 1951, a resolution calling for an international copyright conference was adopted with a view to establish a copyright convention. Such a conference was held in 1952 and the Universal Copyright Convention was signed at Geneva on September 6, 1952. Among the fifty-four countries, at present members of the Convention (Jan. 1, 1969), there are twenty-five developing countries, of which six are also members of the Berne Union.

The aim of the Conference, as well as of the several committees of experts which preceded it, was to lay the basis for a truly universal copyright system, though at times it was suggested to make the new Convention merely a bridge between the Berne and Washington (inter-American) Conventions. To achieve this, rules of less farreaching nature than those of the Berne Convention were obviously required. Such a basic approach was recognized by many delegates and the work was one of conciliation between claims for authors' protection and the urging of many developing countries for easier access, especially for

[51] Thailand, bound by the Berlin text (1908) and Yugoslavia bound by the Brussels text (1948); three developed countries maintain the reservation: Iceland, Japan and Turkey.

educational purposes, to foreign literature, than offered by the Berne Convention. The conciliatory nature of the deliberations were no doubt due to the objects and philosophy of the sponsoring organization. A preliminary statement regarding the work of a 1947 Committee of Experts expressed this in the following words:

> Without omitting to safeguard the rights of creators, UNESCO has as its essential object – and this must be emphasized – the safeguarding of ... free communication of the mind.[52]

An eloquent expression of the desirable approach to the tasks before the Conference, was given by the British delegate, who said, in part, that:

> We will not ask ourselves whether a particular proposal before us is the ideal system of copyright law. We will ask ourselves rahter whether it will create difficulties for other countries. ... The point we now have to think about, if we are going to be successful in this meeting, is not how easy it is for us ... to implement a particular proposal, but how difficult it will be for ... certain other countries to implement that proposal.[53]

As far as the protection of original works and translation rights are concerned, the following rules were agreed upon: the duration of copyright protection was set at "lifetime plus twenty-five years (Article IV)[54] and the right to grant compulsory licenses for translation into the national language(s) was agreed upon for cases where, seven years after original publication, the author has not himself undertaken to publish such a translation. (Article V).

The former rule is an amelioration from the point of view of "importing" countries, but the extent of its positive effect is doubtful. Since these countries need above all educational and scientific literature, which is often quite short-lived, it is questionable whether the supply of it will increase significantly by reducing the time of protection by twenty-five years while maintaining the death date of the author for calculating protection. In other words, twenty-five years of protection more or less when the protection will anyway range from anything

[52] *Unesco Copyright Bulletin*, 1: 64, No. 2, 1948.

[53] UNESCO Copyright Conference, Official Records, p. 123.

[54] A country which on the date of the coming into force of the Convention uses the system of calculating protection from the date of publication (or a prior date of registration) is entitled to maintain that system, provided that the period of protection is not shorter than twenty-five years [Article IV(2)]. "The date of coming into force" appears to be the date at which the Convention becomes applicable in the particular country. Cf. A. Bogsch, *Universal Copyright Convention: An Analysis and Commentary* (New York: R. R. Bowker, 1958), pp. 53–54. A very few countries, among them the United States, use the above mentioned system for calculating the period of protection.

between twenty-five and (say) seventy-five years, is bound to have a limited effect.

The rule concerning the protection of translation rights, providing for the granting of a compulsory license after seven years, is an advance by three years on the ten year period for the protection of translation rights according to the right of reservation contained in the Berne Convention. Whereas the latter rule of ten years, however, means the end of protection, *the seven-year rule of the Universal Convention only establishes the right to grant licenses, under which royalties are due to the author for the whole term of protection of the original work.*

To what extent these two rules of the Universal Convention have, in fact, brought any tangible advantages to the developing countries, may be doubtful.[55] Although nineteen developing countries, not previously members of the Berne Union, have joined the Universal Convention, there are nine others that have joined the Berne Union since 1952 without adhering to the Universal Convention.[56]

The UNESCO initiative in the field of international copyright protection was, as might be expected, not well received by the Berne Union. It was seen as a threat both to its organization and to the principles which had been built up during some seventy years of its existence. It was feared that many Member States would leave the Union and together with other potential members join the rival organization. Thus, the initial reaction of the Berne Union may be compared to that of the Paris Union when the patent question was brought up in the United Nations General Assembly. For several reasons the ensuing policy of the Berne Union changed, leading to a certain cooperation with UNESCO. The strength of the Berne Union, in terms of membership, was not that of the Paris Union some ten years later. Furthermore, the interests behind international patent protection are certainly represented by more powerful pressure groups in national and international politics than those behind copyright protection. Another important reason for the attitude of the Berne Union was the absence of the United States among its members. There existed an interest on the part of both the Berne Union and the inter-American Union to establish closer ties. Though the sometimes made suggestion, that the Universal Convention should constitute a bridge between the two exist-

[55] Though the Mexican delegate to the conference said: "If the Berne Convention has not been ratified by most countries this was due to its uncompromising terms in the matter of translation rights." – UNESCO Copyright Conference, Official Records, p. 164 – this is difficult to understand in view of the reservation allowed.

[56] All of them members of the O.A.M.C.E.

ing Unions and their conventions, only admitting members belonging to any of these two Unions, was not acceptable to UNESCO in view of its stated objectives, there was still a great interest among various countries in the Berne Union to establish relations with the United States.

In order to appease the fears of the Berne Union, that they would lose members to the new organization, a rule was inserted in the Convention ("Appendix Declaration" to Article XVII) saying that any State that withdrew from the Union after 1951 and adhered to the Universal Copyright Convention, would not be given protection according to the latter Convention by Berne Union Members, which have adhered to it. This declaration seems to provide an effective deterrent for any member of the Berne Union considering to leave it and join the new Convention. It is to the same extent effectively preventing developing countries, Members of the Berne Union in 1951, from enjoying the advantages which have been given under the Universal Convention with their particular requirements in view.[57]

3. The response of the Berne Union

At the Brussels Revision Conference, which took place in the year following the first initiative of UNESCO, no signs could be detected of any particular considerations for developing countries, with the possible exception of the retention of the right of reservation concerning the protection of translation rights. The preparations for, and the results of, the subsequent Revision Conference, held at Stockholm in June-July, 1967, have shown a remarkable change in this respect, which must to a large extent be ascribed to the creation of the Universal Copyright Convention.[58]

[57] A resolution passed at the 14th UNESCO Session, however, invited its Director-General to have the possibility of revising the Universal Copyright Convention examined, as far as its Article XVII and the Appendix Declaration are concerned. UNESCO Res. 5.122, Paris, 1966; H. Desbois "La Convention universelle de Genève et la Convention de Berne" *Droit d'Auteur*, 68: 172, 1955, has interpreted the "safe-guard clause" in a very restricted sense. Although the author claims support for such an interpretation (making the clause only apply to works published before the date of withdrawal of a country and thus of only transitory effect) in a writing by A. Bogsch (with no source indication), the latter author has propounded the widely accepted, extensive interpretation in *The Law of Copyright under the Universal Convention* (New York: R. R. Bowker, 1965) p. 116, and also in *Universal Copyright Convention* (New York: R. R. Bowker, 1958) p. 140.

[58] The preoccupations of both the Berne and Paris Unions to become truly universal organizations, which was one basic reason for the recent establishment of the W.I.P.O., undoubtedly also influenced the policy change in favor of developing countries. See further *infra*, pp. 258–65.

What emerged from the Revision Conference at Stockholm was a revised text of the Berne Convention to which was added a *Protocol Regarding Developing Countries*, being in principle an integral part of the Stockholm Text of the Berne Convention. According to this Protocol, developing countries may make certain derogations from the generally applicable rules of the Convention. Subject to certain provisions, the Protocol forms an integral part of the Stockholm text [Article 21(2)]. The new text contains three groups of rules: substantive rules (Articles 1–21); rules concerning administrative provisions for the reorganization of the Berne Union (Articles 22 to 26); and procedural rules (Articles 27 to 38). A country may, when acceding to or ratifying the Stockholm Act, exclude either of the two former groups of rules [Article 28(1) (b)]. If a country excludes the first group containing the new substantive clauses it thereby excludes the applicability of the Protocol to all works of which it is the country of origin (country of origin being the country of first publication). A country may also separately accept the application of the Protocol without, or before, accepting the substantive rules of the new text (article 5 of the Protocol). Thus, the impressive list of derogations from the general rules of the Convention, which the Protocol provides for the benefit of developing countries, will only become effective to the extent that its provisions are accepted by the large exporters of copyright protected works.

During the preparatory work for the Stockholm conference, opinions were divided on the subject of how farreaching concessions ought to be made for the benefit of developing countries. Some countries argued that the Berne Convention ought to be seen primarily as an instrument serving more developed countries (not necessarily developed countries only), while countries, which could not accept the standard of protection provided for in that Convention, could always join the Universal Copyright Convention, for whose benefit that Convention had been established.[59] The majority opinion, however, and that which prevailed, held that it was important that as many countries as possible should adopt intellectual property protection under the auspices of the Berne Union. This latter view was based on the consideration that if a large number of countries remain outside the Union today, there is no certainty that they will adhere later. Another obvious consideration in inducing as many countries as possible to join the Union

[59] Cf. BIRPI Doc. S/1, May 15, 1966, p. 68, and for the opinions of France and Great Britain, BIRPI Doc, S/13, January, 1967, pp. 26–28, 103.

now is the aim of both the Berne and the Paris Unions to be able to claim universality, which together with the creation of the new common organization – W.I.P.O. – it is hoped, will enable the Unions, through that organization, to be recognized *de facto* if not *de jure* as exclusively competent in their respective fields.

The Protocol consists of six articles.[60] The first article, with five paragraphs and a large number of subparagraphs, covers the substantive rules and the rule defining which countries may avail themselves of "protocol treatment," while articles two to six contain procedural rules. Defining the countries, in whose favor the Protocol may be invoked, article one, says, in part:

> Any country regarded as a developing country in conformity with the established practice of the General Assembly of the United Nations ... may ... at the time of making a ratification or accession, which includes article 21 of the Act, declare that it will ... avail itself of any or all of the following reservations.

The five paragraphs of article one concern respectively: (a) the period of copyright protection; (b) translation rights; (c) rights to reproduce the original work; (d) a general restriction of copyright protection for educational purposes and (e) the broadcasting of copyright protected works, only the last of which will not be examined below. In view of the number and complexity of subparagraphs, only the principle of each paragraph will be stated and briefly examined.

(a) The Protocol [paragraph (a)] establishes a minimum copyright protection of "lifetime plus twenty-five years." This possible reduction of twenty-five years from the general provision for such protection is the same as the corresponding rule of the Universal Copyright Convention (Article IV), and its impact is probably negligible from the point of view of developing countries, for the reasons mentioned earlier.[61] In a first preliminary draft, however, it was suggested that developing countries should be able to apply the rule of the 1928 Rome text concerning copyright protection.[62] According to that rule (Article 7), as previously mentioned, countries providing less protection than the principle of "lifetime plus fifty years" were allowed to retain such rules.[63] A member of the Study Group, which submitted this preliminary draft, has explained the suggestion saying:

[60] For a detailed description and analysis of the Protocol, see D. Vignes "Droit d'auteur et aide au développement: Le Protocole à l'Acte de Stockholm pour la protection des oeuvres littéraires et artistiques" *Annuaire Français de Droit International*, XIII: 716–41, 1967.
[61] *Supra*, pp. 248–49.
[62] BIRPI Doc. S/1, p. 68.
[63] Cf. *Supra*, p. 246.

The consideration is that one ought not to require more of the developing countries in this respect, than what was deemed sufficient to require of the industrialized countries up to the adoption of the Brussels text in 1948.[64]

This consideration is thought-provoking. It is based on a fact that is constantly overlooked, when the benefits to developing countries of being members of the Berne and Paris Unions are demonstrated by historical arguments and the experience of now developed countries: that these latter countries had the opportunity to join these Unions when much less restrictive obligations were imposed on Member States.

In further support of the more lenient rule, suggested by the Study Group, was given the fact that those countries, whether developed or not, that have not ratified the Brussels text, continue to be able to apply Article 7 of the Rome text, exempting them from applying the rule of "lifetime plus fifty years" in case their national laws provide a lower level of protection, and containing no provisions for the minimum term of protection in such cases.[65] Nevertheless, the anxiety expressed on various occasions during preparations for a final draft to be submitted to the conference, lest the Berne Union adopt rules providing for less extensive protection than that of the Universal Convention, led to the adoption of the present rule of lifetime plus twenty-five years.

(b) The Protocol [paragraph (b)] establishes a minimum requirement for the protection of translation rights into the national language(s) of ten years, which is equivalent to the rule of the Brussels text [Article 25(3)] according to which a country may make a reservation

[64] T. Hesser, "Det immatriella rättskyddet och u-länderna," *N.I.R.*, 34: 161, 1965. [translated from Swedish]

[65] BIRPI Doc. S/1, p. 69. For the number of countries still bound by the Rome text (or earlier texts), cf. *supra*, n. 50. – The Study Group, in motivating its suggestion according to which the possibility of protecting translation rights for only ten years – at present open to all Member States through Article 25(3) of the Brussels text – should be maintained for developing countries, said, in part: "The fact that the provision has changed its place means that the right of reservation would be more restricted ... as the new article would only operate in favor of developing countries. In this respect, the proposal submitted represents a strengthening of copyright." *Ibid.*, p. 68. (For an argument in similar terms presented by BIRPI in favor of retaining the right of free reproduction of press articles – Article 9(2) of the Brussels text – for the benefit of developing countries, cf. *ibid.*, pp. 73–74.) – A motivation on similar lines would seem appropriate for the suggested rule (be the Study Group) concerning the term of protection of the original work. The much more restrictive rule that was finally decided upon seems all the more difficult to understand, since according to Article 7(7) of the Stockholm text, countries bound by the Rome text may ratify the Stockholm text and still maintain their present possibility of giving shorter protection than the unconditional provision of the Brussels text of "lifetime plus fifty years."

in favor of applying such a short term of protection.[66] Though the ten-year term is longer than the seven-year term of the Universal Convention [Article V(2)] the important difference is that, whereas after ten years, according to the Protocol, all protection of translation rights may cease, the Universal Convention admits only the grant of compulsory licenses after seven years coupled with the obligation to pay royalties for the whole term of protection (i.e., lifetime plus twenty-five years).[67] Thus, and despite the concern that the Berne Convention ought not to provide less protection than the Universal Convention, in this instance, it has clearly gone below the standard set by the latter text. Though the adoption of the ten-year rule may seem logical, considering the existence of a general rule with the same option, the Protocol provides developing countries with a still more favorable option not included in the working document, in that a country enjoying "protocol treatment" may grant compulsory licenses for the translation into the national language(s) *three years* after the date of the first publication of the original work. Thus in opposition to the provision of the Universal Convention, according to which compulsory licenses may be granted after seven years with the obligation to pay compensation for at least the term of "lifetime plus twenty-five years," stands the Protocol admitting compulsory licenses after three years with compensation due for only the remainder of the ten-year period. Provided that the large exporting countries accept the Protocol, the latter clearly offers more advantages than the Universal Convention.[68]

(c) The Protocol [paragraph (c)] provides another possible derogation from the general rules of the Convention, which was not included in the preparatory drafts. This concerns the right to grant a compulsory license, after *three years*, to reproduce and publish the original work *for educational or cultural purposes*, if within three years from the date of the first publication, such a work has not been published locally in its original form. This provision is subject to a limitation, comparable to that concerning translation licenses.[69]

[66] The general applicability of this rule has been retained in the Stockholm text. Article 30(2)(b), with the addition anyhow, that countries are free to apply, as against other countries having availed themselves of that reservation, the same standard of protection.

[67] For that reason, the working document submitted to the Stockholm Conference proposed an identical rule to that of the Universal Convention., *Ibid.*, p. 73.

[68] A factor that may possibly discourage potential translators is the provision – Article 1(b)(vii) – that should the author, between the grant of a compulsory license and the end of the ten-year period, himself publish a translation, the license shall be terminated. For such cases the protection of translation rights will of course run for the whole period of protection of the original work.

[69] Article i(c)(vi). Cf. *supra*, n. 68.

(d) The provision under paragraph (e) appears to be the most extensive concession in favor of developing countries. According to this provision, a country may "reserve the right, exclusively for teaching, study and research in all fields of education, to restrict the protection of literary and artistic works on the condition that compensation is paid to the author." Though the text of this provision seems open to an extensive interpretation,[70] it is difficult to predict its significance. It may anyhow be pointed out that in contrast to the final wording of this provision, the one submitted as a draft to the conference did not require compensation. In this preliminary version, the provision may be seen as a distinctly more farreaching concession than the derogations from the Convention permitted under previous paragraphs of Article one of the Protocol.[71] In introducing the principle of compensation – albeit, in the case of this provision, a compensation "which conforms to standards of payment to national authors"[72] – the extent of additional facilities that it provides over the previous paragraphs of Article 1 of the Protocol was reduced.[73]

Article two says that a country no longer needing to maintain reservations under the Protocol shall withdraw them. Article three permits a country, that is not in a position to withdraw its reservations after an initial ten-year period, to continue to maintain them until it ratifies or accedes to the Act adopted by the next Revision Conference. Article four states that should a country, invoking reservations, cease to be considered in the category which may benefit from the Protocol, the rights to such benefits shall terminate. Article five provides that a

[70] France had objected to a similarly worded provision in the draft submitted to the conference, saying that it could not accept the reservation," which, whatever may be the intention of its authors, would be liable to give rise to an interpretation so wide that it might finally result in the abolition of all protection for intellectual works." BIRPI Doc. S/13, p. 28.

[71] The obvious basis for this provision is the one in the general text of a more limited scope, providing for the inclusion of "excerpts from literary or artistic works in educational and scientific publications," without the requirement of compensation [Article 10(2) of the Brussels text; a comparable provision appears in Article 10(2) of the Stockholm text].

[72] The required compensation according to previously mentioned paragraphs is termed "just"; in the draft such compensation was termed "just and conforming to international standards." BIRPI Doc. S/1. p. 95.

[73] With the introduction of the obligation to pay compensation, the only differences between paragraphs a, b and c and paragraph e are that the standard for compensation is not "just" but that used to compensate national authors, the latter of which may well be lower (in both cases national currency regulations may influence the compensation), and that in the case paragraph e is involved, the authors cannot stop actions by publishing themselves. For an account of how the British delegation managed to introduce the principle of compensation and for other interesting observations on the reported role of the British delegation at the conference. see "Books row: How the 'sell-out' won time for Britain," *Sunday Times*, July 23, 1967, pp. 1, 2.

country may by special declaration accept the Protocol, though it has not yet ratified the Convention or its Articles one to twenty-one. Finally, Article six provides that a country bound by the Protocol and which has declared that the Convention shall be applicable to certain territories, for the external relations of which it is responsible, may in cases of such territory, that can be regarded as analogous to developing countries, declare the Protocol applicable to such territories.

Even from the above-made cursory examination of the Protocol, it becomes clear that the challenge from the Universal Copyright Convention has not only resulted in a remarkable turn-about in the traditional attitude of the Berne Union, but has, in fact, resulted in the adoption of provisions more favorable to developing countries than provided for by the Universal Copyright Convention. Though this development may appear strange, it should be seen in terms of the long-range policy of the Berne Union which will become clear in the following section on W.I.P.O. To the above general characterization of the meaning of the Protocol, it must be stressed again, that the potential impact of the Protocol will depend on the extent to which the developed countries, and in particular the large exporters of copyright protected works, will accept the Protocol. It should also be noted, in comparing the Protocol to the Universal Copyright Convention, that whereas the latter's provisions are general in character and applicable to all countries, the provisions of the Protocol are derogations from general provisions favoring only certain countries and the full utilization of which may conceivably be made difficult through various pressures on the countries in question.[74]

[74] Developments since the Stockholm Conference puts in serious doubt whether the Protocol will, at all, come to play the role meant for it. Of 51 Berne Union Members present at Stockholm, 35 signed the Act and four more countries did become original signatories. Notable exceptions were Great Britain, Australia, and Canada – The United States, never yet a Member of the Union, stated, through its Registrar of Copyrights in December, 1967, that "the opposition in the United States to our joining the Berne Union under the conditions imposed by the Stockholm Protocol is so strong and concerted that I regard our adherance during the forseeable future as impossible." quoted by B. A. Ringer "The Role of the United States in International Copyright," *Copyright*, 4: 225, October, 1968. For the "paradox" between the present United States position and its own history with regard to international copyright protection, see *Ibid.*, p. 226.

On January 1, 1969 no single country had ratified the Stockholm Act. The possibility to declare, separately, the Protocol applicable had at that date been used by two countries. *Thus, as of January 1, 1969, i.e. 18 months after the Stockholm Conference, the Protocol was in force between Bulgaria and Senegal.*

In late 1967, as it became appearant that the developed countries were in no hurry to ratify the Act or declare the Protocol applicable, India asked BIRPI to question all Union Members on their attitudes towards the Protocol. The Indian Registrar of Copyrights in an article in November, 1967, declared, that "if it became clear that the Protocol was blocked . . . a country like India would have no alternative but to denounce both Berne and the

What are the conclusions to be drawn from the developments in the field of international copyright protection, insofar as these developments may provide a precedent for what might happen, under comparable circumstances, in the field of international patent protection?[75] It has been suggested earlier that in order to achieve changes in the

UCC [Universal Copyright Convention] and 'to strike out on its own, or, if possible, sponsor or join a separate Union with other countries similarly placed'." *Ibid.*. p. 225, quoting Krishnamurti: "Protocol Regarding Developing Countries Appended to the Stockholm Act of the Berne Convention," *European Broadcasting Union Review*, 106B: 59, 1967.

Another sign of the restlessness of the developing countries confronted with the present situation regarding the future of the Protocol, is the renewed interest shown within UNESCO in late 1967 for a revision of its Convention, including abolishment of the Art. XVII and the Appendix Declaration. *Ibid.*

At a joint Meeting of the Intergovernmental Copyright Committee (Universal Copyright Convention) and the Permanent Committee of the Berne Union in December, 1967, the Indian Delegate "was of the opinion that the safeguard clause in respect of the Berne Union ... was no longer necessary. Furthermore," he continued, "if developed countries did not accept the application of the protocol adopted at Stockholm, developing countries might be obliged to leave the Berne Union and also denounce the Universal Copyright Convention if Article XVII were maintained." Report of the Meeting in *Copyright Bulletin* [Quarterly Review] II: 11–18, No. 1, 1968.

The American Delegate, however, "considered that application of the protocol would result in a weakening of Copyright without satisfying the needs of developing countries in the field of education." *Ibid.*

The latest development in the field of international copyright protection stems from a resolution adopted at the above Joint Meeting. This resolution, 59(IX), December, 1967, "... considering the increasing complexity of international copyright ... considering the continuing and urgent needs of developing countries ... considering the importance of adequate and effective copyright protection ..." decided that a joint group for the study of matters referred to in the preambule, should be established, as soon as BIRPI had received the answers to its inquiry concerning the attitude of its Members towards the Protocol and as soon as UNESCO had received an answer from the countries, parties to the Universal Copyright Convention, concerning their position with regard to its Article XVII and Appendix Declaration, an inquiry, which was requested in UNESCO Res 5. 122, Paris, July, 1966. As of January, 1969, such a joint study group had not yet met.

The uncertain future of the Protocol is illustrated by the result of the convocation of a "working group" by BIRPI in persuance of a recommendation of the Stockholm Conference, to advice the Director of BIRPI on ways to ensure fair and just compensation to authors, under the Protocol. "This working party [March, 1968] was unable to propose any recommendations, *since it was clearly unwilling to assume that the Protocol would actually come into force.*" *Ibid.*, p. 225, n. 143. (italics added)

[75] The following excerpt from an article by Ch. L. Magnin, "L'Action des Bureaux Internationaux Réunis pour la protection de la propriété intellectuelle et les pays en voie de développement," NIR, 1967: 2, p. 182–83 (written, maybe, before the apparent fate of the Protocol was visible) could word for word be made the basis for an accomodating position towards developing countries, as regards the international patent system: "... s'agissant de pays en voie de développement, c'était dans cette perspective, un impérieux devoir pour les Birpi de tenir compte des conditions spéciales et des nécessités de cette promotion, afin de proposer à ces pays ... des mésures adaptés à leur situation particulière et aptes à les achiminer, dans leur intèret propre, et celui de la Communauté des Nations, vers un plus haut niveau de développement.

. . . .

A ces taches, ils [les Burpi] se consacrent avec désintéressement et dévouement, comme à une oeuvre de promotion humaine qui porte en elle sa justification, et qui, au surplus est, pour les Unions ... riches en promesses de germinations futures."

international patent system for the benefit of developing countries, these countries must display a stronger, more unified stand behind any demands for change, then they have so far shown. With reservation for the differences that exist between the two cases, the above-examined evolution in the copyright field demonstrates that an effective threat to create, or the actual creation of, a rival organization will introduce competitive conditions challenging the established, hitherto exclusive organization. There are obvious dissimilarities between the cases of international protection of copyrights and patent rights. On the one hand, the strength and power of the Berne Union in 1950 (or even today) was much smaller than that of the Paris Union today. Not only is there a great difference in terms of membership – whereas the Berne Union in 1952 had some forty members, the Paris Union today has almost the double, most of the difference anyway made up of developing countries – but more important is certainly the greater economic interests involved in the support and defense of the established patent system. On the other hand, there is today a greater consciousness of both the need and justification for adapting established patterns of international relations in favor of diminishing the present economic, social and technical cleavage between industrialized and developing countries. There also exist today several examples from various fields of international cooperation where such considerations have been put into practice. Finally, and as a consequence of results obtained so far, there is a growing awareness among the developing countries that by concerted action they may successfully claim the implementation of programs designed to reduce the concrete inequalities between their countries and the industrialized part of the world. – Until such concerted action generates enough weight, however, there is little probability for change.[76]

E. THE WORLD INTELLECTUAL PROPERTY ORGANIZATION

Although the Paris Union has so far managed to ward off any attack on its hegemony in the field of international patent protection, the risk that such an attempt will succeed in the future persists. It will remain as long as the organization is less than universal in scope and has not

[76] The occasions where developed countries have raised the possibility of special provisions for developing countries are extremely rare. For one such case, see a Japanese comment on the subject of "Industrial Property in Underdeveloped Countries," I.A.P.I.P. Annual Report, 1965: II, pp. 355–56.

been formally recognized as the exclusively competent body in its field. The same thing is true also for the Berne Union, though in the case of the latter, the UNESCO initiative has already reduced its formerly exclusive position. The combined secretariat of the two Unions and a number of Committees of Experts have been working for the last several years to establish a new organization, common to the two Unions. Its two basic functions would be the coordination of the administrative activities of the Unions and the promotion of all intellectual property rights protected under the Paris and Berne Conventions, as well as those protected by various special agreements. Such an organization was established at the Intellectual Property Conference of Stockholm in June-July, 1967, under the name of World Intellectual Property Organization – W.I.P.O.[77] Particularly since the "Brazilian Resolution" in 1961, the need for a reorganization had been urgently felt, though also the evolution in the copyright field served to indicate what might be expected. The question of reorganization was brought up at the Lisbon Conference (1958), but no action was then taken. In the following year, the Director of BIRPI at the time wrote:

> The intellectual property unions will be able to function to the satisfaction of the states, the public and the creators when they have been given organs capable of winning back the initiative in the field of the international protection of intellectual property.[78]

Writing in 1962, the same author sees the "Brazilian Resolution" as an illustration of what might happen and as an indication of the need for reorganization. The author is aware of two main dangers presented by the traditional structure of the Unions. One is the risk that the basic principles of the Unions may become disintegrated through the being in force of different texts (which the creation of W.I.P.O. anyhow cannot in itself remedy). The other danger of the present structure of the Unions is:

> That new conventions providing for the protection of intellectual property might be initiated within the framework of other international organizations, representing other fields of activities and protecting different interests from those traditionally connected with such property.[79]

In view of the fact that the United Nations, through two articles (22, 27) of the Universal Declaration of Human Rights, has formally

[77] See for text and report *Copyright*, 3: 146–64, August, 1967.
[78] J. Secretan, "Structural Evolution of the Unions for the Protection of Intellectual Property," *P.I.*, 1: 177, July, 1962.
[79] *Ibid.*, p. 173.

recognized the objectives of the protection of intellectual property and thus established the competence of ECOSOC in this field, the Director of BIRPI at the time observes that "if the legal principles which are at the bases of the international unions ... are to triumph" an agreement with the ECOSOC on their exclusive competence must be reached. But he continues:

In order that their exclusive competence be recognized in the industrial property and copyright fields, each Union must become an "agency", i.e., a generally recognized juridical and international body possossing organs fully representative of the States and a secretariat; such transformation must be effected by means of an intergovernmental agreement.[80]

Though the representatives of BIRPI have rarely set out the motive for the new organization so explicitly, later, there can be no doubt that besides the wishes for a new administrative structure, the desire to effectively stop outside organizations from upsetting the present international patent system has been the great driving force.[81] From the beginning it was realized that the most crucial provision of the Convention for the new organization would be the one concerning membership, for only an organization open to all interested countries, it was thought, whether Union members or not, could obtain a status as a Specialized Agency of the United Nations. Though a preliminary draft produced by a Study Group in 1964 therefore suggested membership on an equal footing for all countries in the new organization, a Committee of Experts in the following year could not agree to such an approach. A minority of countries were not prepared to accept the vital viewpoint, according to one author, that:

The only way of demonstrating and safeguarding the world-wide character of the new Organization and its claim to be the only international intergovernmental Organization for the protection of intellectual property, was to include these [non-member] States among its Members, and that this was also the only way of removing any suspicion that the new Organization intended to persue the particular interests of certain groups of States and of preventing the foundation of a competitive organization, for instance through the United Nations.[82]

[80] *Ibid.*, n. 9.

[81] Cf. A. Krieger, "A New International Organization for Intellectual Property? – Efforts to Modify the Structure of the Paris and Berne Unions" *I.P.* 5: 40, February, 1966. As far as Copyright protection is concerned, it may be presumed that the aim is also to win back the control of that field. Though it has been said that UNESCO's present role should be left untouched – cf. "The Proposed Administrative and Structural Reform of BIRPI," *I.P.*, 5: 183, August, 1966 – and though UNESCO representatives have said that it has responsibilities that it cannot decline – cf. "Report on the Work of Main Committee V (World Intellectual Property Organization) of the Intellectual Property Conference of Stockholm 1967," *I.P.*, 6: 186, August, 1967 – how otherwise could the new organization realize its aim to be able to claim to be the sole specialized intergovernmental organization in its field?

[82] Krieger, *op. cit.*, p. 42.

The work of the Expert Committee resulted in a compromise solution on the question of membership. According to this solution, which was retained in the working program submitted by BIRPI to the Stockholm Conference, there should be two categories of members – full and associate – according to whether they were members or not of any of the Unions.[83] The actual denomination of member countries of the new organization into two categories was deleted in the final Convention text. The delimitation of activities and influence of Union and non-Union members proposed in the BIRPI draft and adopted at the Stockholm Conference, makes it doubtful, however, whether the new organization will achieve the aim of becoming recognized as exclusively competent in its field.[84]

The new organization will have four different organs: (1) the General Assembly, consisting of those member states that are also Union members, (2) the Conference, consisting of all members of W.I.P.O., (3) the Coordination Committee, consisting of members of the Executive Committees of the two Unions, and (4) the International Bureau of Intellectual Property.

(1) The General Assembly is the supreme organ of the organization. It meets every three years. Its general function is to carry out one of the two aims of the organization, namely to ensure the administrative cooperation among the Unions and the supervision of the International Bureau of Intellectual Property. Among its functions is to approve reports of the Director General, approve reports of the Coordination Committee and adopt a three-year budget common to the Unions. Members of the organization who are not Union members are admitted as observers.

(2) The Conference consists of all States members of the organization. Its general function is to serve the second aim of the organization, namely the promotion of intellectual property protection and assistance to developing countries in matters concerning intellectual property protection. It will meet every three years.

(3) The Coordination Committee, on which only members of the respective Executive Committees of the two Unions are represented, meets annually. It is the excutive organ of both the General Assembly and the Conference. Among its functions are to prepare the draft agendas of both these organs and the draft program and budget of the Conference.

[83] BIRPI Doc. S/10 of September 16, 1966.
[84] The authors of the working programme evidently believe so, Cf. *Ibid.*, p. 18.

(4) The International Bureau of Intellectual Property will be the secretariat of the organization and take over the present functions of BIRPI.

Since the non-Union members will only be represented at the Conference and the role of the latter, besides taking decisions on assistance to developing countries, is merely to provide a forum for discussions, it seems evident that the influence of non-Union members on the new organization will be small. An illustration of this is provided by an amendment to the draft submitted by BIRPI. The latter body had suggested that the Conference should be able to adopt resolutions and recommendations. The power to adopt resolutions was deleted from the final text "in the belief that the role of the Conference would be better indicated by the single word 'recommendations.'"[85]

The Conference seems to have been of the opinion that once it had removed the actual denomination of Members in two categories, which appeared in the final draft, it thereby assured a non-discriminatory treatment of Members of the new organization.[86] It is doubtful, however, whether mere access to the Conference would satisfy the United Nations Economic and Social Council, through whose specially established Negociating Committee an agreement would have to be reached, if W.I.P.O. would seek recognition as a Specialized Agency, considering also the very limited role of the Conference.[87] In this latter respect,

[85] "Report on the work of Main Committee V ..." *op. cit.*, p. 189. "Le projet des BIRPI prévoyait que la Conférence pourrait adopter non seulement des recommendations, mais aussi des résolutions. Cette dernière disposition a été supprimée; la Conférence ne pourra par conséquence que formuler des recommendations, *ce qui a pour effet d'atténuer quelque peu le caractère impératif que pourraient avoir certaines de ces suggestions.*" A. Chavanne and P. J. Pointet "L'Organisation Mondiale de la Propriété Intelectuelle," *Revue Internationale de la Propriété Industrielle et Artistique*, 70: 213–23, December, 1967, p. 221. [italics added]

[86] "In order to avoid even the appearance of any discrimination, Main Committee V abandoned this terminology." *Ibid.*, p. 187.

[87] Although W.I.P.O. may in genral be found to fulfill the requirements of the U.N. Charter (Art. 57) of having "wide international responsibilities" in "economic, social, cultural, educational, health ... [or] related fields," the limitation on the membership of its most important plenary organ, the General Assembly, puts in doubt its prospects of becoming a Specialized Agency.

No clear and defined rules exist on this matter, but a survey of existing Specialized Agencies shows that all have one or more plenary organs on which all members are represented, "although 'associate' members [where such exists, however, they are only non-selfgoverning territories] may not have a vote." D. W. Bowett, *The Law of International Institutions* (London: Stevens, 1963) p. 102. The fact that with one exception (see below) the real power in existing Specialized Agencies lies with their plenary organs, is emphasized by Bowett, *op. cit.*, p. 105, when he says that "this repository of power with the plenary organ, and the comparative subjugation of the organ of limited composition, is an important feature of these agencies and is well worth the attention of those, who familiar with the UN, tend to think of the organ of limited composition as the executive, effective organ where real power alone lies."

one author compares the final rext with the original plans of making no distinction between members, and says that although the final text might appear to largely correspond to the original plans, "appearances are misleading."[88] Since the new organization as far as non-Union members are concerned, is limited to advisory capacity, "this means," according to the same author, "that the second of the two ideas underlying the original moves has been practically turned into its antithesis," for:

> ... What is now proposed is an Organization whose functions will all be performed by organs on which none but Members of the individual Unions are represented. ...
> Third States will be offered merely a forum for the discussion of general questions ... in a single organ of the new Organization and one that has no powers of decision.[89]

It may also be questioned whether the original aim "of removing any suspicion that the new organization intended to pursue the particular interests of certain groups of States,"[90] has not been unsuccessful.[91]

The appearant exception to this situation is the IMCO, where the actual power rests with an organ of limited composition, rather than with its plenary organ. In the case of IMCO, the Council with restricted membership formulates recommendations while the General Assembly can only add its comments and/or send the proposed texts back to the Council for its further consideration.

Article 17 of the IMCO Constitution regulates the composition of its Council: the six countries having the largest interest in providing international shipping services and the six countries having the largest interest in seaborne trade are each assured a seat in the Council. In addition, the General Assembly shall elect two more countries in each category to be represented on the Council.

Even if an effort were made to apply the IMCO situation on WIPO, there respective systems for making countries eligable to be represented on their organs of limited membership would still show principal differences. While the IMCO criteria for representation on its Council are based on the importance of international shipping to its members, the corresponding criteria for eligability to the General Assembly of WIPO are based on the wholly subjective criteria of adherance or non-adherance to the Paris and Berne Unions. These latter criteria are termed subjective since there is no necessary correlation between membership of one or both of these Unions and a country's effective interest in the international protection of intellectual property. A clear case in point would be India, if its threat to denounce the Berne Union would be carried out.

[88] Krieger, *op. cit.*, p. 44.

[89] *Ibid.*

[90] Krieger, *op. cit.*, p. 42. Cf. *supra*, p. 260.

[91] The claim of non-discrimination may also be disputed. This is recognized by two authors commenting upon the preliminary proposal for two categories of Members (i.e. "Full" and "Associate") as it appeared in the final draft: "En fait, cette distinction se trouve implicitement réalisée dans le project par les règles de fonctionnement de l'Assemblée Générale et du Commité de Coordination. *Elle ne fait donc que souligner inutilement une discrimination entre les états members des Unions et les autres états.*" Pointet and Chavanne "Réforme des structures administratives ...," p. 211. [italics added]

The practical significance of the Conference can probably be described with some generalization as an institutionalized seminar on intellectual property and having the same major purpose as the various regional seminars, so far organized by BIRPI, of convincing developing countries of the claimed benefits of adhering to the Paris and and Berne Unions.[92] Despite all intentions behind the creation of W.I.P.O., it must be finally concluded that, for practical purposes, a State not belonging to one of the Unions will have little power to influence the present international patent system. The only way to attain any influence will still be to join the Paris Union and accept the present system with its built-in brakes on changes.

Therefore it must be hoped that in the interest of the developing countries, whether or not they are members of the Paris Union, neither formal nor tacit recognition will be given to W.I.P.O. as exclusively competent in the field of patent rights and other intellectual property rights.[93]

[92] In a summary of advantages of having non-Union members in the new organization, it has been that: "La présence de non-unionistes dans un organisme international spécialisé dans les droits intellectuels sera en définitif l'anti-chambre de leur adhésion aux Unions." *Ibid.*, p. 6; see also Chavanne and Pointet "L'Organisation Mondiale ..." p 222 (*supra*, n. 85 in fine).

[93] Ratifications of the Act establishing W.I.P.O. have so far been slow. As of January 1, 1969, only three countries have deposited their ratifications: Ireland, Senegal, and the U.S.S.R.

Another reason for believing that the new organization will take long in becoming "worldwide" is the apparently strong opposition against it within certain countries and interest-groups. An article by an American author and well-known personality in the industrial property field, may illustrate this opposition: S. P. Ladas "The Convention Establishing the World Intellectual Property Organization," *Journal of World Trade Law*, 2: 684–94, November-December, 1968. The major, general objection the author makes is that the new organization will be run by government officials, while the existing organization has always been run principally on private initiative, more likely to protect the private property rights of inventors-patentees.

Two comments quoted below from the same author further illustrate the resistance against concessions in favor of developing countries, at least as far as they are not members of the Paris Union. After mentioning one danger to American interests, as the author sees it, from the new organization, he continuous: "But much more important is the admission to the organization of countries which are not members of any Union and the creation of a new organ called 'The Conference' in which these states will be represented on an equal rank with members of the Unions ... These countries, in so far as they refuse adherence to the Paris Convention, will come to WIPO and participate in the Conference largely for the purpose of serving their own interests. [one may ask what the difference in this respect might be between members and non-members of the Unions!]

. . . .

It seems to me that it is unavoidable that the Conference, and particularly the non-member states [sic], will be inspired by political and economic considerations and that the natural

No doubt various pressures will be exercised by the Unions and various other organizations supporting them, to obtain such recognition, and it is essential that the United Nations, and its various bodies interested in questions concerning the transfer of technology, keep open the possibility of initiating independant actions analogous to that taken by UNESCO in the copyright field.

F. A PREFERENTIAL STATUS FOR DEVELOPING COUNTRIES

The use of the term "preferential" in the context of international patent protection and developing countries should be correctly understood. It is used to indicate that there are reasons for giving these countries a special status, but it does not necessarily imply that in such a case these countries would gain advantages from the patent system, which are not open to the industrialized countries and which, objectively seen, would be given at the expense of the industrialized countries. Since the latter would certainly not want a general application of, say, stricter working rules, which would hurt their own patentees abroad as much as it might increase their benefits from giving protection to foreigners, any such rules should be seen as means to decrease the inequality between the two groups of countries, rather than as promoting the interests of one group to the detriment of the other.

Theoretically there exist two principal organizational forms within which a preferential or special status in international patent matters could be offered to the developing countries. Both of them have been illustrated in the field of international copyright protection.

1. A new international Convention sponsored by the United Nations

In view of the powerful support which exists both within and outside the Paris Union for "safeguarding" the principles of the present international patent system, the creation of a new organization, taking due account of all interests that *today* are affected by patent protection, and which will strike a balance between the benefits derived from such protection by various groups of countries, might appear to present the most clear-cut solution. To arrive at this, however, will require a

tendency would be to extract, through their recommendations [i.e. in the Conference], concessions for the developing countries. I cannot be persuaded that these countries, which are promoting what they consider their interests through the United Nations and its Agencies, will suddenly change their attidude when acting on the premises of WIPO."! *Ibid.*, pp. 691–92.

far greater support for such a measure than was mustered up, for instance, for the "Brazilian Resolution" as originally introduced.[94] But whether or not a decision to institute a new convention would be passed over the strong opposition of the industrialized countries, the cooperation of the latter would be indispensable in any such new venture. It is inconceivable that these countries would be willing to substitute the Paris Union and its Convention for such a new organization. Only a unanimous or near unanimous support and determination of the developing countries to achieve a system adapted to their requirements and conditions, might induce the industrialized countries to approve of a new organization in coexistence with the present one. In such a case any "guarantee" against developing countries leaving the Union, comparable to that contained in the "Appendix Declaration" of Article XVII of the Universal Copyright Convention, would not be acceptable.[95] Such a measure would defeat the value of any new arrangement to the extent that the developing countries already belong to the Union. During the preparatory stages of the UNESCO Conference leading to the Universal Convention, the suggestion was made that the two existing Conventions, i.e., the Berne Convention and the (inter-American) Washington Convention might appear in the new Convention as "restricted unions" in the sense in which this concept exists in both the Berne and Paris Conventions.[96] Maybe this would offer a practical solution to the problems of coexistance between the Paris Union and a new organization. In such a case it might also be possible to provide for the inclusion of the Buenos Aires Convention as a restricted union.

2. *A special status for developing countries within the Paris Union*

The Paris Union is unlikely under present circumstances to initiate by itself such a modification of its traditional structure. Despite its power-

[94] It may be recalled that the amendment investing BIRPI with a role in any future development which might have resulted from that resolution – a measure which may have contributed to the negative answer as to whether an international conference should be called – was supported by twenty-one countries, of which three were developing countries, opposed by twenty countries of which seventeen were developing countries, and that out of twenty-five countries abstaining, twenty were developing countries. Cf. p. 174 *supra*.

[95] Cf. *supra*, p. 250.

[96] For the Berne Union, Article 20 (Stockholm text) and for the Paris Union, Article 15 (according to these articles Member States may conclude separate agreements among themselves which offer more extensive protection or anyhow do not contravene the rules of the respective Conventions). Mentioned by D. Sidjanski and S. Castaños, *Droit d'auteur ou Copyright; les rapports entre les différentes systemes en vigeur* (Lausanne: F. Rouge cie., 1954), p. 27.

ful position at present, however, once confronted with the real possibility of the establishment of a competitive organization, the granting of a special status to developing countries within their own organization may be politically more acceptable to the industrialized countries. The creation of W.I.P.O., even without a formal or even tacit recognition of its exclusive competence, may have decreased the possibilities for effective outside influence.[97] Nevertheless, the establishment of a special status for developing countries may conceivably be required as a condition for giving the desired recognition, were it sought.

3. *Possible preferential rules*

Once a decision were taken to adapt the rules of international patent protection, as far as developing countries are concerned, the principle that such measures are justified would be acknowledged. The special provisions which would subsequently be created for the benefit of these countries would then be of less principal interest. What should be important, however, is the recognition that such provisions *should not be considered as gracious gifts* from the industrialized countries, but as wholly justified measures for the participation of developing countries in an international system of patent protection.

It is not the intention here to proceed with an analysis of all possible adaptations of present rules, which may be made for the benefit of these countries. Only a few general considerations will be made to illustrate the inadequacy of the approach so far adopted, when the position of developing countries in the present international patent system has been examined.

Though the text of the General Assembly resolution, which requested the Report, gives no support for an "all-or-nothing" approach to the problem it was asked to deal with, the impression may be gained from the Report, that such an approach was used as far as problems concerning patent grants to foreigners were examined, since in no single instance did the Report suggest measures for the benefit of developing countries, which would have derogated from the existing rules of the international patent system.

For the supporters of the existing system such an approach is the

[97] Another development which might have reinforced the position of the Paris Union is a resolution passed by the Forty-third Session of ECOSOC, whereby the Secretary-General was invited to consider the establishment of more formal ties with such organizations, where he considers it would be helpful to the work of the Council. Reported in *I.P.*, 7: 54, February, 1968.

evident choice. For while it may be easy to show that patent protection as such is likely to have certain advantages, which (by definition) would be absent in the case of no protection, and thereupon draw the conclusion that such protection should be retained, an approach considering marginal changes would be certain to lead to a less unequivocal endorsement of the present system.

The most obvious case in point is the rule concerning working obligations of patented inventions. Though the general motivation for existing rules stresses the necessity for the patentee, and especially so in the developing countries it is often said, to have time to study the possibilities of local exploitation, there may obviously be exceptions. In the Model Law Committee there was a suggestion that a derogation of the normal period of immunity against sanctions ought to be allowed in cases where the foreign patentee, after being requested to do so by the local authorities, does not submit a plan for the exploitation of his patent.[98] Though the commentary to the Model Law, giving this information, does not say so, the suggested derogation would presumably apply to cases where a third party had shown himself prepared to exploit the invention as a licensee. If this were the case, there seems little reason, from the point of view of the local economy, to grant the full period of immunity. Another case which casts doubts on the appropriateness for developing countries of the present unconditional period of immunity of sanctions against non-working, is that of the differences between the general rules of patent protection and those suggested (by the Model Law Committee) for the case of patents of importation.[99]

Though it is frequently maintained that "the patent system, to be effective, must be of general application, and cannot be structured or administered on a case-to-case basis,"[100] this may not be valid for developing countries. To the extent that provisions for patent protection in any one or in all of these countries may be presumed to have a negligible effect on inventive activity and allocation of research resources in the industrialized countries,[101] actions against nonworked patents will have little effect on the intentions of those, who are prepared to work their patented inventions locally.

The ambiguities here mentioned and those analyzed in more detail

[98] *Model Law ..., op. cit.*, p. 58; cf. *supra*, p 208.

[99] Cf. *supra*, pp. 204–06.

[100] U.N. Report, *The Role of Patents in the Transfer of Technology to Developing Countries* (New York: United Nations, 1964), Doc. E/3861I Rev. 1, p. 45.

[101] Cf. *Ibid.*, par. 283.

previously, are, of course, the inevitable result of trying to apply a system originally created for a specific set of conditions to an altogether different situation. Further support for considering changes of the present system would be provided to the extent that contemporary conditions in general may suggest changes of the original rules and principles. G. Akermann has developed an argument along such lines.[102] The interests of the community both to encourage creative activity and to see to it that the resultant benefits are shared by all, may, according to this author, possibly become better balanced if the three-year period were abolished for cases where a public interest made it necessary or useful to have an invention worked.[103]
By way of example, any or all of the following changes might be advantageous for developing countries as far as requirements for the local working of patented inventions are concerned:

(a) the reduction of the automatic period of immunity against sanctions for non-working;

(b) the use of revocation to be permitted concurrently with compulsory licenses as a sanction for non working;

(c) the right to apply sanctions against imports, when it is desirable to have a product manufactured locally;

(d) the right to reduce the automatic period of immunity against sanctions for non-working, in cases where potential licensees exist; and

(e) the recognition that the *quid pro quo* of granting patent protection should be local exploitation by the patentee or else his active cooperation in supplying the non-patented knowhow required for the effective working of the invention by a licensee.

The over-all considerations for an application of an international patent system to the conditions of developing countries must be that the protection granted is intended to protect the exploitation of inventions in the local economy, and not merely to protect the export markets of foreign countries. It must also be recognized that measures against non-working do not necessarily imply an objective fault by

[102] C. Akerman, *l'Obligation d'exploiter et la licence obligatoire en matière de brevet d'invention* (Paris: Sirey, 1936).

[103] *Ibid.*, pp. 153–55. "Le terme de cette évolution est peut-être la consécration internationale d'un systéme de licenses de plein droit inspiré du système actuel des licenses de plein droit ... En tout cas, cela est, d'après nous, fort désirable. Ibid p. 155.

the patentee but that such measures may nevertheless be justifiable on grounds of public policy.

Another measure which ought to be expressly allowed for use in developing countries – and which would be in the best historical traditions of several now industrialized countries! – is the granting of genuine patents of introduction after the expiration of the priority period, to anybody prepared to introduce new technology in the local economy. Such protection should not be dependent upon whether the foreign patent protected article has already been sold locally.

In addition to adaptations of the international patent system as exemplified above, a case of preferences in the traditional sense of that word, might also prove beneficial to developing countries. One of the requirements for efficient industrialization under conditions of economic development is often that the local manufacturing enterprises have opportunities to export perhaps a substantial part of their production. But to the extent that the local producers use foreign-owned, patent protected technology, they will generally be hindered to export their goods either by explicit restrictions or because of the ownership of patents in other countries. Therefore, special facilities enabling local licensees to overcome such restrictions would seem desirable.

Another preferential concession would be for the industrialized countries to abandon unilaterally any working obligations in favor of patentees of developing countries. A radical extention of such a concession would be to set aside such obligations in favor of all imports from these countries. Whereas the former measure would help indigenous industry the latter measure – much less likely to win approval – might induce manufacturers, facing compulsory working obligations in many countries, to set up production in a developing country.

The possibility of arrangements such as these has almost never been raised. A significant exception can be found in an I.C.C. "Working Sheet" on the "Review of Patent, Knowhow, and Trademark Licensing," by S. P. Ladas.[104] Licenses to local enterprises are vital but licensees should be able to penetrate the markets of advanced countries as well as those of other developing countries. Since patent monopolies, however, can be used to allocate national markets and restrict competition, "what devices" Ladas asks "may be suggested to alleviate this condition?" The author then raises the following two possibilities: that licenses might be granted on a regional basis; and that licenses might provide for preferences (presumably for exports to developed

[104] I.C.C. Doc. 450/252, February 27, 1964.

countries) for some time or on a selective basis "for instance, in the case of infant industries."[105] These possible solutions were apparently raised in anticipation of similar proposals being made elsewhere – the document was submitted shortly before the publication of the U.N. Report and the 1964 meetings of UNCTAD and ECOSOC. At none of these events were any similar suggestions made, and nothing further appears to have happened to the possibilities raised by the I.C.C. document. This underlines two important facts: that there is room for imaginative solutions and that modifications of the existing system will not come about unsolicited by those who would benefit from them.

G. COMPLEMENTARY ACTIONS TO INCREASE THE FLOW OF TECHNOLOGY – PATENTED AND UNPATENTED

It is a fact that, in the overall context of the transfer of technology, patent protected inventions play only a part, and perhaps a minor part, even within the areas where patented technology is dominant. On the other hand, though, the unpatented technology and knowhow, which is frequently indespensable for the efficient exploitation of patented inventions, is often, in fact, protected through licensing agreements transferring the patented technology. Even if all the measures suggested above or similar solutions were to be implemented, it would affect only a part of the total technological knowledge required by the developing countries. And even for the part of technology affected by patent protection, its supply would be limited to the purchasing power, on general commercial terms, of the importing countries. One of the passages often quoted from the Report of the United Nations Secretary General, is its final paragraph recognizing the limitations of an approach to the problems of the transfer of technology solely in terms of patented technology:

> In the final analysis, the question of patents must be seen – and dealt with – in the broader context of facilitating the transfer of patented and unpatented technology to developing countries and enhancing the ability of the latter to adapt and use such foreign technology in the implementation of their development programs.[106]

[105] *Ibid.*, p. 2. The possibility to grant licenses to local manufacturers also in other countries to enable them to export, has been suggested by a member of the I.A.P.I.P., but in a different context: "If they [the developing countries] have no foreign currency to pay [royalties with] ... a solution may be to grant them licenses for corresponding patents in other countries in order to enable them to export a – perhaps small – quantity of their production to gain foreign currency with which to pay the royalty."! I.A.P.I.P. Annual Report 1965: II, p. 359.

[106] U.N. Report, *op. cit.*, par. 311.

This part of the Report's conclusions has often been referred to by those intent on defending the present patent system at all costs, as indicating that patented technology and the terms under which it is protected, is of minor importance, and that legislative measures on the national level and general aid policies are what is required to adequately rectify the present technological imbalance between industrialized and developing countries. It must, however, be quite clear from the foregoing that adaptations of the present international patent system as it applies to developing countries are both justified and necessary. Nevertheless, any measures in this direction will only constitute a partial remedy, and supplementary measures are required for a total assault on the present inadequate arrangement concerning the transfer of technology.

Though such measures are strictly outside the subject of patents and their protection, it may nevertheless be of interest to examine some possible forms of supplementary actions. Considerations of such measures are also justified by the impact they may have on the transfer of patented technology. There are evidently a great number of more or less farreaching schemes that could be designed to increase the present flow of technology. Their common denominator would be a modification of the commercial terms under which technological knowledge could be transferred to developing countries. The intention here is to suggest, very briefly and in general terms, one such approach to see how the present patent system might be affected.

1. A world fund of technological knowledge

In a United Nations document entitled "Arrangements for the Dissemination of Information on Industrial Technology," it is said in the introduction that:

> The notion that the United Nations, through the Center for Industrial Development or similar body, should serve as a "clearing house" for industrial technology for the benefit of the underdeveloped countries has been a recurrent theme in reports.[107]

Similar references have been included in the 1964 UNCTAD Recommendation,[108] in the ECOSOC Resolution of the same year,[109] and in

[107] U.N. Doc. E/C.5/51, January 21, 1964, par. 1.

[108] "Additional facilities on and for the transfer of technical documentation and knowhow should be organized within the framework of the United Nations ..." operative paragraph 4 of Recommendation A.IV.26, Doc. E/Conf. 46/141. Vol. I, 3rd Part, Annexes.

[109] Requesting the Secretary General "... to provide additional facilities for information

the General Assembly Resolution of 1965,[110] all concerning the role of patents in the transfer of technology to developing countries. Though these latter references emphasize the supply of knowledge supplementing patent protected technology, the full benefit of an internationally organized transfer or "clearing" of technology could only be realized if the total supply of technological knowledge would be included.

a. Principles of subscription to the fund

Subscription to the fund by industrialized countries could be made in either of two principal forms: through funds to be employed by the organization to buy required technology in the market; or, a much more radical solution as far as patented technology is concerned, through subscription to the fund by these countries of all patents originally granted by them. The first method of support for the fund would obviously be more acceptable to the industrialized countries. It would, in fact, constitute a traditional form of organized support for economic development. As the costs involved would fall primarily on the public authorities and would not affect directly any private interests, such a plan ought not to be objectionable on principle. Such a ready acceptance could in any case not be expected in the case where subscriptions to the fund would partly consist in pledging the rights of all (originally) patent protected inventions by any industrialized country to the fund. The opposition to any such scheme would be in direct proportion to its interference with the vested interests involved and at present protected by the international patent system. And even if the governments of industrialized countries would consent to such a plan, the opposition by private interests might make the acquisition of additional knowhow required to work the inventions difficult. Once agreement in principle were reached, however, governments could probably find means to ensure the supply of needed knowhow.

Such a radical scheme, or even less radical schemes, which would mean a departure from technological transfer on commercial terms, has rarely been suggested. One exception is Penrose, who, writing in 1951, and without any plan for an organized supply of technology, said:

on and for the transfer of technical documentation and knowhow to the developing countries." Operative paragraph 1 of ECOSOC Res. 1013 (XXXVII) July 22, 1964.

110 Requesting the Secretary General to continue his studies of "... national and international action and institutional arrangements including the systematic collection and dissemination of scientific and technological data and material so as to promote the expendious and effective transfer of technology ...," operative paragraph 3 of General Assembly Res. 2091 (XX), December 20, 1965.

In view of the general desirability of facilitating the economic development of "backward" areas, it would be good policy to permit all non-industrial countries freely to use all foreign-originated inventions in industries producing for the domestic market.[111]

The standard comment by delegates to international meetings – whether they represent governments or private parties – to suggestions for measures to increase the flow of technology to developing countries is that, although such developments are desirable, there is little governments can do, because the large majority of patents are owned by private persons.[112] It is one thing to assert that most patents are held by private persons and quite another to thereby imply that governments have no power to influence the exercise of such grants. Those who make this latter implication also thereby express the idea that patents are somewhat comparable to private property rights, or even represent some value more inviolable than private property in general. Those, on the other hand, who argue that patent grants are essentially monopoly privileges granted by the sovereign authority are usually suspected of designs aiming at the socialization of property and the overthrow of free enterprise. And yet it is indisputable that historically patent monopolies were granted as privileges to reward inventors (patentees) for their services, and that it is only due to the dubious theories on the nature of patent grants, that were advanced at the turn of the 18th century and the evolution thereafter, which made patent grants lose their character of privileges.[113] The fact that in most countries today between half and two-thirds of all funds employed in research and development are supplied by the Government would seem to make a reform easier, and make it cover at least such technology resulting from government sponsored research. In the case of research both paid by and undertaken by public agencies this would seem to pose no principal problems,[114] though at present the disposal of patents thus acquired may differ.[115] A limitation of this approach is the rela-

[111] Penrose, *op. cit.*, p. 221.

[112] Cf. however, quotation from D. L. Ladd, *op. cit. supra*, p 236, n 18.

[113] One author, who could not be accused of having had socializing tendencies, has clearly made this point. See W. Röpke, *Die Gesellschaftskrisis der Gegenwart* (Zürich: Rentsch, 1942) pp. 361–62.

[114] One of the recurring suggestions for improving the international exchange of technology has been that there should be free international disclosure of industrial technology developed by public research agencies. Cf. R. T. Terrill, "Cartels and the International Exchange of Technology," *A.E.R.*, 36: 762 ff., May, 1946; E. S. Mason, *Controlling World Trade: Cartels and Commodity Agreements* (New York: McGraw Hill, 1946) pp. 53–55; see p. 189, n. 49.

[115] Terrill, *loc. cit.*, mentions that in the case of the United States, both research employees and contractors may acquire commercial rights to domestic patents and full rights to foreign patents resulting from publicly financed research.

tively small amount of total industrial research undertaken by public agencies in most private enterprise countries. The case of government-financed but privately managed research, which is usually the far greater part of research activities based on public funds, would be more problematical. Finally, however, what is required is the political decision for an agreement among industrialized countries to institute a program along the lines of a world fund for technological knowledge suggested above.

b. Principles for the distribution of technology by the fund.

The acquisition of technology from the fund could be free of charge or against payment. If a price were charged, even on less than commercial terms, it might lead to a certain differentiation of the various fields of technology between countries and lead to some measure of "optimal" allocation of production. Such proceeds could possibly be used to remunerate the original inventors, who thus would be entitled to a certain royalty commensurate to the extent that the invention was being used. Such a system would in fact amount to a generalized system of licenses of right – or why not compare it to a system of authors' certificates, which has recently been accepted by the Paris Union, since "there was no reason to consider the system ... as contrary to the spirit and aims of the Paris Convention."[116] For the alternative of making technology free of charge would speak the fact that the traditional theory of comparative costs, underlying the selection of optimal allocation of production, is not always relevant to an incipient industry, and that the price paid would be merely an additional burden on a country intent on promoting a certain industry despite short-term comparative disadvantages. The payment for fund-distributed technology would further favor the more resourceful countries. Another problem concerning the fund's distribution of technology would be whether it should make all technology available to all countries or whether some measure of planned distribution should be sought.[117] While in theory a planned distribution might be appealing, the problems it would create concerning the definitions and application of criteria for such distribution would be difficult to solve in practice without compromising

[116] Cf. *supra*, pp. 242–44.

[117] This problem was in fact brought up at UNCTAD (1964) in connection with operative paragraph 4 of the Recommendation A.IV.26 (Cf. *supra*, n. 108). It was held by the delegate of Sierra Leone that since many countries of a region had the same resources, an uncontrolled flow of all technology to all countries "would be disasterous for the intraregional trade ..." Doc. E/Conf. 46/C.3. SR 44, p. 6.

the position of these countries. In the case that technology would be distributed free of charge, there would seem to be fewer grounds for objection – the alternative would remain open to buy any required technology directly from the inventor-patentee. The problems of planned distribution might decrease by the growth of the movements within various groups of states for economic cooperation and planned development.

c. Principles for the use of fund-supplied technology

How the technology would be used in the domestic economy would be a concern for each country. There would be several possible alternatives like exclusive use, on a general license basis or completely free. These problems are minor ones and of less principal interest in the present context. More difficult problems would be raised when it comes to exports of products involving fund-supplied technology. One can distinguish between the two cases: of exports to other developing countries and exports to industrialized countries. In the former case, some form of selection or control of the supply of technology by the fund or preferably a form of planned exploitation among the countries themselves would be desirable. The most difficult problems would be raised for the case of exports from developing to industrialized countries, which is often a necessity for the former countries because of their very limited home markets as well as desirable for the purchasing power it accumulates. It is quite unthinkable, even should the principle of the fund be accepted by the industrialized countries, that they would agree unconditionally to imports of goods containing fund-supplied technology (which would in many cases have patent protection which alone would bar such imports). One solution, which also would solve the question of whether fund-supplied technology should be acquired free of charge or against payment, would be to allow such exports against the payment of royalties to the extent that patent protected technology was used in the production of such goods. While not burdening the developing countries by payments for domestically used technology, or the technology that was used in trade with other developing countries, it would contain the principle of payment, equivalent to licenses, when competing in the markets of the industrialized countries. Such an arrangement would appear to be the only possible one and might go a long way to meet objections to the whole fund principle. Such a system would, of course, anyhow require a change in present conditions where such imports are not generally possible.

CONCLUSIONS

The history of the patent institution convincingly demonstrates that the fundamental reason for its introduction was the expected benefits to the national economy from rewarding those who invented and those who introduced foreign-made inventions into the national economy. Although legal considerations have sometimes been held to be equally or even more important, their subordinate nature has been revealed whenever economic interests have conflicted with professed legal principles. The early practice of some countries, which today are highly industrialized, of granting patent protection to those who merely imported foreign technology provided one significant illustration of this.

In creating the Paris Union, its founders aimed at promoting the international exchange of patented technology under the more acceptable form of recognizing the rights of their respective national patentees in the whole territory of the Union. Though the emphasis was put on the protection of the rights of patentees, the ultimate reason for extending protection to foreign patentees was the expected economic benefits from comparable protection of national patentees abroad. The fact that the most advanced countries have been those urging increased protection for patentees while many less developed countries, claiming lack of reciprocity in terms of economic benefits, have been opposed to such extension, is sufficient illustration of this point. In this respect, the situation of developing countries is not new.

The contention that the traditional system of international patent protection provides a suitable international vehicle for the transfer of patent protected technology to developing countries appears, a priori, implausible. It implies that the rules, originally created and later developed with the dominant objective of securing the interests of patentees abroad, at the same time may adequately serve the interests of the local economy of developing countries. Since a developing country will benefit from granting patent protection to foreigners only when such protection will lead to the effective introduction into the local economy of the patent protected technology, all cases where, for whatever reason, such a transfer does not take place, will increase the potential costs of the system to those countries.

The finding that the rules regulating the obligation to work patented inventions and the sanctions against non-working, permissible under the Convention, may be effective only under special conditions, justifies the conclusion that the present international patent system is inadequate for the needs and requirements of developing countries. Changes of the present system for the benefit of developing countries may be justified on two separate though complementary grounds. For one thing, the particular rules may be adapted to the conditions of these countries. It ought to be acknowledged, for instance, that in return for obtaining patent protection in a developing country, the foreign patentee should either undertake to work the patented invention himself or else actively cooperate with local manufacturers in introducing the technology involved, In cases of non-compliance with such a requirement, and in cases where the patent protected technology cannot usefully be worked locally, patent protection should be denied or revoked.

Besides the adaptation of specific rules to the conditions of developing countries, changes for their benefit may also be motivated on the ground ot preferential treatment. The same reasons underlying the general trend in international economic relations between industrialized and developing countries away from strict legal equality and towards conditions of real economic equality, justify such an approach also within the field of international patent cooperation.

The opposition to any fundamental changes of the present international patent system is formidable. Despite the fact that today more than half of the members of the Paris Union are developing countries, the voting procedures for altering the existing rules of the Convention, together with the unanimous opposition of industrialized countries, effectively inhibit any change. The only possibility for developing countries of obtaining a more equitable position will lie in effectively challenging the dominant position of the Paris Union. Earlier efforts in this direction have come to nothing and only a concerted action by all developing countries, whether or not members of the Paris Union, may be able to challenge the power of the Union and the organizations uncompromisingly defending the present system.

ABBREVIATIONS USED IN THE BIBLIOGRAPHY

A.E.R.	American Economic Review
B.I.R.P.I.	Bureaux Internationaux Reunis pour la Protection de la Propriété Intellectuelle (United International Bureaux for the Protection of Intellectual Property)
E.C.O.S.O.C.	United Nations' Economic and Social Council
G.R.U.R.	Gewerbliche Rechtsschutz und Urheberrecht
G.R.U.R.: Ausl.	Gewerbliche Rechtsschutz und Urheberrecht – Auslands- und Internationalen Teil
I.A.P.I.P.	International Association for the Protection of Industrial Property
I.C.C.	International Chamber of Commerce
IDEA	Patent, Trademark and Copyright Journal of Research and Education [since Vol. VIII (1964)]
I.P.	Industrial Property [periodical]
I.S.E.A.	Institut de Science Economique Appliquée
J.P.O.S.	Journal of the Patent Office Society
N.I.R.	Nordiskt Immatriellt Rättsskydd [periodical]
P.I.	Propriété Industrielle [periodical]
R.I.P.I.A.	Revue Internationale de la Propriété Industrielle et Droit d'Auteur
U.N.	United Nations
U.N.C.T.A.D.	United Nations Conference on Trade and Development

BIBLIOGRAPHY

SOURCES

DOCUMENTS

A. UNITED STATES SENATE

1. Committee on the Judiciary, Studies of the Sub-committee on Patents, Trademarks and Copyrights:
   Machlup, F., "An Economic Review of the Patent System," Study No. 15. Washington: Government Printing Office, 1958.
   Melman, S., "The Impact of the Patent System on Research," Study No. 11. Washington: Government Printing Office, 1958.
   Neumeyer, F., "Compulsory Licensing of Patents under some Non-American Systems," Study No. 19, Washington: Government Printing Office, 1959.
   Vernon, R., "The International Patent System and Foreign Policy," Study No. 5. Washington: Government Printing Office, 1958.
2. Temporary National Economic Committee:
   Hamilton, W. H., "Patents and Free Enterprise", Monograph No. 31. Washington: Government Printing Office, 1941.

B. UNITED NATIONS

1. United Nations Conference on Trade and Development 1964:
   Selected Summary Records of Committee III. Documents E/Conf. 46/C. 3/SR. 44, 49.
   Report of Committee III. Document E/Conf. 46/141, Vol. I., Annex F.
   "Transfer of Technology", Recommendation A. IV. 26 of the Conference. Document E/Conf. 46/141, Vol. I., Part III, Annexes.
2. United Nations Economic and Social Council:
   Selected Summary Records of Committee VI of the Economic and Social Council at its Thirty-seventh Session, July, 1964. Documents E/AC. 6/SR. 341–44.
   "The Role of Patents in the Transfer of Technology to Underdeveloped Countries". Resolution adopted by the Council. Document Res. 1013 (XXXVII), July 22, 1964.
3. United Nations General Assembly:
   "The Role of Patents in the Transfer of Technology to Underdeveloped Countries,". Brazilian [original] Draft Resolution introduced at the Sixteenth Session of the United Nations General Assembly. Document A/C. 2/L. 565, November 8, 1961.

General Assembly, Official Records, Sixteenth Session, Second Committee, 778–889th Meetings, December, 1961.
"The Role of Patents in the Transfer of Technology to Underdeveloped Countries,". Resolution adopted by the General Assembly at its Sixteenth Session. Document Res. 1713 (XVI), January 8, 1962.
General Assembly, Official Records, Twentieth Session, Second Committee, 999th Meeting, December, 1965.
"Transfer of Technology". Resolution adopted by the General Assembly at its Twentieth Session. Document Res. 2091 (XX), December 20, 1965.

4. United Nations Secretariat:
"Patents and the Economies of Underdeveloped Countries." Interim Report of the Secretary General. Document E/C. 5/35, April 30, 1963.
"The Role of Patents in the Transfer of Technology to Developing Countries." Report of the Secretary General. New York: United Nations, 1964. Document E/3861/Rev. 1, March, 1964.

C. UNITED INTERNATIONAL BUREAU FOR THE PROTECTION OF INTELLECTUAL PROPERTY

Actes de la Conférence de Lisbonne 1958. Genève: Bureau de l' Union Internationale pour la Protection de la Propriété Industrielle, 1963.
Actes de la Conférence de Londres 1934. Berne: Bureau de l'Union Internationale pour la Protection de la Propriété Industrielle, 1934.
Actes de la Conférence de La Haye 1925. Berne: Bureau International de l'Union, 1926.
Actes de la Conférence de Washington 1911. Berne: Bureau International de l'Union, 1911.
Actes de la Conférence de Bruxelles 1897–1900. Berne: Bureau International de l'Union, 1901.
Conférence Internationale pour la Protection de la Propriété Industrielle de Paris 1883. Paris: Ministère des Affaires Etrangères, 1883.
Conférence Internationale pour la Protection de la Propriété Industrielle de Paris 1880. Paris: Ministère des Affaires Etrangères, 1880.
Intellectual Property Conference of Stockholm, 1967. International Convention for the Protection of Literary and Artistic Works. Proposals for Revising the Substantive Copyright Provisions (Articles 1–20). (Prepared by the Government of Sweden with the assistance of BIRPI.) Document S/1, May 15, 1966.
Intellectual Property Conference of Stockholm, 1967. International Convention for the Protection of Industrial Property. Proposal for amending Article 4 of the Convention. (Prepared by the Government of Sweden with the assistance of BIRPI.) Document S/2, April 15, 1966.
Intellectual Property Conference of Stockholm, 1967. Convention Establishing the International Intellectual Property Organization. Proposals for Establishing the Organization. (Prepared by BIRPI at the request of the Government of Sweden.) Document S/10, September 16, 1966.
Intellectual Property Conference of Stockholm, 1967. International Convention for the Protection of Literary and Artistic Works. Oberservations of the Governments on Proposals for Revising Substantive Copyright Provisions (Document S/1). Document S/13, January, 1967.
Intellectual Property Conference of Stockholm, 1967. Report on the Work of Main Committee II (Protocol Regarding Developing Countries) of the Intelec-

tual Property Conference of Stockholm, 1967. *Copyright*, 3: 222–24, October, 1967.

Intellectual Property Conference of Stockholm, 1967. Report on the Work of Main Committee V (World Intellectual Property Organization) of the Intellectual Property Conference of Stockholm, 1967. *I. P.*, 6: 185–95, August, 1967.

Model Law for Developing Countries on Inventions. Geneva: BIRPI, 1965.

Paris Convention for the Protection of Industrial Property. Manual of Industrial Property Conventions. Geneva: BIRPI, 1966.

"The Role of Patents in the Transfer of Technology to Underdeveloped Countries". Note submitted by BIRPI at the United Nations Conference on Trade and Development 1964. U.N. Document E/Conf. 46/101, April 10, 1964.

D. COMMISSION ON THE INTERNATIONAL PROTECTION OF INDUSTRIAL PROPERTY OF THE INTERNATIONAL CHAMBER OF COMMERCE

"The Lisbon Conference." Draft Report by S. P. Ladas. Document No. 450/163, January 13, 1959.

Summary Records of Meeting November 23–24, 1961.
Document No. 450/212, November 24, 1961.

"The Role of Patents in the Transfer of Technology to Underdeveloped Countries." Statement adopted by the Commission. Document No. 450/210 Rev., November 24, 1961.

"The Role of Patents in the Transfer of Technology to Underdeveloped Countries." Note from International Headquarters. Document No. 450/213, February 22, 1962.

"The Role of Patents in the Transfer of Technology to Underdeveloped Countries." Copy of a letter sent by the Secretary General of the ICC to U. Thant, Secretary General of the United Nations, dated: October 14, 1963. Document No. 450/243, October 28, 1963.

"Review of Patent, Trademark and Knowhow Licensing." Working Sheet submitted by S. P. Ladas. Document 450/252, February 27, 1964.

"The Role of Patents in the Transfer of Technology to Underdeveloped Countries: Report of the Secretary General of the United Nations." Summary by S. P. Ladas. Document No. 450/253, March 5, 1964.

"Model Patent Law." Memorandum on the Geneva Meeting of the Committee of Experts, submitted by S. P. Ladas and P. J. Pointet. Document No. 450/262, December, 15, 1964.

"Modern Technology and Industrial Property." Draft Memorandum prepared by S. P. Ladas. Document No. 450/264, April 26, 1965.

E. INTERNATIONAL ASSOCIATION FOR THE PROTECTION OF INDUSTRIAL PROPERTY

Annual Reports 1961: II
1963: I, II
1964: II
1965: II
1966: I, II

F. MISCELLANEOUS

Ayyangar. S. R., *Report on the Revision of the Patents Law*. New Delhi: Government of India, 1959.

Manual for the Handling of Applications for Patents, Designs, and Trademarks throughout the World. Amsterdam: Octrooibureau Los en Stigter, 1927 [brought up to date: April, 1967].

WORKS

A. BOOKS

Akerman, C., *L'Obligation d'exploiter et la licence obligatoire en matière de brevet d'invention*. Paris: Sirey, 1936.

Ayyangar, S. R., *Report on the Revision of the Patents Law*. See under Documents, Miscellaneous.

Bennett, W. B., *The American Patent System: An Economic Interpretation*. Baton Rouge: Louisiana State University Press, 1943.

Börlin, M., *Die Volkswirtschaftliche Problematik der Patentgesetzgebung, unter besonderer Berücksichtigung der Schweizerischen Verhältnisse*. Zürich und St. Gallen: Polygraphischer Verlag, 1954.

Casalonga, A., *Traité technique et pratique des brevets d'invention*. Paris: Librairie Générale de Droit et de Jurisprudence, 3 vols., 1949–1958.

Dame, E., *Die volkswirtschaftliche Bedeutung des Systems des Ausführungszwanges im Patentwesen*. Berlin: Verlag Chemie, 1929.

Fox, B. G., *Monopolies and Patents: A Study of the History and Future of the Patent Monopoly*. Toronto: University of Toronto Studies, Legal Series, Extra vol., 1947.

Godenhielm, B., *Utlänsk och internationell patenträtt*. Stockholm: Institutet för Utlänsk Rätt, 1953.

Hexner, E., *International Cartels*. Chapel Hill: University of North Carolina Press, 1946.

Isay, H., *Die Funktion der Patente im Wirtschaftskampf*. Berlin: Franz Vahlen, 1927.

—. *Die Patentgemeinschaft im Dienst des Kartellgedankens*. Mannheim: J. Bensheimer, 1923.

Kruse, L. F. V., *The Right of Property*. [translated from Danish by P. T. Federspiel] London: Oxford University Press, 1939.

Ladas, S. P., *The International Protection of Industrial Property*. Cambridge: Harvard University Press, 1930.

—. *Propiedad Industrial y Desarrollo Económico*. Bogotá: Brigard y Hurrutia, 1963.

Le Grand, L., *Etude économique de la propriété industrielle: Fondement et fonction économiques de cette "propriété"*. Paris: Sirey, 1937.

Machlup, F., *The Political Economy of Monopoly: Business, Labor and Government Policies*. Baltimore: Johns Hopkins, 1952.

Mason, E. S., *Controlling World Trade: Cartels and Commodity Agreements*. New York: McGraw Hill, 1946.

Meynaud, J., *Les groupes de pression internationaux*. Lausanne: [chez l'auteur], 1961.

Mousseron, J.-M., *Le droit du breveté d'invention: contribution à une analyse objective*. Paris: Libraire Générale de Droit et de Jurisprudence, 1961.

Neumeyer, F., *Patent, reflexioner kring patent-institutionens uppkomst, utveckling och ställning i vår tid.* [Studier och Debatt, No. IV, 1958] Stockholm: Studieförbundet Näringsliv och Samhälle, 1958.

Patentschutz und Entwicklungsländer: Dokumente und Materialien, Max Plank-Institut für ausländisches und internationales Patent-, Urheber-, und Wettbewerbsrecht, Vol. XV. Munich: Carl Heymanns Verlag, 1966.

Penrose, E. T., *The Economics of the International Patent System.* Baltimore: Johns Hopkins, 1951.

Plaisant, M., *Traité de droit conventionnel international concernant la propriété industrielle.* Paris: Sirey, 1949.

— and Jacq, F., *Le nouveau régime internationale de la propriété industrielle.* Paris: Sirey, 1927.

— *Les brevets d'invention en droit international.* Paris: Sireay, 1931, third edition.

Ripert, G., *Les forces créatrices du droit.* Paris: Libraire Générale de Droit et de Jurisprudence, 1955.

Roubier, P., *Le droit de la propriété industrielle.* Paris: Sirey, 2 vols., 1952–54.

Silberstein, M., *Erfindungsschutz und merkantilistische Gewerbsprivilegien.* Zürich: Polygraphischer Verlag, 1961.

Toulmin, H. A. J., *Invention and the Law.* New York: Prentice Hall, 1936.

Troller, A., *Die mehrseitigen völkerrechtlichen Verträge im internationalen gewerblichen Rechtsschutz und Uhrheberrecht. Studien zum Immaterialgüterrecht, Vol. VI.* Basel: Verlag für Recht und Gesellschaft, 1965.

Union Internationale pour la Protection de la Propriété Industrielle; Mémoire publié par le Bureau International pour la Protection de la Propriété Industrielle à l'occasion du cinquantenaire. Berne: Bureau International de l'Union, 1933.

Vojáček, J. A., *Survey of the Principal National Patent Systems.* New York: Prentice Hall, 1936 [addenda: 1951, 1956].

Waline, M., *L'Individualisme et le droit.* Paris: Domat Montchrestien, 1945.

Walleser. F., *Die Patentfähigkeit als rechtsteleologisches Problem.* Bern: Stämpfli, 1963.

Whittlesey, Ch., *National Interest and International Cartels.* New York: Macmillan, 1946.

B. PARTS OF BOOKS, CHAPTERS, PAPERS

Blum, E., "Abuse of Monopolies and its Prevention," *Souvenir – Indian Patents Centenary 1856–1956.* Calcutta: Patent Office, 1956., pp. 54–56.

Bodenhausen, G. H. C., "A Model Patent Law for Developing Nations," *Creative Ferment in World Patent Systems, Conference of the National Association of Manufacturers, June, 1965.* New York: National Association of Manufacturers, 1965., pp. 24–29.

Bose, A., "Compulsory Licensing of Patents," *Souvenir – Indian Patents Centenary 1856–1956.* Calcutta: Patent Office, 1956., pp. 57–59.

Carter, C. F., "Economic Incentives for and Consequences of Technical Invention," *Scientific Change, Symposium on the History of Science, University of Oxford 9–15 July, 1961.* [A. C. Crombie ed.] London: Heinemann, 1963, pp. 678–90.

Daudé, B., "L'importance actuelle de la recherche dans l'économie et les caractéristiques de l'industrie de la découverte," *La Rentabilité de la recherche, Cahiers de l'Institut de Science Economique Appliquée, No. 148.* Paris: I.S.E.A., April, 1964., pp. 107–70.

Edwards, C. D., "America's Postwar Policy Toward International Cartels,"

International Cartels and Private Trade Agreements, America's Place in the World Economy. [A. J. Zurcher, R. Page, eds.] New York University, Institute on Postwar Reconstruction, Conferences, fourth series, 1945.

Finniss, G., "Conclusions du Colloque," *La propriété industrielle et le marché commun, aspects économiques; Colloque Université – Industrie, 19–20 novembre, 1965, Lyon.* Paris: Dunod, 1966., pp. 189–92.

Friedmann, W., Verloren van Themaat. P., "International Cartels and Combines," *Anti-trust Laws, A Comparative Symposium.* [ed. W. Friedmann] Toronto: Carswell, 1956., pp. 469–515.

Frost, G. E., "Patent Rights and the Stimulation of Technical Change," *Patents and Progress, The Sources and Impact of Advancing Technology.* [eds. W. Alderson, V. Terpstra, S. J. Shapiro] Homewood, Ill.: Richard. D. Irwin, 1965., pp. 61–86.

Frumkin, M., "The Early History of Patents for Invention," *Paper Presented at a Joint Meeting of the Chartered Institute of Patent Agents and the Newcomen Society, London, 1947.* 25 pp.

Gather, G., "Reform der Patentgesetzgebung," *Jahrbuch für die Ordnung von Wirtschaft und Gesellschaft, Vol. II* [ORDO] Godesberg: Helmut Kupper, 1949., pp. 270–307.

Hamilton, W. H., "Patents and Free Enterprise," See under Documents, United States Senate.

Kahn, J. L., "Découverte scientifique et propriété industrielle," *Les brevets d'invention dans l'économie. I – Caractères institutionnels et problématique économique. Cahiers de l'Institut de Science Economique Appliquée, No. 116.* Paris: I.S.E.A., August, 1961., pp. 69–72.

Kronstein, H., "A Reevaluation of the International Patent Convention," [1948] *Law and Economic Power, Sellected Essays.* Karlsruhe: C. F. Müller, 1962., pp. 357–75.

Kust, M. J., "Industrial Property Rights," *Foreign Enterprise in India; Laws and Policies.* Durham: University of North Carolina Press, 1964., pp. 419–31.

Ladas, S. P., "The Revision of the Paris Convention," *ICC Brochure, No. 206.* 1959, 20pp.

Ladd, D. L., "Industrial Property and the Iron Curtain Countries," *Adress to World Patent System Conference,* [Sponsored by the] *National Association of Manufacturers, New York, 1964.* New York: National Association of Manufacturers, 1964, 7pp.

Machlup, F., "An Economic Review of the Patent System," See under Documents, United States Senate.

– "The Nature of the International Cartel Problem," *A Cartel Policy for the United Nations.* [ed. C. D. Edwards] New York: Columbia University Press, 1945., pp. 1–24.

— "Patentwesen – I. Geschichtliche Überblick [und] II. Wirtschaftsteoretische Betrachtung", *Handwörterbuch der Sozialwissenschaften, Vol. VIII.* Göttingen: G. Fischer, J. C. B. Mohr, 1962. pp. 231–52.

Markham, J. W., "Inventive Activity: Government Controls and the Legal Environment," *The Rate and Direction of Inventive Activity: Economic and Social Factors; Nation Bureau of Economic Research, Special Conference Series, Vol. XIII.* Princeton: Princeton University Press, 1962., pp. 587–608.

Melman, S., "The Impact of the Patent System on Research," See under Documents, United States Senate.

Neme, C., "Pénétration des produits sous marque ou licence et unification des marchés dans la C.E.E.," *La propriété industrielle et le marché commun, aspects économiques; Colloque Université – Industrie, 19–20 novembre, 1965, Lyon.* Paris: Dunod, 1966., pp. 121–55.

Neumeyer, F., "Compulsory Licensing of Patents under some Non-American Systems," See under Documents, United States Senate.

Opie, R., "A Critical Appraisal of the International Cartel," *International Cartels and Private Trade Agreements, America's Place in the World Economy.* [eds. A. J. Zurcher, R. Page] New York: New York University, Institute on Postwar Reconstruction, Conferences, Fourth Series, 1945., pp. 124–36.

Plaisant, M., "De la protection internationale de la propriété industrielle," *Académie de Droit International, Recueil des Cours,* 39: I, 1932., pp. 357–549.

Plaisant, R., "L'Evolution des conventions de propriété intellectuelle," Les Unions Internationales pour la Protection de la Propriété Industrielle, Littéraire et Artistique 1883–1963. Genève: BIRPI, 1962., pp. 47–115.

Pretnar, S., "La Notion d'intérêt public et la Convention d'Union," [offprint from] *Mélanges Marcel Plaisant,* Paris: Sirey, 1960., 10pp.

Rondon de Sanso, H., "Influencia de la protección de las patentes y las marcas sobre la economía nacional de los diversos Estados de la America Latina," *Ponencia al Congreso Latinoamericano de Propiedad Industrial,* Bogotá, 1964, 29pp.

Sola Pool, de, I., "The Social Environment for Sustained Technological Growth," *Patents and Progress, The Sources and Impact of Advancing Technology.* [eds. W. Alderson, V. Terpstra, S. J. Shapiro] Homewood, Ill.: Richard D. Irwin, 1965., pp. 19–34.

Vernon, R., "The International Patent System and Foreign Policy," See under Documents, United States Senate.

C. ARTICLES

Bodenhausen, G. H. C., "La Union de París para la protección de la propiedad industrial," *Revista Mexicana de la propiedad industrial y artistica.* 3: 259–68, July–December, 1965.

Brown, R., "Whither Goes the United States Patent System?," *IDEA,* 9: 251–71, No. 2, 1965.

Casalonga, A., "Forfeiture of Patents for Non-Working," *J.P.O.S.,* 33: 714–28, October, 1951.

Deller, A. W., "Social and Economic Impact of Patents," *J.P.O.S.,* 46: 424–57, June, 1964.

Fatouros, A. A., "International Law and the Third World," Virginia Law Review, 50: 783–823, June, 1964.

Finniss, G., "The Impact of Research Policy upon Economic Expansion and the Standard of Living," *I.P.,* 5: 88–92, April, 1966.

Frumkin, M., "Les anciens brevets d'invention: les pays du continent européen au XVIIIe siècle," *Bijblad bij De Industriële Eigendom,* 23: 46–49, April, 1955.

Gariel, G., "Après la Conférence de La Haye: les taches du lendemain," *P.I.,* 42: 146–52, July, 1926.

Gilfillan, S. C., "The Prediction of Technological Change," *Review of Economics and Statistics,* 20: 368–85, November, 1952.

— "The Root of Patents or Squaring Patents by Their Roots," *J.P.O.S.,* 31: 611–23, August, 1949.

Habachy, S., "Protection of Trademarks and Patent Rights in the Middle East: History, Geography and Economics," *Patent, Trademark and Copyright Journal of Research and Education,* 6: 347–67, No. 3, 1962.

Hesser, T., "Det immatriella rättsskyddet och u-länderna," *N.I.R.*, 34: 153–68, 1965.

Kahn, A. E., "Fundamental Deficiencies of the American Patent Law." *A.E.R.*, 30: 475–91, September, 1940.

Krause, L. B., "Industrial Property Relations with the Less Industrialized Nations: An Economist's View," *IDEA*, 9: 205–09, Conference number, 1965.

Krieger, A., "A New International Organization for Intellectual Property? – Efforts to Modify the Structure of the Paris and Berne Unions," *I.P.*, 5: 37–48, February, 1966.

Lachmann, K,. "The role of Industrial Property in the Dissemination of Technical Information in the World Context: A United Nations View," *IDEA*, 9: 180–88, Conference number, 1965.

Ladas, S. P., "The Fundamental Bases of the International Protection of Industrial Property," *P.I.*, 70: annex, 4pp., April, 1954. [original text of "Les bases fondamentales de la protection internationale de la propriété industrielle," *P.I.*, 70: 93–97, April, 1954.]

— "The Lisbon Conference for Revision of the International Convention for the Protection of Industrial Property," *Trademark Reporter*, 48: 1291–1319, November, 1958.

Machlup, F., Penrose, E. T., "The Patent Controversy in the 19th Century," *Journal of Economic History*, 10: 1–29, January, 1950.

Maclaurin, W. E., "Patents and Technical Progress: A Study of Television," *Journal of Political Economy*, 58: 142–57, No. 2, 1950.

Magnin, Ch., "Une mise au point des notions de base de la propriété industrielle," *P.I.*, 68: 142–47, October, 1952.

Mandich, G., "Venetian Patents (1450–1550)," *J.P.O.S.*, 30: 166–224, March, 1948.

Markham, J. W., Worley, J. S., Brothers, D. S., "The Value of the American Patent System: An Inquiry into Possible Approaches to its measurement," *Patent, Trademark and Copyright Journal of Research and Education*, 1: 20–56, No. 1, 1957.

Mascareñas, C. E., "Las modificationes de Lisboa al Convenio de París para la Protección de la Propiedad Industrial," *Boletín del Instituto de Derecho Comparado de México*, 12: 37–53, January–April, 1959.

Massel, M. E., "Evolving Needs for the Protection of Industrial and Intellectual Property: An Economist's View," *IDEA*, 9: 34–38, Conference No., 1965.

Moser, von, R., "Der Sinn des Patentrechts und die Patentrechtsteorien," *G.R.U.R.*, 34: 1331–45, December, 1929.

Neumeyer, F., "Die Rolle von Patenten in internationalen Kartellen," *Wirtschaft und Recht*, 4: 219–37, No. 3, 1953.

— "Die historischen Grundlagen der ersten modernen Patentgesetze in den U.S.A. und in Frankreich," *G.R.U.R.: Ausl.*, 58: 241–52, June, 1956.

L'Obligation d'exploiter les brevets d'invention," *P.I.*, 40: 65–75, 86–99, 118–23, April–June, 1924.

Plant, A., "The Economic Theory Concerning Patents for Inventions," *Economica*, New Series, 1: 30–51, No. 1, 1934.

Pohlmann, H., "The Inventor's Right in Early German Law," *J.P.O.S.*, 43: 121–35, February, 1961.

Pointet, P. J., "Du défaut d'exploitation des brevets d'invention." *Revue Suisse de la Propriété Industrielle et du Droit d'Auteur*, pp.: 24–40, May, 1952.

— "L'Influence sur le développement économique d'une législation appropriée en matière de brevets et de marques," *R.I.P.I.A.*, 69: 146–51, October, 1961.

— "The Role of Industrial Property in the Economic Development of States," *I.P.*, 6: 60–71, March, 1967.

— Chavanne, A., "Réforme des structures administratives des BIRPI," *R.I.P.I.A.*, 74: 204–11, December, 1966.

Prager, F. D., "A History of Intellectual Property from 1545 to 1787," *J.P.O.S.*, 26: 711–60, November, 1944.

Pretnar, S., "The International Protection of Industrial Property and the Different Stages of Economic Development of the States," [translation supplied by BIRPI of "La protection internationale de la propriété industrielle et les différents stades de développement économique des Etats," *P.I.*, 69: 213–21, December, 1953]. 10pp. [BIRPI library]

— "More on the Legal Protection of Industrial Property," *I.P.*, 71: annex, 5 pp., January, 1955. [translation supplied by BIRPI, of "Nochmals zur Frage des gewerblichen Rechtsschutzes in der Struktur des heutigen Weltwirtschaft," BIRPI library]

"The Proposed Administrative and Structural Reform of BIRPI," *I.P.*, 5: 183–86, August, 1966.

"The Role of Industrial Patents in the Transfer of Technology to Developing Countries," *Industrial Research News*, 1: 28–33, No. 1, 1966.

Rondon de Sanso, H., "The Effect of Patent Protection on the National Economy of a Developing Country," *I.P.*, 4: 114–17, May, 1965.

Roubier, P., "Droits intellectuels ou droit de clientèle," *Revue Trimestrielle du Droit Civil*, 34: 251–304, No. 2, 1935.

— "The Law of the Union for the Protection of Industrial Property," *Journal du Droit International*, 78: 667–769, 1041–1119, No. 3, 4, 1951.

Secretan, J., "Structural Evolution of the Unions for the Protection of Intellectual Property," *I.P.*, 1: 170–78, July, 1962.

Terrill, R. T., "The American Trade Proposals: Restrictive Business Practices," *Department of State Bulletin*, March 24, 1946, p. 455 ff.

— "Cartels and the International Exchange of Technology," *A.E.R.*, 36: 745–67, May, 1946.

Troller, A., "Intellectual Property and Justice," *I.P.*, 3: 119–24, April, 1964.

Vander Haeghen, A., "Partage des droits intellectuels en propriété industrielle et en droit d'auteur," *L'Ingénieur Conseil*, 44: 189–201, 237–45, November–December, 1954.

Vaughan, F. L., "International Cartels – Discussion," *A.E.R.*, 36: 777–83, May, 1946.

Vignes, D., "Droit d'auteur et aide au développement: Le Protocole à l'Acte de Stockholm pour la protection des oeuvres littéraires et artistiques" *Annuaire Français de Droit International*, XIII: 716–49, 1967.

"War and Peace and the Patent System," *Fortune*, 51: 103 ff., August, 1942.

Addendum:

GPSR Compliance

The European Union's (EU) General Product Safety Regulation (GPSR) is a set of rules that requires consumer products to be safe and our obligations to ensure this.

If you have any concerns about our products, you can contact us on ProductSafety@springernature.com

In case Publisher is established outside the EU, the EU authorized representative is:

Springer Nature Customer Service Center GmbH
Europaplatz 3
69115 Heidelberg, Germany

Batch number: 10830943

Printed by Printforce, the Netherlands